FIRST EDITION | 2014

ACTIVE EQUITY MANAGEMENT

Xinfeng Zhou

Sameer Jain

Authors: Xinfeng Zhou and Sameer Jain
Title: Active Equity Management©
          First Edition, 2014

ISBN-13: 978-0-692-25928-3
ISBN-10: 0-692-25928-7

In memory of my sister,
Xinli Zhou
(1975-2003)

Preface

Active equity management has been well studied over the past decade and a reasonable body of literature now exists on this topic. However, most of the literature tilts towards theory rather than practice. Surprisingly few practical guides exist for accessing the benefits of active management. Recognizing the need we have written this book to bridge the gap between theory and practice for investment professionals, researchers, active investors, and students. It is intended for readers who have knowledge of finance theory and markets but want to delve deeper to enhance their understanding of equity investing.

As equity markets have evolved, the pursuit of skill-based returns (alpha) has been no easy task. Our goal is to introduce readers to market inefficiencies and examine the theoretical and practical background of active investing. Drawn from academic research, financial literature and our own practitioner insights, we discuss a wide variety of seasonal effects, economic and market indicators, as well as technical and fundamental signals that may be used to create profitable risk-controlled trades.

We showcase methods to extract signals from disparate information sources and rigorously test the signals using scientific methods. By providing relevant practical illustrative examples, some historical and others hypothetical, we clarify important concepts for discerning readers. We also provide the building blocks to assist active investors improve their general understanding of the equities market, better recognize both technical and fundamental investing signals, derive an information edge and independently arrive at new insights to interpret and act on market indicators. Armed with the necessary building blocks for actively investing in equities, we go on to further draw attention to important issues surrounding forecasting, dynamic signal timing, portfolio construction and optimization, risk control, while successfully managing implementation and trading costs.

Besides covering long/short equity strategies in great detail, we survey statistical arbitrage, risk parity, commodities, and currency trading to extend the active equity management framework to other investment strategies.

While some approaches outlined in this book are quantitative in nature, this book goes beyond demonstrating the efficacy of the quantitative methods. Rather, we focus on the intuition behind the methods. Those with knowledge of statistics will enjoy delving deeper into the mathematical and modeling sections, while others may skim the technical detail without loss of comprehension.

We thank our current and former colleagues, those in academia whose work we have built upon, and are grateful to the many friends who have spent invaluable hours reviewing this book.

If you have any suggestions or comments, please send them to our email addresses xinfeng.zhou@sloan.mit.edu and sameer.jain@sloan.mit.edu. We are grateful for your feedback and will post your constructive ideas on the book's companion website http://www.activeequitymanagement.com.

We hope you enjoy reading this book!

Xinfeng Zhou, 2014
Sameer Jain, 2014

About the Authors

Xinfeng Zhou manages a global long/short equity portfolio at Point72 Asset Management. He has designed and implemented profitable trading strategies by integrating fundamental long/short ideas, quantitative stock selection signals, portfolio optimization, risk management, and algorithmic trading. Formerly with SAC Capital Advisors, Goldman Sachs, Barclays Global Investors, and Cambridge Alternative Investments, he employs financial engineering methodologies, investment theory, and applied mathematics to trading signal development, trading cost analysis, derivative trading, securities lending, and asset allocation.

Mr. Zhou is a Chartered Financial Analyst (CFA), Financial Risk Manager (FRM), and has a Ph.D. from Massachusetts Institute of Technology.

Sameer Jain is Chief Economist & Managing Director at American Realty Capital. His executive management responsibilities include heading risk management, firm strategy and direction development, as well as alternative investments. He has 18 years of investing experience where his responsibilities have included the formulation of investment strategy, the development of risk management practices and asset allocation models, creating thought leadership, and the assessment and engagement of real estate, private equity and hedge fund managers. Prior to this he headed Investment Content & Strategy at UBS Alternative Investments, where he was also responsible for all illiquid investing across the platform. Prior to UBS he was at Citi Capital Advisors, Cambridge Alternative Investments and SunGard System Access. He has written academic and practitioner articles on alternative investments, many of which are available in the public domain at SSRN.

Mr. Jain is a graduate of Massachusetts Institute of Technology and Harvard University.

Contents

Notations

$A \Rightarrow B$	whenever A is true, B is also true
s.t.	such that
$\displaystyle\sum_{i=1}^{n} x_i$	$x_1 + x_2 + \cdots + x_n$
$\displaystyle\prod_{i=1}^{n} x_i$	$x_1 \times x_2 \times \cdots \times x_n$
$\ln(x)$	natural logarithm of x
$E[x]$	expected value of x
$\mathrm{var}(x)$	variance of x
$\mathrm{std}(x)$	standard deviation of x
$\mathrm{cov}(x, y)$	covariance of x and y
$\mathrm{cor}(x, y)$	correlation of x and y
$\displaystyle\int f(x)\,dx$	indefinite integral of $f(x)$
$\displaystyle\int_{a}^{b} f(x)\,dx$	definite integral of $f(x)$ from a to b
$N(\mu, \sigma^2)$	normal distribution with mean μ and variance σ^2
cdf	cumulative density function
pdf	probability density function
A'	transpose of a vector or matrix A
A^{-1}	inverse of a square matrix A
e	$N \times 1$ column vector with all elements equal to 1
$\forall$	for each/for every/for all

Chapter 1

Introduction

Market Efficiency

In 1970, Eugene Fama proposed the Efficient Market Hypothesis (EMH) in a landmark paper *Efficient Capital Markets: A Review of Theory and Empirical Work*. The fundamental idea behind the EMH is that securities markets are efficient in incorporating all information that determines the value of a security. As a result, investors cannot achieve better risk-adjusted returns than by holding the market portfolio. EMH has three versions. (i) The weak form of the EMH says that the asset price fully reflects all *past market price* information. If the weak EMH holds, technical analysis that relies on past price actions cannot outperform the market on a risk-adjusted basis. (ii) The semi-strong form of the EMH posits that the asset price reflects all *publicly* available information. If the semi-strong EMH holds, fundamental analysis that relies on public accounting information is futile. (iii) The strong form of the EMH claims that the asset price reflects *all* information, including all non-public information. If the strong EMH holds, no investor can outperform the market on a risk-adjusted basis.

The EMH triggered an on-going debate within the academic community. Since corporate insiders with material non-public information can capture higher risk-adjusted returns, researchers generally agree that the strong EMH does not hold. There is no consensus on whether the weak EMH and the semi-strong EMH hold. Defenders of the weak EMH and the semi-strong EMH argue that any inefficiency in the market will be immediately arbitraged away by smart market participants. Sharpe and Alexander (1990) defined arbitrage as "the simultaneous purchase and sale of the same, or essentially similar, security in two different markets for advantageously different prices." In other words, if there are any market anomalies—patterns in the financial market that contradict the EMH—that produce high risk-adjusted returns, investors will immediately act on them and restore the market efficiency if the information is publicly available. Naturally, many empirical studies by critics of the EMH are dedicated to identifying market anomalies that reflect possible market inefficiencies. In this book, we will discuss a variety of successfully identified anomalies. The existence of these anomalies casts serious doubt on the EMH.

Other critics question the very foundation of the EMH which is based on the premise that investors are always rational and value securities without biases. In reality, investors have biased views, often have limited attention to analyze all relevant information, and sometimes do make emotional decisions instead of rational ones. Some well-documented behavioral phenomena are overconfidence, anchoring effect, confirmation bias, loss aversion, and the disposition effect:

- **Overconfidence**: Investors tend to overestimate their knowledge and skills in forecasting asset price moves and underestimate the risks. For example, many investors are inclined to attribute successful investments to their superior skills and attribute unsuccessful ones to bad luck. Overconfidence leads investors to trade excessively and take unnecessary investment risks.

- **Anchoring effect**: Investors tend to become attached to, or anchored on one piece of information when making decisions. One typical example is the anchoring effect of analysts' target prices for stocks. Overenthusiastic analysts sometimes arrive at unrealistically high target prices; investors recognize that the target prices are too high, yet they still tilt their own estimates towards such analyst recommendations.

- **Confirmation bias**: Investors tend to pay special attention to information that confirms their preconceptions and ignore the information that is at odds. In other words, investors actively seek out information that confirms their personal beliefs; at the same time, they tend to downplay information that contradicts their beliefs. They tend to interpret objective information in a biased way to favor their beliefs. Moreover, investors are often influenced by less frequent but more extreme events (anecdotes) instead of conducting deeper analysis that includes all similar events. Consequently, such biases result in under-reaction and over-reaction to new information.

- **Loss aversion**: Investors tend to prefer avoiding losses to acquiring gains. Studies have shown that a loss has more than twice the impact on a person as a gain of equal magnitude. Loss aversion dissuades investors from participating in investments with high risk-adjusted returns because of the potential risks. Loss aversion also contributes to herding among institutional investors. For many portfolio managers, it is a much bigger career risk to bet against popular opinion. When a portfolio manager suffers losses along with peers, general market conditions may be used to explain the loss; underperformance versus peers, on the other hand, is much more difficult to explain. Therefore, the investments of a portfolio manager are often influenced by the investments of other portfolio managers.

- **Disposition effect**: Investors tend to sell winning stocks too soon and sell losing stocks too late. Some investors believe that as long as they hold on to losing stocks, hoping those stocks will subsequently recover, unrealized losses will remain just paper losses. They believe that only when they sell the losing stocks, paper losses will turn into actual real losses. Some investors even actively average down by buying more shares of the same losing stocks. When it comes to winning stocks, they believe that a bird in the hand is worth two in the bush. Thus, they are eager to sell winning stocks to lock in gains. Empirical evidence shows that such tendency is detrimental to performance since stock returns are more likely to exhibit momentum: winning stocks often continue to outperform the market and losing stocks continue to underperform the market.

Besides investors' behavioral biases and irrationality, the market structure also contributes to sustained mispricing of assets. For instance, there are institutional obstacles to the dissemination of negative information about stocks. Since analysts need access to senior managers of a firm to have a competitive edge in gathering information about the firm, they are more reluctant to make sell recommendations than to make buy recommendations; this way, they maintain good relationships with the management. Index funds and mutual funds may help sustain mispricing as well. Almost all index funds replicate value weighted benchmarks. When the price of a stock is driven up by irrational exuberance, an index fund is not allowed to reduce the holdings of that stock since its market value increases proportionally with the stock price. Most mutual funds and pension funds have short sale restrictions that prevent them from short selling overvalued stocks. Another market reality is that most individual investors do not routinely short stocks. Hence, a stock can stay overvalued for a long time before correction. For some illiquid asset classes such as real estate, few instruments exist for investors to short the assets. As a result, the price reaction of assets reflects more of the view of optimistic investors instead of the view of all investors; this contributes to bubble and bust cycles.

The weak EMH and the semi-strong EMH are based on the assumption that any inefficiency in the market will be immediately arbitraged away by smart market participants. In reality, there are limits to arbitrage because exploitation of market inefficiencies involves significant costs and risks. Pure arbitrage opportunity without costs and risks is extremely rare as this type of inefficiency will be immediately arbitraged away. Small inefficiencies, however, can be persistent for a long time because of information costs, transaction costs, noise trader risk, idiosyncratic risk, and event risk.

- **Information costs**: In order to identify possible mispriced securities, investors need timely access to a large amount of data. The collection, dissemination, and analysis of the data come at a cost to active investors—investors who try to actively select stocks to generate better risk-adjusted returns instead of passively investing in the market portfolio—often adding up to millions of dollars a year.

- **Transaction costs**: Active investments also require substantially more trading than passive investments. Trading costs such as commissions, bid-ask spreads, and market impact costs limit arbitrageurs' ability to explore market inefficiencies. Active investors also spend huge amounts a year on trading costs. These steep costs often prevent investors from trading mispriced assets.

- **Noise trader risk**: Noise traders are investors who have little insight into stock valuations and make irrational buy and sell trading decisions. Many mispriced stocks are caused by the excessively optimistic or pessimistic views of noise traders. The irrational sentiment that creates mispricing can sustain or even exacerbate the mispricing for long periods of time. In order to exploit mispricing, investors need to be willing to bet against the noise traders and effectively manage potential losses caused by sustained mispricing without losing confidence in their trades.

- **Idiosyncratic risk and event risk**: In order to make a pure bet on a single anomaly or a group of anomalies, investors need to hedge other risks, which is a difficult task. Since the idiosyncratic risk—asset return volatility that cannot be explained by common risk factors—and the event risk (e.g., acquisition, bankruptcy) of one asset is uncorrelated with the risks of other assets, investors cannot find good substitutes to hedge unwanted risks. As a result, idiosyncratic risk and event risk pose limits on arbitrage as well.

The EMH has had a huge impact on the financial industry. It has contributed to the growing popularity of index products including passive index funds and exchange-traded funds (ETFs). Within the financial industry, however, there is greater consensus that market inefficiency exists. The key question for practitioners is not *whether* the market is efficient, but *how* efficient it is? If the market inefficiency is so small that the costs and the risks outweigh the benefits of exploiting the inefficiency, low cost passive investment is a better choice. On the other hand, if the benefits from exploiting the inefficiency are more than sufficient to compensate for the costs and the risks, investors may elect to pursue an active investment strategy.

A number of factors deter   mine the market efficiency of an asset class. One factor is the complexity of the product. The more complex the financial instrument is, the less efficient its market is. For example, the exotic derivatives market is less efficient than the stock market and the collateralized debt obligation market is less efficient than the mortgage rate market. The composition of market participants also impacts its relative efficiency. A market dominated by rational, profit-motivated investors is more efficient than a market with many non-profit seeking participants. For example, currency markets tend to be less efficient because many of the participants—central banks, corporate hedgers and tourists—are not motivated by profits when they trade currencies. Stock markets, on the other hand, are more efficient because they are dominated by profit seeking investors. The liquidity of the underlying instruments and the market transparency influence market efficiency, too. Over-the-counter financial products are less transparent and less efficient whereas large cap stocks traded on the New York Stock Exchange are highly liquid and more efficient.

All these suggest that stock markets, especially those of developed countries, are relatively efficient. It is difficult to find bargains in the stock market. As a consequence, it is not an easy task for an active investor to deliver alpha—the return in excess of the compensation for the risk taken. In order to generate better risk-adjusted returns than passive investors, successful active investors need to have one or more of the following edges over average investors:

- **Information edge:** Delivering consistent alpha through active management depends on a manager's expertise to collect and analyze all information that impacts a company's revenues and profits. The best active managers collect information that may go far beyond the basic financial information that typical investors use in investment strategy formulation. Some managers also incorporate information that average investors do not have access to, for such information is costly to obtain or may require industry knowledge to acquire. They often rely on detailed information about a company's suppliers, customers, and competitors to make better decisions than average investors.

- **Insight edge**: Some investors have a better understanding of the interaction between different pieces of information. As new information arrives, they are better at estimating the impact and making educated bets with better odds than average investors' bets.

- **Implementation edge**: Some investors are good at controlling trading costs and manage risks better than others. Effective cost reduction and risk management allow for exploitation of market anomalies that other investors cannot take advantage of. When a strategy has low alpha and requires leverage, access to low-cost financing also adds to implementation edge.

- **Conviction edge**: Some investors are better at adhering to their own disciplined investment approaches than others are. Investors often judge investment strategies and managers using short-term performance instead of a long-term track record. Although the old Wall Street saying "You are only as good as your last trade" is a little extreme, average investors are quick in chasing returns and abandoning a valid strategy after periods of low returns or losses. It takes a deep understanding of the market and conviction to build investment strategies which work in the long run, and to resolutely stick to them, despite short-term losses.

Needless to say, developing such edges is not an easy task. Before fees and trading costs, active management is a zero-sum game; for every winning bet, there is a corresponding losing bet. That means when some investors generate positive alpha, other investors generate negative alpha. Active management leads to higher turnover and higher trading costs. When trading costs are taken into consideration, the aggregated alpha generated by active management is slightly negative.

Since the aggregated alpha is negative, the success of some smart active investors depends on the existence of a sufficient number of "less smart" investors who place losing bets. If less sophisticated active investors get out of the active management markets, it naturally becomes more difficult for sophisticated investors to generate better risk-adjusted returns, for remaining market players will have their own sources of investing edge. The 2008 financial crisis hit active equity funds hard and, given poor performances and client redemptions, many funds did not survive the crisis. After the crisis, it was a difficult environment for active funds to generate alphas. Retail investors, especially those who invested in stocks, were slow to come back to the market. The surviving funds had to build new edges over their leaner, meaner competitors. Although all major indices recovered, the performance of active equity funds remained less than sterling.

Managers who currently have an edge over others would still need to constantly improve their investment processes in order to maintain competitive advantage. Although the market is not fully efficient, it is adaptive. If an investor identifies a stock selection signal using novel data or constructs a creative signal from readily available data, it is only a matter of a time before other investors gain access to the same data and construct similar signals. Therefore, the predictive power of a signal often decays or even completely disappears over time. In order to maintain the edge, investors have to constantly explore new data sources, pursue smarter and faster ways to collect and analyze information, investigate new portfolio construction and risk management ideas and increase implementation efficiency. Even for firms with large teams of professionals who devote countless hours to research, success is far from guaranteed.

Technical Analysis versus Fundamental Analysis

For decades, active investors who explore market inefficiencies have had an on-going debate: the relative value of technical analysis versus fundamental analysis. Fundamental analysts analyze the fundamentals of companies to select stocks that are traded either at an absolute discount to intrinsic value, or at a relative discount to other similar stocks. Technical analysts focus on price and volume actions in the market. Many fundamental analysts believe that the weak EMH holds and technical analysis adds little value. They draw upon their industry knowledge and deep understanding of individual companies in looking for attractive investment opportunities. They painstakingly collect detailed information on a company, its suppliers, its customers, and its competitors to evaluate its intrinsic value. Some technical analysts contend that the fundamentals causing the stock price move are already reflected in price/volume actions. With price/volume information available, fundamental analysis adds little extra value. An argument against fundamental analysis is that sentiment—fear and greed—and investors' perception of a company often have larger impact on stock prices than the fundamentals. Economist John Keynes[1] once said "The market can stay irrational longer than you can stay solvent". For example, the dot-com bubble persisted for years before it finally burst in 2000. Similarly, a stock may stay relatively cheap for months or even years until a catalyst triggers investors' interests.

We believe that fundamental and technical signals complement and reinforce each other since they both capture underlying forces driving stock prices. In the long term, a stock's price is determined by its merit: its absolute value or relative value to other stocks. Ultimately, a stock's price will converge towards its value. Fundamental analysis can help investors filter out false technical signals, which are rather frequent, and increase the success rates of investments. In the short term, a stock's price may be determined by popularity contest (supply and demand) instead of meritocracy. Since stock fundamentals do not change much in the short term, technical signals and sentiment signals play larger roles in stock price movements. In order for a stock's price to rise, there must be more buyers who want to buy the stock than sellers who want to sell, or short sell the stock. Understanding technical signals helps investors determine the timing of entries and exits. Since a combined approach increases investing edge, we will discuss both technical signals and fundamental signals in this book.

Quantitative Analysis

Many investors distinguish quantitative analysis from both technical and fundamental analysis and treat it as a distinct type of investment analysis. From our point of view, quantitative analysis is a systematic and efficient approach to test and implement technical and fundamental signals instead of a different type of investment analysis. Using quantitative analysis, the value of an idea or a trading system can be tested using statistical measures. Technical analysts have long adopted quantitative analysis to backtest technical signals, optimize parameters, estimate profits, evaluate risks, and reduce drawdowns. Fundamental portfolio managers and quantitative portfolio managers explore similar information with different focus. Successful fundamental portfolio managers tend to become experts in analyzing a number of stocks, usually no more than 50 to 100, and progressively acquire higher stock selection skills within that universe. Successful quantitative portfolio managers, on the other hand, systemically invest in hundreds or even thousands of stocks. Although their skills in selecting individual stocks may be lower, the diversification benefit of the large investment universe substantially reduces portfolio risk. The lower risk compensates the difference in expected alpha and yields similar information ratios—the ratio of the expected active return to the active risk.

Exhibit 1-1 shows the general framework for quantitative equity portfolio management. Quantitative portfolio management starts with a variety of information and data used by

---

[1] Keynes also developed the Keynes's General Theory: the modern capitalist economy does not automatically work at top efficiency, but can be raised to that level by the intervention and the influence of the government. The theory is widely cited in the justification of government bail-outs and stimulus packages in response to recessions.

technical and fundamental analysts. Popular inputs are price/volume data, fundamental financial data, news, and analyst recommendations. These data are fed into a systematic model to generate alpha forecasts for stocks. The alpha forecasts are combined with risk estimations and trading cost estimations to construct a final portfolio using portfolio optimization techniques. Portfolio managers then select suitable trading venues to execute trade baskets.

Exhibit 1-1 Overview of quantitative portfolio management

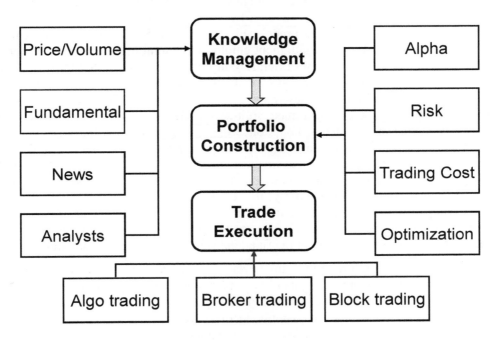

A popular misconception about quantitative investment is that it, unlike fundamental analysis, relies purely on computer models instead of human judgment to make investment decisions. While it is certainly true that quantitative investors heavily use systematic approaches to analyze the data and build investment models, human judgment nevertheless plays a crucial role in every step of the investment process. Ultimately, investors decide on which signals to test, establish criteria to analyze the statistical significance of the signals, decipher ways to combine different signals, build methods to control the portfolio risk as well as arrive at a view on efficiently implementing trading strategies.

Quantitative investment does have its limitation for not all information is quantifiable. For instance, the impact of management team changes, new product launches, or competitors' strategic shifts are all difficult to be systematically evaluated and included in a quantitative model. The best fundamental analysts, on the other hand, frequently incorporate such qualitative information in making investment decisions. Many successful quantitative portfolio managers accept statistician George Box's saying that "all models are wrong, but some are useful." Most quantitative models are based on solid economic theories and built upon sensible assumptions. At the same time, portfolio managers recognize that even sensible assumptions are too simple to capture the full market complexity. Furthermore, markets are not only complex, but are also adaptive. If other competitors explore similar strategies, the strategies become increasingly less profitable. As other market participants respond to the trading flows generated by the strategies, the market dynamic changes and the profit potential may erode or completely disappear. Thus, successful managers continuously analyze market conditions, adjust their strategies in response to market changes, and develop new strategies to maintain their competitive edge.

Another limitation is that quantitative strategies tend to be slow to respond to rapid market changes, especially changes triggered by events. In order to remove behavioral biases, quantitative models follow a predefined set of rules. Sometimes, the rules may break down. In those cases, human judgment employing common sense makes for better decisions. Since quantitative strategies often rely in large part on rigorous statistical tests using long-term data to arrive at investment decisions, it often takes long periods to accumulate a sufficient number of new data points to change the investment decision. Fundamental traders, in contrast, can make split-second decisions in response to news or make quick decisions in a matter of hours once they have established the impact of the event. For example, if an earthquake hits a region, fundamental traders immediately assess the direct damage to companies in the region and estimate the impact on their production (revenues). Once a crude estimation is made, they may make trading decisions on the companies directly impacted by the earthquake. In the days following the earthquake, they may also further evaluate the indirect impact on suppliers or customers to sharpen their initial analysis. Quantitative strategies in comparison may have to wait for weeks until the impact shows up in the financial statement or in other statistics.

In practice, investors can improve investment returns and better manage risks when they effectively combine fundamental analysts' experience and quantitative analysts' modeling skills. To address the limitation of quantitative portfolio management, quantitative portfolio managers increasingly incorporate a discretionary overlay to the investment process. Information derived from fundamental analysis is often used to add or eliminate individual stocks from the portfolio or to adjust the weights of stock selection factors. Increasingly fundamental portfolio managers are adding quantitative analysis into their stock picking process as well. Quantitative analysis also helps fundamental portfolio managers with position sizing and risk management. The quantitative approach provides a disciplined foundation to effectively combine ideas recommended by economists, fundamental researchers and technical analysts.

Active Mutual Funds and Hedge Funds

Active mutual funds have long been a dominant force behind active equity investments. In recent years, equity hedge funds have gradually become an important player in active investments as well. In 2014, the total assets under management (AUM) of hedge funds[2] were more than $2 trillion, with equity funds accounting for over $1 trillion in AUM. Alfred Winslow Jones is widely believed to have started the first hedge fund in 1949. His hedge fund invested in long equity positions that were hedged by short positions to reduce the market risk. Today, the term hedge funds refers to a variety of investment

---

[2] AUM numbers for hedge funds are from Barclay Hedge (www.barclayhedge.com), a leading provider of information on alternative investments.

vehicles, mostly limited partnerships, for sophisticated accredited individual investors and institutional investors to invest in a variety of asset classes. Similar to active equity mutual funds, equity hedge funds invest in global stock markets. As we will discuss in the following chapters, equity hedge funds explore the same strategies and build similar investment processes as traditional active equity mutual funds or institutional funds. The difference lies in a hedge fund's flexibility to short sell, use leverage, and trade derivatives as well as in performance evaluation:

- Most active mutual funds are long only vehicles and harvest positive alpha by investing in stocks that are expected to outperform the market. Equity hedge funds short individual stocks or indices to hedge market/industry exposure as well as harvest the negative alpha of individual stocks.

- Most active mutual funds do not use leverage while equity hedge funds routinely use leverage to boost total expected returns. They hedge unwanted risks, which reduces the total risk of the portfolio allowing for the employment of greater leverage.

- Most active mutual funds do not trade in derivatives. Equity hedge funds have the flexibility to use derivatives to hedge tail risks or to leverage their bets.

- Most active mutual funds track specific benchmark indices and are evaluated by active returns against indices. Equity hedge funds are often evaluated by their absolute returns instead of active returns against specific market benchmarks.

Equity long/short hedge funds on average still have a significant long bias. Jain, Yongvanich, and Zhou (2011) studied the market beta of the HFRI Equity Hedge Index[3] using Kalman Filter[4] and 36-month rolling regressions of the index return against the stock market return. The study showed that equity hedge funds on average had 50-60% market exposure. As shown in Exhibit 1-2, the HFRI Equity Hedge Index returned 10.1% a year in 1994-2013, 1.6% higher than S&P 500's return of 8.5%. Furthermore, the annual volatility of the index was only 9.3%, substantially lower than the S&P 500's annual volatility of 15.5%.

A particular subtype of the equity hedge fund strategy referred to as "market neutral", usually keeps the portfolios close to cash neutral (dollar values of long positions close to dollar values of short positions) and beta neutral (net market beta exposure close to zero). Since the market neutral strategy does not capture the positive market risk premium, the return of market neutral funds in 1994-2013 was 5.6%, about half of the Equity Hedge Index returns. Nevertheless, because of tight risk management, the annual volatility of market neutral funds was only 3.2%, about one third of the volatility of the Equity Hedge Index. Therefore, the market neutral funds had a higher return-to-volatility ratio than the HFRI Equity Hedge Index.

Another type of equity hedge fund trading strategy called "short biased" has negative market exposure. Since short-biased funds have negative exposure to the stock market,

---

[3] Published by Hedge Fund Research Inc., the HFRI Equity Hedge Index includes seven sub-strategies: equity market neutral, fundamental growth, fundamental value, quantitative directional, energy/basic materials, technology/healthcare, short-biased, and multi-strategy.
[4] Kalman Filter is a statistical model that better captures the time-varying market beta of the equity hedge fund index than rolling regressions.

they have negative returns in the long run. The return of the short-biased funds was -1.9% in 1994-2013. Because of negative long-term returns, short-biased funds account for only a tiny fraction of equity hedge funds. Investors who have high market exposures in other investments, however, may use short-biased funds to reduce market exposures and hedge market risks.

Exhibit 1-2 Historical returns of equity hedge fund indices

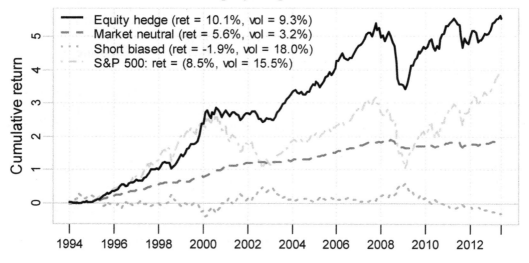

Fundamental Law of Active Management

The information ratio is the ratio of the expected active return to the active risk and measures the risk-adjusted return of a strategy. The information ratio is an important measure of a strategy's long term success. It is therefore important to know the key attributes that determine the information ratio. The Fundamental Law of Active Management, originally developed by Richard Grinold and extended by other researchers, provides a theoretical framework for predicting the ex-ante information ratio of a strategy.

The original Fundamental Law of Active Management predicts the information ratio using the following formula:

$$IR = IC \times \sqrt{N}$$

where IR is the information ratio;

IC is the information coefficient;

N is the number of independent forecasts.

The Information Coefficient (IC), a measure of skill or performance, measures the correlation between assets' predicted returns and actual returns. It is measured on a scale between 0 and 1. In practice, the linear correlation coefficient or rank correlation coefficient between stock selection signal values (or expected alphas) and realized future returns is often used as an estimate for IC. Higher IC values indicate higher predictive powers and higher skills. A strategy with an IC of 1 means that the strategy has perfect prediction of the actual returns and a strategy with IC close to 0 suggests it has no forecasting power.[5] In practice, a monthly IC—correlation between forecasted returns and forward one-month realized returns—higher than 3-4% is sufficient for a strategy to be profitable. The number of independent forecasts (N), a measure of breadth, measures how many independent bets investors can make in a year. For strategies with similar ICs, the more independent bets that investors can make, the higher the information ratio. The relationship can be roughly explained by the central limit theorem: as the sample size N increases, the expected value of average returns stays constant, but the standard error of the average is proportional to $1/\sqrt{N}$ and the information ratio increases with the square root of the independent bets, $\sqrt{N}$.

The relationship between the IR and the breadth suggests that investors can improve the IR by making many small bets on a large number of independent trades instead of making large bets on a small number of trades. Since N is the number of independent bets in a year, it has two aspects: the number of cross-sectional bets on different assets at any point in time and the number of independent bets on the same asset across time. At any point in time, investors may make multiple bets on all assets that are included in their investment universe. However, the number of independent bets does not grow linearly with the number of assets because common factors (e.g., the market) impact the returns of all stocks. In fact, the effective number of bets is substantially lower than the number of assets since the number of common factors is much lower than the number of assets. Investors can also make multiple bets on the same asset in a year. The number of independent bets does not grow linearly with the number of portfolio rebalances either. Consider, for example, the case where an investor uses price-to-earnings (P/E) ratio as the single criterion to build a long/short portfolio and rebalances the portfolio every week. Since the P/E ratio tends to be similar from one week to the next, the new portfolio has high correlation with the old portfolio after the rebalancing, which means that a bet made each new week is not an independent bet. Therefore, the number of independent bets is often much lower than the number of rebalances.

Clarke *et al.* (2002) added an extra term, transfer coefficient, in the information ratio prediction equation:

$$IR = IC \times \sqrt{N} \times TC$$

The Transfer Coefficient (TC), a measure of implementation, measures the extent to which a strategy can incorporate its predictions into a portfolio. A strategy with no constraints can have a transfer coefficient close to 1. In reality, portfolio managers face many constraints. A long-only constraint and a limited risk budget are two main constraints in many investment mandates that limit the transfer coefficient. Some asset managers have marketed balanced alpha (120/20 to 150/50) funds to expand the active management beyond long only funds. For each dollar of capital, a 130/30 fund has $1.3 exposure to long positions and $0.3 exposure to short positions. The goal is to adapt existing knowledge and practices to increase the transfer coefficient. Expanding the active strategy from long only to long/short allows for investing in assets with negative alphas through short positions. The inclusion of short positions as well as the increased

---

[5] Alternatively, a scale between -1 and 1 can be used. An IC of -x, $0 < x \leq 1$, is as valuable as an IC of x since we can simply reverse the sign of the positions to yield a positive IC if the original IC is negative.

exposures to assets with positive alphas leads to a higher transfer coefficient. Overall, it is estimated that by relaxing the long only constraint, a 130/30 strategy can increase the information ratio by ~50%.

Kroll *et al.* (2005) further expanded the Fundamental Law of Active Management to include trading costs in the information ratio prediction:

$$IR = IC \times \sqrt{N} \times TC - (TCost \times TR \times 2 / TE)$$

where TCost is the average trading cost per transaction as a fraction of trade value

TR is a measure of the annual portfolio turnover

TE is the portfolio tracking error (expected volatility of alpha)

Portfolio turnover is a measure of trading activity. It is defined as the ratio of the average of the total amount of new securities purchased and the amount of securities sold in a particular period to the market value of the portfolio. The total trading is $TR \times 2$ and the total trading cost as a fraction of portfolio value is $TCost \times TR \times 2$. In other words, trading costs reduce the alpha by $TCost \times TR \times 2$ and reduce the information ratio by $TCost \times TR \times 2/TE$.

The Fundamental Law of Active Management explains the different approaches that fundamental portfolio managers and quantitative portfolio managers use to achieve good information ratios. Fundamental portfolio managers tend to have higher ICs and lower breadth. They focus on stocks they know well and have more concentrated portfolios. Since fundamental stock picking requires deep knowledge of the stocks being analyzed, diversification often means less depth in research and leads to lower skills. Warren Buffett once said, *"Diversification is a protection against ignorance. It makes very little sense for those who know what they're doing."* He believes that those investors who understand their stocks well should put their investments in the stocks with greatest profit potential instead of blindly diversifying their portfolios. At the end of March 2014, Berkshire Hathaway, held only 45 stocks in the $105 billion portfolio. The top four stocks, Wells Fargo, Coca Cola, American Express and IBM, accounted for more than 60% of the portfolio weight. Similarly, many fundamental portfolio managers keep their portfolio small and focus on the assets with highest expected returns. As a result, they often hold no more than 50 stocks and skew portfolio weights towards a few high conviction stocks. Quantitative portfolio managers tend to have lower ICs and higher breadth. They often have more diversified portfolios and actively limit the maximum weight of individual stocks to manage risk. Since systematic quantitative analysis can be applied to all the stocks in the investment universe, it is a simple task to estimate the forecasted returns of thousands of stocks. The accuracy of the forecast in each stock, however, tends to be lower. Portfolio optimization is often used to control risk exposures and to address the uncertainty in forecasts. It is for this reason quantitative portfolio managers tend to hold more stocks in their portfolios, often as high as several hundred.

Although expressed as an equation, the Fundamental Law of Active Management is not an exact formula to determine the information ratio of a portfolio. Instead, it is a general framework to estimate the impact of different contributors to the information ratio. Even though the number of independent bets cannot be quantified, it does not prevent us from qualitatively evaluating strategies using the Fundamental Law of Active Management.

Investors can increase the IR by finding factors that have better predictive power than the ones in their existing models to increase information coefficient. They can also find factors that are less correlated with the ones in their existing models to increase breadth. Alternatively, investors can increase the IR by reducing constraints that are detrimental to returns to increase the transfer coefficient. For those trading strategies that have high turnover, finding better trading algorithms to reduce trading costs is often the most effective way to boost the information ratio.

Conclusion

Active equity management explores different market inefficiencies with the goal of achieving better adjusted returns for investors. In order to achieve this goal, successful active investors need to build and maintain their information edge, insight edge, implementation edge, and conviction edge. Following the Fundamental Law of Active Management, the theme of the book is to help investors improve the information coefficient (IC), breadth (N), the transfer coefficient (TC), and reduce trading costs (TCost and TR) to achieve better risk-adjusted returns:

- Chapter 2 covers a variety of common data sources typically used in investment process.

- Chapters 3-7 examine a wide variety of seasonal effects, economic and market indicators, technical signals, fundamental signals, and other signals useful to build investment skills.

- Chapters 8-11 discuss signal construction, signal combination, portfolio optimization, management of portfolio risks and constraints, and dynamic factor timing to effectively improve information coefficients, increase breadth, and manage transfer coefficients.

- Chapters 12-13 survey statistical arbitrage and other investment strategies that help investors further broaden their stock selection skills and apply them to other asset classes.

- Chapter 14 discusses trading cost analysis, management of portfolio turnover, and trading strategies that help investors reduce trading costs.

Chapter 2

Data

Successful implementation of investment strategies depends heavily on the utilization of good data. Whether we want to test a technical trading system, or estimate the value of a company using a discounted cash flow model, or build a complex quantitative portfolio, we need clean and well-organized data. In order to make investment decisions, sophisticated investors routinely examine dozens or even hundreds of qualitative or quantitative data sources. From exploring a new idea using fresh data to implementing a trading strategy using market data, managing large amounts of high-quality data effectively is a key ingredient to success. In this chapter, we discuss commonly used data in investment processes, the sources of these data, as well as popular approaches to data management.

Asset Identifiers, Descriptions, Prices and Volumes

Let us begin with the basic data used to build and test investment strategies. Asset identifiers and descriptions are basic information that helps investors understand asset characteristics. Prices and volumes are basic market data that help investors understand the performance of different assets.

Asset Identifiers

Asset-specific data are associated with one or more asset identifiers. The identifier that stock investors are most familiar with is the ticker. For US common stocks, American depository receipts (ADR), exchange-traded funds (ETF) traded on US exchanges, tickers with one to five letters are used to uniquely identify these assets on a given day. Some tickers may contain a dot to distinguish different share classes. For example, the ticker of Berkshire Hathaway B shares is BRK.B[6] and the ticker of the corresponding A shares is BRK.A. Since a ticker identifies a unique tradable asset on a US exchange, it is the most common identifier for trading. However, a stock's ticker may change when there are corporate actions such as mergers and acquisitions. Even when there are no corporate events, a ticker may change if the issuer chooses to do so. For example, PowerShares QQQ Trust, a popular ETF that tracks NASDAQ-100 index, changed its ticker from QQQ to QQQQ on December 1, 2004 and then again changed its ticker back to QQQ on March 23, 2011. Furthermore, the ticker of a delisted company may be recycled for another company. These inconsistencies pose a challenge in using the ticker as the identifier for time series data. It is therefore crucial to identify ticker changes in order to guarantee the continuity of other key information (*e.g.*, prices and volumes) of an asset.

---

[6] Not all data sources use a dot before the share classes. For example, Yahoo Finance uses BRK-B. The inconsistency in tickers among data sources is a reason why it is difficult to map different data sources using tickers.

Reuters Instrument Code, RIC, is an identifier related to ticker. For a stock, its RIC is usually its ticker followed by a dot and the exchange code of the exchange that the stock is traded on. For example, the RIC of Citigroup stock (Ticker: C) traded on New York Stock Exchange (NYSE) is C.N. The following lists some exchange codes in the US market:

Exchange	NYSE	NASDAQ	AMEX	Pacific	Boston
Code	N	O	A	P	B

CUSIP (Committee on Uniform Securities Identification Procedures) is another popular identifier for North American securities. CUSIP is an 8- or 9-character code that identifies a stock or a bond. The first 6 characters identify the issuer; the 7th and the 8th characters identify the exact issue (numbers are usually used for equities and letters are used for fixed income securities); the 9th character, if it is included in the CUSIP, is a check digit calculated from the first 8 characters (it can be used to detect errors in the CUSIP). Multiple share classes of the same company have the same first 6 characters. Thus, CUSIP provides an easy way to identify different share classes of the same company. Similar to the ticker, the CUSIP of an asset can change over time as well. For instance, on July 1, 2009, AIG had a 1-for-20 reverse split to make its stock more appealing to a broader set of investors (the close price of AIG on June 30th was $1.16). Its ticker remained the same, but the CUSIP was changed from 026874107 to 026874784. The first six characters for the issuer stayed the same so that other securities issued by AIG did not need to change CUSIPs; but the 7th and the 8th characters changed to reflect the reverse split. From this example we can see that since the CUSIP may change over time, if we use CUSIP as the identifier for time series data, we need to track CUSIP changes as well.

ISIN, International Securities Identification Number, is an identifier related to CUSIP for securities beyond North America. An ISIN has 12 digits: the first 2 characters are the ISO (International Organization for Standardization) country code; the next nine characters identify the security (For a US or Canadian asset, CUSIP is used); the last digit is a check digit. Another popular identifier for global securities is **SEDOL** (Stock Exchange Daily Official List). SEDOL is a 6- or 7-character code with the 7th character being a check digit.

Combining data from different sources often requires a robust identifier mapping system so that different pieces of information about a stock can be stored together in a table. To address the identifier change issue, many data providers adopted their own identifiers to track an asset's history and provide a mapping to other identifiers over time. For example, CRSP (Center for Research in Security Prices) uses **PERMNO**, a unique permanent security identification number for each stock. As the name suggests, PERMNO does not change during a stock's trading history and is not recycled after the stock is delisted or ceases to exist. That is, PERMNO does not change when the same stock changes its ticker or CUSIP. If a stock is delisted, its PERMNO will not be used by any other stock in the future. PERMNO allows researchers to easily track the performance of a stock through years of history. The existence of a permanent identifier and a daily mapping to other identifiers such as ticker and CUSIP have contributed to CRSP's popularity among academic researchers and financial practitioners. Besides CRSP, major data providers such as Thomson Reuters, Bloomberg, and S&P all have their own versions of permanent identifiers.

Why do different data providers develop their own permanent identifiers instead of collaborating to make a standard one? One reason is that there is no consensus as to which "permanent" identifier is the best. Instead, each provider makes a judgment call on whether a corporate action constitutes a fundamental change to an asset that requires an identifier change. An example of such a judgment call is how to deal with mergers and acquisitions. If a large company acquires a small company, the combined company usually keeps the identifier of the acquirer. The merger of two companies of similar sizes sometimes does not have a clear answer. On October 1, 2010, United Airlines (UAUA traded on NASDAQ) merged with Continental Airlines (CAL traded on NYSE) to form United Continental Holdings (UAL traded on NYSE). Some providers treated the combined company as a new entity whereas others treated it as a continuation of the United Airlines.

Asset Descriptions

Besides names and identifiers, data vendors also provide descriptions to help investors classify different assets. Depending on investment objectives, active managers tend to focus on specific types of assets. For example, managers whose strength resides in being able to time markets tend to trade ETFs or index futures instead of individual stocks. Fundamental portfolio managers and research analysts often focus on one industry or on one sector. The following are some of the common descriptions that investors use to classify different equities.

Security type: Typical security types for equities are common stock, ADR, ETF, real estate investment trust (REIT), preferred stock, mutual fund, and closed-end fund.

Exchange: The exchanges are where stocks are traded. For equities that are traded in the United States, most of the stocks with sufficient market caps are traded on exchanges such as NYSE, NASDAQ, NYSE Arca (formerly Archipelago/Pacific Exchange), and NYSE AMEX (formerly American Stock Exchange); other stocks are traded over the counter (OTC).

Shares outstanding and market cap: Since shares outstanding and market cap play a major role in determining an asset's liquidity, risk and potential alpha opportunity, some funds only invest in liquid large-cap (market cap over $10 billion) and mid-cap (market cap between $2 billion and $10 billion) stocks. Other funds, to ostensibly capitalize on market inefficiencies, invest in small-cap (market cap below $2 billion) stocks.[7]

Sector/industry classification: Since stocks in the same industry usually tend to move in tandem, investors often group stocks by sectors or industries. Jointly developed by S&P and MSCI, GICS (Global Industry Classifications Standard) is a popular choice for industry classification. In the GICS system, each company is assigned an 8-digit GICS code: the first 2 digits identify the sector; the first 4 digits identify the industry group; the first 6 digits identify the industry; the full 8 digits identify the sub industries. The GICS system includes 10 sectors, 24 industry groups, 68 industries, and 154 sub industries. The

---

[7] This is just one way of classifying stocks by market cap. Other investors may choose different market cap thresholds or use market cap rankings instead.

GICS sectors are energy, materials, industrials, consumer discretionary, consumer staples, health care, financials, information technology, telecommunication services, and utilities. Overall, GICS classification is reasonably good at explaining stock return co-movements within the same industry and return differences among industries. Another popular choice is North American Industry Classification System (NAICS). Developed as a joint effort of the United States, Canada, and Mexico, NAICS classifies each company using a 6-digit code: the first 2 digits identify the sector; the first 3 digits identify the subsector; the first 4 digits identify the industry group; the first 5 digits identify the NAICS industry; the full 6 digits identify national industries.

There is no consensus as to whether single industry classification is a good choice for conglomerates with subsidiaries in different industries. Risk models often adopt a multi-industry approach by assigning positive weights to one or more industries with total industry weights adding up to 1. The multi-industry approach is a valid choice for risk management as the weights of different industries reflect the sensitivity of stock returns to the returns of the different industries that the stock has exposure to.

Price, Volume, Dividends and Splits

All investors need information on prices, volumes, dividends, and splits to estimate investment returns and the liquidity of the underlying assets. Prices and volumes are also key inputs in building technical signals. Individual investors have access to free daily information on prices, volumes, and dividends through a number of providers. For example, finance.yahoo.com is a popular data source for historical prices and volumes that individual investors use to test their trading ideas. Besides publishing information on open, high, low, close and volume, many data vendors also provide daily return or cumulative return information. For example, Yahoo provides adjusted close prices that adjust historical prices by incorporating cash/stock dividends and splits. When a stock pays dividend, the adjusted price in Yahoo makes the following adjustment:

Let T be the ex-dividend date[8] and $T-1$ be the last trading day before T. All prices before T is adjusted by a multiplier $\dfrac{C_{T-1} - d_T}{C_{T-1}}$, where C_{T-1} is the close price at $T-1$ and d_T is the dividend per share.

For rigorous analysis, free data sources have their limitations. The data from free sources are usually of lower quality than the commercial data. Data vendors spend significant resources on cleaning the data so that they have more accurate prices and are better at incorporating corporate actions such as dividends, splits, spin-offs, and rights offerings. Thomson Reuters, Bloomberg, and CRSP all maintain a comprehensive collection of daily security prices, returns, volumes, dividends, and other company distributions such as rights offering and spin-offs for stocks. These data include historical information for stocks that no longer exist or are delisted (delisted stocks may still be traded over the counter) from the exchanges—this ensures that data are free of survivorship bias. They also provide information on stock indices, Treasury bonds and mutual funds.

---

[8] Ex-dividend date is the first date that the buyers of a stock will not receive the dividend. That is, if an investor buys the stock on the day before the ex-dividend date, he is entitled to the dividend; if he buys the stock on the ex-dividend date, he is not entitled to the dividend.

Trade and Quote (TAQ) Data

TAQ data include all intraday trades and quotes for stocks listed on NYSE, AMEX and NASDAQ. The trade data include all tick-by-tick transactions and the quote data include detailed bid/ask information. High-frequency firms were early users of TAQ data. The huge size of the data, often several gigabytes a day, made it extremely unwieldy to work with and exploit. However, with recent strides in computing technology, mid-frequency and low-frequency fund managers have increasingly recognized the potential benefits of using TAQ data and indeed many have now incorporated it in their research.[9] For example, 5-min bars—summary of open, high, low, close, volume, and volume-weighted average price for 5-minute periods—constructed from TAQ trade files can be used to estimate average execution prices; they are usually more representative of trade prices than daily open and close prices.

The usage of TAQ data is straightforward except that it is necessary to remove the out-of-order or erroneous data points from the analysis. In one instance, we researched an intraday trading strategy that traded SPY (the most liquid ETF that tracks S&P 500 index) with limit orders for entry and exit. An initial analysis without data cleaning produced an annualized return of 150%. Once the spikes from late trade reports—trades that happened earlier and were reported later with a later timestamp—were removed, all the profit disappeared from this strategy. Further examination of the detailed data revealed the systematic bias: The initial analysis assumed that limit buy orders were executed at negative spikes caused by late trade reports and limit sell orders were executed at positive spikes. In reality, limit orders couldn't be executed at the favorable prices indicated by the late trade reports.

The NBBO file contains continuous national best bid and offer (NBBO) updates and consolidated trades and quotes. The quote file, which is more than ten times larger than the trade file, contains all quotes reported to the consolidated tape (the consolidated tape includes a stock's trades and quotes from all exchanges instead of just the primary exchange). One can also extract the NBBO information from the quote file. If we need detailed quote information, the quote data can be used to derive the entire order book, which shows the series of all open bids/offers and their corresponding quantities at a given time. The order book, in turn, can be used to estimate a stock's liquidity and identify the imbalance between supply and demand of a stock at any given time.

Fundamental Data

Fundamental data refer to any data that capture the fundamentals of individual companies. Traditional fundamental data include information from income statements, balance sheets, and cash flow statements as well as analyst estimates and recommendations. Besides analyst recommendations, institutional ownership, insider trades, and short interests are also broadly used to estimate investor sentiment. A variety of industry-specific data are widely used by investors who conduct detailed analysis on individual companies as well.

---

[9] Traditional row-based SQL databases are less efficient in handling TAQ data. The development of column-based database such as Kdb+ has facilitated the usage of TAQ data.

Financial Reports

Standard & Poor's Compustat is a major provider of fundamental data. It covers quarterly and annual income statements, balance sheets, cash flow statements, and supplemental data items on more than 70,000 securities and 90% of the world's tradable stock market values. The database includes hundreds of variables ranging from earnings per share (EPS) to the number of employees. CRSP and Compustat also provide a merged database that simplifies matching the security price data with the fundamental data. Besides collecting data from company filings such as annual and quarterly reports, Compustat also obtains information not available in the reports through their contacts with corporate insiders. Furthermore, Compustat standardizes the data collected from different companies by removing reporting variability (e.g., accounting differences) and bias to make data items more comparable across companies.

Another major source for financial report data is Thomson Reuters's Worldscope, which covers similar information as Compustat. Worldscope also takes into consideration a variety of accounting conventions to facilitate comparisons between companies and industries within and across countries. Before 2000, Compustat covered more companies than Worldscope but now the difference in coverage is rather small between these two data sources. Generally, Compustat is considered to have slightly better coverage of US and Canadian companies while Worldscope is perceived to have better coverage of international companies.

Analyst Estimations

The Institutional Brokers Estimates System (I/B/E/S) provides consensus and detailed analyst-by-analyst forecasts. Although I/B/E/S does not directly compensate analysts for providing their forecast data, analysts receive exposure to the broad base of I/B/E/S subscribers. So I/B/E/S has a good coverage of analyst recommendations. Besides headline numbers for analysts' earnings per share forecasts, buy/sell recommendations and price targets, it also reports detailed forecasts for revenues, cash flows, and long-term growth projections. The detailed information is updated several times a day to provide up-to-date information on analyst revisions. There is sometimes a delay between the time that an analyst revision is released and the time that the data become available in I/B/E/S. A comparison between I/B/E/S and Bloomberg indicates that analyst revisions tend to be available in Bloomberg earlier than in I/B/E/S. Besides, some analysts are not included in the I/B/E/S database. Hence, large institutions often have alternative sources for analyst data. One popular choice for real-time broker research data and analyst estimations is Thomson Reuters's First Call product.

Institutional Ownership and Insider Trades

Investment managers with at least $100 million assets under management are required to file a quarterly Form 13F to report their long positions within 45 days of the end of a quarter. Raw institutional ownership data are available in SEC EDGAR (electronic data-gathering, analysis, and retrieval) system. The 13F data are widely used as information on institutional holdings and hedge fund ownership. The total holdings of a stock by all funds, active funds, or a selected group of "successful" hedge funds, as well as the breadth of fund participation in specific stocks, are closely followed by investors. Active weights (the difference between weights in institutional holdings and weights in a market index) by sector and style (e.g., small cap versus large cap, value versus growth) are reported by many brokers as well.

Officers, directors, and owners of more than 10% of the stocks of a company are required to file Form 4 to report their ownership changes (purchases and sales of stocks, grants or exercises of stocks or stock options) within two days of the ownership change. The raw data for insider trades are also available in the EDGAR system. Retail investors can find insider trades for stocks on websites such as www.insidercow.com. Most institutional investors use vendor-compiled databases for institutional ownership and insider trades since it is easier to retrieve holdings data of a stock, or of a fund, as well as the time series of holdings from a database than from the EDGAR system. For example, the FactSet LionShares Global Ownership database and the Thomson Financial CDA/Spectrum database both provide summary and detailed ownership data of institutions and insiders.

Short Interest

NYSE, AMEX and NASDAQ publish short interest data twice a month for short positions settled on the last business day on or before the 15th and on the last business day of the month. The data usually become available to the public eight days later through a variety of data providers. For example, www.shortsqueeze.com compiles the short interest data and estimates short squeeze risks—the risk of price spike if short sellers have to cover their positions in a short period of time—using a variety of other information such as institutional ownership and stock price volatility.

When short sellers short a security, they need to borrow the security from a broker or from institutional investors and deliver the security to the purchaser. Thus, the short interests of stocks can also be estimated from the securities lending data. For daily securities lending and short interest information, Data Explorers is a leading provider. Initially, Data Explorers only distributed data to subscribers who contributed their own securities lending[10] or borrowing data to the database, so its usage was limited to large banks, asset managers and some hedge funds. The participant list has been growing over the years and it is estimated that its participants now represent over 80% of the securities lending market. In recent years, Data Explorers has also been selling non-contributor access to most of the securities lending data: the main difference is that contributors receive cost to borrow securities (fees) and non-contributors receive only cost to borrow scores of 1-10 (lowest cost-highest cost). The data cover more than 95% of the US listed stocks as well as most of the actively traded international stocks. Information embedded in the data includes available supply (shares available to borrow and the number of suppliers), demand (shares on loan), utilization (percent of total used and unused supplies that is currently on loan), and costs (fees are available to contributors and cost buckets are available to non-contributors). SunGard's Astec Analytics is another provider of daily securities lending data. Although SunGard has less coverage than Data Explorers, it does not require user participation in order to receive data and it provides cost to borrow to

---

[10] Many prime brokers, asset managers, and custodian are suppliers of shares. They set up securities lending desks to lend securities to short sellers and get compensated by charging fees on the shares that the short sellers borrow.

non-contributors. Thus, it is an alternative choice for users who prefer not to disclose their own information to a third party.

Risk Models

To estimate portfolio risk, institutional investors often use factor risk models. Factor risk models use either fundamental factors or macroeconomic factors to explain stock returns, volatility, and correlation between different stocks' returns. Fundamental factor models use stock attributes such as size, book-to-price ratio, dividend yield, and industry classification. Barra, Axioma and APT provide data on stocks' exposures to a wide variety of fundamental factors as well as country and industry factors, the covariance matrix of these factors, and the daily returns of these factors. Macroeconomic factor models, by contrast, use economic factors instead. For instance, the Northfield Macroeconomic Equity Model includes the following market and economic factors: inflation, industrial production, slope of interest rate term structure, investor confidence, foreign exchange rates, housing starts, and oil prices.

Industry-Specific Data

Investors who focus on specific sectors or industries also explore a large number of industry-specific data. Compustat provides industry-specific factors for a variety of industries such as airline, gaming, health care facilities, oil and gas, and retail. These industry-specific factors tend to focus on the data that shed light on a company's ability to generate current and future revenues and on a company's expenses. For example, the oil and gas industry is divided into three sectors: upstream, midstream, and downstream. The upstream sector focuses on the exploration and production (E&P) of oil and gas; the midstream sector focuses on the transportation and storage of oil and gas products; the downstream sector focuses on refining crude oil, processing raw natural gas, and marketing final products such as gasoline and diesel. For upstream E&P companies, Compustat reports current production of oil and gas as well as the proved reserves for future production on the revenue side and the exploration expenses on the expense side.

Other data vendors provide more specialized and detailed data for selected industries. For the retail industry, some investors use SymphonyIRI Group's retail tracking data and store sales data. SymphonyIRI collects point-of-sale data from thousands of grocery stores, drug stores, and department stores. Once the data are processed and validated, SymphonyIRI delivers the price and volume information on different products to investors so that investors can better estimate different companies' revenues and profits. For pharmaceutical and biotechnology companies, investors focus on existing drug or medical device sales and new drug developments. Revere Healthcare™ provides information on these companies by tracking existing drugs, medical devices, and drug pipelines. The following is some information included in the data:

- Trade names and generic names of approved drugs and drug candidates
- Historical sales of different drugs and drug patent expiration dates

- Information on New Drug Application (NDA), Biological License Application (BLA), Prescription Drug user Fee Act (PDUFA) dates, and FDA Advisory Committee meetings[11]

Patents

Many companies, especially the ones in information technology and healthcare sectors, depend heavily on technological innovation as a source of competitive advantage. These companies tend to release new products earlier than their competitors and attract more loyal customers. The number of patents and the number of patent citations are commonly used as measures of innovation. The number of patents measures the concrete output of a company's research and development. The number of patent citations measures the importance of these patents. Although patent filing information is readily available, mapping patents to companies poses a major challenge because many patents are filed in the name of subsidiaries of the parent companies. Some data providers offer both detailed patent information and aggregated quantitative measures for evaluating innovations. One leading provider, Patent Board, provides Patent Scorecard. The Patent Scorecard uses a systematic approach to quantify the intellectual property of companies and provides scores to rank the technology innovation of different companies.

Additional Data

In addition to the price and volume data used in technical analysis and fundamental data used in fundamental analysis, active investors continue to look for new data sources to extract useful information and to gain an edge over competitors. Some investors use news feeds and internet data to quickly capture new information and gauge market sentiment; some analyze economic links among different companies; some others explore information from other markets such as the options market.

News Data

Given the impact of news on stock prices, institutional investors and individuals have long incorporated news in making investment decisions. CNBC and Bloomberg TV are broadcasted on many trading floors around the globe. News feeds from Reuters, Bloomberg, and Dow Jones are followed by many practitioners as well. Although fundamental portfolio managers and technical analysts have traded on news for decades, quantitative portfolio managers have been late adopters of news analytics. The main reason is that news is communicated in words instead of numbers. An experienced trader can respond to news almost instantaneously by watching or reading the news. Quantitative portfolio managers need to convert those words to numbers before the information can be incorporated into portfolio construction and acted upon. Such conversion is called natural language processing. Large scale natural language processing requires both sophisticated algorithms and computational power/speed that has only became feasible in the past decade.

One of the leading providers of news analytics is RavenPack. RavenPack scans news content from a variety of sources (newswires, corporate releases, papers, rating agencies,

---

[11] These are different key filings and dates for drug developments and clinical trials.

investment banks, and regulatory agencies), processes it in real time using natural language processing algorithms, and publishes the extracted information. Key information used by investors includes relevance score, novelty score, and sentiment score. If a company is mentioned in a news story, a relevance score between 0 and 100 indicates the relevance of a news story to the company. A score of 100 means that the company is the focus of the news story; a score close to 0 means that the company is only passively mentioned in the story. Novelty score measures how new or novel the news story is over the past 24 hours. The first story that hits the news has a novelty score of 100 and subsequent similar stories have novelty scores quickly decay towards 0. Sentiment score measures news sentiment for the company using words in the story. A score close to 100 indicates positive sentiment and a score close to 0 indicates negative sentiment.

Internet Data and Social Media Data

Besides deciphering information from news, many investors also turn to websites and social media sites such as blogs, Facebook, and Twitter to look for information. For example, Google Trends provides weekly and daily (hourly for the top 20 hot searches) updates on the search volumes of different search terms such as industry activities, company names, and brands. Therefore, Google Trends can provide timely information on economic activities and consumer interests for specific industries and companies. Motley Fool is a website for investors to make recommendations on their stock picks. Motley Fool CAPS pools the resources of tens of thousands of members in the community to identify stocks to buy or sell. Through the website, www.caps.fool.com, members make predictions on whether particular stocks will outperform or underperform the market and the time frame for such predictions to occur. CAPS system analyzes the hit rate of the each member's historical picks and the returns of those picks to assign ratings to members. Besides distributing detailed recommendations of all contributors, CAPS also assigns a rating for each stock (one star for stocks with the least favorable ratings to five stars for stocks with the most favorable ratings) by aggregating members' recommendations. The aggregation gives higher weights to members who had more accurate forecasts in the past. To access a plethora of data on the internet, some sophisticated investors build web crawlers to systematically scan numerous websites. If the websites have standard templates, these web crawlers can automatically capture the up-to-date information from the websites. Since many updates are not always available through newswires, capturing these updates may help these investors gain the information edge and make investment decisions before other investors do.

Economic Links

A company is economically linked to many other companies. It relies on suppliers for raw materials, depends on customers for revenues, and competes with other firms in the industry. It is important for investors to understand a firm's economic links in order to understand its financials. Information on a company's economic links is scattered in a company's earnings reports, SEC filings, and press releases. For example, SFAS (Statement of Financial Accounting Standards) 131 requires companies to report their major customers. Several data sources also compile such information and make them available for clients. The popular Bloomberg terminal provides a supply chain analysis function SPLC that shows customers, suppliers, and competitors of a selected company in a chart or in a table. Credit Suisse's PEERS database and Revere Supply Chain Relationships™ also provide data on customers, suppliers, competitors, partners (e.g., joint ventures, distributors), and equity investment relationships between securities as well as characterize the importance (high, moderate, or low or in specific percentages) of the relationship.

Option Data

Because of the inherent linkage between stock market and equity derivatives market, investors use information from options trading to forecast stock returns. OptionMetrics's Ivy DB is a widely used database of historical price, implied volatility, and sensitivity for US listed index options and equity options. It provides raw end-of-day pricing information such as bid/ask quotes, trading volumes, and open interests (total number of outstanding option contracts that are held by market participants) as well as calculated fields such as implied volatility, Delta, Gamma, and Theta. The implied volatility is calculated using a binomial tree model that takes discrete dividend payments and possible early exercises of options into consideration. In collaboration with Chicago Board Options Exchange (CBOE), Tick Data (www.tickdata.com) provide investors with Tick Options Data (TOD). TOD contains historical tick-by-tick option trades and market-level bid/ask prices for US equity and index options. Similar to TAQ data for stocks, TOD allows option traders to dig into intraday trades and quotes to test and improve their trading strategies.

Data Management

Investors often must decide on whether to collect raw data and calculate the factors using the raw data or to purchase processed data and even pre-calculated stock selection signals from data vendors. The former approach requires a lot of effort. Since the raw data are seldom of high-quality and well-organized, investors have to build a system to extract information from the original data. In addition, investors need to clean the data and combine different pieces of data to calculate a signal. Purchasing processed data and pre-calculated signals, on the other hand, saves investors the time and resources needed for raw data collection and cleaning. Using vendor-processed data has potential drawbacks though. Raw data give us the flexibility to create a stock selection signal with different flavors. Since we are restricted by what the vendor provides, processed data do not afford as much flexibility as the raw data. Because the vendor needs to collect the data and calculate the signals, the pre-calculated signals may not be as timely as the signals that investors can calculate using the raw data. The delay in the vendor data can also lead to lower alpha, if other investors who process the raw data themselves act earlier on the same information.

To get earnings in a traditional value measure, the price to earnings (P/E) ratio, we have a number of options. Theoretically investors can directly collect the numbers from press releases or SEC filings (company annual/quarterly reports). In reality, few managers manually collect the data from the press releases or the official filings. Instead, managers use earnings data provided by data providers such as Bloomberg and Compustat. We can also directly obtain P/E ratios from vendors that sell calculated signals. To use vendor calculated P/E ratios, we need to better understand the definition of earnings. This is because a vendor may decide to include or exclude some types of accounting earnings such as profits or losses from extraordinary items, discontinued operations, and other non-recurring events. With raw accounting data, we can easily calculate different versions of P/E ratios by combining different information in the income statement. In some cases, there is also a delay between the time that the earnings data become available and the time that the data are distributed by vendors. To guarantee data quality, a data provider may not use the preliminary results included in the press releases and wait for the official filings instead. Alternatively, the preliminary data may need to go through a data validation process before they are released. Therefore, the vendor data may sacrifice speed for quality. Such a trade-off works for investors who bet on long-term post-earnings price drifts. The trade-off, however, does not work for investors who bet on immediate price responses to earnings surprises (the difference between a company's reported earnings and analysts' forecasted earnings).

Investors rely on different financial ratios (e.g. book-to-price ratio) or the changes of financial data (e.g., year-over-year earnings per share change) to analyze companies and make investment decisions. To facilitate investment research, many vendors provide pre-calculated financial ratios and stock selection signals besides raw financial data and analyst estimates. For example, Ford Equity Research, an independent equity research firm, provides calculated financial ratios for stock valuation along with raw sales, earnings, and balance sheet data. Furthermore, Ford Equity Research provides a number of proprietary stock selection signals calculated from historical prices and financial data. Quantitative Service Group (QSG) distributes a collection of ~300 stock selection factors that include a variety of value, growth, sentiment, quality, and momentum signals. Standard & Poor's Capital IQ has a similar alpha factor library to provide raw, ranked, and z-scored factors for more than 400 stock selection factors. Since the factors are calculated using the underlying data that Compustat and Capital IQ publish, the alpha factor library has full transparency in the definitions that describe each signal's formulation. The equity research teams of traditional brokers also provide their clients with some of the underlying data behind their research reports and recommendations. Some large banks such as Deutsche Bank and JP Morgan have dedicated quantitative strategy teams to systematically investigate stock selection signals. These groups publish their research findings and share their signals with clients. At the same time, data providers have been reducing latency in their data delivery. Instead of waiting for official filings, Compustat and Capital IQ publish initial accounting results and financial ratios using preliminary press releases to improve the timeliness of the data. These developments have encouraged more investors to adopt processed data and pre-calculated signals provided by vendors.

Large financial institutions collectively spend billions of dollars a year on data collection and data management. Researchers spend countless hours on understanding the underlying data and building rigorous systems to correct erroneous data and fill missing data. Some data problems are easy to identify. For instance, researchers routinely remove logically inconsistent data points from the price/volume data:

- Remove the quote prices if the bid price is higher than the ask price.
- Remove trading volumes if they are less than 0.
- Remove the tick prices that are out of the range of the low price and the high price.

Although extreme and unreasonable data points are easy to detect and correct, we need to be more careful when we deal with outliers. In statistical analysis, the three-sigma rule is often used to identify outliers: any data points that are more than three standard deviations away from the mean are considered outliers as such outliers account for less than 0.27% of all data points in a normal distribution. Nevertheless, such an approach to identify outliers does not apply to most of the financial data since most of the financial data do not follow normal distributions. Instead, financial data tend to have fat tails. Although the daily standard deviation of stock returns is usually less than 4%, it's not unusual for a stock's price to rise more than 20% (five standard deviations) because of good news; it is also not unusual for a stock's price to drop more than 20% because of bad news. On April 19, 2012, GlaxoSmithKline PLC (GSK.L) announced a hostile takeover bid for Human Genome Sciences (HGSI) for $13 a share, an 81% premium to the previous close price of HGSI, $7.17. The board of HGSI immediately rejected the offer as too low but signaled willingness to discuss the offer further. The stock price went up as high as $14.61 before closing at $14.17. The one-day return to HGSI investors was 98%. Knight Capital (KCG), a leading market maker and electronic execution provider, had a technology breakdown on August 1, 2012. Even though the breakdown lasted for just an hour, it cost KCG $440M. Once news about KCG's breakdown gradually spread among investors, many investors sold or shorted the KCG stock. On August 1, KCG stock price dropped to $6.94 from the previous close of $10.33. After a loss of 33% on August 1, KCG opened at $3.27 on August 2 and close at $2.58.[12] The two day cumulative loss to investors was 75%. Unlike in many other fields, in finance, investors cannot simply remove these outliers from their analysis as these price jumps have significant impact on investment returns.

Researchers have limited resources to fully clean all the available data. Fortunately, in most cases, the 80/20 rule applies.[13] For example, errors in daily total returns of stocks are common because of failure to adjust for dividends or splits. Failure to adjust for splits often results in large errors (e.g., failure to adjust a 1-for-2 split yields -50% return) and failure to adjust for dividends often yields small errors as quarterly dividends for stocks are typically below 2%. In practice, failures to adjust for dividends happen far more frequently than failures to adjust for splits as splits are far less common. Small random errors caused by occasional missing dividends usually have little impact on the final results. Accordingly, suave managers focus on examining stocks with significant returns (e.g., ±15%) to capture the small percentage of errors that have significant impact on the final results. If one has access to multiple data sources that contain the same information, comparing the same data from different sources is the simplest and the most effective way of identifying data errors. For critical data such as prices and returns, institutional investors routinely use multiple sources to cross-check the validity of the data. For example, one may check the price data from Reuters against the data from Bloomberg. When there are significant discrepancies, one can further manually examine prices with the help of TAQ data and decide which price to be included in the final data.

---

[12] This incident also demonstrated market inefficiency. Better informed investors began to dump KCG stocks on the morning of August 1 before less informed investors had the opportunity to respond to the news.

[13] 80/20 rule states that 80% of the effects result from 20% of the causes. In business, it means that we should focus on the 20% that really matters in order to generate 80% of the benefit or to fix 80% of the problems.

Occasionally, full validation is infeasible because of limited resources and time. When a company has a rights offering, the value of the rights is sometimes hard to price and different sources may give quite different values. In rare cases, we get the same incorrect price data from different sources. Smaller data errors are less obvious and often get passed to investors by exchanges and data suppliers. In most cases, they have limited impact in backtests. Investors, however, should not discount the existence of such errors, especially when a method shows just a slight advantage or when data errors may introduce a systematic bias. For example, if a strategy selects stocks with high dividend yields, using total daily returns that miss some dividends likely results in an underestimation of the strategy's returns.

We should avoid look-ahead bias when including fundamental data and economic indicators in research. Look-ahead bias is a bias created by using information that would not be available at the time to make the investment decision. When backtesting investment strategies, it is crucial to only use the data that are available when the portfolio is constructed. By US regulation, a company has up to 45 days after the fiscal quarter ends to file the quarterly report, 10-Q, and up to 90 days after the fiscal year ends to file the annual report, 10-K. Delays are allowed though if a company needs more time to prepare the reports. Therefore, a lag up to three months is often needed to account for the time difference between the end of a fiscal quarter and the time that the financial data become available. To make the matter more complex, a company's fiscal year may not coincide with the calendar year. For instance, the fiscal year of Walmart (WMT) ends on January 31 instead of December 31. In addition, a firm may change its fiscal year schedule during the period of analysis. Goldman Sachs (GS) changed its fiscal year from ending in November to ending in December at the end of 2008 when it converted from an investment bank to a bank holding company. The change created a stub month for December 2008 that was not included in either fiscal year 2008 or fiscal year 2009.[14] Some data providers such as I/B/E/S include the publication dates of these reports so that users can determine the earliest available date of the fundamental information included in the reports, which mitigates the look-ahead bias problem. Even when the report dates are available, we need to be careful with determining which date is day 0—the date an event happens. For example, the majority of US earnings releases happen after market close and the rest mostly happen before market open. If earnings are released after market hours, we can only trade on the earnings information the next day; if the earnings are released before market open, we can trade on the earnings information the same day. In many cases, stocks gap up or down in response to earnings announcement. If the time stamp is not available, we may have to assume that we can only trade on the information the second day. For example, when Apple had a negative earnings announcement on January 23, 2013 after the market close, the price reduced by 10%. If a signal mistakenly assumes that the earnings information was available before the close and triggered a sell at the close price of $514.01, it has 10.5% positive return bias built into it since the next day's open price was $460.00. To avoid look-ahead bias, we need to either obtain accurate timestamp on the data or take a conservative approach in estimating the dates that the data become available.

---

[14] Goldman Sachs reported heavy losses for December 2008. Therefore, some critics accused it of packing all the losses into the stub month to generate positive earnings for the first quarter of 2009.

A more difficult problem is to avoid look-ahead bias due to revisions. Many macroeconomic indicators are revised after the initial releases. Similarly, financial statements are sometimes revised or restated after the initial releases to correct problems identified by the company, the auditor, or in rare cases, the SEC. Studies have shown that using the final revised numbers, which are often the default choices provided by data sources, with the initial release dates tend to yield better forecasting powers. Yet if we do so, we introduce look-ahead bias as the revised numbers are not available at the initial release dates. To remove the look-ahead bias, we need to use the initial unrevised economic and financial data with the initial release dates.

Conclusion

In this chapter, we examined various data used in technical and fundamental analysis and discussed approaches to managing them. Over the years, data availability and data delivery methods have been constantly improving. As new data sources become available, we have also observed significant consolidation among data providers. Large data providers such as Bloomberg, Thomson Reuters, and Standard & Poor's have been actively building their own platforms to deliver other vendors' data in a standardized interface. Such changes facilitate the dissemination of data and the integration of the data from different sources. These changes have reduced the time that investors spend on collecting, cleaning, and integrating the data. At the same time, these changes also increase competition among investors, as the data that historically only few investors had access to have now become widely available. In order to maintain their information edge, investors have to constantly look for new data sources, which in turn motivate data providers to identify and supply new data. Given these trends, we expect to see even more changes to the financial data in the future.

Chapter 3

Seasonal Effects

Before we dive into economic, technical and fundamental indicators, let us briefly discuss an easy topic: market seasonality. Market seasonality refers to the tendency for the aggregated stock market or a group of stocks to go up or down during specific periods in an election cycle, a year, a month, or even during the course of a day. Seasonal effects are widely cited by the financial press. The existence of such effects poses a direct challenge to the efficient market hypothesis. Therefore, whether seasonal effects do in fact exist, and if they do exist, the reasons for such effects have been heatedly debated over the years. In this chapter, we establish the statistical significance of popular seasonal effects and discuss possible explanations. Critics often point out that some observed seasonal effects may be a result of data mining: investors research thousands of seasonal effects, so it is but natural that some of them are statistically significant at 95% or 99% confidence levels. Besides, most seasonal effects have high standard deviations, which suggest that these effects have high year-to-year volatility. That said, a few well-known seasonal effects continue to perform after their publication and have plausible behavioral explanations. We believe that seasonal effects are likely to continue to exist in the future and an understanding of the seasonal effects can help investors fine tune return and risk expectations.

Seasonality in Market Returns

Historically, stock market returns tend to exhibit seasonal patterns. In this section, we examine several documented calendar effects, test whether these effects are statistically significant, and discuss plausible explanations.

Presidential and Mid-Term Election Effect

The US stock market tends to perform well after the mid-term election. The historical 1-month, 3-month and 1-year return starting from the mid-term election have been better than average.[15] As shown in Exhibit 3-1, the average 1-year S&P 500 index (SPX) return after a mid-term election is 15.5% and the Sharpe ratio is 1.9; furthermore, all 1-year returns are positive. In comparison, the 1-year return after the Presidential election is 6.4% and the Sharpe ratio is only 0.4. The 3-month and 1-year return differences after the mid-term elections versus after Presidential elections are statistically significant at 99% confidence level.

Since this calendar effect is related to the election, the political ramification of mid-term elections is often used to explain the higher returns. One hypothesis is that it is more likely to have political gridlock after midterm election—the White House, the Senate, and

---

[15] The stock market was closed on election days every year through 1968 and closed on Presidential election days between 1972 and 1980. All returns are calculated using the close prices of the Mondays before the election days as the starting prices.

the House of Representatives are not controlled by the same party. The Presidential election often gives the President and his/her party mandates to pass controversial new laws and new regulations favored by their party's base. New laws introduce instability to the market and new regulations sometimes have unintended negative impact on businesses. Opposition to new laws and regulations often energize the base of the opposite party and sometimes alienate independent voters. For instance, the party of the President on average lost 23 house seats and 3 Senate seats in midterm elections between 1962 and 2010. Because of political gridlock after midterm elections, Congress is less likely to act on controversial issues, which actually maintains policy stability and boosts the market. Another hypothesis is government stimulus or the anticipation of government stimulus. After a midterm election, the party in power has the incentive to promote fiscal stimulus to improve the economy until the next Presidential election. Since promoting economic growth is not a controversial issue, the party that is not in power often supports stimulus measures. Therefore, the political environment after the mid-term election is better for economic growth and market returns.

Exhibit 3-1 Stock market returns after Presidential and mid-term elections

Presidential Election				Mid-term Election			
Election Day	S&P 500 Change			Election Day	S&P 500 Change		
	+21 day	+63 day	+253 day		+21	+63	+253 day
11/8/1960	1.9%	12.9%	28.6%	11/6/1962	7.9%	13.8%	24.8%
11/3/1964	-1.2%	2.9%	8.4%	11/8/1966	1.6%	8.7%	12.9%
11/5/1968	4.2%	0.6%	-5.8%	11/3/1970	6.0%	15.5%	11.1%
11/7/1972	4.1%	0.6%	-6.1%	11/5/1974	-7.8%	6.2%	20.5%
11/2/1976	-1.0%	-0.5%	-11.4%	11/7/1978	2.4%	3.0%	7.0%
11/4/1980	5.8%	-0.3%	-3.3%	11/2/1982	2.4%	7.3%	20.6%
11/6/1984	-3.8%	7.1%	14.1%	11/4/1986	3.3%	12.3%	4.1%
11/8/1988	1.5%	9.4%	21.4%	11/6/1990	4.9%	11.7%	24.1%
11/3/1992	1.7%	4.7%	11.0%	11/8/1994	-2.6%	3.8%	27.1%
11/5/1996	5.4%	11.7%	32.9%	11/3/1998	5.4%	14.4%	21.2%
11/7/2000	-5.6%	-6.4%	-21.9%	11/5/2002	1.0%	-7.1%	16.0%
11/2/2004	5.4%	5.2%	6.8%	11/7/2006	2.4%	5.0%	7.0%
11/4/2008	-9.9%	-13.9%	8.2%	11/2/2010	1.8%	10.4%	5.8%
Average	0.6%	2.6%	6.4%	Average	2.2%	8.1%	15.5%
Std Dev	4.8%	7.3%	15.9%	Std Dev	4.0%	6.1%	8.0%

For example, the bill to extend the Bush era tax cut was bogged down in Congress for months before the 2010 mid-term election because Democrats and Republicans could not reach a compromise on whether to extend the tax cuts for families making more than $250,000 a year. After the election, the Obama administration soon reached an agreement with House Republicans. Following the Republicans' demand, all tax cuts were extended for two years and the estate tax was lowered for a year. In return, the Republicans agreed to a one-year social security tax cut and the extension of unemployment benefits. Despite adding costs to the national debt, the compromise injected hundreds of billions of dollars into the economy and provided much needed boost to markets.

Sell in May and Go Away

An old adage "Sell in May and Go Away", also known as the Halloween indicator since it recommends getting into the market on October 31, is yet another seasonal anomaly. This observation suggests stock market returns are higher between November and April than returns in the rest six months. Exhibit 3-2 shows the average monthly returns in the 53 years between 1961 and 2013. The average monthly SPX return in the period between November and April, 1.11%, was significantly higher than the average monthly return in the period between May and October, 0.16%. In fact, the average monthly return in the period between May and October was not significantly different from zero and was lower than the average T-bill return.

Exhibit 3-2 Average SPX monthly return (1961 - 2013)

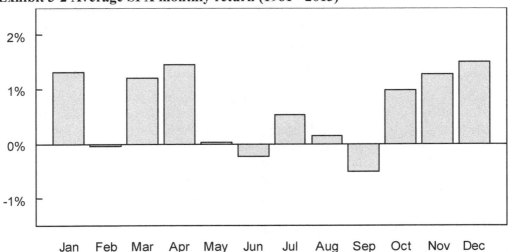

Although frequently cited in financial press, "Sell in May and Go Away" remains a puzzle. This phrase was born decades ago before quantitative analysis, as we understand it now, became popular—earlier than 1980—and it still held for the last 10 years. This perhaps suggests that we cannot simply discredit it as a result of data mining. Using data between January 1970 and August 1998, Bouman and Jacobsen (2002) demonstrated that returns in the period between November and April were substantially higher than in the period between May and October in 36 out of 37 countries that they examined. Maberly and Pierce (2004) disputed Bouman and Jacobsen's results as artifacts from outliers such as the October 1987 market crash and the August 1998 collapse of hedge fund Long-Term Capital Management. They argued that, after removing outliers, this seasonal pattern was not an exploitable trading strategy after taking trading costs into consideration. However, the choice to remove one-side (negative-side) outliers from May to October returns is questionable since there were also negative outliers in November to April returns. Instead of removing outliers, Witte (2010) used three robust regression methods to mitigate the impact of outliers and found that the Halloween effect was still statistically significant. Doeswijk (2008) provided a hypothesis that an optimism cycle is the cause of this seasonal pattern: Investors start looking forward to the next year as the current year winds down, often with an optimism bias to overestimate economic growth, which in their view drives the stock market higher. A few months into a new year, such optimism bias gradually disappears, which causes lackluster returns in the rest six months. At least two of his observations support the optimism cycle hypothesis.

(i)   The first was that cyclical industries outperformed defensive industries by 0.56% a month between November and May during the 1970-2003 period (cyclical industries usually perform better when investors are optimistic about the economic growth) and the strategy worked 65% of the time.

(ii)   The second observation was that analysts' forecast of twelve-month rolling forward earnings growth rate tended to increase in the winter and decrease in the summer.

Let us consider a simple timing strategy—one that held SPY (ETF that tracks S&P 500) between November and April and switched to hold long-term Treasuries between May and October[16]. Exhibit 3-3 shows the performance of SPY, long-term Treasuries, and the timing strategy in the 20 years between the inception of SPY in 1993 and 2012. The annualized geometric return of the timing strategy was 13.8%, which was 68% higher than SPY returns. The strategy also had lower volatility and lower drawdown. In fact its return-to-risk ratio[17] is twice that of the return-to-risk ratio of passively holding the SPY.

An analysis of the Treasury monthly returns reveals that Treasuries are also exposed to the optimism cycle; the average monthly Treasury return in the period between November and April, 0.33%, is significantly lower than the average monthly return in the period between May and October, 1.13%. In other words, during the period that stocks underperform, Treasuries tend to outperform. It is unlikely that long-term Treasuries will continue to have a return of 8.7% in the future: The 30-year Treasuries yield gradually decreased from ~14% in 1981 to ~3% in 2012, boosting the longest bull market for Treasuries in history. Since the nominal yield cannot fall below 0, the potential return of Treasuries in the following years will not reach 8.7%.

If we are to believe that the optimism cycle continues, we will continue to see that stocks outperform between November and April and Treasuries outperform between May and October.

---

[16] We use the Bloomberg/EFFAS US Government 10+ Year bond index as a proxy since long-term Treasury bond ETFs do not have a 20 year history.
[17] The return-to-risk is calculated as annualized return divided by annualized standard deviation. Essentially it is the Sharpe ratio with zero as the reference rate instead of risk-free interest rate.

Exhibit 3-3 Return summary of SPY, long term Treasuries and timing strategy

Strategy	Timing	SPY	Treasuries
Geometric Return	13.8%	8.2%	8.7%
Annualized Std Dev	12.0%	15.1%	9.9%
Return/Risk	1.15	0.55	0.88
Worst Drawdown	30.8%	50.8%	13.3%

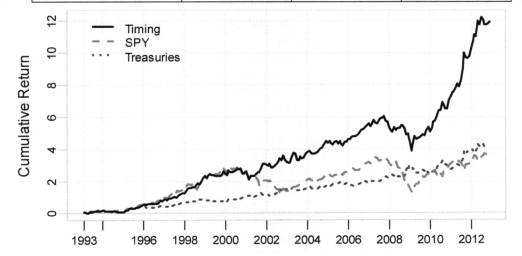

Santa Claus Rally

Exhibit 3-2 also reflects interesting monthly return patterns. For example, the stock market tends to have positive returns in December and January. In fact, the days around Christmas and New Year's Day are among the best periods for the stock market, which is often called the Santa Claus rally. Although some question whether the Santa Claus rally is still statistically significant as it has become a well-known anomaly among investors, a number of possible reasons continue to boost market return during the period. Besides the optimism people have during the holiday season, December and January are also the months that many investors, including investment professionals of many financial firms, collect their year-end bonuses. Such bonuses bring extra money flows into the securities market. The period between Thanksgiving and New Year's Day is also the busiest period for retailers as consumers spend more during the period. Retailers often hire temporary workers to manage increased consumer demand, which adds extra employees to the payroll and decreases unemployment rates. Since these underlying driving forces will stay in place in the future, the stock market may continue to have better expected returns around the New Year.

January Effect

There are actually different versions of the January effect. One version is similar to the Santa Claus rally: the stock market tends to go up in January. An extra argument for the January rally is that individual investors often sell losing stocks before the end of year to claim investment losses for tax reasons and institutional investors may sell losing stocks for window dressing purposes. Window dressing is a strategy used by fund managers to improve the appearance of their portfolio before end-of-quarter positions are reported. One way to achieve better appearance is to get rid of losing stocks from the portfolio before the end-of-quarter portfolio holdings are reported to investors. As fund managers buy back some of the stocks in January, the buying pressure pushes up the stock market. But as Exhibit 3-2 shows, the average market return in December is actually higher than January (the difference is not statistically significant though). Therefore, we are inclined to treat the January effect as part of the Santa Claus rally.

Another January effect is January Barometer. The return of January is considered to be an indicator of how the market will perform in the following eleven months. For example, between 1961 and 2010, in 70% of the years, the signs of February to December returns of S&P 500 index were consistent with the signs of January returns. Furthermore, for the 30 years that the S&P index had positive returns in January, the S&P index had positive returns between February and December in 26 years of those 30 years (which was 86.7% of the years). When January returns were negative, the forecast was less strong. For the 20 years that the S&P index had negative returns in January, only 9 years had negative returns between February and December. If we apply a chi-square test to test whether the sign of January return is independent of the sign of February to December return, it yields a p-value of 3%, which means we can reject the null hypothesis that the sign of January return does not predict the sign of February to December return at the 95% confidence level but not at the 99% confidence level. The January Barometer may not help the long-term investor much in making investment decisions. Although it may offer some confirmation that an investor can hold long positions for the rest of the year after a positive January, it does not tell investors how to invest after a negative January. In fact, the average February to December return when January returns were negative was still higher than T-bill returns. So even with negative January returns, a buy-and-hold strategy still has higher expected returns during the rest of the months.

Turn-of-the-month Effect

Historically, stock market returns during the four days at the turn of the month, the last trading day of the month to the third trading day of the following month, are significantly higher than returns over other days of the month. Using 1897-1986 Dow Jones Industrial Average daily returns, Lakonishok and Smidt (1988) found that the total return over those four days was 0.473%, whereas the total return was 0.0612% for a random four day period. Using 1987-2005 US CRSP data, McConnell and Xu (2008) showed that turn-of-the-month effect continued to exist. They showed that the market cap weighted average daily return during the turn of the month was 15 bps whereas for other days the average daily return was 0 bps. They further demonstrated that the turn-of-the-month effect occurred in both small- and large-cap stocks, among both high- and low-price stocks, and at both quarter ends and other month ends. Using SPX daily return between 1961 and 2012, we confirmed that the average daily return during the turn of the month was 10.5 bps, which was significantly higher than the rest of the days' average return of 1.1 bps (p-value < 0.0001).

Ogden (1990) proposed an explanation for the turn-of-the month effect: the turn of each month includes typical pay dates for wages, dividends, and interests. As investors put their income into the stock market, the market moves higher. Pension fund rebalancing may also contribute to the turn-of-the-month effect. Many pension funds have strategic asset allocation requirements that allocate a predefined percentage or a percentage range of funds to equities. For example, a pension fund may have a policy to invest 50% of the capital in equities and 50% in bonds. If equities underperform bonds in a period, bonds will have higher than 50% of the weight. To maintain the 50/50 allocation target, the pension fund will buy equities and sell bonds. Furthermore, pension fund assets drop as the stock market drops and the fund becomes underfunded. Such underfunding often happens during difficult economic times when it is difficult for companies to put more money into their pension funds. In order to make up the difference, some pension funds change their policy to give higher allocation to equities to boost expected returns. So they rebalance from bonds to equities. Such rebalances often happen at the end of a month or at the end of a quarter. As a result, rebalancing provides support to stock prices at the turn of the month if the stock market is in turmoil. When the equity market has high returns, the pension funds may become overfunded. Instead of selling equities, companies often choose to reduce future funding, which has a smaller negative impact on stock returns.

Option Expiration Week

Monthly options expire on the third Friday[18] of the month. The third Fridays of March, June, September, and December are called triple witching days since options, index futures such as E-mini S&P 500 futures (ES), and options on index futures all expire on those days. Buying at the close on the Friday prior to the option expiration week and selling at the close of option expiration week was a strategy with better risk-adjusted returns than other weeks. For example, between 1991 and 2010, SPX had an average return of 0.38% in the option expiration week with a standard deviation of 2.41%. In comparison, the index had an average return of 0.16% for a random week with a standard deviation of 2.38%. Since the option expiration week includes the 15th day of the month, it includes the pay dates for workers who receive semi-monthly wages. Hence, the pay dates may contribute to the higher return of the option expiration week.

Holiday Effect

Holiday effect refers to the observation that the market tends to perform well on the trading day before a public holiday. Ariel (1990) documented that the average return on the trading day prior to holidays was 9 to 14 times the average return of the remaining days of the year. Using SPX daily return between 1961 and 2012, we also confirmed that the average daily return on the day before a US public holiday was 17.8 bps, which was significantly higher than the rest of the days' average return of 2.9 bps (p-value = 0.0003). Despite higher average daily return than turn-of-the-month effect, it is difficult to exploit the holiday effect. The turn of the month covers four trading days with an average total return of 42 bps; the holiday effect, on the other hand, covers a single day. When we take the trading cost into consideration, the turn-of-the-month effect is likely to be more significant than the holiday effect. Besides, the trading days before New Year's Day, Independence Day, and Labor Day are significant contributors to the holiday effect. These trading days are also days at the turn of the month. Swinkels and Vliet (2010)

---

[18] Technically, they expire on the Saturday following the third Friday of the month. Since the market is closed on Saturday, Friday's close prices are used.

studied the interaction between the Halloween indicator, the turn-of-the-month effect, and the holiday effect. They found that the holiday effect became insignificant once they incorporated the Halloween indicator and the turn-of-the-month effect in return analysis.

Seasonality in Cross-Sectional Stock Returns

Besides the absolute returns of the overall stock market, the relative returns of different industries and individual stocks also exhibit seasonal patterns.[19] If stock-level relative seasonality exists, we would expect that the same group of stocks is likely to outperform (underperform) the market in the same period of a year. Indeed, Heston and Sadka (2008) showed that the stocks that outperformed (underperformed) the market in a month during a year tended to outperform (underperform) the market in the same calendar month in the subsequent years. A zero-investment strategy that longed (bought) the stocks with the highest returns and shorted (sold) the stocks with lowest returns based on their one-month historical return 12 months ago had 1.15% per month return before transaction costs. The tendency of the same group of stocks to outperform (underperform) the market in a month supports the hypothesis that cross-sectional stock returns exhibit seasonal patterns.

Industry Return Seasonality

Seasonality in industry returns is a main contributor to seasonality in individual stock returns. Part of the sector seasonal patterns can be explained by the market optimism cycle. For example, in his study of the Halloween indicator, Doeswijk (2008) demonstrated that cyclical industries outperformed defensive industries between November and April and underperformed between May and October. Using the returns of MSCI US Sector indices since 1995, we found that cyclical sectors (materials, industrials, consumer discretionary, and information technology) outperformed defensive sectors (consumer staples, health care, utilities and telecommunication services) by 5.7% between November and April and underperformed defensive sectors by 3.3% between May and October.[20] Therefore, a strategy that longed defensive sectors and shorted cyclical sectors between May and October and then longed cyclical sectors and shorted defensive sectors between November and April was profitable. Although such a strategy would have yielded 300% cumulative returns since 1995, higher than the return of an average long/short hedge fund, exploiting such a strategy would have been far from a smooth ride. As shown in Exhibit 3-4, the strategy suffered a 30% drawdown starting from 2003 to 2005 and it took almost seven years for the strategy to reach a new high. As a result, the information ratio of this strategy was only 0.6. The low information ratio and the lengthy drawdown prevent large funds from relying on the seasonal sector rotation and other seasonal patterns as a main source of alpha. Although an individual with high conviction may stick to the strategy, it is unlikely that investors would have stayed with a portfolio manager after a drawdown of 30%.

---

[19] Because of the popularity of seasonality analysis, the Bloomberg terminal provides a function SEAG for investors to visually compare absolute and relative seasonal patterns.

[20] Energy and Financials are not included in this analysis as there is no consensus on whether they should be classified as cyclical or defensive sectors. Financials used to be a defensive sector before the banks substantially increased their leverage in the late 1990s. Energy sector return is driven more by energy prices and tends to have its own seasonal patterns.

Exhibit 3-4 Cumulative return of seasonal sector rotation

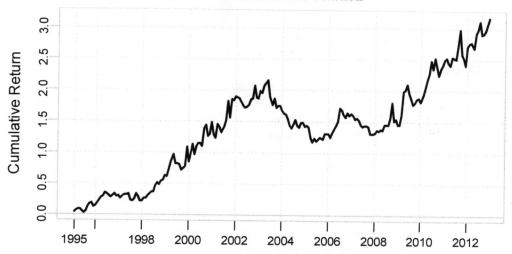

Weather conditions and holidays may contribute to the seasonal patterns of some industries as well. For example, energy stocks tended to outperform in the spring: as shown in Exhibit 3-5, the energy sector return was 2.1% per month between February and May and 0% per month between June and October. Low inventories of heating oil, natural gas and gasoline in the spring may offer an explanation. The winter heating season consumes heating oil and natural gas inventories, which pushes inventories to the lowest level in the spring. The Environmental Protection Agency regulation requires refineries to switch to summer-grade fuel at around one of the busiest traveling holidays, Memorial Day. As refineries shut down their facilities for the switch in the spring, the gasoline inventory is also lower and the retail gas price often goes up, which brings more profits to energy companies.

Exhibit 3-5 Average cumulative year-to-date return (1995-2012)

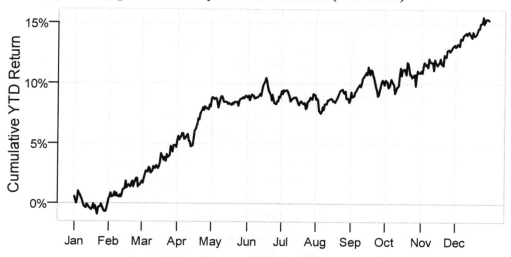

January Effect – Market Cap

Market cap also plays a role in the seasonality of relative stock returns. Another version of the January effect refers to an observation that small cap stocks—and in general higher risk stocks—tend to outperform large cap stocks in January. As described earlier, one hypothesis is that investors sell losing stocks close to the end of the year for window dressing or tax benefit purposes and buy them back in January; such buying pressure has significantly higher impact on less liquid small-cap stocks which helps to push up their prices. As a result, small cap stocks tended to perform better than large cap stocks in January. Since the documentation of small cap stock outperformance in January by Reinganum (1983), we observed significant weakening of the outperformance of small-cap stocks (Russell 2000 index, RUT) versus large-cap stocks (S&P 500 index, SPX). Between 1961 and 1982, RUT outperformed SPX by 2.2% in January; between 1983 and 2013, the outperformance was only 0.4%. Besides, between 1983 and 2013, RUT outperformed SPX by 1.1% in December. The outperformance of small-cap stocks in December puts the liquidity hypothesis in question. Instead, the outperformance of RUT in December and January in the past thirty years may be linked to the market optimism cycle as well: RUT underperformed SPX by 2.3% between May and October and outperformed SPX by 2.9% between November and April. Since small-cap stocks are more risky than large-cap stocks, the better performance of small-cap stocks between November and April reflected investors' willingness to invest more in riskier stocks between November and April.

Options Max Pain

Options max pain is a theory on cross-sectional returns related to the option expiration week. The theory says that the stock prices tend to move toward the max pain prices on the option expiration date. The max pain price is the price at which that all outstanding options of a given month expire at the least aggregated value. In other words, it is the price level that causes the option buyers the maximum losses (or minimum profits) and brings in maximum pain. On the expiration date, the total profit and loss between option buyers, which include many hedgers and individual investors, and sellers, which are dominated by market makers, is a zero-sum game. If option sellers as a group can manipulate the stock price to achieve the max pain, the max pain price serves as a center of gravity for the stock price. Besides possible market manipulations, hedging strategies also play a role in max pain. If an option is in the money, most investors close the position before the expiration date to avoid delivery. For in-the-money call options, their strike prices are lower than the stock price. Market makers usually hedge the risk of short call positions with long stock positions. When investors sell their calls back to market markers, market makers have fewer short call positions to hedge and they sell stocks to reduce the hedge, which puts negative pressure on the stock price. Indeed, Ni et al. (2005) presented evidence that on option expiration dates, the closing prices of stocks with listed options tended to cluster at option strike prices. They also provided evidence that both hedge rebalancing and stock price manipulation contributed to the clustering.

Despite a solid following among investors and our own anecdotal observations of price moves towards the max pain prices before the closes of option expiration dates, it may be difficult to explore the cross-sectional return differences using a systematic approach. Using the near-month open interest data from 2005 to 2012, we calculated the max pain prices for all S&P 500 stocks at the close of the second Friday. We then tested a strategy that longed stocks with max pain prices at least 5% higher than the close prices and shorted stocks with max pain prices at least 5% lower than the close prices. The long/short portfolio was closed at the close of the third Friday. The average one week return spread between the long portfolio and the short portfolio was ~29 bps and the standard deviation was 180 bps. Once we took the trading costs into consideration, the strategy yielded little.

Intraday Return

Intraday relative stock return patterns are likely driven by temporary imbalance in buying and selling activities. Heston et al. (2011) found that stocks with high relative returns versus the market in a given half hour on one day were more likely to have high relative returns in the same half hour on subsequent days. Such positive correlation was stronger at the first of and the last of the half hours. One likely explanation is that investors buy the same assets at the same time over multiple days. Indeed, many funds tend to rebalance the portfolio at the same time of the day and use the same algorithm with fixed trading horizon. Since large trades are often split and traded over multiple days, the split introduces similar intraday order flow patterns over multiple days, which in turn drives the prices of these stocks up during the same half hours.

Conclusion

Overall, we believe some seasonal effects do exist, but these are far from infallible. Most effects have high volatility year over year and may have returns opposite to their long-term expectations for multiple years. Among the seasonal effects, the Halloween indicator and the turn-of-the-month indicator pass the statistical significance test and the underlying investor behavioral biases are likely to continue to support historical patterns in the future. Investors may therefore incorporate such information to tilt the market exposure of their portfolios over time. We also suggest that it is difficult for investors to exploit short-term seasonal effects such as intraday return patterns because of trading costs. Nevertheless, these patterns are useful for investors to make better trading decisions.

Chapter 4

Economic and Market Indicators

Economic indicators are statistics about the economy. Stock markets tend to respond positively when economic indicators signal improving economic prospects, easy monetary/fiscal policy, and strong consumer sentiment as these conditions are favorable for economic growth. Besides their value in forecasting stock market direction, economic indicators are often used as top-down factors in industry selection and stock selection as different industries and stocks respond to economic changes in different ways. For example, cyclical stocks are often hit harder than defensive stocks in a recession and export industries often outperform import industries when easy monetary policy weakens the local currency.

In this chapter we discuss important economic indicators that investors follow closely. Dozens of economic indicators are released every month. What makes some of them more important than others? Five factors determine the importance of an indicator:

Relevance: Indicators that provide a clear picture of the entire economy, the market, or a major part of the economy grab investor attention.

Timeliness: Investors crave timely information. The shorter the time span between the date that an indicator is measured and the date that it is released, the more timely the indicator is. For example, although the weekly jobless claim report only measures the number of individuals who filed for unemployment insurance in a week, it attracts a lot of interest since the data are published less than four business days after the week.

Accuracy: Investors assign higher weights to more accurate data. Some indicators rely on actual data and others rely on surveys. In general, the economic indicators collected from surveys, especially the ones that reflect participants' opinions or confidence, are less reliable and often more volatile than indicators extracted from actual data. The sample size used to estimate the indicator also impacts accuracy. Overall, indicators that rely on large samples have higher reliability.

Revisions: In order to release the economic data to the market as early as possible, government agencies and private data providers often release initial preliminary results, many of which rely on incomplete or even inaccurate information, and revise the results later. There is often a trade-off between timeliness and accuracy. In most cases revisions are not closely watched (GDP revision is one of the exceptions) since the revisions are no longer timely information. Interestingly, there may be consistent bias in initial releases. For example, between 2000 and 2012, 80% of the times the subsequent revisions to the initial jobless claims were upward revisions. This suggests that the initial release numbers were likely to be lower than the final claim numbers. A statistician may draw the conclusion that the estimation model for the initial releases had systematic bias; a cynical investor may draw the conclusion that the Department of Labor manipulated the initial release data to paint a more optimistic picture of the job market. Regardless of the reasons for revisions, we must decide whether to adjust the initial numbers with the updated revisions when we use historical economic data for back-testing. If we do make adjustments, we have to know both the dates of the initial releases and the dates of the revisions to avoid look-ahead bias. Since the more accurate revised data only become available after the initial release dates, we need to use the initial release numbers with the initial release dates and the revised numbers with the revision release dates to avoid look-ahead bias.

Surprises: Many academic papers have long established strong correlation between contemporaneous economic factors and stock market returns. Nevertheless, reported economic factors have much weaker predictive power for future stock market returns. Since an economic indicator is published after its measurement period, the indicator always has a time lag. Before the result is released, many economists have their own estimates and their consensus estimate is available to investors. Therefore, these estimates have been incorporated in stock prices before the data are released. If the released data are in line with the consensus, the release has little immediate impact on the market. On the other hand, if the released data are significantly different from the consensus, the release has an immediate impact on the market. For models that predict short-term stock returns, surprises—the difference between the reported data and the consensus estimates—are often used as inputs. For longer-term models that rely on economic conditions, the reported data are often directly used as inputs.

Economic Activity Indicators

Economic activity indicators measure the production, the distribution, and the consumption of goods and services. GDP provides a full picture of all economic activities; retail sales and housing activities provide information on critical components of the economy; employment situation report and other labor statistics show the level of economic activity and the utilization of the labor force; Purchasing managers index and consumer confidence index measure the overall sentiment of businesses and consumers.

GDP

GDP (Gross Domestic Product) measures the value of goods and services produced in a country. GDP is the broadest measure of the overall health of the economy. The numbers are published in both nominal dollars and inflation-adjusted real dollars. GDP is published quarterly by the Bureau of Economic Analysis, Department of Commerce. The initial release is in the final week of the month following the end of a quarter and the report is revised in the following months. Historically, a real GDP growth rate above 2.0-2.5% indicates that the economy is growing at a healthy rate. A decline of GDP of two or more consecutive quarters is an unofficial definition of recession.[21]

A healthy GDP growth rate usually means strong demand from consumers, businesses, and the government, which translates to strong corporate profits and boosts the stock market. On the other hand, a recession is typically accompanied by a bear market. Considering that GDP measures the overall health of the economy, market participants pay close attention to GDP releases, including revisions. Before each release, economists

---

[21] Officially, the beginning and the end of a recession is determined by economists at National Bureau of Economic Research who rely on GDP numbers as well as other economic indicators.

also spend significant effort forecasting GDP growth and revise their forecasts as more information becomes available. If the reported number is much better or worse than economists' consensus, the market reacts to the surprise. For example, on July 29, 2011, the Department of Commerce released the Q2 GDP number and revised the Q1 GDP number. The GDP growth figure for Q2 at 1.3% was much lower than the consensus estimate 1.9%; the GDP growth figure for Q1 was revised down from 1.9% to 0.4%. The disappointing numbers shocked investors, which, combined with a subsequent US debt downgrade by S&P, triggered market turmoil and the market dropped close to 20% in August and September.

Besides the impact of the headline numbers on the market, the detailed changes about different components of the GDP also attract investors' interests. The GDP can be split to different expenditures:

$$GDP = C + I + G + (X - M)$$

where C is personal consumption including consumption of durable goods, nondurable goods, and services;

I is private business investment including fixed investment (e.g., equipment, software, buildings) and inventory changes;

G is government spending;

(X − M) is net exports, the difference between gross exports (X) and gross imports (M).

Investors may look at increasing consumption of durable goods as a sign of consumer confidence, which is beneficial to cyclical industries. Others may treat increasing business investment as a sign of business confidence. On the other hand, consecutive quarters of business inventory buildup without corresponding personal consumption (final sales) increases suggest that business may have to cut spending in the future, which leads to lower GDP growth.

Retail Sales

In the US, consumer spending accounts for around 70% of all economic activity. Of this, retail sales account for close to one half of the consumer spending making it a very important economic indicator. The advance retail sales report comes from information collected in Monthly Retail Trade Survey (MRTS) conducted by the US Census Bureau, which covers approximately 5,000 retailers. The initial release of the advance retail sales report is published about two weeks after a month ends, which makes it an early indicator on consumer spending. The report adjusts for seasonality, holiday and trading day difference, but it does not adjust for inflation. The real growth rate can be estimated by taking the Consumer Price Index into consideration. The advance report is often revised later to reflect a more accurate picture.

The headline numbers that many investors watch are month-over-month changes of sales, with or without auto sales. The reason for publishing a number without auto sales is that about one quarter of retail sales are auto sales which tend to be more volatile. Government and car manufacturer incentive programs also distort auto sales. For example, in the summer of 2009, the US government implemented the Cash for Clunkers program that provided incentives (~$2500-$4500) for buyers who traded in less fuel-efficient vehicles for new fuel-efficient ones. The end result was to pull future car purchases earlier. After the program ended, sales dropped significantly in the following months.

In general, robust month-over-month retail sales growth indicates a healthy economy and higher corporate revenues/profits, which are good for the stock market. Many investors, especially those who focus on industry selection, also look into detailed breakdowns by businesses (e.g., store retailers versus non-store retailers) to estimate the relative strengths of different industries. Top-down data from government statistics, such as retail sales, can be used for stock selection as well. Monthly top-down data are more timely and frequent than quarterly financial statements from companies. The drawback is that the data are aggregated at the industry level instead of the company level and is often restricted to a small subset of industries (e.g., manufacturing and retail). So, investors need to analyze whether the statistics reported for an industry is indicative of a specific company's performance.

Housing Activities

The start of the housing bubble in early 2000s pulled the US economy out of the recession, but the subsequent slowdown in 2006 and the housing crisis that started in 2007 led to the worst recession since the Great Depression. The lack of housing market recovery subsequently became a major obstacle to the economic recovery following the 2008 recession. Needless to say, the US economy is closely tied to the housing market. In response, investors use a plethora of indicators to track housing market activity.

 Housing starts, new building permits, and new home sales are all important indicators for the housing market. When homebuilders build new homes, they not only hire more construction workers but also increase demand for building materials such as wood, steel, and copper. It is estimated that the construction of each new house generates four to five direct and indirect employment opportunities. The Census Bureau publishes data for housing starts—the number of new home constructions—and building permits—the number of future constructions approved by local governments—in the middle of the month for the prior month's data. The Census Bureau also releases a new home sales report close to the end of each month for the prior month's estimation. When home builders slow down new home construction, related industries are negatively impacted. Such slowdowns often precede recession. When home builders begin to build more homes, the related industries are positively impacted. This increase boosts economic recovery. When home builders apply for more permits, housing starts are likely to increase in the following months. Hence, the number of building permits is a leading economic indicator. The Census Bureau defines the sale of a new house as the signing of a sales contract or the acceptance of a deposit. When buyers buy new homes, home builders get their investments back and invest the proceeds in building more homes, which in turn stimulates related industries. For typical families, buying a home is their single largest purchase decision. Home sales increase reflects buyers' confidence in job security and income growth, so new home sales index is also an indicator of consumer confidence.

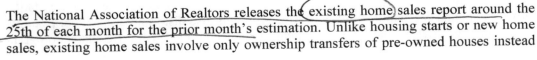 The National Association of Realtors releases the existing home sales report around the 25th of each month for the prior month's estimation. Unlike housing starts or new home sales, existing home sales involve only ownership transfers of pre-owned houses instead

of new construction. Nevertheless, existing home sales do bring more income for real estate agents, home renovation businesses, and mortgage bankers. More importantly, since existing home sales represent ~85% of home sales, they are a good measure of housing activity and consumer confidence. However, existing home sales are a lagging indicator as sales are included only after closing: it often takes four to ten weeks between the signing of the home purchase contract and the final closing. To address the lag, the National Association of Realtors began to report pending home sales index in 2005 as a leading indicator of housing market activity. Pending home sales track the number of homes that have signed contracts and are awaiting closing. The limitation of the pending home sales index is that some sales contracts fail with the percentage of failure rates varying over time. In January 2011, for instance just under 10% of home contracts failed. Even though mortgage rates continued to decline to record low in 2011, banks tightened their credit standards and fewer people could get loans. In January 2012, more than 30% of home contracts failed as an increasing number of home purchasers could not obtain financing from the banks. In order to properly use pending home sales index, investors need to take the prevailing failure rate into consideration.

S&P/Case-Shiller Home Price Indices track the changes in the value of homes nationally and in 20 major metropolitan areas using same home repeat sales. The data are published on the last Tuesday of every month with a two month lag. Because of the lag, the market seldom has had an immediate response to the releases. The long-term trend of home prices has a profound impact on consumer spending and consumer confidence. When housing prices trend up, home owners have more wealth in their homes (at least on paper) and are more confident about the future. Many home owners also take home equity loans to finance other spending, which promotes economic growth. When housing prices trend down, home owners see their wealth decline and many go underwater (the market value of the home is less than the mortgage principal). In response, existing home owners cut back spending and potential home owners postpone buying homes, which hinders economic growth.

Employment Indicators

Employment situation report: The employment situation report, also known as the jobs report, is published by the Department of Labor. The initial report for a month is released at 8:30 am on the first Friday of the following month, which makes it a timely report to gauge both the job market and the economy. The results are derived from both a household survey of 60,000 households to collect employee information and an establishment survey of more than 400,000 businesses and government agencies to collect employer information. The nonfarm payroll number and unemployment rate from the establishment survey are closely watched indicators in the employment situation report. Unemployed people and underemployed people have less income to spend than fully-employed people do. When the nonfarm payroll number grows at a dismal rate or shrinks, consumer spending is unlikely to have healthy growth. The unemployment rate also impacts consumer psychology. When consumers worry about the possibility of losing their jobs, even those who are currently employed spend less. A steady increase in nonfarm payroll and a decrease in unemployment rate are signs of an expanding economy, which are often associated with a bull market. But as the job market reaches full employment, companies often have to deal with wage inflation and high borrowing costs; then the unemployment rate change has less correlation with the stock market. Another reason why the employment situation report is actively followed by investors is that it is not unusual to see reported numbers different from economists' consensus. When surprises hit, the stock market responds immediately.

The employment situation report contains rich detail that goes far beyond simple headline numbers. For example, average hours of work have direct impact on total economic output and incomes as well. An increase of hours of work from 33.5 to 33.6 increases the economic output by an amount similar to an increase of 0.3% in nonfarm payroll. When the economy is close to full employment, average hourly earnings become a gauge of labor costs and reflect potential inflation rates. Therefore, large increases in average hourly earnings are detrimental to corporate earnings and stock prices.

ADP national employment report: Automatic Data Processing, Inc. (ADP) is one of the major providers of payroll services. It collects payroll information on ~340,000 private companies that cover more than 20 million workers in all private nonfarm sectors. Its partner Macroeconomic Advisers, a corporation that specializes in macroeconomic forecasting and policy analysis, processes the data, makes seasonal adjustments, applies statistical analysis, and compiles the final report on private payrolls. The headline number is the month-over-month change in private payrolls. The main reason for broad interest in the ADP report is its timeliness. The initial report for a month is released at 8:15 am on the first Wednesday of the following month, which is two days before the employment situation report and makes it one of the earliest economic indicators. Overall, the ADP payroll changes have good correlation (~0.9) with the employment situation report's nonfarm employment numbers, and serve as a valid early indicator of the labor market. Economists also adjust their employment forecasts in response to the ADP report.

Initial claims: In recent years, initial claims have gained prominence as a timely economic indicator because of sustained high unemployment rates. Published by Department of Labor, the initial claims are first released on every Thursday at 8:30 AM to track the number of people who filed new claims for unemployment insurance benefits in the week ended on the previous Saturday. The number of initial claims is part of the Leading Economic Indicators. High initial claim numbers indicate that many people have recently lost their jobs and that businesses are reducing investment, which in turn reduces future spending and lowers consumer confidence. The weekly frequency of initial claims makes it a timely report as the full employment situation report is only released monthly. Nevertheless, weekly numbers can be easily distorted by holidays, quarter ends, or weather conditions; economists often use four-week moving averages to reduce the noise in trend analysis.

Purchasing Managers Index (PMI) and Consumer Confidence Index

The PMI of a month is released at 10 AM on the first business day of the following month, which makes it the first and the most timely monthly report on the economy. The PMI is based on an Institute for Supply Management (ISM) survey of hundreds of purchasing managers regarding manufacturing activities. The composite index is calculated as the average of seasonally adjusted diffusion indexes of five indicators: new orders, production, employment, supplier deliveries, and inventories. The diffusion index measures month-over-month change: it is the sum of the percentage of respondents that report higher activities and half of the percentage of respondents that report no change in activities. For example, if 35% of the respondents report higher new orders and 39%

report same level of orders, then the index is 35 + 39/2 = 55.5. Overall, a PMI number above 50 indicates that the economic activity is expanding and a number below 50 indicates that economic activity is shrinking. The PMI index is a particularly important index to watch during a recession or in the early stage of a recovery. In those periods, the stock market usually reacts positively to a positive surprise in PMI.

The Conference Board publishes a monthly Consumer Confidence Index on the last Tuesday of each month. This is based on a survey of 5000 consumers' perceptions of business condition, employment, and income. Compared with retail sales, the Consumer Confidence Index is a less important economic indicator even though it is a forward-looking measure. Since it relies on a survey of different individuals each month, part of the volatility in the index is due to sample noise. As a result, changes in Consumer Confidence Index are sometimes not good predictors of retail sales changes and tend to have less impact on the market. That said, it still has moderate value. A significant change in Consumer Confidence Index often indicates a potential change in consumer spending and a reversal of market direction; a consecutive month-over-month change in the same direction often confirms the existing market trend.

Inflation, Interest Rate, and Currency Indicators

A country's economic health, monetary policies, and fiscal policies have significant impact on stock market returns. Since the economic health, monetary policies, and fiscal policies are reflected in inflation rates, interest rates, and exchange rates, investors closely follow these rate changes as well.

Price Indices and Commodity Prices

Consumer Price Index (CPI) and **Producer Price Index (PPI)** are price indices closely followed by the market. Published by the Bureau of Labor Statistics, CPI measures inflation from consumers' perspective and PPI measures inflation from businesses' perspective. The top-level price index is derived from dozens of sub-indices, each of which estimates the price level change of one type of goods or services. Seasonal adjustments are made to correct the effect of price variations caused by calendar effects, such as climatic conditions and holidays. Stock markets often respond negatively to a sharp increase in CPI. Although high inflation may increase the nominal values of revenues, it leads to tightening monetary policy and higher interest rate, which increases business borrowing costs as well as cost of capital. Negative inflation, deflation, is also bad for the market. Deflation reflects that the demand for goods is much weaker than supply and suggests a weakening economy. Modest and steady inflation, on the other hand, indicates a stable growing economy—something that investors prefer. Some investors focus more on year-over-year price index changes to avoid potentially inaccurate seasonal adjustments. Other investors also study the sub-indices to infer their impact on different industries or even specific companies. The revenue of a company is the quantity of the goods sold times the average price of the goods sold. Generally, the interaction between price and quantity means that higher price leads to lower quantity demanded of goods or services. But the exact relationship depends on price elasticity: price changes have larger impact on the revenues of defensive sectors than of cyclical sectors. Since the quantity is less elastic to the price changes for defensive sectors, revenues grow faster as prices go up.

Commodity prices, especially oil prices, are tightly linked to the economy. Oil price directly impacts consumer sentiment through "pain at the pump". When oil price rises, consumers spend a larger percentage of their disposable income on gas and heating oil and have to cut back spending on other products. Furthermore, high oil price often puts a negative dent on consumer confidence. Less consumer spending and lower consumer confidence reduce corporate revenues and corporate earnings. Oil price hikes have thus contributed to many recent recessions. Besides the impact on the overall economy, oil price has differential impacts on different industries. High oil price directly increases the costs of companies that consume oil and oil-related products; an oil price hike is especially detrimental to industries such as airlines and trucking. Its impact on financial and information technology companies is much smaller. For the energy sector, the correlation between oil prices and earnings is positive. Higher oil prices lead to higher revenues for oil producing energy companies. But even within the energy sector, the impact is uneven. For example, crude oil price hikes often squeeze the profit margin of oil refiners in the short term as retail gas price tends to be sticky and increases less than the crude price hike.

Interest Rate and Yield Curve

Investors also closely monitor interest rate changes and yield curve changes. The yield curve refers to the relationship between interest rate and time to maturity of US Treasuries. Short-term interest rates are usually lower than long-term rates. But occasionally, the interest rate curve is inverted: short-term interest rates are higher than long-term rates. An inverted yield curve indicates that investors and businesses are pessimistic about future economic growth. If investors believe that the economy is slowing down or even going into a recession, they are willing to accept lower long-term interest rates to lock in future income; at the same time, businesses are unwilling to issue long-term debt in order to reduce financial risk, which in turn reduces the supply of long-term debt. It is for this reason investors closely watch the shape of the yield curve and extract economic growth information implied by the yield curve. For example, the difference between the ten-year Treasury note yield and three-month Treasury bill (T-bill) yield is used to forecast the GDP growth rate. Researches by Estrella and Mishkin (1996) showed that when the spread between interest rates on the ten-year Treasury and the three-month Treasury bill was less -1% (inverted yield curve), a recession was likely to follow four quarters later. Indeed, the interest rate on the ten-year Treasury fell more than 1% below the interest rate on three-month Treasury bill prior to almost all recent recessions, including the ones in 2001 and 2008.

The relationship between interest rate levels and stock market returns is less clear cut. Lower interest rates mean lower borrowing costs for both businesses and consumers, which boosts business investments and consumer spending. For instance, lower interest rates translate to lower mortgage rates, making housing more affordable for homeowners. But low interest rates may also reflect investors' overall pessimism about the economy and their willingness to accept low returns in government bonds to avoid taking risks. The risk aversion also leads banks to tighten their credit standards and grant fewer loans to small businesses or potential homeowners. Fewer loans in turn hinder economic growth and add more uncertainty to the stock market. The impact of interest rate levels on different industries requires detailed analysis as well. For example, low interest rates are good for commercial banks since they can collect deposits at low rates and charge a spread when they make loans. Sustained low interest rates are detrimental for insurance companies though. The reason for this is that their liabilities are often structured as annuities and universal life policies which pay policy holders guaranteed rates. Sustained low interest rates make it difficult for insurers to pay existing policy holders such higher guaranteed rates.

Currency Movement

Currency exchange rates have long been major market indicators. Real-time currency exchange rates are readily available from currency market makers. The Federal Reserve also publishes a daily broad index that measures the value of the US dollar relative to a trade-weighted basket of currencies of major US trading partners.

Overall, weak trade-weighted local currency is good for a country's equity market. This is because exports become more competitive due to lower pricing in foreign currency terms. At the same time, profits from overseas operations are repatriated at a higher value in local currency terms. However, not all stocks are impacted by currency movements in the same way, or even in the same direction. US dollar depreciation is good for industries and companies with significant percentage of overseas sales and earnings but bad for those with significant percentage of overseas costs. Therefore, when the US dollar is weak, domestic US investors ought to overweigh global sectors that generate larger percentages of sales overseas and overweigh domestic sectors when the US dollar is strong.

Although exchange rates are widely available and relative level of foreign sales to total sales ratio by industry groups are published by investment banks, incorporation of currency movements into stock selection is not an easy task. With globalization, more and more companies derive their revenues from multiple countries and incur costs in those countries as well. Coupled with the lack of data on foreign currency exposure of companies' costs, it is difficult to estimate the impact of currency movements on earnings without deep knowledge of the company. Besides, weak local currency often reflects global investors' negative view on the future economic growth or fiscal situation of the country, which in return impacts foreign investors' interest in investing in that country. Since foreign ownership is often higher in global sectors, a negative outlook may reduce foreign demand for the underlying securities. Furthermore, large currency movements are often associated with market events (e.g., announcement of quantitative easing) that attract market participants' attention. Compared with gradual small changes, large jumps are more likely to be priced in. Because of the complexity involved in estimating different aspects of currency movements, financial analysts often rely more on qualitative instead of quantitative analysis to forecast their impact on industry returns or individual stock returns.

Monetary and Fiscal Policies

The Federal Open Market Committee (FOMC) meets eight times a year to make decisions on interest rates and other monetary policies. After each meeting, they make an official policy announcement. The announcement happened at ~2:15 PM for meetings before April 2011 and at 12:30 PM since April 2011. The FOMC meeting sets a target for the Federal Funds Rate, the overnight interest rate at which a depository institution lends immediately available funds (at the Federal Reserve) to another. FOMC also actively buys and sells Treasuries in the market in order to control interest rates. When the Federal Reserve sets an expansionary monetary policy, the FOMC lowers the Federal Funds Target Rate and increases the supply of money by buying Treasuries. Needless to say, investors pay close attention to these decisions and actively speculate their impact before and after the announcements. Over the past two decades, the Federal Reserve has time and again implemented policies to stabilize or boost the financial market. Using data from February 1994 to March 2011, David Lucca and Emanuel Moench (2013), two economists at the Federal Reserve Bank of New York, found that the 24-hour return (8 out of 252 trading days) before the FOMC announcement accounted for more than 80% of the equity premium—the difference between equity return and T-bill return—during that period.

In the short term, government intervention through monetary and fiscal policies usually yields desired results. For instance, on September 15, 2010, Japan intervened in the foreign-exchange market by selling Yen to stop its surge. Before the intervention, the Yen had risen 11% against the dollar since May 2010. On the day of the intervention, the Yen was down 1.5% against the dollar and the Nikkei index was up 2.3%. Longer term, such interventions often fail in the fight against market forces. In the following months after September 2010, even with more Japanese central bank interventions, the Yen appreciated another 8% against the dollar.

In addition, many interventions have unintended longer-term consequences. In response to the burst of the internet bubble and the subsequent recession, the Federal Reserve implemented a series of cuts in Federal Fund Rates between 2000 and 2002 to (the then) historical lowest rate of 1% in 2002. One goal of the rate cut was to stabilize the housing market. During the same period, the US Congress and the Bush administration also started a wide range of tax incentives and subsidy programs to promote home ownership. The monetary policy and the fiscal policy yielded targeted results as the housing market became the stabilizing force during the recession. In Fed Chairman Alan Greenspan's testimony to Congress in November 2002, he stated,

"Stimulated by mortgage interest rates that are at lows not seen in decades, home sales and housing starts have remained strong... Besides sustaining the demand for new construction, mortgage markets have also been a powerful stabilizing force over the past two years of economic distress by facilitating the extraction of some of the equity that homeowners had built up over the years."

In retrospect, despite the success of those monetary and fiscal policies in the early 2000s, they ultimately contributed to the housing bubble and led to the subprime mortgage industry collapse in 2007 and the financial crisis in 2008. In order to stabilize the economy and the housing market, the government again implemented similar but more drastic measures. The Federal Reserve lowered and kept the Federal Funds Rate to essentially zero. At the same time, the US Congress and the Obama administration initialized another round of tax incentives including a tax credit of up to $8000 for new home buyers in 2010 and subsidy programs to stabilize the housing market. Needless to say, these policies helped slow down the housing price decline in the short term. But the policies had limited long-term effect on the housing markets as prices continued to decline after the incentives ended before the market finally stabilized in 2013.

Market Sentiment Indicators

The stock market can be roughly classified by two regimes: the bull-market regime has higher expected return, lower volatility and lower correlations between individual stock returns; the bear-market regime has lower expected returns, higher volatility, and higher correlations between stock returns. There are a variety of market sentiment measures that try to gauge the market regime. Trend followers follow the sentiment in making their investment decisions to avoid taking positions against the market sentiment. Contrarian investors, on the other hand, use sentiment indicators to measure overbought and oversold market conditions and take opposite positions. They argue that if everyone agrees that the market will rise and has fully participated in the market, there will be no extra capital inflow to push the market even higher. As a result, the market is likely to fall in the near future.

Volatility index (VIX): VIX is the weighted implied volatility of near-term S&P 500 index options (front month and second month expirations) at different strike prices. It measures the market's expectation of 30-day volatility. As shown in Exhibit 4-1, there is a strong negative contemporaneous correlation between daily S&P 500 returns and daily VIX changes. Since the spike of VIX often coincides with steep drop in stock markets, it is a commonly used as a fear index. Despite their strong negative same-period return correlation, the VIX is sometimes used as a short-term contrarian indicator since an extreme increase in VIX and a corresponding market decline often indicate an oversold market. We studied the relationship between VIX changes and future SPY returns. Between 1993 and 2013, when the VIX closed at a level 10% or more above its 10-day moving average, SPY on average returned 64.5 bps in the following week. When the VIX closed at a level 10% or more below its 10-day moving average, SPY returned -8.3 bps in the following week. For other days, the average one-week forward return was 15.8 bps. The results are consistent with Warren Buffett's teaching: *"Be fearful when others are greedy and greedy when others are fearful."* When the VIX is significant higher than its short-term moving average, investors are fearful and the market is likely to be oversold. As a result, the market often rebounds in the following days.

Exhibit 4-1 Rolling one-year correlation of daily SPX returns and VIX changes

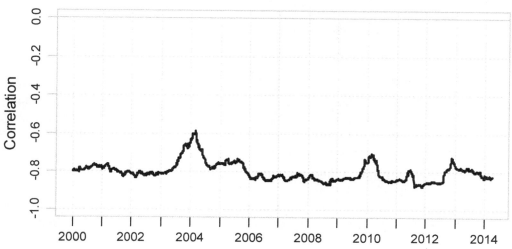

Variance risk premium (VRP): VRP, the difference between option-implied variance (VIX^2) and realized S&P 500 index variance estimated from daily returns of the past month, is another measure of the risk appetite. The correlation between VRP and forward 1-month market return is positive: high VRP indicates higher expected future returns and low VRP indicates lower expected future returns. Higher VRP may indicate higher tail risk for the market and equity investors need to be compensated by a higher risk premium. Between 1993 and 2012, when VRP closed higher than the 12-month median, the average next month S&P index return was 1.23%; otherwise, the average next month return was 0.26%. Since daily data for one month history include only ~21 data points, the estimation error using daily data may be large. Instead, some researchers recommend using five-minute interval returns (close-to-open overnight return is treated as the return of one interval) for the realized volatility estimation. Bollerslev et al. (2009) found that VRP calculated using five-minute interval returns had better forecast power to predict future market returns than variance risk premium calculated using daily returns.

TED spread and credit spread: The TED spread is the difference between the three-month LIBOR rate and three-month T-bill rate, which is the premium that banks pay for unsecured borrowing over the risk-free interest rate. The TED spread goes up when the perceived default risk of the banks goes up. Therefore, TED spreads often widen as the stock market enters into a bear market. Similarly, the credit spread measures the yield difference between corporate bonds and US Treasuries of similar maturity. Investors also use the spread between the yield of a high-yield bond index and Treasuries as a sentiment indicator. When investor sentiment is bullish, investors are more willing to take risks—risk-on market regime—and credit spread decreases; when investor sentiment is bearish, investors are less willing to take risks—risk-off market regime—and credit spread increases.

Trading index (TRIN): developed by Richard Arms, TRIN is a short-term market indicator. The most popular daily TRIN uses NYSE data and is calculated as the following:

$$TRIN = \frac{\text{Number of advances / Number of decliners}}{\text{Advancing volume / Declining volume}}$$

where Number of advances is the number of stocks that close up on a day;

Number of decliners is the number of stocks that close down on a day;

Advancing volume is the total trading volume of the advancing stocks;

Declining volume is the total trading volume of the declining stocks.

A TRIN reading below 1 indicates more volume (in shares) is moving into advancing stocks and a TRIN reading above 1 indicates more volume is moving into declining stocks. If TRIN values stay above (below) 1 for several consecutive days, it is often used as a short-term oversold (overbought) signal.

Retail money market funds: When retail investors are unwilling to take risks, they often move their money out of stock funds and park the money in money market funds. Since the daily NAV (net asset value) of mutual funds and ETFs is readily available, investors can monitor whether capital is flowing into or out of money market funds. High dollar value invested in retail money market funds indicates bearish investor sentiment.

IPO indicator: Companies tend to go public when the market sentiment is bullish and investors are willing to accept high IPO valuations. High number of IPOs, high first-day return versus the IPO price, and high growth rate implied in the IPO pricing (high P/E ratio) are all signs of strong investor sentiment.

Bull/Bear ratio and Put/Call ratio: Published by Investor's Intelligence, the Bull/Bear ratio is the ratio of bullish advisors to the total number of bullish plus bearish advisors covered in a survey of investment advisors. Extreme optimism, a high Bull/Bear ratio, often coincides with market tops and is a bearish signal; extreme pessimism, on the other hand, often coincides with market bottoms and is a bullish signal. Put/Call ratio is the ratio of total CBOE put volume to total CBOE call volume. A high put/call ratio indicates investor pessimism as investors are actively buying insurance against future expected stock price drops.

Conclusion

Economic data provide useful information on the current market regime to enable better investment decision making. The macroeconomic view helps investors make top-level asset allocation decisions, which is still the main driver of differences in long-term investment returns. For equity investments, the popular top-down investment also starts with looking at the big picture before digging into industries and individual stocks. For example, the big picture helps investors make sector rotation decisions. Defensive sectors are less influenced by cyclical shifts in disposable income and consumer confidence; therefore, they outperform the market when the economy slows down. Cyclical sectors, on the other hand, benefit more when consumers have more disposable income and are confident about the future; therefore, they outperform the market when the economy recovers from a recession.

Although the US economy remains the world's largest, the economic stability and the growth of other countries are becoming increasingly important in an interconnected world. In recent years, the European debt crisis and potential solutions (or temporary fixes) have impacted the US stock market outlook. The slowdown of the Chinese economy has also played a role in the US stock market. As a result, investors have increasingly begun to take a global view and now closely monitor international economic indicators.

Chapter 5

Technical Signals

Financial market behavior is not completely random, and there are stable and robust patterns which can be identified and traded on. Technical analysis uses past market actions such as price and volume information to forecast future price trends. Technical analysts use both technical signals (e.g., moving average, Bollinger Bands, and relative strength index) and chart patterns (e.g., support or resistance level, head and shoulder pattern, and trend line) to search for buy and sell opportunities. This chapter focuses on technical signals since they are more amenable to systematic analyses and tests.

Pure technical analysts believe that price and volume provide all necessary information to make investment decisions. They argue that price moves ultimately depend on supply and demand. The supply and demand of stocks materializes through trading and leads to distinct price and volume patterns. By studying and understanding the supply and demand driving distinct patterns, investors gain an edge in investments. Within the financial industry, technical analysis has loyal followers. Moreover, since price and volume data are far more readily available than fundamental data and require fewer resources to analyze, technical analysis has long been a favorite choice for individual investors. Yet some academics have held a skeptical view on the real value of technical analysis since many well-known technical trading rules tend to break down under rigorous statistical testing. The myriad of commercial trading systems that have flooded the market—most sell for a few thousand dollars and have little value—has further raised skepticism. Nevertheless, after the internet bubble, the housing bubble, and the subsequent market crashes, increasingly academics have come to realize the limitation of fundamental analysis and have begun to accept the value of technical analysis as part of the investment process.

A criticism of technical signals is that they are self-fulfilling prophecies: technical signals work if and only if many investors follow and act on those signals. Such criticism does not entirely negate the value of technical signals. If a sufficient number of investors follow a technical trading rule or a price pattern, the supply and demand from these investors helps determine stock price moves. As long as investors adopt a technical signal that captures the overall market supply and demand and make an educated guess about a stock's future trading pattern, they may stand to gain an edge in making investment decisions. The gradual shift of active managers to make shorter-term investments in pursuit of fleeting alpha opportunities also explains the growing popularity of technical analysis. Compared with fundamental accounting information that is available on a quarterly basis, price and volume provide timely daily and intraday information. Short-term direction and volatility are more important for short-term traders with holding periods less than a few weeks since the fundamental value of a stock changes slowly. Portfolio managers who mostly rely on fundamental analysis for investment decision making have started using technical analysis to determine entry/exit points as well. At the same time, many technical analysts have also come to recognize the limitation of traditional technical trading rules. As markets have become more sophisticated and trading speeds have increased, they have quickly striven to adapt their trading strategies to changes in the market environment.

Price, Volume and Volatility Measures

Most daily technical indicators are constructed using open, high, low, and close prices. Some indicators also add trading volume into the mix. In this section, we cover the notations and the derived price information used in technical analysis.

C_t : Close price is the trade price at the close of trading[22]

O_t : Open price is the trade price at the opening of trading

H_t : High price is the highest trade price from the opening to the close of trading

L_t : Low price is the lowest trade price from the opening to the close of trading

V_t : Volume is the number of shares traded from the opening to the close of trading

TP_t : Typical price is the mean of close, high and low prices, $TP_t = (C_t + H_t + L_t)/3$

$LL_{t,N}$: N-day low is the lowest low price of the past N days

$HH_{t,N}$: N-day high is the highest high price of the past N days

$$LL_{t,N} = \min(L_{t-N+1}, L_{t-N+2}, \cdots, L_t), \; HH_{t,N} = \max(H_{t-N+1}, H_{t-N+2}, \cdots, H_t)$$

$\Delta O_t, \Delta H_t, \Delta L_t$, and ΔC_t are one-day open, high, low, and close price changes:

$$\Delta O_t = O_t - O_{t-1}, \; \Delta H_t = H_t - H_{t-1}, \; \Delta L_t = L_t - L_{t-1}, \; \Delta C_t = C_t - C_{t-1}$$

Price volatility is included in many technical indicators. In general, when the market is volatile, incorporation of volatility in a technical indicator makes the entries and exits less sensitive to price moves. The standard deviation of N-day close price changes is often used as a measure of volatility:

$$\sigma_{t,N} = \sqrt{\frac{1}{N}\sum_{i=0}^{N-1}(\Delta C_{t-i} - \overline{\Delta C})^2}, \text{ where } N\text{-day mean price change } \overline{\Delta C} = \frac{1}{N}\sum_{i=0}^{N-1}\Delta C_{t-i}$$

Besides standard deviation, mean absolute deviation and average true range (ATR) are common choices of volatility measures as well. Mean absolute deviation is calculated as the average absolute distance to the mean (or the median) of price changes:

$$D_{t,N} = \frac{1}{N}\sum_{i=0}^{N-1}\left|\Delta C_{t-i} - \overline{\Delta C}\right|$$

ATR is calculated as an exponential moving average of the true range (TR):

---

[22] In US, major stock exchanges open at 9:30 AM Eastern Time and close at 4:00 PM Eastern Time. The official pre-market trading is between 8:00 AM to 9:30 AM and the after-market trading is between 4:00 PM to 8:00 PM.

$$ATR_{t,N} = \frac{N-1}{N} \times ATR_{t-1,N} + \frac{1}{N} \times TR_t,$$

where $TR_t = \max(|H_t - L_t|, |H_t - C_{t-1}|, |C_{t-1} - L_t|) = \max(H_t, C_{t-1}) - \min(L_t, C_{t-1})$

Trend Following Signals

Although there are hundreds of technical signals used by investors, they mostly fall into two categories: trend following signals and mean reversion signals. Trend following signals assume that the existing trend will continue unless it shows clear signs of reversing. Mean reversion signals, on the contrary, try to identify potential reversal points as a trend becomes exhausted or overextended.

Trend following strategies attempt to identify current trends in order to make investments in the same direction as the trend. If the current trend continues long enough before it reverts, a trend following strategy is profitable. Trend following strategies have long been the backbone of technical analysis. Dow Theory—developed by the founder of Dow Jones, Charles Dow, back to the 1800s—states that major trends have three phases: an accumulation phase, a public participation phase, and a distribution phase. In the accumulation phase, smart investors actively accumulate long or short positions before other market participants do. During this period, the stock price does not demonstrate a clear trend. The new fundamentals may support a new trend, but investors underreact to the fundamentals because of anchoring bias. In the public participation phase, other investors gradually embrace the smart investors' view and the stock price trends. This is the phase that trend followers usually participate in. In the distribution phase, many speculators jump in and the herding effect pushes the stock to become overbought/oversold. Smart investors begin to lock in their gains by trading out of their positions as the trend reverts. The goal of a trend following strategy is to enter the trade at an early stage of the participation phase and exit when the stock price trend shows signs of reverting.

The start of a new market trend often coincides with major market-level changes such as interest rate changes, economic activity changes, as well as implementation of new government policies (e.g., quantitative easing). The start of a new trend in a stock's price may be triggered by both broad factors such as industry rotation or demographic changes as well as asset-level factors such as new product releases or the entry of new competitors. Nevertheless, when new information triggers a new trend, trend followers do not respond to the information immediately. Instead they wait for market confirmation of the new trend before entering the trade. Similarly, when new information reverses an existing trend, trend followers wait for market confirmation of the trend reversal before exiting the trade. Although the entry misses some profits from the start of the trend and the exit suffers some losses from the trend reversal, properly executed trend following strategies capture most major trends and associated profits.

Moving Averages (MA)

Moving average crossover, momentum indicator and channel breakouts are examples of popular trend-following strategies. When the stock price moves mostly in one direction, a trend is established. Because of the volatility of daily stock prices, moving averages are often used to smooth price moves and to identify the price trend. There are several types of moving averages. The most basic one is the simple moving average (SMA). The N-day SMA of a time series of close prices at the close of day t is the average close price of past N days:

$$SMA_{t,N} = \frac{1}{N} \sum_{i=0}^{N-1} C_{t-i}$$

For example, a 3-day SMA at t is $(C_t + C_{t-1} + C_{t-2})/3$. A potential drawback of SMA is that it treats all the prices of the past N days equally instead of giving more recent data higher weights. To mitigate this problem, we can use the exponential moving average (EMA). The EMA of the close prices with decay factor α is calculated as the weighted average of C_t and the previous day's EMA, $EMA_{t-1,\alpha}$:

$$EMA_{t,\alpha} = \alpha \times C_t + (1-\alpha) \times EMA_{t-1,\alpha} \text{ where } 0 < \alpha < 1$$

In EMA, the weight of each data point decreases exponentially as time goes by. Another approach to increase the relative weights of more recent data points is the weighted moving average (WMA). The N-day WMA assigns weight N to the latest price, $N-1$ to the second latest, down to 1 for the price $N-1$ days ago:

$$WMA_t = \sum_{i=0}^{N-1} w_i C_{t-i} \bigg/ \sum_{i=0}^{N-1} w_i, \text{ where } w_i = N-i$$

For example, a 3-day WMA at t is $(3C_t + 2C_{t-1} + C_{t-2})/(3+2+1)$.

By design, SMA, EMA, and WMA all lag the latest data point. The lag of SMA is $(N-1)/2$; the lag of EMA is $(1-\alpha)/\alpha$; the lag of WMA is $(N-1)/3$. To make an EMA have the same lag as an N-day SMA, we can set $\alpha = 2/(N+1)$ to make $(1-\alpha)/\alpha$ the same as $(N-1)/2$. The N-day EMA[23] is calculated as

$$EMA_{t,N} = \frac{2}{N+1} C_t + \frac{N-1}{N+1} EMA_{t-1}$$

Faster moving averages—smaller N and larger α—have smaller lags, but they are noisier and generate more false signals; slower moving averages are smoother, but they have larger lags and are slower to capture trend changes. 50-day SMA and 200-day SMA are widely followed by investors. Both are considered important support and resistance levels and are used to estimate the market trend. The 200-day SMA is often considered a long-term market trend line: if the market closes above its 200-day SMA line, the market is in uptrend; if the market closes below its 200-day SMA line, the market is in downtrend. The number of days used in technical analysis is the number of business days. Since the US stock market is open ~252 days a year, some investors use 10-month moving average as the trend line. Similarly, 50-day SMA acts as a medium-term trend line and 10-day

---

[23] We should point out that some technical signals, e.g., average directional index, simply uses $\alpha = 1/N$ for N-day EMA instead of $\alpha = 2/(N+1)$. It is important to understand the exact decay factor when implementing a technical signal involving EMA.

SMA acts as a short-term trend line. A SMA with fewer than 10 day smoothing tends to be choppy and is more likely to whipsaw instead of trending.

A basic trend following strategy is to long a stock when its close price is above the N-day moving average, where N varies from ten days for short-term trading to a year for long-term trading. One potential problem is that single day stock prices tend to be noisy. When the market has no clear trend, stock prices simply fluctuate within a range. As the stock price swings close to the top of the range, it closes above the N-day moving average even though the price is likely to revert. To reduce noise, two moving averages are sometimes used instead:

- Buy when the M-day moving average of C_t crosses above the N-day moving average ($N > M > 1$) of C_t

- Sell or short sell when the M-day moving average of C_t crosses below the N-day moving average ($N > M > 1$) of C_t

The short-term M-day moving average smoothes the stock's close price and reduces whipsaws.

By design, moving average crossover does not try to pick the market top or the market bottom. Instead it waits until the market trend is established and exits when the market has already topped. The goal is to capture the middle part of a trend. Exhibit 5-1 shows the daily close prices of SPY and the 200-day SMA of SPY in 2000-2012. The 200-day SMA captures the market trend well. Between January 2008 and May 2009, the SPY price stayed below the 200-day SMA line and the market was down ~33% during that period. The exhibit also shows that the moving average crossover does not try to capture the price bottom. Instead, the crossover signal waited until the new uptrend was established: even though SPY bottomed on March 9th, 2009 at 68.11, the price did not cross above the 200-day moving average until June 1 when SPY closed at \$94.77 and the uptrend was established.

Besides fixed-length moving averages, some investors also use dynamic moving averages. They believe that the number of the periods used for smoothing should vary over time. When the prices have a strong trend, the moving average should use a shorter period to capture the trend earlier; when prices have no clear trend, the moving average should use a longer period to avoid whipsaws. A general formula for variable moving average (VMA) is

$$VMA_{t,\alpha} = (\alpha \times VI_t) \times C_t + (1 - \alpha \times VI_t) \times VMA_{t-1,\alpha}$$

VMA introduces a volatility index (VI) to adjust the decay factor when the volatility or the trend strength changes. For example, Perry Kaufman (1995) recommended the efficiency ratio as an input to adjust the decay factor:

Efficiency ratio = Direction/Volatility

where $\text{Direction} = |C_t - C_{t-N}|$ and $\text{Volatility} = \sum_{i=0}^{N-1} |C_{t-i} - C_{t-i-1}|$.

When the trend is strong and the price moves mostly in the same direction in the past N days, the efficiency ratio is close to 1; when the price is range-bound and fluctuates within a range instead, the efficiency ratio is close to 0. The VMA decreases the decay factor to increase the number of days in the smoothing when the efficiency ratio is close to 0 and increases the decay factor when the efficiency ratio is close to 1.

Exhibit 5-1 SPY and 200-day SMA of SPY

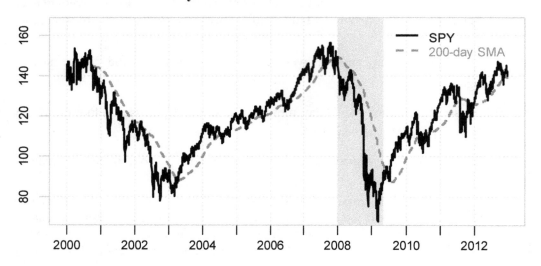

To produce a moving average without lag requires a peek into the future. Nevertheless, some investors create zero-lag moving averages using mathematical approximation. One approximation is **Double exponential moving average (DEMA)**. DEMA includes both a single EMA component and a double EMA component:

$$DEMA = 2 \times EMA1 - EMA2,$$

where EMA1 = N-day EMA of close prices

EMA2 = N-day EMA of EMA1

A simple dissection of DEMA reveals the reason for zero lag:

$$DEMA = EMA1 + (EMA1 - EMA2)$$

EMA1 itself has N-day lag. Since EMA2 is the N-day EMA of EMA1, it further lags EMA1 by N days. EMA2 has a lag of $2N$ days and (EMA1 − EMA2) has a lag of -N days, which compensates the lag of EMA1. Conceptually, the first component is a normal EMA and the second component captures the momentum. As the price trends up, EMA1 lags the close price and EMA2 further lags the price. So the difference between EMA1 and EMA2 is an additional momentum term aiming to capture the trend and to remove the lag.

Exhibit 5-2 compares the weights of lagged prices in EMA and DEMA to demonstrate why DEMA has zero lag. The momentum component, EMA1 − EMA2, increases the weights of the most recent data and forces the data points in distant history to have negative weights: the latest price has a weight of 0.2 in EMA and a weight of 0.36 in

DEMA; the price 16 days ago has a weight of 0.0056 in EMA and a weight of -0.0079 in DEMA.

Exhibit 5-3 plots the close prices, EMA and DEMA ($N = 9$) of SPY from January 2009 to April 2009. Overall, it demonstrates that DEMA follows the trend of the close price series more closely than EMA. For example, between February 10th and March 9th, EMA lags the SPY prices while DEMA smoothed out the short-term volatility and followed SPY prices closely. However, we should point out that DEMA only captures the existing trend. If the trend reverses, it takes time for DEMA to catch up to the reversal. When the SPY price trend reversed after the market bottomed on March 9th, both EMA and DEMA lagged the close prices. It took two weeks for DEMA to closely follow SPY prices again.

Exhibit 5-2 Weights of lagged prices in EMA and DEMA with $N = 9$

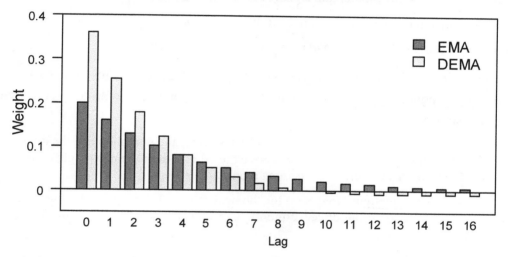

Exhibit 5-3 Close prices, EMA, and DEMA of SPY

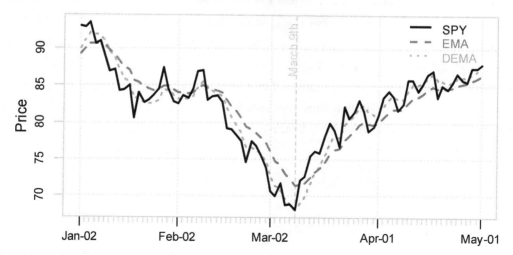

Momentum

The momentum indicator simply measures the difference between the current price and the price N days ago:

$$\text{momentum}_t = C_t - C_{t-N}$$

A related measure, rate of change (ROC), measures the difference as a fraction of the price N days ago:

$$ROC_t = \frac{C_t - C_{t-N}}{C_{t-N}}$$

A trading rule using the momentum signal is fairly straightforward:

- Buy when the N-day momentum or ROC is positive

- Sell or short sell when the N-day momentum or ROC is negative

Despite their simplicity, moving average crossover and momentum strategies have proven to be powerful technical signals. Let us consider two simple long-only trend following strategies:

- 10-Month moving average crossover: Hold SPY for the next month if the dividend-adjusted close price[24] of a month is above the 10-month moving average; otherwise, hold long-term Treasuries for the next month.

- 12-Month momentum: Hold SPY for the next month if the dividend-adjusted close price is higher than the price 12 month ago; otherwise, hold long-term Treasuries for the next month.

Exhibit 5-4 shows that both the 10-month crossover and 12-month momentum strategies yielded substantially better returns and had lower standard deviations than a buy and hold strategy that held SPY between 1994 (SPY started trading at the end of 1993) and 2012. Both strategies also cut the maximum drawdown of the portfolio from 50.8% to less than 20%. The 10-month crossover strategy moved to Treasuries for 12 times and 12-month momentum strategy moved to Treasures for only 4 times. The main reason for the success of these simple strategies is that they prevented investors from catching a falling knife during the 2000-2002 and 2008-2009 bear markets.

---

[24] For our tests, we use time series of cumulative total returns instead of time series of close prices. Total return time series take the cumulative effect of dividends into consideration and measure the performance of the underlying asset by assuming that all dividends are reinvested in the asset at the ex-dividend date.

Exhibit 5-4 Performance of 10-month moving average crossover and 12-month momentum strategies

Strategy	10-month crossover	12-month momentum	buy and hold
Geometric Return	12.2%	12.7%	7.8%
Annualized StDev	12.2%	12.8%	15.4%
Return/StDev	1.00	0.99	0.51
Worst Drawdown	18.2%	16.2%	50.8%
% Time in SPY	71.9%	76.7%	100%

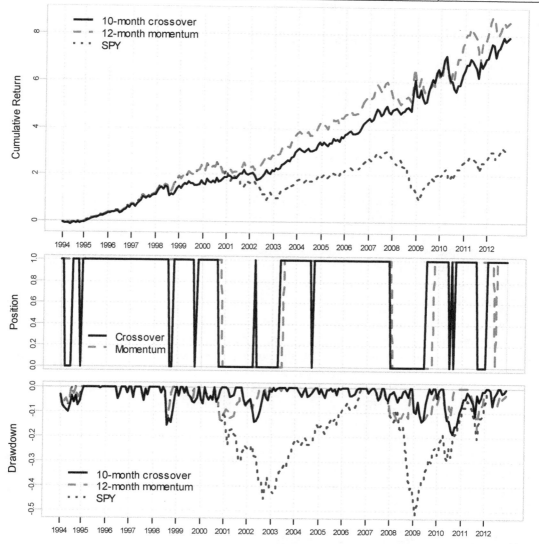

Interestingly, if we change the moving average crossover strategy from a monthly rebalance to a daily rebalance (e.g., use 210-day moving average crossover with daily data), we get higher turnovers and lower returns. One explanation is that daily returns actually exhibit a mean reverting pattern. If one day's positive return pushes the SPY prices above the 210-day moving average in one day, the price is more likely to go down in the following day. Therefore, daily rebalance that closely follows the moving average crossover actually leads to lower returns than monthly rebalance.

Channel Breakouts

It is widely believed that stock prices bottom when investors stop selling. It may be weeks or even months before a sufficient number of new investors begin to accumulate shares and start an uptrend. Although occasionally stock prices do reverse vehemently, such scenarios are more likely to be caused by drastic market sentiment reversal. More often than not, after the stock price bottoms, it is likely to go sideways for weeks or months with little investor interest before we see a new trend. Successful investors do not need to pick the stock at its bottom; instead they wait for the confirmation of a new trend.

Channel breakout is a popular choice for the confirmation of a new trend. Channel breakout calculates the rolling N-day highest high and the rolling N-day lowest low as the channel with the following entry and exit rules:

- Enter a long position when today's high is the N-day highest high and exit the long position when today's low is the M-day lowest low ($M < N$).

- Enter a short position when today's low is the N-day lowest low and exit the short position when today's high is the M-day highest high ($M < N$).

This simple strategy is believed to be the key ingredient in the Turtle trading system. In 1983 and 1984, to settle a debate with his friend on whether trading could be taught to "ordinary people" to make them successful traders, Richard Dennis taught about twenty "turtles" (people with little or no trading experience) a trend following system that was based on channel breakouts for two weeks. After that, he funded them and let them trade commodities, bonds, and futures using the system. In five years, the "turtles" generated over $200 million profit!

Despite its popularity, channel breakout signals have had less success in recent years. The back test results for breakout strategies are mixed because of false breakouts—stock prices reach new highs or new lows but then quickly reverse direction. In order to revive channel breakout signals, some technical analysts seek volume confirmation, e.g., at least 50% higher trading volume on the breakout day than average daily volume, when they use the breakout signal. High volume indicates high market participation and investor enthusiasm. Therefore, the breakout is less likely to reverse. Some wait for the retracement test before entry: if the stock price decisively breaks out of the previous N-day highest high, that price level becomes a support level. A real breakout may have pullbacks before the up trend continues, but the pullbacks should be small and there should be buyers defending the price at the support level. If the support level holds, the initial breakout is less likely to be a false breakout and it is safer to enter a long position.

Trend Strength Indicators and Whipsaw Reduction

Moving average crossover and channel breakout do not work if a stock's price moves sideways in a range. Instead, buy signals are often triggered when the stock prices are at the top of the range and sell signals are often triggered when the stock prices are at the bottom of the range. In these cases, trend following signals lead to losses.

How do we then determine whether the stock price shows a significant trend and the strength of the current trend? Average directional index (ADX) is one measure of trend strength. It is calculated using the following steps.

Positive directional movement:

$$+DM_t = \begin{cases} H_t - H_{t-1}, \text{if } H_t - H_{t-1} > L_{t-1} - L_t \text{ and } H_t > H_{t-1} \\ 0, \text{otherwise} \end{cases}$$

Negative directional movement: $-DM_t = \begin{cases} L_{t-1} - L_t, \text{if } L_{t-1} - L_t > H_t - H_{t-1} \text{ and } L_{t-1} > L_t \\ 0, \text{otherwise} \end{cases}$

Average true range: $ATR_t = \text{EMA of } TR_t$

Positive directional indicator: $+DI_t = \text{EMA of } (+DM_t / ATR_t)$

Negative directional indicator: $-DI_t = \text{EMA of} (-DM_t / ATR_t)$

Directional index: $DX_t = \dfrac{|+DI_t - -DI_t|}{+DI_t + -DI_t} \times 100$

Average directional index: EMA of DX_t

In the original 14-day ADX proposed by J. Welles Wilder, the decay factor was chosen to be 1/14 for ATR and the positive/negative directional indicators. ADX ranges between 0 and 100. When ADX is below 20, the market is range-bound or the trend is weak; when ADX is above 30, the trend is strong. Although ADX itself only measures the strength of the trend instead of the direction, it is easy to get the direction by comparing $+DI_t$ with $-DI_t$.

Another measure of trend strength is the reverse arrangement test (RAT). For price series $C_1, C_2, \ldots, C_n$, reverse arrangement test compares the price changes, $C_j - C_i$, for all pairs of intervals, $1 \le i \le j \le n$, and calculates the trend using the average of the signs of the changes:

$$\tau_n = \frac{\displaystyle\sum_{j=i+1}^{n} \sum_{i=1}^{n-1} sign(C_j - C_i)}{n(n-1)/2}, \text{ where } sign(C_j - C_i) = \begin{cases} 1, & \text{if } C_j > C_i \\ 0, & \text{if } C_j = C_i \\ -1, & \text{if } C_j < C_i \end{cases}$$

If the prices monotonically increase, $sign(C_j - C_i) = 1$ for all $1 \le i < j \le n$ and $\tau_n = 1$. If the prices monotonically decrease, $\tau_n = -1$. When the prices have no clear trend, τ_n is close to 0.

Although sound in principle, ADX and RAT have their limitations and are mainly used as supplementary signals to confirm other trend indicators. ADX and RAT tell us that the prices display a trend; but they do not tell us whether the trend will continue. If the trend does not last for a sufficient period of time in the future, establishment of an existing trend does not help forecast future returns. Besides, ADX and RAT are slow at generating meaningful signals. When they become significant, the trend may have exhausted or even reverted. Instead of relying on trend strength indicators, investors often adopt the following ad-hoc approaches to reduce whipsaws:

Confirmation pattern: Such a system seeks confirmation before entering or exiting a position. For example, instead of entering a position on a day when the close price crosses above the 50-day SMA, investors can wait for a second day and only enter a long position if the second day's close price remains above the 50-day SMA.

Moving average channel: In such a system, investors construct a channel around the moving average. The close price needs to cross above the upper channel for a buy entry signal; the close price needs to cross below the lower channel for a sell entry signal. For example, we can use a percent envelope as the channel. The size of the envelope is calculated as a percentage of the moving average. The system generates a buy signal when the close price crosses above the upper channel (e.g., 2% higher than the moving average) and generates a sell signal when the close price crosses below the lower channel (e.g., 2% lower than the moving average).

Triple moving average crossover: In such a system, we only enter a long position if the short-term moving average closes above the medium-term moving average and the medium-term moving average closes above the long-term moving average. For example, we long a position if the 5-day SMA is higher than the 50-day SMA and the 50-day SMA is higher than the 200-day SMA; we short a position if the 5-day SMA is lower than the 50-day SMA and the 50-day SMA is lower than the 200-day SMA; we take no position otherwise.

Hysteresis: Hysteresis denotes that the current state of a system depends not just on its current environment, but also on its past. In essence, besides the current snapshot of information, historical information is included in determining the current state. For example, Abrams and Walker (2010) used a moving average trend channel to determine whether the market is in uptrend or downtrend. Instead of comparing the close price with the 200-day SMA of close prices, the trend channel uses the following method to determine market regime:

Let $\mu_{H,t} = \dfrac{1}{N}\sum_{i=0}^{N-1} H_{t-i}$ and $\mu_{L,t} = \dfrac{1}{N}\sum_{i=0}^{N-1} L_{t-i}$ be the N-day simple moving average ($N = 200$) of the daily high prices and the daily low prices. The market regime is defined as

$$\tau = \begin{cases} 1\,(\text{uptrend}) \text{ if } C_t > \rho_t \\ -1\,(\text{downtrend}), \text{ otherwise} \end{cases}, \text{ where } \rho_t = \begin{cases} \max(\mu_{L,t}, \rho_{t-1}), \text{ if } \tau_{t-1} = 1 \\ \min(\mu_{H,t}, \rho_{t-1}), \text{ if } \tau_{t-1} = -1 \end{cases}$$

Essentially, the calculation of the threshold value ρ depends on the previous day's market regime, τ_{t-1}. In an uptrend environment, the moving average trend channel is determined by the moving average of the low prices and the threshold value ρ is only allowed to increase. In a downtrend environment, the moving average trend channel is determined by the moving average of the high prices and ρ is only allowed to decrease.

For moving average crossover to work, the trend should last longer than the lag of the moving average. Despite efforts to reduce whipsaws, no method is fail-safe. When the price reverses rapidly or fluctuates between uptrend and downtrend, investors still get caught in the whipsaws. As a result, the percentage of winning trades in a good trending system may be below 50%. However, the profit to loss ratio by trade of a successful trend following system should be high since such a system often has many small losses and a few large winning trades that more than compensate the small losses. Trend following strategies such as moving average crossover and channel breakout capture major market moves and the profits from these moves are often substantial. Statistically, trend following strategies tend to work because the returns have fat tails and these strategies effectively capture these fat tails.

Mean Reversion Signals

Mean reversion strategies generate signals when a trend is likely to reverse or when it becomes exhausted or overextended. The assumption is that an oversold stock is likely to bounce back from its lows and an overbought stock is likely to fall from its highs. So mean-revision indicators focus on identifying situations where prices are unusually high (overbought) or unusually low (oversold). Bollinger Bands, relative strength index, and stochastic oscillator are popular mean reversion indicators.

Bollinger Bands

Bollinger Bands(N, K) are volatility bands used to measure the price relative to its moving average. Bollinger Bands(N, K) consists of a middle band, an upper band, and a lower band:

Middle band = N-day SMA of close prices, $SMA_{t,N}$

Upper band = N-day SMA + $K \times N$-day price volatility[25], $Upper_{t,N} = SMA_{t,N} + K\sigma_{t,N}$

Lower band = N-day SMA − $K \times N$-day price volatility, $Lower_{t,N} = SMA_{t,N} - K\sigma_{t,N}$

The default values for N and K are 20 and 2, respectively.

Bollinger Bands are valuable tools for chartists to visually identify potential overbought and oversold conditions. The following trading strategy uses Bollinger Bands:

- Enter a long position when the close price falls below the lower band and exit the long position when the close price rises above the middle band.

- Enter a short position when the close price rises above the upper band and exit the short position when the close price falls below the middle band.

Exhibit 5-5 shows SPY close prices and Bollinger Bands between May 2012 and November 2012. On June 1, SPY price fell below the lower band, which indicated an oversold condition. Indeed, the price soon reverted and rose 3.9% in a week to push the price to cross above the middle band. On July 3, SPY rose above the upper band, which indicated an overbought condition. In the following week, the price fell 2.4% to push the price below the middle band. Although statistical analysis indicates that Bollinger Bands

---

[25] The volatility is the N-day standard deviation of the prices. Bollinger Bands use the population method to calculate the standard deviation. Thus, the divisor in the standard deviation calculation is N, not $N - 1$.

are indeed good mean reversion indicators, they do not always work as expected. For example, on November 8, SPY price fell below the lower band. Yet in the following week, the price continued to fall another 2% before the price trend reverted.

Exhibit 5-5 SPY prices and Bollinger Bands

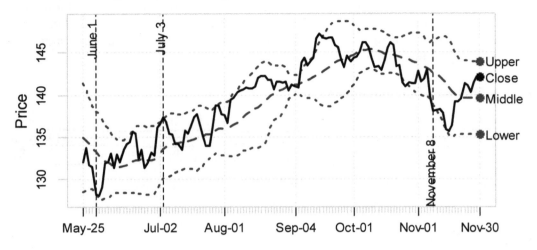

Bollinger Bands themselves are less amenable to quantitative analysis. Instead, the Bollinger z-score indicator is often used as a technical signal:

$$z_B = (C_t - SMA_{t,N})/\sigma_{t,N}$$

Essentially, the z-score measures how many standard deviations the price lies from its moving average. Another related indicator, Bollinger %B, measures the price relative to the upper and lower Bollinger bands:

$$\%B = \frac{C_t - Lower_{t,N}}{Upper_{t,N} - Lower_{t,N}} = \frac{C_t - SMA_{t,N}}{2K \times \sigma_{t,N}} + 0.5$$

When Bollinger z-score is less than -2 and Bollinger %B is less than 0 (for $K = 2$), the price falls below the lower band and the stock is oversold; when Bollinger z-score is higher than 2 and Bollinger %B is higher than 1, the price rises above the upper band and the stock is overbought.

Relative Strength Index

Relative strength index (RSI) is a momentum oscillator developed by J. Welles Wilder. N-day RSI is calculated using the following steps:

$$gain_t = \begin{cases} C_t - C_{t-1}, & \text{if } C_t > C_{t-1} \\ 0, & \text{otherwise} \end{cases} \text{ and } loss_t = \begin{cases} C_{t-1} - C_t, & \text{if } C_t < C_{t-1} \\ 0, & \text{otherwise} \end{cases}$$

$$\text{mean gain}_t = \frac{1}{N} \times \text{gain}_t + \frac{N-1}{N} \times \text{mean gain}_{t-1} \text{ with initial mean gain}_N = \frac{1}{N} \times \sum_{i=1}^{N} \text{gain}_i \text{ }^{26}$$

$$\text{mean loss}_t = \frac{1}{N} \times \text{loss}_t + \frac{N-1}{N} \times \text{mean loss}_{t-1} \text{ with initial mean loss}_N = \frac{1}{N} \times \sum_{i=1}^{N} \text{loss}_i$$

$$RSI_t = 100 - \frac{100}{1+RS_t} = 100 \times \frac{\text{mean gain}_t}{\text{mean gain}_t + \text{mean loss}_t} \text{ where } RS_t = \frac{\text{mean gain}_t}{\text{mean loss}_t}$$

Wilder recommended $N = 14$. The RSI oscillates between 0 and 100. A value close to 100 shows that the prices have multiple up days with no pullback or only small pullbacks in between; a value close to 0 shows that the prices have consecutive down days with no recovery or only small recoveries in between. The market is considered to be overbought when the 14-day RSI, labeled as RSI(14), is above 75 and oversold when RSI(14) is below 25. In a bull market the threshold for overbought is increased to 80 and in a bear market the threshold for oversold is decreased to 20.

Exhibit 5-6 SPY close prices, RSI(4) and RSI(14)

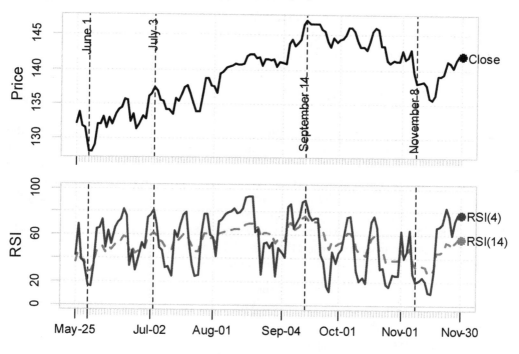

Nevertheless, the market has changed since the publication of RSI in 1978. One significant change is the increase in daily trading volume and trading speed. Investors

---

[26] There is no standard as to how the initial mean gain is calculated. We adopted the recommendation by stockcharts.com. We can also set mean gain$_1$ = gain$_1$ as the initial value. Because of the initial mean gain calculation, the RSI value may differ depending on the number of days included in the calculation. When $t \geq 5N$, the initial mean gain and mean loss have little impact on RSI.

react much faster to new information and market sentiment responds to news much faster as well. Although still a popular choice, the traditional RSI(14) is often too slow to capture short-term overbought or oversold conditions. As shown in Exhibit 5-6, the RSI(14) mostly fluctuated between 30 and 70 from May 2012 to November 2012. During the half year period, it never fell below 25 and only reached 75 once on September 14, in which case SPY did fall 2.7% before the RSI(14) fell below 50. Some technical analysts recommend faster-moving RSI signals instead. For example, we can use 4-day RSI and use 80/20 as thresholds for overbought/oversold conditions. RSI(4) identified several other overbought/oversold conditions, including the oversold condition on June 1 and the overbought condition on July 3 that the Bollinger Bands also identified.

Stochastic Oscillator

Stochastic oscillator measures the location of the close price relative to the range defined by the highest high and the lowest low of the past N days. The fast stochastic oscillator includes two components: Fast %K and Fast %D. Fast %K is the ratio of the difference between today's close price and the N-day lowest low to the difference between the N-day highest high and the N-day lowest low:

$$\%K_{t,N} \ Fast = \frac{C_t - LL_{t,N}}{HH_{t,N} - LL_{t,N}} \times 100 \ \text{(default } N = 14)$$

Fast %D is the n-day SMA of Fast %K:

$$\%D_{t,N} = \frac{1}{n}\sum_{i=0}^{n-1}\%K_{t-i,N} \ \text{(default } n = 3).$$

Both Fast %K and Fast %D range from 0 to 100. A value close to 100 means that the close price is near the N-day highest high. A value close to 0 means that the close price is near the N-day lowest low. Values above 80 indicate potential overbought conditions and values below 20 indicate potential oversold conditions. Strategies involving stochastic look at both the absolute level of the stochastic and the crossover of the Fast %K and the Fast %D lines. A long position may be triggered when the Fast %K line rises above 20 and the Fast %K line crosses above the Fast %D stochastic (momentum bullish reversal). A short position may be triggered when the Fast %K line falls below 80 and the Fast %K line crosses below the Fast %D stochastic (momentum bearish reversal).

Although the fast stochastic oscillator is the original version of stochastic, it is too sensitive to price moves. To reduce the sensitivity, technical analysts introduced the full stochastic oscillator:

Full %K = m-day SMA of Fast %K

Full %D = m-day SMA of Full %K

m is called the %K slowing period as it smoothes Fast %K to reduce the sensitivity. When m is set to 1, the full stochastic oscillator is the fast stochastic oscillator. When m is set to 3, it is often called slow stochastic oscillator. When the Full %K is close to 100, it indicates that the close prices for the past m days stayed close to the highs; when the Full %K is close to 0, it indicates that the close prices for the past m days stayed close to the lows. Therefore, the full stochastic oscillator, stoch(N, m, m), is a popular oscillator to identify overbought and oversold conditions.

Exhibit 5-7 shows SPY close prices, the full %K line, and the Full %D line of stoch(14, 3, 3) between May 2012 and November 2012. On June 9, the full %K line rose above 0.2 and crossed the full %D line. The momentum bullish reversal generated a buy signal three business days after the Bollinger z-score and RSI(4) generated the buy signal on June 1. As a result, the stoch(14, 3, 3) did not capture the 2.9% return between June 1 and June 6. In November, the stoch(14, 3, 3) generated the buy signal on the 19th whereas the Bollinger z-score and RSI(4) generated the buy signal on the 8th. As a result, the stoch(14, 3, 3) avoided the initial loss between November 8 and November 15.

Exhibit 5-7 SPY close prices, stoch(14, 3, 3) full %K and full %D

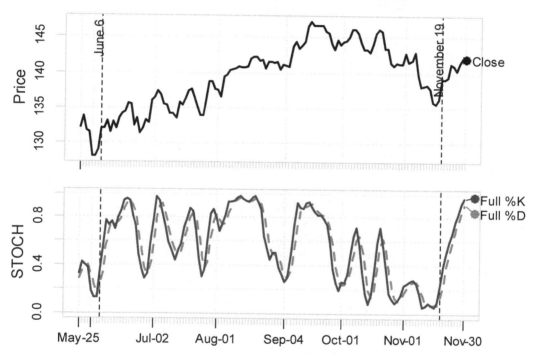

Besides the three popular mean reversion signals discussed in this section, there are many other signals (e.g., moving average convergence divergence) that try to capture overbought and oversold conditions and potential trend reversals. How does one decide which signal to choose? The simple answer is to choose whichever signal one feels most comfortable with. As long as we choose parameters for different signals to capture overbought/oversold conditions in similar time frame, these signals often yield similar results. The signals are often triggered at the same day or within several days. Some signals work better than others in certain times and some work better than others for certain assets. But no signal has consistently outperformed other signals at all times or for all assets.

Volume-Adjusted Technical Indicators

Volume-adjusted technical indicators attempt to combine price movements with volume changes to yield better indicators. Investors often monitor trading volume changes. The general argument is that volume should confirm the trend. In an uptrend, volume should increase as the price moves higher and decrease as the price falls; in a downtrend, volume should increase as the price falls and decrease as the price moves higher. A volume spike—significantly higher volume than recent average daily volume—indicates a spike in investor interests, which often occurs around significant news or corporate events.

On-balance Volume (OBV)

On-balance volume is a simple technical indicator to estimate whether the volume is flowing in or out of a stock:

$$OBV_t = \begin{cases} OBV_{t-1} + V_t, & \text{if } C_t > C_{t-1} \\ OBV_{t-1}, & \text{if } C_t = C_{t-1} \\ OBV_{t-1} - V_t, & \text{if } C_t < C_{t-1} \end{cases}$$

Since the price move is ultimately determined by the supply and demand of the stock, the stock price rises when there is more demand from buyers than supply from sellers. A day's volume is added to OBV if the price closes higher than the previous day's price and subtracted from OBV if the price closes lower. In other words, it is the cumulative sum of signed volumes. OBV is used to confirm the price trend. If the price is rising, increasing OBV (volumes are higher on the days that the prices increase) confirms the trend and decreasing OBV suggests potential reversal since smart money may have started to exit the trades. Increasing prices and decreasing OBV are considered a bearish divergence since the volume pattern does not confirm the price pattern, indicating possible reversal. Decreasing prices and increasing OBV are considered a bullish divergence since the volume pattern again does not confirm the price pattern, indicating possible reversal.

Chaikin Accumulation/Distribution Line (ADL) and Chaikin Money Flow

Developed by Marc Chaikin, accumulation/distribution line is a more complex version of volume-based indicator. Instead of multiplying the volume by the sign of close price change as in OBV, ADL multiplies the volume by the close location value (CLV).

Close location value: $CLV_t = \dfrac{(C_t - L_t) - (H_t - C_t)}{H_t - L_t} = 2 \times \dfrac{C_t - (H_t + L_t)/2}{H_t - L_t}$

Money flow volume: $MFV_t = CLV_t \times V_t$

Accumulation/distribution line: $ADL_t = ADL_{t-1} + MFV_t$

Chaikin Money Flow: $MFI_{t,N} = \sum_{i=0}^{N-1} MFV_{t-i} \Big/ \sum_{i=0}^{N-1} V_{t-i}$

Ranging between -1 and 1, CLV measures where the close price lies between the high price and the low price. If the close price is higher than the average of the high price and the low price, CLV is positive. If the bull is in charge and pushes close price to be the high price, CLV is 1. On the other hand, if the close price is the low price, CLV is -1. Similar to on-balance volume, accumulation/distribution line is also used to confirm the price trend: when ADL moves in the same direction as the price, it confirms the price trend; when ADL moves in the opposite direction of the price, it indicates that the trend is exhausted and likely to reverse. Chaikin Money Flow is the cumulative money flow volume over the past N days (default $N = 20$) divided by the total trading volume over the same period. When the money flow is above 0, it indicates that there is more buying than selling; when the money flow is below 0, it indicates that there is more selling than buying.

In many cases, ADL and OBV yield similar information. But sometimes they may produce different trends. Since ADL does not take the overnight price move into consideration, the multipliers for ADL and OBV may have different signs if the stock price gaps up or gaps down at the open. For example, if the price gaps up at the open but closes below the average of the high price and the low price, ADL decreases but OBV increases. There is no evidence that one is better than the other. Instead, they reveal different information and as all other technical indicators, they are not infallible.

Money Flow Index (MFI)

The money flow index also combines the volume with the direction of the price move. The calculation of MFI is as follows:

$$\text{Positive money flow: } + MF_t = \begin{cases} TP_t \times V_t, & \text{if } TP_t > TP_{t-1} \\ 0, & \text{otherwise} \end{cases}$$

$$\text{Negative money flow: } - MF_t = \begin{cases} TP_t \times V_t, & \text{if } TP_t < TP_{t-1} \\ 0, & \text{otherwise} \end{cases}$$

$$\text{Money flow index: } MFI_{t,N} = 100 \times \left(\sum_{i=0}^{N-1} + MF_{t-i} \right) \Bigg/ \left(\sum_{i=0}^{N-1} + MF_{t-i} + \sum_{i=0}^{N-1} - MF_{t-i} \right)$$

MFI is defined as the ratio of the positive money flow to total money flow during a selected period. Instead of using close prices, MFI incorporates high and low prices by determining the sign of the volume using typical price changes. Money flow is positive if the typical price is higher than the previous typical price and negative if the typical price is lower than the previous typical price. Traditional MFI is calculated using daily data and the default value for N is 14. With intraday data, we can also calculate the money flow index using 5-minute bars. The formula of MFI is similar to RSI. Its difference from RSI is that the formula is applied to signed dollar volumes instead of price changes.

MFI is often used as an oscillator with values ranging from 0 to 100. A value of 80 is often considered overbought and a value of 20 is considered oversold. Divergences between MFI and price trend are also considered significant. For instance, if the price makes a new high but the MFI is less than its previous high, it may indicate a weak trend and possible trend reversal.

Exit Strategies

For a technical trading system to work, deciding when to exit a trade is as important as deciding when to enter a trade. The basic idea behind many of the good exit rules is to lose the least amount possible when the price moves against us and to capture a large percentage of the profit when the price moves in our favor.

Signal Reversion

The premise guiding us to enter a trade provides information for us to exit a trade as well. We exit a trade when the original reason for entering the trade no longer exists. If we enter a long position because the stock price is trending up, we should exit the trade when the price is no longer trending up; if we enter a long position because the stock is oversold, we should exit the trade when the stock is no longer oversold. For example, if we bought a stock after the price moved above the N-day moving average and the price subsequently moves against us, the price move itself will naturally trigger a crossover when the price falls below the N-day moving average and will change the signal from buy to neutral or sell. On the other hand, if the price continues to trend up, the price will stay above the N-day moving average and the long position will stay open. Similarly, signal reversion can be used to determine exits for mean reversion strategies. If we enter a long position when a stock is oversold as indicated by an RSI value below 15, we can exit the position when the stock is no longer oversold as indicated by an RSI value above 50. If we enter a long position when a stock is oversold as indicated by a Bollinger z-score less than -2, we can exit the position when the stock is no longer oversold as indicated by a Bollinger z-score higher than 0.

Stop Loss and Trailing Stops

Stop loss is often used to complement signal reversion as an exit signal. Stop loss gives us guidance on how to respond to losses when the price moves against us. Most trend followers recommend "cut your losses and let your profits run". Naturally, trend following strategies have embedded stop loss signals. If we enter a long position following a trend, the reversal of the trend causes losses. But the trend reversal also causes us to exit the trade or even to take an opposite position. Therefore, the signal change keeps maximum loss small relative to the potential gain. Mean-reversion strategies do not have embedded stop loss signals. On the contrary, when the price moves against us, the signals become stronger. For instance, if we entered a long position when the Bollinger z-score reached -2, what should we do if the price keeps on falling? If we still believe in the original mean-reversion premise, the opportunity looks more attractive as the z-score falls below -3 and we should hold or even add to the long position. Yet if we believe that the premise no longer holds as there are fundamental changes that drive down the price, we need to ignore the "attractive" z-score and cut our losses. There is no standard answer as to how to manage losses for mean reversion strategies. Analysis of historical z-score ranges may help. If the z-score falls below the historical minimum, we may need to question the premise and cut the losses. For example, if historical z-scores did not fall below -3 and the current z-score reaches -3.5, it is likely that news or fundamentals drive investors' negative view on the stock and the price often does not revert. Some investors also closely monitor news and other events so that they cut their losses instead of doubling down on the long position if newly released bad news triggers more sell-off after they enter a long position.

There are two types of stop losses: initial stop loss and trailing stop loss. The initial stop loss is the maximum risk that we are willing to accept before we take steps to protect the principal. Most high-probability trading strategies recommend that the potential profit be at least as large as the initial risk. A stop loss of 8-10% is often suggested for single stock strategies. A typical stock has daily volatility of 2-4%, so 8-10% is approximately 2-4 standard deviations. Such a stop is sufficiently away from the current price to make the stop less likely to be triggered by normal market fluctuation and still provides adequate principal protection. A fixed percentage stop loss does not take the volatility of the stock into consideration though. A volatility-based stop loss directly includes volatility—standard deviation of close prices or average true range—in setting the stop loss price. A stop loss of three times of the average true range from the entry price is a reasonable choice for single stock strategies. Once the price moves in our favor, a trailing stop can be used to protect the profit. Many traders emphasize that trailing stop is necessary to avoid turning a winning trade to a losing trade.

Let us consider an example where we set the trailing stop loss to be $2 when the stock price is $30 to protect a long position. The initial trailing stop price is $28. If the stock price rises, the stop price rises with the stock price; but if the stock price falls, the stop price stays the same. In other words, the trailing stop price is set to $2 below the highest price since the inception of the trailing stop loss. If the stock price first rises to $35, the stop price rises to $33. If the stock price then falls from $35, the trailing stop price stays at $33 and we exit the long position when the stock price falls below $33.

We note that the true loss is often higher than what the stop price indicates if a stop loss is triggered. Stock prices often have overnight gaps and news events can cause price jumps. Furthermore, market irregularity sometimes makes using stop price a risky choice. Physical stop loss orders—stop loss orders placed with brokers to trigger sells if the stock price falls below the stop price— were a likely contributing factor for the flash crash of May 6, 2010. In the 15 minutes before 2:46 PM on that day, stocks suffered heavy losses and drove the S&P index down by more than 7% only to recover most of the losses in the following minutes. As stock prices dropped, many stop sell orders were triggered, which in turn created more sell orders and further drove down prices. Consequently, many investors sold their shares at very low prices even though the stock prices soon recovered to previous close prices. For example, Procter & Gamble (PG) dropped more than 30% in a couple of minutes and then rebounded to the original level in five minutes.

When different investors place a large number of physical stop loss orders at similar stop prices, traders with access to the order book information may exploit a stop loss hunting strategy. These traders actively influence or even manipulate the stock price to trigger the stop loss orders placed by the investors. When stop loss orders are triggered, the cascade of market sell orders drive price down rapidly because of the temporary imbalance in order flows. As a result, investors sell their shares at the worst prices and the traders who buy the shares reap a profit as the imbalance dissipates and the price recovers. Stop loss hunting strategy is rare in normal market conditions, but the risk is significantly higher when market liquidity is low. Investors who invest in low-liquidity stocks or who leave stop loss orders open after market close are more vulnerable to become victims of such strategies since traders can move the market price with a small number of trades. Instead of physical stop loss orders, many investors use mental stops. They predetermine the stop loss price in their mind but do not physically place stop loss orders in a trading system. When the stock price touches the stop loss price, they respond to the loss. Mental stop, however, requires a good monitoring system to alert investors when the stop price is triggered and requires them to make timely and sound decisions under stress at a time when the trade suffers heavy losses.

Price Targets

Some investors use a price target to determine when to exit a trade. Price targets are often based on key support and resistance levels. A support level is the price level where the demand is likely to be sufficiently strong to prevent the price from falling further; a resistance level is the price level where the supply is likely to be sufficiently strong to prevent the price from rising further. For example, the past 50-day highest high (lowest low) is a potential resistance (support) level, especially if the market has tested that price several times and failed to break out. Another popular choice for support and resistance levels is 50-day or 200-day moving average. If an investor believes that the sell pressure is likely to push the stock price down once it reaches a key resistance level, he may put a limit sell order with a limit price slightly below the resistance level to exit the trade once the limit price is reached. Besides the N-day highest/lowest prices and moving averages, some more complex and controversial methods use Elliott Wave Theory and Fibonacci retracements to estimate price targets.[27]

Time Stops

Many strategies, especially mean-reversion ones, only allow a position to stay in the market for up to a predefined number of days. If the signal is not reversed and the stock price does not hit either the price target or the stop price before the time stop, the position is closed. The appropriate time stop can be estimated using a conditional probability approach from historical data: if the position had not been closed by other rules after a predefined number of days, how did it perform in the following days? For example, if historical results show that when a reversion strategy worked, there was 90% chance that it worked in less than ten days. Conditioned on that it did not work in ten days, its average return in the following ten days was negative. In this case, it is appropriate to set the time stop to be ten days to free up cash for more profitable trades.

Momentum versus Mean Reversion Strategies

Most technical strategies can be categorized as either momentum or mean reversion. The general principle of momentum strategies is to buy high and sell higher; the general principle of mean-reversion strategies is to buy low and sell high. That raises the question of why two strategies with seemingly opposite principles can both work in practice. At least two factors help explain the paradox.

Trending regime versus mean-reversion regime: One observation from historical stock price moves is that stock prices sometimes show strong trends and sometimes trade

---

[27] In our tests, we found no value in Fibonacci retracements. However, we cannot rule out the possibility other investors find ways to successfully explore Fibonacci retracement signals.

sideways with no clear uptrend or downtrend. If a trader can identify whether the market will be in a trending regime or be in a mean-reversion regime, he will successfully explore both momentum strategies and mean-reversion strategies: he will be a trend follower if the market will be trending and be a contrarian if the market will be mean reverting. In reality, a trader's forecasts are far from perfect. Successful momentum traders try to stay away from the market when the markets trade sideways and avoid taking positions opposite to the forecasted market trend. When a momentum trader enters a trade, the trader has a positive profit expectation as long as the momentum signal sufficiently increases the odds that the stock price will continue the trend after the entry. Mean reversion traders, on the other hand, try to capture the reversion when the market is likely to enter a mean-reversion regime and avoid betting against the market when the market continues the existing trend. Similarly, when a mean-reversion trader enters a trade, the trader has a positive profit expectation as long as the mean-reversion signal sufficiently increases the odds that the stock price will reverse the trend after the entry.

Long-term momentum versus Short-term mean reversion: Another observation from historical stock price moves is that prices tend to exhibit long-term momentum and short-term mean reversion patterns: if a stock went up in the past three to eighteen months, its return in the following month tends to be positive; if a stock had abnormally high positive returns in the past few days, its return in the following days tends to be negative. Technical analysts, especially the ones who focus on high probability trading strategies, have long explored dual time frame momentum strategies. The idea is to trade in the direction of long-term momentum but execute the trade in the direction of short-term reversal. Strategies that buy (sell) at short-term oversold (overbought) conditions when the longer-term trend is up (down) tend to have good return to risk ratios. For example, Kestner in his Quantitative Trading Strategies (2003) book recommended a signal called divergence index:

$$\text{Divergence index} = \frac{10\text{ - day price momentum} \times 40\text{ - day price momentum}}{\text{variance of daily price changes in the past 40 days}}$$

The strategy enters a long position when the divergence index is less than -10 and the 40-day momentum is greater than 0. In other words, it longs a stock when the longer-term 40-day trend is up, the 10-day momentum is negative and the absolute values of both momentums are large relative to daily price volatility. Kestner showed that the divergence index strategy yielded a Sharpe ratio of 0.73 on futures markets and generated profits in 11 out of the 12 years that he tested.

Dual time frame momentum strategies increase the odds of individual trades and reduce risks by requiring the confirmation of both longer-term signals and shorter-term signals. Shorter-term mean-reversion signals identify temporary overbought or oversold conditions. The risk of position entry using mean reversion signals is that the market stays at overbought or oversold conditions for an extended long period of time. An overbought condition simply means that the bullish momentum is strong and it may remain strong; an oversold condition means that the bearish momentum is strong and it may remain strong as well. By trading in the direction of the longer-term momentum, investors reduce the likelihood of catching a falling knife and increase the odds that the overbought or oversold conditions will revert soon.

Let us now consider a 3-day RSI strategy for SPY that explores the short-term overbought/oversold conditions, but only bets in the direction as indicated by the long-term 6-month moving average crossover signal:

Trade	Entry	Exit
Buy	If the close price is above the 6-month SMA, buy 1 unit if RSI(3) is below 20; buy another unit if we already long 1 unit and RSI(3) falls below 10	If the price is above 5-day SMA, sell the long position
Sell	If the close price is below the 6-month SMA, sell 1 unit if RSI(3) is above 80; sell another unit if we already short 1 unit and RSI(3) rises above 90	If the price is below 5-day SMA, buy to cover the short position

Exhibit 5-8 Positions and returns of dual time frame RSI(3) strategy

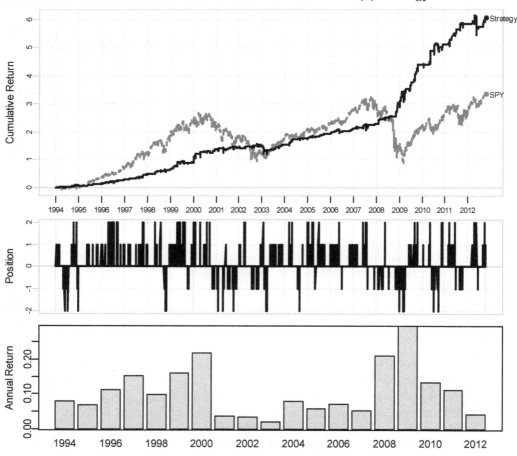

Exhibit 5-8 shows the cumulative return and position information of this dual time frame RSI(3) strategy. The strategy yielded 11% annualized geometric return from 1994 to 2012 and a cumulative return of 600% before trading costs even though the strategy was only in the market for 13.4% of the time. The annualized volatility was 9.5% and the

Sharpe ratio was 1.15. Furthermore, the maximum drawdown was only 14% and every year's return was positive.

Besides the dual time frame momentum, this strategy also implements another idea commonly used by technical analysts: scale-in. Instead of committing full position size at the beginning, we start with a smaller initial investment. If the market moves against our trade, we may get a stronger entry signal and have the capacity to commit more capital at a better price. Position sizing further lowers the risk of the trading strategy. It achieves the risk reduction with the possibility of losing some potential gains. The risk reduction allows us to use leverage (up to 200% leverage is used in this strategy) and to achieve higher risk-adjusted returns.

Technical Signals for Quantitative Portfolio Management

Technical analysts use technical signals mostly for deciding entry and exit points for individual securities. Quantitative portfolio managers, on the other hand, use technical signals mainly for cross-sectional stock selection. Momentum signals and mean reversion signals have long been explored by quantitative portfolio managers. Numerous studies document that cross-sectional stock returns tend to have long-term (3-12 months) momentum and short-term (< 1 month) reversal. Technical signals, especially short-term mean-reversion signals, have low or even negative correlations with other groups of stock selection signals, which make them excellent candidates in multi-factor stock selection models. For instance, short-term mean reversion signals are often negatively correlated with both growth factors and sentiment factors. The diversification benefit of adding negatively correlated signals to a multifactor model leads to similar returns at lower risk or higher returns at similar risk. Furthermore, when many other types of stock selection signals lost their predictive power, short-term reversion signals excelled during the financial crises. Hence, technical signals continue to attract the interest of quantitative investors.

Some technical signals are amenable to cross-sectional analysis. For example, relative strength index ranges from 0 to 100 for all stocks. Therefore, we can directly treat RSI as an input for cross-sectional stock selection. Other signals require adjustments, often by proper scaling, to make the signals of different stocks comparable. One example is building a cross-sectional signal using moving averages. Moving average crossover—buy when M-day moving average of close price crosses above N-day ($M < N$) moving average and sell when M-day moving average crosses below N-day moving average—is one of the simplest technical trading rules. But how do we convert it to a cross-sectional signal? A simple approach is to assign a value of 1 to stocks with M-day moving averages above N-day moving averages and a value of -1 to stocks with M-day moving averages below N-day moving averages. For quantitative analysis, such an approach has its limitation though. The binary value provides no differentiation for stocks within the same group and the signal is a discontinuous function of the price as a tiny price change around the moving average can trigger a signal change from -1 to 1. A bull or bear market also introduces a large imbalance between the two groups. Let us consider the basic 200-day simple moving average crossover ($M = 1$, $N = 200$). When the market bottomed on March 9, 2009, fewer than 2.5% of the Russell 1000 stocks had prices above their corresponding 200-day moving averages, which means few stocks had a signal value of 1. To address the discontinuity and the imbalance problem, we can convert the moving average to a signal called percentage price oscillator (PPO)[28]:

PPO = (M-day moving average – N-day moving average)/N-day moving average

PPO measures the difference between the shorter-term moving average and the longer-term moving average as a percentage of the longer-term moving average. PPO is positive when the M-day moving average is higher than the N-day moving average and the signal around the crossover is continuous. Since stocks have different percentage moves, the signal has a wide range of values. When we further normalize the percentage moves by removing the average percent moves of all stocks, we have a well-balanced signal with sufficient number of stocks on the positive and the negative side. Similarly, as we discussed in the section for Bollinger Bands, Bollinger Bands themselves are good for visual representation but not for quantitative analysis. Extracting the price information into the Bollinger z-score indicator or Bollinger %B makes the signals comparable across stocks.

Momentum Signals

Jegadeesh and Titman (1993) first systematically documented that strategies that bought past 3- to 12-month winners—stocks with the highest returns—and shorted past losers—stocks with the lowest returns—generated significant positive returns over the next 3 to 12 months. To eliminate the short-term mean reversion effect, the most recent month return was removed from the signal. For example, a 12M-1M momentum signal at t used the 11-month returns between $t-12$ month and $t-1$ month. Using CRSP data between 1965 and 1989, they showed that a portfolio that longed the stocks in the highest decile of 12-1M returns and shorted the stocks in the bottom decile yielded an average return of 1.31% per month in the next 3 months and yielded 1.14% per month in the next 6 months.

Multiple sources contribute to the profitability of momentum signals. The momentum of the overall market is one contributor. A bull market or a bear market usually lasts more than a year. In a bull market, stocks with higher betas[29] tend to have higher returns than stocks with lower betas. So the momentum portfolio has a positive beta bias as the market moves up. In a bear market, stocks with lower betas tend to have higher returns than stocks with higher betas as stocks with lower betas lose less. So the momentum portfolio has a negative beta bias as the market falls. Industry-level momentum also contributes to the momentum anomaly. Since stocks within the same industry tend to move together as a group and the underlying factors driving the industry move rarely change overnight, the trend for stocks within an industry lasts for months or even years. Therefore, the cross-sectional momentum signal also works for industry selection. Jegadeesh and Titman argued that the market's under-reaction to firm-specific news was a contributor to the momentum anomaly as well. Indeed, residual returns after removing beta returns and industry returns also have long-term momentum. Investors initially underreact to

---

[28] It is called an oscillator because it is often used as a short-term mean reversion signal defined as the difference between the 12-day EMA and the 26-day EMA divided by the 26-day EMA. If we make $N > 3$ months, it can be used as a momentum signal.

[29] Market beta measures the sensitivity of a stock's price volatility in relation to the market volatility. If a stock's beta is higher than 1, the stock tends to go up (down) more as the market goes up (down).

fundamental news that has long-term impact on a firm's profitability: some smart investors act on the news first and establish the initial trend; as more and more investors participate in the trend, the stock returns begin to have long-term momentum.

Since the basic versions of momentum factors only require historical returns, their simplicity makes them a popular choice for quantitative funds. As a result, their profitability has decreased over time. Besides, the returns of the momentum factors depend on the state of the market. Using 1929-1995 data, Cooper et al. (2004) showed that a six-month momentum strategy yielded a monthly return of 0.93% in up markets and -0.37% in down markets. Although they used a three-year market return to determine the market states, the results were robust when one-year or two-year market returns were used. The subsequent two bear markets again confirmed their observations. The 2009 stock market rally—often called junk stock rally—from the March 9th low made 2009 (market state was down) a horrendous year for many funds that heavily relied on momentum factors as classic momentum factors lost more than 40% that year. Stocks with the worst balance sheets (as measured by leverage ratio) suffered the heaviest losses during the financial crisis because of perceived bankruptcy risk, subsequently had the largest rebounds. In other words, loser stocks with the worst trailing returns before the market bottom had the best returns when the market direction reversed.

Despite the risk involved with cross-sectional momentum signals, they are still actively pursued by investors. Besides industry momentum and individual stock momentum, momentum signals have been shown to work in country selection, style factor selection, and asset allocation across multiple asset classes. Chen and De Bondt (2004) demonstrated that investment styles such as size, book-to-market ratio, and dividend yield all had long-term momentum. Furthermore, style momentum is distinct from price and industry momentum. Besides the momentum of total returns, we can also use alternative momentum measures that rely on residual returns (e.g., residuals returns from CAPM model) for cross-sectional stock selection. Rachev et al. (2007) found that momentum strategies based on risk-adjusted performance measures (e.g., Sharpe ratio) provided better risk-adjusted returns than momentum strategies based on total returns in most situations. We can also use the percentile of the current stock price relative to the daily stock prices of the past year as the momentum signal. These alternative signals are profitable in the long run. Some of them also generate returns that have low correlation with returns generated by total-return momentum signals, which make them good choices to form a composite momentum signal.

Many strategies, including many indices, actively or unwittingly exploit momentum signals. For example, market cap weighted indices dynamically allocate capital among different industries and increase the weights of best performing industries in the indices. In other words, market-cap weighted indices incorporate an implicit view that recent outperformers will continue to outperform.

Short-Term Mean Reversion Signals

Short-term mean reversion signals have long been used by quantitative investors as well. For example, in their study of momentum signals, Jegadeesh and Titman noticed that stock returns demonstrated short-term reversal at one month horizon and removed the last month return from the 12M-1M momentum signal. Since then, short-term reversals from one-day to one-month horizons have been confirmed by numerous studies.

One possible explanation of short-term reversals is investor overreaction. If investors overreact to news and rush to buy (sell) a stock right after news releases even though the news may not have long term impact on the stock, the stock becomes overbought (oversold) and the stock price subsequently reverts. Another possible explanation is liquidity. Institutional investors often trade large blocks of stocks over one to several days. When they rebalance their portfolios, their order flows drive the stock prices. After the order flows stop, the stock price tends to revert. By trading in the opposite direction, contrarian traders essentially provide liquidity to institutional investors and get compensated for being liquidity providers.

Since industry-level momentum contributes to the mid-term momentum anomaly, one may guess that industry-level reversal contributes to short-term reversal anomaly. In reality, industry-level returns show short-term momentum instead of short-term reversal. Similarly, many factor returns (e.g. book-to-market ratio) also demonstrate short-term momentum instead of short-term reversal. The short-term mean reversion signal is caused by individual stock return reversal within industries. As a result, a strategy that buys losers within each industry and sells winners within each industry yields better risk-adjusted returns than a strategy that buys losers across industries and sells winners across industries. We can further combine short-term industry momentum with short-term individual stock reversal: buy losers within the winning industries and sell winners within the losing industries to yield better returns.

Investors can also examine whether short-term price moves are caused by new information or driven by liquidity demand and short-term sentiment. If there is no new information that changes investors' view on future earnings in the direction of the price move, a large short-term price move is likely to revert. On the other hand, stock prices adjust to changes in a firm's fundamentals or investors' consensus view on a firm's fundamentals. Therefore, price moves caused by the release of new information are less likely to revert. For example, stock prices go up after positive earnings surprises and go down after negative earnings surprises. The post-earnings drifts are often consistent with earnings surprises: prices continue to go up (down) after the initial response to positive (negative) earnings surprises in the following weeks. If we do not have direct information about events that may trigger price moves, we can rely on trading volume as a proxy. Since news events often trigger spikes in volumes around the event dates, we can incorporate volume information to calculate volume-adjusted returns:

$$\widetilde{R}_{t,i} = (R_{t,i} \times ADV_{t,i})/V_{t,i}$$

where $R_{t,i}$ is the return of asset i on day t;

   $V_{t,i}$ is the trading volume of asset i on day t;

   $ADV_{t,i}$ is the historical average daily volume of asset i;

   $\widetilde{R}_{t,i}$ is the volume-adjusted return of asset i on day t.

Volume-adjusted returns reduce the absolute values of the returns on high volume days. Since news events such as earnings announcements usually trigger higher trading volumes, volume-adjusted returns assume that large price movements accompanied by large volumes are less likely to revert. The adjustment is also consistent with common views of technical analysts: high volume confirms breakout to the upside or the downside of price ranges and these breakouts are less likely to revert. If we have direct information about news events such as earnings announcements and analyst revisions, we can improve the performance of short-term mean reversion signals by removing stocks with large price moves that are consistent with the directions of earnings surprises or analyst revisions.

For investors to take advantage of short-term mean reversion signals, it is crucial to control trading costs as these strategies have high turnover. In fact, high turnover is a natural result of the success of such strategies: investors buy recent losers with the expectation that they will outperform—move out of the loser group—and sell recent winners with the expectation that they will underperform—move out of the winner group. If the strategies are successful, recent losers will become winners and the positions need to be reversed. Furthermore, mean-reversion signals such as RSI and Bollinger z-scores are most effective in illiquid stocks. The stocks that fall into the top and bottom deciles of RSI and Bollinger z-scores tend to be smaller and more illiquid compared to average stocks in the investment universe. These illiquid stocks have higher bid-ask spreads and higher market impact costs. Therefore, strategies that mostly rely on mean reversion signals may have limited capacity and effective trading algorithms that can reduce trading costs are often critical for their success.

Unlike long-term momentum signals, which tend to break down during a high volatility environment and market reversals, short-term reversal signals thrive during those periods. During the 2008 market crisis and subsequent recovery in 2009, most of the fundamental signals and momentum signals failed to yield positive returns; short-term mean reversion signals, on the contrary, had high returns and high information ratio during those two years.

Technical Analysis for Fundamental Portfolio Management

More and more fundamental managers are incorporating technical analysis as part of their entry/exit signals. Although in the long run, stock prices converge to their fundamental values, the convergence often takes months or years. Since the market can stay irrational for years, to bet against the market trend, even if an investor is right in the end, may be a painful process. Successful fundamental portfolio managers often try to bet on stocks with fundamental signals consistent with the current technical trend. If they decide to bet against the current trend, they wait for market catalysts (e.g., earnings releases) that trigger a reversal of the current trend. Others look for short-term or intraday overbought (oversold) opportunities to enter long (short) positions at favorable prices.

Portfolio managers who ignore technical indicators may get caught on the wrong side of the market trend. Many investors recognized the dot-com bubble in the late 1990s, but most of the brave investors who shorted technology stocks in late 1990s had to give up their short positions as the NASDAQ index went up another 150% in 1999 and early 2000 before the bubble finally burst.

Another example is value investor Whitney Tilson's bet against Netflix. In 2008, Netflix, a major player in the DVD rental business, began to offer online streaming of TV shows and movies to subscribers and gradually added more contents to its streaming as it struck deals with content providers. The new business model made Netflix a darling of Wall

Street analysts and investors. As the enthusiasm pushed the price up from $30 at the beginning of 2009 to $180 in December 2010, Whitney Tilson published an in-depth report titled "Why We're Short Netflix". In the report, he wrote,

"In short, because we think the valuation is extreme and that the rapid shift of its customers to streaming content (vs. mailing DVDs to customers) isn't the beginning of an exciting, highly-profitable new world for Netflix, but rather the beginning of the end of its incredible run. In particular, we think margins will be severely compressed and growth will slow over the next year."

Essentially, he studied Netflix's valuation and believed Netflix's price was too high even with an optimistic growth rate expectation. Besides, his own estimation of growth rate and profit margin for Netflix was much lower than the optimistic expectation. So his fund took a large short position in Netflix. The report attracted a lot of interests and triggered Netflix's founder Reed Hastings to write a response in defense of his company. Two months later, the stock price was up another 25% and Tilson had to close his short position at a loss in February 2011. The stock continued to climb up and reached its peak at above $300 by mid-July at a price-to-earnings ratio close to 80 before reality finally set in. As Netflix's subscribers expanded, the content providers naturally asked for higher content licensing fees for the rights to stream content, which severely compressed Netflix's profit margin. In hope of generating more revenue, Netflix announced an ill-fated plan to split the pricing of its standard DVD plans and video-stream plans on July 12. A combined plan that had cost $9.99 a month would change to two separate plans for $15.98 a month in total (an increase of 60%). Subscribers revolted and many cancelled their subscriptions, which forced Netflix to abandon its plan to split its services in October. But the damage was done. The stock price fell consistently and closed at $69.29 by the end of 2011. It turned out that Tilson was correct in his analysis about Netflix's profit margin and the growth rate, but the timing of his short was wrong from a technical analyst's perspective as he was betting against the market trend.

Conclusion

In this chapter, we discussed how investors can build technical trading strategies using a variety of momentum and mean reversion signals. Although no technical signal or chart pattern is infallible, some have produced positive returns in the past and are likely to have positive returns in the future. The key to identifying and exploiting such patterns is rigorous scientific research. The research typically involves testing investment strategies using historical price/volume data and analyzing performance history using statistical tools. We also demonstrated the value of some simple technical trading strategies as well as the value of technical signals to both quantitative and fundamental portfolio managers.

Chapter 6

Fundamental Signals

Numerous articles and books have been written about selecting stocks using fundamental signals ranging from simple formulas based on a single financial ratio to complex systems that have more than a dozen rules. For example, the "Dogs of the Dow" strategy is based on the premise that blue chip stocks with high dividend yield outperform the Dow-Jones index: at the end of each year, the strategy looks at dividend yields, defined as dividend divided by price, of all thirty stocks in the Dow-Jones Industrial Average, invests equal dollar values in the ten stocks with the highest dividend yields, and holds them until the end of the next year. In *The Little Book That Beats the Market*, Greenblatt (2005) recommended a "magic formula" that used the rank of return on capital plus the rank of earnings yield to select stocks. The strategy recommends that investors buy stocks with high return on capital and high earnings yield at the beginning of each year.[30] The general principle behind the formula is that companies with high return on capital are good companies and stocks with high earnings yield are good stocks.

Both the "Dogs of the Dow" and the "magic formula" are examples of value investing strategies. Other strategies bet on companies with good growth prospects. CANSLIM, a strategy developed by William O'Neil (2002), looks for several growth-related characteristics of the stock and the market when investing in a stock:

- **C = Current earnings**: the most recent quarter's earnings per share (EPS) should be at least 20% higher than the same quarter's EPS one year ago.

- **A = Annual earnings**: annual earnings should have increased over 25% in the last five years and no more than one year has had decreased earnings.

- **N = New product**, new service, new management, or new high price: there should be indications that the company is well positioned for future success.

- **S = Supply and demand**: the company should be of small to medium size for potential future growth.

- **L = Leader or laggard**: the company should be a market leader in its industry and its relative price strength rank—measured as the rank of its past year return versus other stocks—should be above the 70th percentile.

- **I = Institutional sponsorship**: the stock should have at least some institutional ownership to indicate that professional investors have an interest in holding the stock.

- **M = Market direction**: the overall market should be expected to be in an uptrend.

---

[30] Return on capital is defined as earnings before interest and taxes (EBIT) divided by the sum of net working capital and tangible assets (intangible assets such as goodwill are excluded from the capital). Earning yield is defined as EBIT divided by the enterprise value (total market value of stocks and bonds of a company).

Unlike traditional value strategies, the principle of CANSLIM is "buy high, sell higher". It invests in stocks that have had higher growth as well as higher price appreciation relative to the market in recent years and expects that these stocks to continue to outperform the market.

In this chapter, we discuss a variety of fundamental signals that investors track in making investment decisions.

Financial Statements

The majority of fundamental signals rely on information from financial statements, primarily the balance sheet, the income statement, and the statement of cash flows. Fundamental analysts also look into the details in the notes to the financial statements and management's discussion and analysis for more information. Before we discuss stock selection signals built on financial ratios, let us review the top-level summaries of the balance sheet, the income statement and the statement of cash flows.

The balance sheet is a snapshot of a company's financial condition. On the left side of the balance sheet are all the assets owned by the firm. On the right side are the firm's liabilities and shareholders' equities. The basic equation for the balance sheet is that assets equal liabilities plus shareholders' equities. Exhibit 6-1 shows a simplified version of the balance sheet.

Exhibit 6-1 Simplified version of the Balance Sheet[31]

Assets	Liabilities + shareholders' equities
Current assets = Cash & cash equivalent	Current liabilities = Accounts payable
+ Inventories	+ Short-term debt
+ Accounts receivables	+ Long-term debt due in a year
+ Prepaid expenses	+ Other current liabilities
Fixed assets = Property, plant & equipment	Long term liabilities = Long-term debt
+ Investments	+ Other long-term liabilities
+ Intangible assets	
	Shareholders' equities = Preferred stock
	+ Common stock

A number of financial measures and financial ratios rely only on information available in the balance sheet:

Book value = Total assets – Total liabilities

Capital employed = Total assets – Current liabilities

---

[31] Investments are a company's investments in the assets or securities of other firms; intangible assets include goodwill, patents, and trademarks. Other current liabilities include accrued taxes, wages payable, etc. Other long-term liabilities include long-term lease obligations, pension and employee benefits, and deferred taxes, etc.

Operating asset = Total assets – Cash and cash equivalent

Working capital = (Current assets – Cash and cash equivalent) –

(Current liabilities – Short-term debt)

≈ Inventory + Accounts receivable – Accounts payable

Debt to equity ratio = (Long-term debt + Short-term debt) / Shareholders' equities

Debt to asset ratio = (Long-term debt + Short-term debt) / Total assets

Current ratio = Current assets / Current liabilities

Quick ratio = (Cash and cash equivalent + Accounts receivables) / Current liabilities

Cash ratio = Cash and cash equivalent / Current liabilities

Operating liabilities = Total liabilities – Short-term debt – Long-term debt

Book value is the value of all assets booked on the balance sheet minus the liabilities. It is equivalent to **shareholders' equities**. In practice, some investors exclude intangible assets such as goodwill to yield tangible book value and use tangible book value in financial ratios. For companies with preferred stocks, the book value of the preferred stocks is often removed to yield book value of the common stocks. In the **book to market ratio (B/P ratio)**, common stock book value is used since the market value does not include preferred stocks.

Capital employed refers to the investment required for a business to function. It is defined as long-term funds used by the company. Since current liabilities are obligations that are due within a year, they do not contribute to a company's future revenue and profit. Therefore, they are removed from the calculation of the capital employed.

Operating assets are defined as total assets minus cash and cash equivalent. Essentially these are the non-cash assets that are needed to maintain the firm's operating activities.

While accounts payable reduces a company's cash needs, inventory and accounts receivable tie up a company's cash. Hence, working capital[32], calculated as the difference between inventory plus accounts receivable and accounts payable, reflects the cash that needs to be set aside for daily operations and is often used as a measure of a company's operational efficiency.

Debt to equity ratio and debt to asset ratio are two measures of a firm's financial leverage and financial risk. Current ratio, quick ratio, and cash ratio are liquidity ratios that measure a company's ability to cover its current liabilities.

A company's liabilities can be classified as either financial liabilities or operating liabilities. Financial liabilities are short-term debt or long-term debt borrowed from the lenders. Operating liabilities are the consequence of operating activities. For example, accounts payable represent liabilities to the suppliers; wages payable represent liabilities to the employees; deferred taxes represent liabilities to the government.

---

[32] Working capital is usually defined as the difference between current assets and current liabilities. We remove cash and cash equivalent from the current assets as they generate risk-free returns; we also remove short-term debt and long-term debt due in a year as they require interest payments. Such a definition is also called non-cash working capital.

The income statement summarizes a firm's revenues for an accounting period, the associated expenses and the resulting income. Exhibit 6-2 shows a simplified version of the income statement.

Exhibit 6-2 Simplified version of the Income Statement

	Gross sales
−	Returns, allowances & discounts
=	Net sales
−	Cost of goods sold (COGS)
=	Gross profit
−	Operating expenses (selling, general and administrative expenses)
=	Earnings before interest, taxes, depreciation and amortization (EBITDA)
−	Depreciation and amortization
=	Operating income
+	Non-operating income (FX adjustment, sale of securities, royalties, etc.)
=	Earnings before interest and taxes (EBIT)
−	Interest expenses
=	Income before income taxes
−	Income taxes
−	Minority interest
=	Income from continuing operations
+	Extraordinary items and discontinued operations
=	Net income

Gross sales are often also called the top line since it is the first line in the income statement; net income is often called the bottom line since it is the last line in the income statement. The difference between gross sales and net income is broken down to into different components of expenses associated with the firm's current or future revenue generation.

When we combine the information from the income statement and the balance sheet, we get a variety of financial ratios:

Gross profit margin = Gross profit / Net sales

Operating profit margin = EBIT / Net sales

Basic earning power = EBIT / Average total assets[33]

Return on assets (ROA) = (Net income + Interest expense) / Average total assets

Return on equity (ROE) = Net income / Shareholders' equities

Payout ratio = Dividend / Net income

Receivables turnover = Net annual sales / Average receivables

Inventory turnover = COGS / Inventory

Payables turnover ratio = COGS / Average account payables

Asset turnover = Net sales / Average total assets

Fixed asset turnover = Net sales / Average net fixed assets

Business risk = Standard deviation of operating income / Mean operating income

Cash flow statement shows how balance sheet changes and income affect cash and cash equivalents. It breaks down the cash and cash equivalent changes into cash flow from operations, cash flows from investing activities, and cash flow from financing activities. Exhibit 6-3 shows a simplified version of the cash flow statement.

Exhibit 6-3 Simplified version of the Cash Flow statement

	Cash flow from operations
+	Cash flow from investing
+	Cash flow from financing
=	Change in cash and cash equivalent

Cash flow from operations (CFO) includes cash inflow and outflow for all operating activities such as payments to suppliers for goods, payments to employees, interest expenses,[34] and receipts from sales of goods. Cash flow from operations can be directly calculated from detailed cash payments and receipts of different operating activities. Alternatively, we can start with net income and add back the non-cash charges:

CFO ≈ Net income + Noncash charges

where noncash charges ≈ depreciation and amortization – change in working capital

Depreciation and amortization are non-cash charges since there is no cash inflow or outflow involved in depreciation and amortization. Increases in inventory increase cash outflow: raw materials need to be purchased and workers need to be paid to make the final goods. Increases in accounts receivable reduce cash inflow: earnings are booked when goods are sold but cash flow does not increase until the customers pay for the goods

---

[33] Average total assets (and other averages) are calculated as the mean of the total assets at the beginning of the fiscal period and total assets at the end of the period.

[34] Financial Accounting Standard Board (FASB) decided to include interest expenses in cash flow from operations instead of cash flow from financing even though many believe it is more logical to include interest expenses as part of cash flow from financing.

in cash. Increases in accounts payable reduce cash outflow: as the company buys raw materials on credit, the company pays less cash to suppliers. Since working capital is defined as the sum of inventory and accounts receivable minus accounts payable, the increase in working capital decreases cash flow from operations.

Cash flow from investing includes cash inflow and outflow for all investing activities such as purchases or sales of property, plant and equipment, loans to customers, and payments related to mergers and acquisitions. Cash flow from financing includes cash inflow and outflow for all financing activities such as payment of dividends, repurchase of stocks, payments or new issues of debt.

A popular cash flow measure derived from the cash flow statement and the income statement is free cash flow. Free cash flow is calculated as operating cash flow minus capital expenditures:

Free cash flow (FCF) = Cash flow from operations – Capital expenditure

= CFO – (Fixed capital investment + Working capital investment)

It measures the cash flow that a company generates after investment in maintaining its asset base and reflects the company's ability to pay dividend or to finance future growth.

Although the inputs used in these formulas look straightforward and most financial reports follow Generally Accepted Accounting Principles (GAAP), to compare different companies' accounting data is a difficult task in practice. The reason is that GAAP gives companies some discretion in accounting decisions such as when costs and revenues are booked and how assets are valued. Moreover, companies have greater freedom in determining the impact of uncertain events such as litigations. In order to make a financial ratio comparable between companies, numerous financial adjustments are often needed. For example, some research expenses can either be treated as costs in the year that the expenses occur or be amortized over a number of years. Immediate expensing, a conservative accounting choice, reduces net income in the year in which expenses occur, but leads to higher net income in the future. If one company chooses immediate expensing and another chooses amortization, their net incomes are not directly comparable without adjusting for the accounting difference. To address the problem, financial analysts dig into the details in the financial statements and make adjustments in order to make the numbers comparable for different companies.

Factor Models and Residual Returns

Since Harry Markowitz (1952) introduced Modern Portfolio Theory (MPT) in his paper *Portfolio Selection*, portfolio diversification has been widely accepted by investors. MPT separates an asset's risk to two components: systematic risk and specific risk. Systematic risk is the risk common to all securities that cannot be diversified away. Specific risk, also called idiosyncratic risk, is the risk associated with the individual asset that can be diversified away. Building upon MPT, William Sharpe (1964) developed the Capital Asset Pricing Model (CAPM). The key concept of the CAPM is that since specific risk can be diversified away, investors should not get compensated for taking specific risk. Rather, they should only be compensated for taking systematic risk. The expected excess return of a stock is proportional to the expected market excess return and the stock's beta:

$$r_{pt} - r_{ft} = \alpha + \beta_m(r_{mt} - r_{ft}) + \varepsilon_{pt} = \alpha + \beta_m MKT_t + \varepsilon_{pt}$$

where r_{ft} is the risk-free rate[35] in period t;

$r_{pt} - r_{ft}$ is the stock return premium;

$MKT_t = r_{mt} - r_{ft}$ is the market return premium;

$\beta_m = \dfrac{\text{cov}(r_{pt} - r_{ft}, MKT_t)}{\text{var}(MKT_t)}$ is the sensitivity of $r_{pt} - r_{ft}$ to MKT_t;

α is the intercept;

ε_{pt} is the estimation error.

If the CAPM holds, the expected value of α for all assets is 0 and we have

$$E[r_{pt} - r_{ft}] = \beta_m E[r_{mt} - r_{ft}]$$

The derivation of the CAPM depends on a number of simplifying assumptions:

- All investors are rational and are risk averse;
- All investors have access to all information at the same time;
- All investors can borrow and lend money at the same risk-free rate;
- All investors can invest in all available assets;
- All assets are infinitely divisible;
- All transactions have no transaction costs or taxes.

Most of these assumptions clearly do not hold in the real world. Therefore, the CAPM does not fully explain the expected return premium of individual stocks but that in itself does not diminish the value of the CAPM. For passive investors, the CAPM enforces the idea of diversification and the value of the market portfolio. For active investors, it provides a benchmark to evaluate the value added by a strategy or a portfolio manager. For active management, the CAPM distinguishes between return premium from market exposures and the residual return premium. The former is beta, which can be easily achieved at little cost; the latter is alpha, which reflects managers' skills and is difficult to achieve.

Arbitrage pricing theory (APT) expands the systematic risk beyond the market risk. It states that the expected return of an asset can be modeled as a linear function of various systematic factors, which lays the foundation of quantitative investment management. In two of their papers *The Cross-Section of Expected Stock Returns* and *Common Risk Factors in the Returns on Stocks and Bonds*, Eugene Fama and Kenneth French (1992, 1993) proposed a three-factor regression model to explain the stock return premium:

---

[35] For US market, 1-month T-bill rate is often used as the risk-free rate.

$$r_{pt} - r_{ft} = \alpha + \beta_m MKT_t + \beta_s SMB_t + \beta_h HML_t + \varepsilon_{pt}$$

where $r_{pt} - r_{ft}$ and MKT_t have the same definition as in the CAPM model;

> SMB_t (small minus big) is the return on a portfolio of small-cap stocks minus the return on a portfolio of large-cap stocks;
>
> HML_t (high minus low) is the return on a portfolio of high book-to-market stocks minus the return on a portfolio of low book-to-market stocks;
>
> β_m, β_s, and β_h are the estimated slopes on MKT_t, SMB_t, and HMT_t, respectively.

Fama-French three-factor model expands the CAPM with two extra systematic risk factors: small minus big and high minus low.

Carhart (1997) further extended the Fama-French three-factor model to a four-factor model by adding price momentum as an extra factor:

$$r_{pt} - r_{ft} = \alpha + \beta_m MKT_t + \beta_s SMB_t + \beta_h HML_t + \beta_o MOM_t + \varepsilon_{pt}$$

where MOM_t is the return on a portfolio of past winners minus the return on a portfolio of past losers and β_o is estimated slope on MOM_t. The time interval to determine past winners and losers is often month $t-12$ to month $t-1$. For example, at the end of August 2012, returns between the end of August 2011 and the end of July 2012 are used to determine winners and losers.

Small minus big, high minus low, and momentum factors continued to explain stock return differences after the wide publication of these factors. For example, in the twenty years between 1991 and 2010, S&P 500 index (SPX) had an annualized geometric return of 6.9% and the small-cap Russell 2000 index (RUT) had a return of 9.3%. Small-cap stocks do have higher systematic risk. In the same twenty years, the annualized volatility of RUT was 21.5%, which was higher than the volatility of SPX, 18.7%. Hence, the market cap (size) is usually considered to be a risk factor instead of an alpha factor. The residual returns that are not explained by systematic risk factors are also called abnormal returns. Besides total returns, abnormal returns from the CAPM, the Fama-French factor models, and other risk models are often used as the returns to investigate the forecasting power of stock selection factors.

Value Factors

Value factors compare the value of an asset with that of another. The general idea is that assets with similar earnings, sales, cash flows, or book values should have similar prices. In other words, firms with similar characteristics should have similar price to earnings, price to sales, price to cash flow, and price to book ratios. In the stock market, temporary dislocations between the intrinsic value and the price can happen for a number of reasons:

- Investors incorrectly equate a good company with a good stock without sufficiently taking the price into consideration.

- Investors have the tendency to extrapolate recent over-optimistic or over-pessimistic growth rate far into the future.

- Investors may overreact or underreact to news or fundamental changes in a company.

But in the long run, the price will converge to the intrinsic value. Investors looking for bargains will invest in undervalued stocks; corporations will take over cheaply priced targets; companies with cash will buy back their own shares. Such market actions drive convergence. As convergence happens, stocks with higher relative values outperform stocks with lower relative values. Since Graham and Dodd laid the foundation for value investing in their book *Security Analysis* in 1934, value strategies have been at the core of many actively managed portfolios. Exhibit 6-4 shows some value factors used for stock selection.

Exhibit 6-4 Relative value factors

Factor	Description
E_0/P (earnings yield)	Past 12 months' earnings / Market cap
FY 1/2 earnings yield	Forecasted next 12 months' earnings / Market cap
EBIT/EV	EBIT / Enterprise value
EBITDA/EV	EBITDA / Enterprise value
Gross profit/EV	Gross profit / Enterprise value
Cash flow yield	Operating cash flow / Market cap
FCF/EV	Free cash flow / Enterprise value
S/P	Sales / Market cap
Dividend yield	Dividend per share / Price
B/P	Book value of common equities / Market cap
Capital employed/EV	Capital employed / Enterprise value
S/EV	Sales / Enterprise value

In many value measures, the denominator is either the market cap or the enterprise value. Enterprise value is the sum of the market values of common stock, preferred stock and debt minus cash and cash equivalents. It is the theoretical value that an acquirer pays when taking over the target company. Although the official definition for EV uses market value of debt, the book value of debt is often used in practice because it is difficult to obtain the current market value of debt.[36] The rationale for subtracting cash and marketable securities is that cash and cash equivalents directly reduce the costs to a potential acquirer. Some investors use excess cash (for example, cash in excess of 5% of sales) instead, since they believe that certain amount of cash is required as working capital to maintain day-to-day business operations.

---

[36] Companies often have multiple issues of corporate debt, most of which are thinly traded.

Earnings/sales based measures

Equity value-based measures directly compare returns to shareholders. Enterprise value-based measures give the deleveraged perspective on sales and earnings, which are valuable when we compare companies with significant differences in their debt levels. For enterprise value-based measures, both the numerator and the denominator are firm level aggregated values. For equity value-based measures, the denominator can be either share price or market cap. If the denominator is share price, the numerator needs to be expressed as per share value (e.g., earnings per share); if the denominator is market cap, the numerator needs to be firm level aggregated value (e.g., net income).

The numerator measures a company's intrinsic value such as earnings and cash flows. Earnings measures include net income (E), earnings before interest and taxes (EBIT), earnings before interest, taxes, depreciation and amortization (EBITDA), and gross profit. Net income is used as the earnings measure in the most important value signal—earnings yield. The pre-interest expenses and pre-tax measure EBIT removes the impact of different tax rates and financial leverage. EBITDA further removes the impact of choices regarding depreciation & amortization. Some investors find EBITDA/EV to be a valuable factor in evaluating stocks across industries with significantly different capital expenditure. For example, telecommunication companies often rely on heavy capital expenditure and have higher Depreciation & Amortization costs than financial companies. Therefore, EBITDA/EV may be a better choice to compare companies in these two industries than EBIT/EV. Some analysts also use EBITDA/EV and EBIT/EV as a measure of relative takeover attractiveness of a company within an industry. The gross profit to enterprise value ratio is a less commonly used factor. Compared with EBITDA, gross profit adds back selling, general and administrative expenses (SG&A), which includes research and development, advertisement, and marketing expenses. Research and development expenses are often considered to be investments instead of current period expenses. For many companies, advertisement and marketing are crucial expenses to attract new customers and grow future sales. Therefore, advertisement impacts earnings beyond the current period as well. Higher gross profit may indicate that a company has lower cost of goods sold than its peers. Companies with a lower cost structure tend to maintain that advantage over several years as the cost structure changes slowly. Higher gross profit may also indicate a company's pricing power compared to its competitors. The price premium of a company's products indicates that consumers consider its products to be more desirable. As a result, the company's products have better growth potential. As we gradually move up the income statement from net income to gross profit, we also reduce the impact of management discretion since there are fewer accounting choices included in the reported numbers.

Compared with earnings, sales measure removes costs and may be a better proxy for a longer term view since the management team has more control in reducing long-term costs. For example, in 2009 and 2010, many companies were able to implement significant cost cutting measures to restore profits back to pre-recession level. Sales also help identify potential acquisition targets as the acquirer has more flexibility to cut costs. During periods of recession and subsequent recovery, earnings often change rapidly and earnings yield becomes a less reliable measure. In such periods, the sales to price ratio often outperforms the earnings yield signal. Sales are also more relevant for companies with negative net incomes, especially for new companies with higher expenses. Hence, sales to price ratio is one of the most consistent value signals in selecting stocks that outperform the market.

It is worth noting that earnings yield (E/P) instead of the popularly quoted P/E ratio is used as a stock selection factor. The reason is that the P/E ratio is undefined for assets with negative earnings. Let us consider three stocks traded at $100 and with earnings $10, $5, and -$5. If we use the P/E ratio, the order becomes undefined as their P/E ratios are 10, 20, and -20. We would naturally prefer to buy the stock with a P/E ratio of 10 to the stock with the more expensive P/E ratio of 20. But we would prefer the stock with P/E ratio of 20 ($5 earnings) to the stock with P/E ratio -20 (-$5 earnings) even though the former has higher P/E ratio. If we use earnings yield, the order is consistent: Their earnings yields are 0.1, 0.05, and -0.05; a stock with higher earnings yield is preferred to a stock with lower earnings yield. Similarly, most relative value measures have prices and enterprise values as the denominator and performance measures such as gross profit as the numerator.

For earnings, we may either use historical earnings or forecasted earnings. Since annual reports have a significant time lag, historical earnings (E_0) are calculated as aggregated earnings of the trailing four quarters in the 10-Q reports. To incorporate information that impacts future earnings, investors also use analyst estimates of future earnings. Analysts may have earnings forecast for up to five fiscal years. FY1 (fiscal year 1) earnings E_1 is the forecasted earnings for the following fiscal year: If t is the fraction of the year that has passed since the last annual reporting date, E_1 is the forecasted earnings for the past t year and the following $(1-t)$ year. The Forecasted next 12 months' earnings are $E_{1/2} = (1-t) \times E_1 + t \times E_2$ and the FY 1/2 earnings yield is $E_{1/2} / \text{Market Cap}$.

Essentially, the forecasted next 12 months' earnings are dominated by E_1 (forecast for the current fiscal year) at the beginning of the fiscal year and are dominated by E_2 (forecast for the next year) by the end of the year. For some assets, earnings forecasts beyond FY1 are not available. In which case, E_1 is used as $E_{1/2}$. Although FY 1/2 earnings yield is forward-looking compared with historical earnings yield, empirical evidence indicates both have similar predictive power for future stock returns. One reason is that FY 1/2 earnings yield relies on analysts' forecasts, which contains uncertainty as the realized future earnings can be different from forecasts. We do, however, find that FY 1/2 earnings yield adds value in helping investors avoid investing in companies with significant earnings deterioration.

Cash flow based measures

Besides earnings, cash flows are common choices as numerators in the value signals. The adage "cash is king" is often used to describe the importance of cash flow in evaluating the value of a company. A firm's value depends on its ability to generate cash flows in the future. Compared with earnings, cash flows are less susceptible to management manipulation. A company that generates positive earnings without positive cash flows usually warrants further investigation. Cash flow yield, the ratio of operating cash flow to price can be used as the cash flow counterpart of the earnings yield.

Let us consider the case of two companies that have just invested in a new building. One chooses to depreciate the cost over 17 years and the other chooses to depreciate the costs over 25 years. The company that chooses a longer depreciation period has lower depreciation and amortization costs, which increases the current net income. Nevertheless, the accounting choices have no impact on operating cash flows. So the operating cash flows for both companies are the same despite different choices in depreciation years. Besides operating cash flow, free cash flow is another common choice for calculating cash flow yield. Free cash flow is the cash available to a company after it invests in capital expenditure to maintain the ongoing business. A company's enterprise value should equal the sum of the present values of all future free cash flows discounted at the weighted average cost of capital (WACC, the average rate the company is expected to pay to debt holders and equity holders). In recent years, cash flow based factors such as free cash flow to enterprise value ratios have been valuable additions to stock return forecast beyond traditional earnings or book value based factors.

Dividend based measures

Dividend yield (D/P) is another value measure. Dividends represent all future cash flows available to shareholders. The Dividend Discount Model values the stock price as the sum of the present value of all expected future dividends. Cash dividend indicates a company's ability to generate cash instead of just paper earnings. Many investors also believe that high dividend payout indicates that the management is more shareholder oriented: instead of blindly growing the business, they actively distribute excess cash to shareholders. Similar to earnings, the dividend yield can be calculated using either dividends in the past 12 months (D_0) or the forward looking analyst estimates for the next 12 months ($D_{1/2}$). Some investors also prefer dividend payments for income streams because dividends have lower tax rates. Hartzmark and Solomon (2011) hypothesized that dividend clienteles are more likely to buy dividend stocks before the ex-dividend day and are more likely to sell after the ex-dividend day. They found that dividend-paying stocks had 53 bps per month abnormal returns in the months that those stocks are expected to pay dividends than non-dividend-paying stocks—with the majority of the abnormal returns on actual declaration day and ex-dividend day. They also found negative returns after the ex-dividend day. Both results are consistent with their hypothesis.

Stocks with highest dividend yields do not have the highest expected returns. Some stocks with the highest dividend yields have unsustainable dividends as the payout ratio is higher than 100%. When the net income is less than the dividend, the dividend payment is return *of* capital instead of return *on* capital. Some companies even use cash proceeds from secondary offering of stocks to pay dividend, which raises the question whether the business is a "Ponzi scheme". Some stocks have high dividend yields because of large price depreciations in the past year instead of dividend appreciations. The price depreciation is often caused by rapid deterioration of revenues and profits. In response, these companies are likely to cut future dividends to preserve cash. Some stocks do not pay dividends. These are often companies with high earnings growth rate, in which case it is sensible to plow the profits back rather than return the capital back to investors in the form of dividends. When we include the payout ratio as part of the input, the dividend yield signal has better predictable power: stocks with high dividend yields and low payout ratios tend to have higher expected returns. So we can use payout adjusted dividend yield estimated from a linear regression as a value factor:

$$D/P = \beta \times \text{payout ratio} + \beta_i \times I_{industry,\,i} + \varepsilon$$

where $I_{industry,i}$ is an indicator function that equals 1 if the asset belongs to industry group (sector) i and 0 otherwise;

Coefficients β and β_i are estimated using linear regression on all stocks.

The residual ε indicates whether a stock is overvalued or undervalued relative to other stocks in the same industry[37]: positive ε indicates that the stock is undervalued and negative ε indicates that the stock is overvalued.

Book value based measures

The book to price ratio (B/P) and capital employed to enterprise value ratio are often used to examine the liquidation/restructuring value of a company. These factors are especially useful when current earnings are misleading. A company can temporarily have depressed earnings for a variety of reasons. A cyclical company may have negative earnings during a recession but will become profitable as the economy recovers. A company may be going through restructuring with significant immediate costs but will be able to restore profitability once the restructuring is complete. Even an ill-managed company with a high cost structure may have valuable assets, distribution channels, or patents that make them an attractive acquisition target.

B/P is a traditional value measure and a factor in the Fama-French factor model. Book value is a proxy of liquidation value for shareholders. If all of the firm's assets are liquidated at values listed on the balance sheet and all the liabilities are paid off, shareholders will receive the book value. B/P measures the liquidation value for the shareholders to the market value. So assets with higher B/P are expected to be relatively undervalued and appreciate more in the future. Fama and French (1992) observed that book to price ratios were positively correlated with future stock returns. Since then, the B/P ratio has been a key ingredient in many value strategies.

Capital employed, is the capital investment that the company currently has, and is often calculated as total assets minus current liabilities. Compared with B/P ratio, capital employed to enterprise value ratio adds the long-term debt to both the numerator and the denominator. Hence, we can consider it a unleveraged version of B/P.

Avoiding the value trap

Although it is well established that many value signals yield positive long-term returns, not all investors believe that a value premium reflects market inefficiency. Some argue that the value premium is really a compensation for bearing systematic risk instead of mispricing on account of investor bias. For example, stocks with high book-to-price ratios have higher distress risk. Furthermore, value stocks on average have a smaller market cap, lower analyst coverage, and higher price volatility. These exposures indicate that the value premium may be a compensation for taking on systematic risk.

The returns of value signals are also volatile over time. Gray and Vogel (2011) analyzed EBITA/EV, E/P, FCF/EV, and B/P from 1971 to 2010. They not only confirmed that these value signals did have long-term positive returns with EBITA/EV offering the best

---

[37] We can also include other risk factors such as size in the regression to better identify the peers of a stock.

risk-adjusted return, but also discovered that all signals suffered maximum drawdowns of more than 50% and the worst one-year loss of more than 40%.

Although value models are at the core of many actively managed portfolios, we suggest that value signals alone are not sufficient to generate high risk-adjusted returns. A number of reasons contribute to the limitation of value signals. Many stocks appear undervalued relative to other stocks or their own historical earnings yields, but they continue to have lower returns. Stocks with above average value measures but negative earnings momentum often see further price deterioration instead of price appreciation. This phenomenon is often referred to as the value trap. Essentially, in these cases high value measures are caused by deteriorating fundamentals and falling prices instead of increasing sales and profits. Unless there are catalysts to reverse the trend, future value measures revert to the mean not by an increase in the denominator—i.e., prices—but unfortunately by a decrease of the numerator— i.e., earnings, book values and sales.

To avoid value trap stocks that are unlikely to recover, Joseph Piotroski (2000) proposed nine criteria to score "true" value stocks—stocks in the highest book-to-price quintile. A stock gets a score of 1 if it passes a criterion and 0 otherwise. The following are the criteria.

1. **Net income**: net income (or return on asset) is positive.

2. **Operating cash flow**: operating cash flow is positive.

3. **Return on asset**: return on asset is higher than prior year.

4. **Earnings quality**: operating cash flow is higher than net income.

5. **Gross margin**: gross margin is higher than prior year.

6. **Asset turnover**: asset turnover is higher than prior year.

7. **Leverage**: debt to asset ratio is lower than prior year.

8. **Current ratio**: current ratio is higher than prior year.

9. **Shares outstanding**: split-adjusted shares outstanding are no higher than prior year.

These criteria incorporate profitability, operating efficiency, earnings quality, risk, and sentiment factors. FSCORE, the sum of the individual scores, can help identify good value stocks. Piotroski classified any value stocks with FSCORE between 8 and 9 as good and stocks with FSCORE between 0 and 1 as bad. Good value stocks outperformed average value stocks by 7.5% a year and outperformed bad value stocks by 23% a year between 1976 and 1996. Since the publication of the paper in 2000, values stocks with high FSCORE have continued to outperform unfiltered value stocks (the volatility of the return difference has been high though). As a result, Piotroski scores have a large investor following.

Investors also examine the details of earnings numbers and book values to determine whether earnings represent the true earning power of a company as well as whether the book value represents the liquidation value to shareholders. If earnings are the results of accounting adjustments and the book is filled with impaired assets that cannot be recovered, the earnings yield and B/P ratio have no power in predicting future returns.

Many of the earlier described value factors do not apply to financial firms since the book values of the financial assets that a firm holds are often different from their market values and earnings are often distorted by accounting adjustments. The accounting standard allows companies to account for their own financial liabilities at fair value (also known as mark-to-market accounting) and reports the gains/losses as part of the income if the fair values of liabilities change.

Let us consider a company with $5 billion long-term liability. In the past quarter, the company suffered a string of losses and its financial future became gloomy, its credit rating deteriorated and the credit spread increased. As a result, its liability is now worth $4 billion in the market. If the company chooses fair value option, it books $1 billion "profit"! Fair value accounting has large impact on banks because they carry significant liabilities. For instance, in 2008, HSBC reported $6.6 billion "profit" on its own debt as its credit spread jumped up. Most of those gains were reversed in 2009 as HSBC's credit spread decreased. Overall, the fair value option helps smooth earnings: it increases reported earnings as a company's fiscal situation deteriorates and decreases reported earnings as the fiscal situation improves.

Besides liabilities, banks often report their assets at mark-to-market value. Nevertheless, many illiquid assets or derivatives in a bank's books have no objective market value as these financial instruments have little or no trading activity. Therefore, model prices are often used as market prices. In 2005-2007, the mark-to-market rule allowed banks to book huge, sometimes fictitious, profits. As the market value of many assets fell in 2008, the mark-to-market rule forced many banks into bankruptcy as they wrote down their assets. In the Emergency Economic Stabilization Act of 2008—better known as the bank bailout— Congress required a review of mark-to-market accounting. Soon, the Financial Accounting Standards Board updated accounting rules to allow companies to use significant leeway in valuing assets when the market is unsteady or inactive. The changes allowed many banks to reduce the write-down on mortgage-backed securities and derivatives. Consequently, the book values of assets were often significantly different from their market values or liquidation values. To cope with the failure of standard value signals for financial firms, investors developed industry-specific factors to examine earnings and the book values of financial firms. For example, nonperforming asset ratio, business mix, and capital strength all provide valuable information to evaluate financial firms.

Profitability and Efficiency Factors

Profitability ratios measure a company's ability to generate earnings and cash flows on its revenues, assets, and (book value of) equities. Efficiency ratios measure how effectively a firm uses its assets to generate revenues and how well it manages its liabilities. A company with higher profitability and higher efficiency relative to its peers is more attractive to investors. Similar to value signals, the numerators for profitability ratios are earning measures ranging from net income to gross profit. The denominators, however, are sales, total assets, and book value of shareholders' equity instead of market value of shareholders' equity or enterprise value. Gross margin, operating margin, net margin, cash flow margin, and free cash flow margin are different ways to measure how much profit a company generates on each dollar of sales.

Exhibit 6-5 shows some profitability and efficiency factors that investors follow for stock selection:

Exhibit 6-5 Profitability and Efficiency Factors

Factor	Description
Gross margin	Gross profit / Sales
Operating margin	Operating income / Sales
Net margin	Net income / Sales
Cash flow margin	Operating cash flow / Sales
Free cash flow margin	Free cash flow / Sales
Return on equity (ROE)	Net income / Average shareholders' equity
Return on asset (ROA)	Net income / Average total assets
Return on operating assets	(Net income + Interest Expense × (1 − tax rate)) / Operating assets
Gross profit to assets	Gross profit / Average total assets
Asset turnover	Net sales / Average total assets
Inventory turnover	Costs of goods sold / Average inventory

Return on equity (ROE), net income/average shareholders' equity, measures the profitability of the money that shareholders have invested in the company. Net income can be either earnings of the past four quarters or consensus earnings of the next fiscal year. The average shareholders' equity is the average of shareholder's equity at the beginning and at the end of the period. For companies with preferred stocks, the preferred dividend is often removed from the net income and preferred equity is excluded from the shareholders' equity to yield return on common equity. A company that has a consistent high ROE indicates its ability to generate profits by effectively managing its resources. It is a high-level number that combines profitability, operating efficiency and leverage as shown in the DuPont analysis:

$$\text{ROE} = \frac{\text{net income}}{\text{equity}} = \text{profit margin} \times \text{asset turnover} \times \text{financial leverage}$$

$$= \frac{\text{net income}}{\text{sales}} \times \frac{\text{sales}}{\text{total assets}} \times \frac{\text{total assets}}{\text{equity}}$$

Chen *et al.* (2011) showed that for stocks with similar market cap and investments-to-asset ratios, high ROE stocks outperformed low ROE stocks by 71 bps a month between 1972 and 2010.

Return on assets provides a deleveraged view of how profitable a company is relative to its total assets. Companies with high financial leverage often yield high ROE in the years when earnings are good; they also have low ROE during the years when earnings become negative. Therefore, ROA is valuable when we compare companies with significant differences in their debt levels.

Another unleveraged profitability measure is return on operating assets:

$$\text{Return on operating assets} = \frac{\text{net income} + \text{interest expenses} \times (1 - \text{tax rate})}{\text{total assets} - \text{cash and cash equivalent}}$$

If a firm had financed all its operating activities using equities, it would not have paid interest expenses; but those saved interest expenses would have been subjected to corporate tax. Thus, the numerator adds after tax interest expenses to net income as unleveraged profits. If we replace net income with operating cash flow, we have cash flow return on operating assets:

$$\text{Cash flow return on operating assets} = \frac{\text{operating cash flow} + \text{interest expenses} \times (1 - \text{tax rate})}{\text{total assets} - \text{cash and cash equivalent}}$$

Besides earnings, investors also use other profit measures to estimate a company's profitability. For example, Robert Novy-Marx (2010) found that stocks with higher gross profit to asset ratios had higher future growth in earnings and free cash flow. He also showed that the gross profit to asset ratio had similar power as book to market ratio (B/P) in predicting cross-sectional stock returns. Furthermore, the gross profit to asset signal generally has positive returns when B/P signal suffered large drawdowns, which makes it a complementary signal to the B/P signal.

When we combine value factors and profitability factors, we get better information on possible mispricing. Value factors tend to select stocks that have low profitability and the stock prices of these companies often stay low instead of recovering. The difference between market value and book value often reflects the difference between ROE and the required cost of capital:

$$P = B \times \exp^{T \times (ROE - K_e)} \Rightarrow \ln(P / B) = T \times (ROE - K_e)$$

where K_e is the required cost of capital;

   T is the number of periods that ROE exceeds the firm's cost of capital.

If a firm's ROE is higher than the firm's required cost of capital, the firm generates value-added to its shareholders beyond the book value. On the other hand, if the ROE is lower than the firm's required cost of capital, the value-added is negative and the market value can be lower than the book value. Longer term, a firm will lose its competitive advantage and the ROE will converge to the cost of capital. Hence, the value-added is limited to a certain number of periods. Since T is unknown, we use a regression to estimate T and calculate residuals:

$$\ln(P / B) = T \times ROE + \beta_i \times I_{industry,i} + \varepsilon$$

where $I_{industry,i}$ is an indicator that equals 1 if the asset belongs to industry group (sector) i and 0 otherwise. T and β_i are estimated using linear regression on all stocks. The residual ε indicates whether the stock is overvalued or undervalued relative to other stocks in the same industry: positive ε indicates that the stock is overvalued and negative ε indicates that the stock is undervalued.

Companies with better operating efficiency and productivity levels often have competitive advantages over their competitors on pricing and brand name, which leads to higher cash flow generation and higher growth rates. Asset turnover measures a company's efficiency in generating sales with its assets. A company with higher asset turnover than its peers has higher return on assets if it charges the same profit margin. Alternatively, a company with higher asset turnover can maintain the same return on assets with lower profit margins, which means it can charge a price lower than its peers to attract more customers. Since companies in different industries have vastly different asset turnovers, it is important to compare a company's asset turnover with peers in the same industry to evaluate its relative efficiency.

Inventory turnover is another operating efficiency measure. If a firm is more efficient at managing its supply chain than its peers, it has a higher inventory turnover and less capital tied to inventory. The phenomenal growth of Walmart around the turn of the century was largely fueled by its leadership in supply chain management. By managing its supply chain more efficiently, Walmart was able to take full advantage of economies of scale, reduce its inventory, and offer better prices to customers than its competitors could. High inventory may be a sign that the company has difficulty in selling its products, which results in poor profit in the future. Inventory turnover also varies substantially across industries: retailers have most of their capital invested in inventory; financial service firms by contrast have very little inventory. Hence, it is more effective to compare inventory turnover within industries where inventory accounts for a significant percentage of total assets, than to compare inventory turnover across industries. Besides cross-sectional comparison of asset turnover and inventory turnover, investors also track trends in their changes. Firms with increasing operating efficiency are likely to become more profitable in the future and are viewed favorably.

Growth and Fundamental Momentum Factors

Growth has always been an inherent component in stock price valuation. A company's current value can be calculated as the net present value of all future cash flows discounted at risk-adjusted cost of capital. A simple discounted cash flow model using dividends as cash flows is the Gordon growth model. Stock price with a constant dividend growth rate can be calculated as the sum of the present values of all future dividends:

$$P = \sum_{t=1}^{\infty} \frac{D_t}{(1+K_e)^t} = \sum_{t=1}^{\infty} \frac{D_0 \times (1+g)^t}{(1+K_e)^t} = D_0 \times \frac{1+g}{K_e - g} = \frac{D_1}{K_e - g}$$

where P is ex-dividend value of the stock immediately after dividend D_0 is paid;

D_t is the expected dividend at time t;

g is the growth rate of dividends;

K_e is the cost of capital.

Although no assets have a steady growth rate of dividends forever (multistage dividend discount models are more common), the model demonstrates the relationship between the growth rate and the value of the stock: as the growth rate becomes higher the stock becomes more valuable.

Companies with above-average growth rate in sales, earnings, and cash flows are often competitive companies with growing market share. Some are also market leaders in growth industries. Although most high growth companies have already had good price appreciation in the past, many are likely to further appreciate in the future. Growth factors capture the changes in a firm's sales, earnings, and cash flows. Fundamental momentum factors capture the changes in a firm's fundamentals such as efficiency and profitability. They measure whether a firm is becoming more effective at using its resources to generate profits. Exhibit 6-6 shows growth and fundamental momentum factors.

Exhibit 6-6 Growth and fundamental momentum factors

Factor	Description
Historical earnings growth	1-year to 5-year historical EPS growth rate
Forecasted growth	Forecasted 1-year (or long-term) EPS growth rate
Sales growth	$(Sales_t - Sales_{t-1}) / Sales_{t-1}$
Dividend yield growth	$Dividend\ yield_t - Dividend\ yield_{t-1}$
Past forecast error	(Realized EPS – Consensus forecast 1 year ago) / Price
Change in gross margin	$Gross\ margin_t - Gross\ margin_{t-1}$
Change in cash flow margin	$Cash\ flow\ margin_t - Cash\ flow\ margin_{t-1}$
Change in ROE	$ROE_t - ROE_{t-1}$
Change in asset turnover	$\ln(asset\ turnover_t) - \ln(asset\ turnover_{t-1})$
PEG	(P / E) / Expected annual earnings growth rate

The 1-year historical earnings growth is defined as the year-to-year percentage growth of earnings per share (EPS):

1-year earnings growth rate = Current year EPS/Last year EPS – 1

The 3-year to 5-year historical EPS growth rate is also used to measure a firm's long-term growth. In general, m-year earnings growth rate is calculated as

$$m\text{-year earnings growth rate} = \sqrt[m]{(current\ year\ EPS)/(EPS\ m\ years\ ago)} - 1$$

Growth needs to be calculated using split-adjusted per share numbers instead of firm level numbers. A firm can grow its assets by issuing more shares to make new investments, which will likely lead to higher total revenues and earnings. But unless these new investments increase the earnings of existing shareholders, the increase in total earnings adds no value to existing shareholders. The impact of EPS growth is simple: companies with higher EPS growth rates are more attractive as they create more value-add beyond the book value for shareholders. Besides earnings growth, investors look for growth in other profit measures as well as growth in revenues. Some popular choices are growth in sales, cash flows and dividends. These factors are especially useful in the market environment where investors focus on growth—often when economic growth slows down and overall corporate profits stall. Interpretation of sales growth requires a little extra effort though. We cannot assume that rapid sales growth always reflects superb fundamentals. It is easier to grow revenues when a company sells products for less than cost. Many companies do pursue a strategy of selling products below cost in hope of gaining market share and achieving economies of scale to reduce costs in the future. More often than not, such a strategy fails to produce future profits. Therefore, companies with high revenue growth without corresponding earnings growth and cash flow growth require further scrutiny.

Similar to value signals, investors look at forecasted growth rates in sales, earnings, and cash flows along with historical growth rates as the future growth potential of a company can be different from its historical growth. Using analysts' forecasted earnings for the next fiscal year, we can arrive at the forecasted earnings growth rate. Besides, analysts also publish long-term earnings growth forecast for companies. The drawback of forecasted growth rates is that they depend on analysts' estimates and may not accurately capture real future growth rates. In fact, the past forecast error itself is a stock selection signal. Past forecast error is the difference between realized EPS for the past four reported quarters and the forecasted EPS for those quarters one year ago. The signal is normalized by the stock price. When the realized growth rate is higher than the forecasted growth rate, if investors have not already fully incorporated the higher growth rate into the price, the stock may be undervalued.

Changes in gross margin, cash flows margins and ROE capture improvements or declines of a firm's profitability. Improvements in profitability indicate that the firm is becoming more competitive. For example, an increase in cash flow margin shows that the firm is making higher operating profits per unit of sales in the current year than in the previous year, which makes the firm more attractive to invest in. Since asset turnover is one of the components in the DuPont decomposition of ROE, the change in asset turnover signal captures the improvement or the decline in asset turnover that drives the change in ROE.

A common criticism of relative value signals, such as earnings yield, is that they do not take growth into consideration. Since the current market value of a stock is the discounted value of future cash flows, growth rate is a critical component in valuation. In general, a company with a higher growth rate commands a higher P/E ratio. The PEG ratio, price/earnings to growth ratio, directly incorporates the trade-off between the P/E ratio and the growth rate. PEG is the core ingredient in Growth at A Reasonable Price (GARP) strategy, a stock selection strategy popularized by Fidelity fund manager Peter Lynch. GARP investors seek out stocks that have a PEG of 1 (a stock with a P/E ratio of 10 and 10 percent forecasted growth rate has PEG ratio of 1) or less. Since the growth rate in PEG is the forecasted long-term growth rate by analysts, it is less accurate and subject to large changes as market conditions change. The PEG ratio also has no meaning for companies with negative earnings, no growth, or those with negative growth. The main advantage of the PEG ratio is to identify fairly priced growth stocks. It makes evident that value and growth are not mutually exclusive strategies as most market participants like to invest in companies with high expected future growth rate. Nevertheless, if the market has already overpriced the growth rate, those stocks are likely to underperform in the future. In fact, a rationale behind value investing is investors' tendency to extrapolate recent over-optimistic or over-pessimistic growth rate far into the future. As they overpay for hyped stocks, the expected future abnormal returns become negative. By taking the price into consideration, investors avoid hyped stocks and invest in stocks with good growth rate and good valuation.

Since a company with a higher growth rate can generate more future cash flows from the same assets, investors are willing to pay a higher price for the same book value. Consequently, the book to price ratio is often used as a proxy for growth, for growth stocks tend to have lower book to price ratios. Nevertheless, one needs to avoid paying too high a price for a growth stock as many investors unfortunately do. Investors who blindly buy high-flying stocks with high historical growth rate often underperform the market.

How does one select good growth stocks? Partha Mohanram (2005) proposed eight criteria to score growth stocks—stocks in the in the lowest book-to-market quintile. A stock gets a score of 1 if it passes a criterion and 0 otherwise. The following are the criteria.

1. **Return on asset**: return on asset is higher than the industry median.
2. **Operating cash flow**: operating cash flow to assets ratio is higher than the industry median.
3. **Earnings quality**: operating cash flow is higher than net income.
4. **Earnings variability**: variance of return on assets in the past 3-5 years is lower than the industry median.
5. **Growth stability**: variance of sales growth in the past 3-5 years is less than the industry median.
6. **R&D intensity**: R&D expenses to total asset ratio is higher than the industry median.
7. **Capital expenditure**: capital expenditure to total asset ratio is higher than the industry median.
8. **Advertising intensity**: advertising costs to total asset ratio is higher than the industry median.

GSCORE, the sum of individual scores, can help identify good growth stocks. Mohanram classified growth stocks with GSCORE between 6 and 8 as good[38] and stocks with GSCORE between 0 and 1 as bad. In his study, good growth stocks outperformed bad growth stocks by 21% a year between 1977 and 2005. Thus, some investors use the GSCORE to screen growth stocks.

Sentiment Factors

The behavior of informed market participants such as financial analysts, corporate managers, and professional investors often conveys information about a company's future

---

[38] GSCORE are left skewed since many growth companies do not report advertising costs or do not have sufficient history to calculate earnings variability.

performance. Therefore, their opinions as well as their actions influence investor behavior and impact stock prices. Exhibit 6-7 highlights common sentiment factors.

Exhibit 6-7 Sentiment Factors

Factor	Description
Up-down signal	(Up revisions – Down revisions) / Total revisions
Target price implied expected return (TPER)	Consensus target price / Current stock price – 1
Earnings surprise	(Actual earnings – Mean of estimated earnings) / Price
Standardized earnings surprise	(Actual earnings – Mean of estimated earnings) / Standard deviation of analyst estimates
Shares issuances	Shares outstanding / Shares outstanding 12 months ago – 1
Shares repurchase	Shares repurchase / Shares outstanding 12 months ago
Insider trading	Insider buying as a positive signal
External financing	(Net increase in long term and short-term debt + Net increase in equity) / Average total assets
Days to cover	Short interest / Average daily volume
1-Month change in short interest	Month-to-month short interest change / Shares outstanding

Analyst Estimates

Analyst reports include a plethora of information about the current financial situation of a company and forecasts for future financials. Commonly used analyst estimates include buy/sell recommendations and forecasts for EPS, cash flow, sales, and dividend. There are several reasons why analyst estimates may carry new information about future returns. First, analysts are evaluated by their ability to collect new information about the firms they cover and make forecasts using collected information, so they have strong incentives to be right the majority of the time; otherwise they will not be able to stay in business for long. Second, analysts often take a conservative approach towards revisions: when they revise their forecast, they often release the revisions in smaller steps instead of one large step. Some even argue that analysts have incentives to revise forecasts in steps so that they can claim multiple correct forecasts over time instead of one correct forecast. Historical evidence does suggest positive autocorrelation in analyst revisions: positive revisions tend to lead to more positive revisions by the same analyst or other analysts and negative revisions lead to more negative revisions.

One top level summary of an analyst's view on a stock is a numeric value that represents a buy/sell recommendation:

1. Strong Buy
2. Buy
3. Hold

4. Underperform

5. Sell

Assigning numeric values (1-5) to analyst recommendations makes the calculation of consensus recommendation easy. Many stocks are covered by multiple analysts. Their recommendations and estimates are often different from each other. Consensus recommendation is the average of all analysts. The consensus recommendation—especially if we use the recommendation to make buy/sell decisions for stocks within the same industry—has predictive power for future stock returns. Besides the recommendation itself, we can also use recommendation revisions as a signal. When an analyst changes his rating to a lower number such as from 3 (hold) to 2 (buy), it is an upgrade; when an analyst changes his rating to a higher number, it is a downgrade. For a stock, the up-down signal is calculated as

$$UpDn_t = \frac{Up_t - Down_t}{Up_t + Down_t}$$

where Up_t and $Down_t$ are the number of analyst upgrades and downgrades in the signal construction period—usually three months to a year. Besides the vanilla version of up-down signals, we can further take revision time into consideration and reduce the weights of earlier revisions by introducing a time-weighted (e.g., exponential decay with 3-month half-life) up-down signal.

Another top level summary is the target price, which is the projected price that an analyst believes the stock will reach in a year. Using the target price, we calculate the target price implied expected return (TPER) as

TPER = consensus target price/current stock price − 1

The absolute valuation implied by TPER often has little bearing on realized returns. But Da and Schaumburg (2011) showed that the relative valuation implied by TPER was a valuable tool in predicting relative stock returns within the same sector or industry: The top 1/9 of stocks with highest TPER within each sector outperformed the bottom 1/9 of stocks within each sector by 1.8% a month in 1997-2004.

Earnings announcements are closely followed by investors. When announcements release information different from market consensus, stock prices move up or down in response to the new information. Most of the abnormal returns from earnings surprises—difference between the actual earnings and the consensus earnings—concentrate on the immediate price jumps when earnings are announced, which cannot be effectively captured by investors unless they have better forecast than the consensus and take positions (and risks) before the earnings announcement. After earnings announcements, stocks still experience weak post earnings announcement drift: stocks with positive earnings surprises tend to outperform stocks with negative earnings surprises in the weeks after the announcements. In earnings surprise signals, the earnings surprise is the numerator. To normalize the dollar value of the earnings surprises, the following denominators are recommended:

- Stock price before the earnings announcement

- Standard deviation of historical actual quarterly earnings

- Standard deviation of analyst earnings estimates for the current quarter

- Standard deviation of historical earnings surprises

There is little empirical evidence that one denominator is consistently better than the others. I/B/E/S uses the standard deviation of analyst earnings estimates for the current quarter as the denominator. Such an approach tends to yield extreme scores if analyst estimates are close to each other, which is especially problematic for small stocks with only one or two analyst forecasts. Standard deviation of historical actual quarterly earnings or historical earnings surprises take the earning variability and uncertainty in analyst forecasts into consideration, but they require at least three years of data to calculate the standard deviation.

In recent years, the post earnings drift has been weaker since the market is more responsive to earnings surprises. Besides, earnings announcements now include information beyond earnings numbers. More frequently, a firm's management holds conference calls after earnings releases to give guidance on future performance, which dilutes the value of current quarter earnings. If a company's earnings beat the consensus for the current quarter but the management warns lower future revenues and earnings, its share price is likely to fall. Investors also increasingly examine other data such as top line sales numbers. If a company's earnings beat analysts' consensus but the sales number falls short, the price reaction is often muted or even negative. In response, many investors have built an equivalent surprise signal for sales to capture the new information embedded in sales data.

Since earnings announcements only happen every quarter and analysts revise their earnings forecast more frequently, some investors combine earnings surprises and earnings revisions to yield a monthly surprise/revision signal:

$$S_t = \begin{cases} (A_t - E_{t-1})/P_{t-1}, \text{ if earnings are released between } t\text{-}1 \text{ and } t \\ (E_t - E_{t-1})/P_{t-1}, \text{ otherwise} \end{cases}$$

where E_t and E_{t-1} are the consensus earnings per share forecasts for the current quarter (not reported yet) at the end of month t and $t - 1$ and A_t is the announced earnings per share for the latest completed quarter. Essentially, if there is no new quarterly earnings release between $t - 1$ and t, earnings revision is used as E_t and E_{t-1} are forecasts for the same quarter; if there is quarterly earnings release, earnings surprise is used as A_t and E_{t-1} are the realized and the forecasted earnings for the same quarter.

In August 2000, the SEC ratified Reg FD (Regulation Fair Disclosure) that required publicly traded companies to disclose material information to all investors at the same time. The regulation prevented companies from giving material non-public information to selected analysts. The passage of Reg FD has had a significant negative impact on the usefulness of signals that rely on analyst recommendations and forecasts. Increased access to real-time analyst recommendations and their active exploitation also make them less effective signals. Stock prices do still respond to analyst recommendation changes, but the speed of price adjustments makes it difficult for investors to profit from price moves. In other words, the continued price drift after analyst revisions is much smaller or even insignificant to exploit.

In order to revive signals based on analyst forecasts, investors continue to dig deeper into the data trying to find smarter estimates that perform better than simple consensus. One approach is to differentiate analysts by their skills. If an analyst had consistent good forecasts of a company's sales and earnings, he is given a higher weight than an analyst who did not have a good track record. StarMine, a firm that provides analytics on sell-side research, uses this approach for their earnings surprise forecast: StarMine puts more weights on recent forecasts of top-rated analysts to calculate "SmartEstimates" and uses the differences between SmartEstimates and simple consensus estimates to predict earnings surprises: since SmartEstimates are better forecasters than consensus estimates, the sign of the difference between SmartEstimates and simple consensus is likely to have the same sign as the earnings surprise. There is also evidence that revisions away from the current consensus carry more information—it takes higher conviction to break away from the herd. If an analyst with a good track record revises his forecast away from the consensus, that revision is assigned higher weight. On the other hand, if an analyst with a poor track record revises his forecast to the consensus, that revision is assigned little weight as the analyst is likely just catching up with others. One reason that revisions work is the autocorrelation of revisions—therefore models that better forecast future analyst revisions may have some value. One such model building approach is to identify possible persistent bias in analysts' estimates. Since the majority of analysts adjust their views slowly or have systematic bias in estimating a company's earnings, the forecasts have a persistent bias too. When an analyst's historical forecast errors (actual earnings – forecasted earnings) were consistently negative or consistently positive, a model can correct the persistent bias by exploring the positive correlation of forecast errors.

Stocks without analyst coverage, often called neglected stocks, on average have higher returns than stocks with analyst coverage after adjusting for market risk. Schutte and Unlu (2009) found that part of the premium was compensation for higher information risk though. Analyst coverage provides investors with more company-specific information and reduces the proportion of noise-motivated trades, which reduces volatility and leads to lower risk. Hence, stocks without analyst coverage have higher systematic risk and need to be compensated with higher returns.

Management Actions and Statements

Senior managers (CEO, CFO, President, etc.) and corporate directors are always more informed about their own companies than other investors since they have access to both public and private information. Consequently, insider buying indicates that managers and directors have positive views on the company's future, which is a positive sign for the future stock price, while insider selling may reflect negative views. In practice, raw insider buying and insider selling signals have limited success in forecasting cross-sectional returns. One main reason is the noise introduced by buys and sells that are unrelated to insiders' views on the company's future. Given the broad use of stocks and stock options as part of the executive compensation, many insiders routinely sell stocks from compensation programs to meet their own cash flow needs or to reduce concentrated exposure to their own company. Such sales often do not reflect a negative view about the company's future. Some companies allow employees to purchase company stocks at a discounted price as part of the compensation, which triggers buys that do not necessarily reflect a positive view about the company's future. So, it is important to eliminate less informative trades and keep only the ones that are informative for stock selection. In practice, investors have to infer the intention of insider trades from historical trading patterns. Cohen et al. (2010) defined insider trades as routine if the same insider made the same trades in the same month of both of the last two years and the rest of the insider trades as opportunistic. After removing 56% of the insider trades that were identified as routine, they found that a portfolio using opportunistic insider trades yielded an abnormal return of 0.71% a month. Overall, the more information asymmetry corporate insiders have versus other investors, the more informative the insider trades are. Wu and Zhu (2011) showed that insider returns were higher in firms with less transparency, with high analyst forecast dispersion, and with high idiosyncratic risk. There is also evidence that insider trades are more informative for firms with higher R&D costs and uncertain R&D outcomes (e.g., biotech firms). Insider buys of stocks with high book-to-price ratio also generate higher returns than stocks with low book-to-price ratios. Insider buying signal is often calculated as the total insider purchases or the net purchases (buy − sell) over the past six-month to twelve-month period. Besides net purchases, we can also include the number of insiders in a signal. Buys or sells in the same direction by multiple insiders often yield a stronger signal than trades by a single insider.

For companies that grant stock options or stocks as part of the executive compensation, stock price moves around the grant date may also have some predictability. Since the price used to calculate the units of stocks to be granted and the strike price of the options are often the market price of the stock on the grant date, managers may have an incentive to accelerate the release of "bad news" before the grant date and delay the release of "good news" until after the grant date. As a result, there may be negative abnormal returns in the days before the grant date and positive abnormal returns after it. Using data between 1996 and 2008, Jansen and Sanning (2010) showed that exploring such a strategy could generate annualized abnormal returns of 1.4-5.2% net of transaction costs.

Besides paying attention to the actions taken by managers, investors also pay special attention to statements made by managers. A Bank of America study using data between 2001 and 2009 showed that S&P 500 companies that issued positive profit guidance were twice as likely to beat expectations in the following quarter. Furthermore, management guidance often leads analyst revisions. Consequently, the study argued that management guidance is a better predictor than analyst revisions. The mutual confirmation of management guidance and analyst revisions is useful information as well. When management guidance is above the consensus and analysts are making revisions to increase their estimate, it is a bullish signal for the company.

Investors also closely monitor firms' financing activities that introduce changes to shares outstanding or debt outstanding. A number of events contribute to the change in shares outstanding: secondary offering, warrant exercise, stock option exercise, conversion of convertible bonds, stock-for-stock mergers, and shares repurchases. Open market share repurchase announcements and secondary offerings are reported in the Mergers & Acquisitions database of Securities Data Corporation (Thomson SDC). Investors often use share repurchase as a positive indicator for stock returns. When there are few new profitable projects to invest in, responsible managers will distribute the cash back to investors instead of investing in less profitable projects. Share repurchase is one way of achieving that goal. Managers also use share repurchase to signal their belief that the share price is undervalued. Shares repurchased reduce the number of shares outstanding, which means each remaining share represents a higher percentage of the company's future cash flows. In one of Warren Buffett's letters (1984) to Berkshire Hathaway shareholders, he wrote, *"When companies with outstanding businesses and comfortable financial positions find their shares selling far below intrinsic value in the marketplace, no alternative actions can benefit shareholders as surely as repurchases."* Indeed, historically, stocks tended to have positive abnormal returns following repurchase announcements.

On the other hand, managers are more likely to raise capital by issuing new shares to finance new projects or acquisitions when they view the current stock price as adequately valued or even overvalued. Because the cost of capital is higher for stocks than internal financing and debt, firms choose secondary offerings often as a last resort when internal financing and debt issuance are not available. Secondary offering is usually issued at prices lower than the prevailing market price of the stock and naturally dilutes existing shareholders' interests, which often leads to lower short-term and intermediate-term returns. Therefore, secondary offering is a negative indicator—historically stocks tend to have negative abnormal returns following secondary offerings.

Instead of looking at each event individually, a simpler approach is to directly look at changes in shares outstanding after adjustments for stock dividends and stock splits. Net stock issuance often indicates that the stock price is overvalued and has negative future abnormal returns. An earlier study by Loughran and Vijh (1997) showed that firms that completed stock-for-stock mergers earned significantly negative excess returns of -25.0% in the five-year period following the acquisition. Pontiff and Woodgate (2008) used the log of annual share change as a proxy for share issuance:

$$ISSUE_t = \ln(\text{adjusted shares}_t) - \ln(\text{adjusted shares}_{t-12})$$

where $ISSUE_t$ is the share issuance measure at t;

adjusted shares$_t$ and adjusted shares$_{t-12}$ are shares outstanding adjusted for splits at time t and $t-12$ month.

They found that $ISSUE_t$ was a more statistically significant factor than size, book-to-market, or momentum factors in predicting cross-sectional stock returns.

The external financing signal expands the equity dilution signal by including net changes to debt. One reason that management may use external financing is to fund new investments. These new investments often have lower marginal profitability than existing ones, which leads to lower future return on assets. Another possible reason to use external financing is to preemptively fund future cash flow shortfalls. When management is pessimistic about a company's prospects, they are more willing to raise capital to address the potential cash shortfall before the cash flow problem becomes apparent. In those cases, raising capital before a liquidity crisis is a responsible choice since it is much more expensive or even impossible to raise capital in distressed situations. But it also indicates weakness in a firm's financial situation. The liquidity crisis was the catalyst that brought down Bear Stearns. Bear Stearns relied heavily on overnight borrowing for its funding needs. When the market began to question its capital adequacy, the company launched a public relationship campaign to deny the problem instead of raising equity or increasing longer-term debt. Three days after the CEO Alan Schwartz declared that *"there is absolutely no truth to the rumors of liquidity problems"*, Bear Stearns was bailed out by the Fed and sold to JP Morgan on March 14, 2008. Lehman Brothers suffered similar fate on September 16. One week after Lehman's collapse, Goldman Sachs took a $5 billion cash infusion from Warren Buffet's Berkshire Hathaway as preferred stock at a 10% dividend yield (Berkshire also got warrants to buy over 43 million shares of Goldman Sachs stock at $115, which produced handsome returns for Berkshire shareholders) and issued $5 billion in new stock. In other words, when a company relies on new external financing for survival, its outlook is usually bleak, at least in the near future. Companies that generate sufficient cash to reduce external financing tend to have stable or growing profits. Reducing external financing increases return for shareholders in the future.

The values of the simple shares repurchase signal and the secondary offering signal have weakened significantly in recent years. Not all share repurchases are in the best interests of shareholders. In another Warren Buffett's letter (1999) to Berkshire Hathaway shareholders, he wrote,

"It appears to us that many companies now making repurchases are overpaying departing shareholders at the expense of those who stay. In defense of those companies, I would say that it is natural for CEOs to be optimistic about their own businesses. They also know a whole lot more about them than I do. However, I cannot help but feel that too often today's repurchases are dictated by management's desire to show confidence or be in fashion rather than by a desire to enhance per-share value."

Because of the agency problem[39], management may also use shares repurchases to artificially maintain stock prices at the shareholders' expenses as management compensation is often tied to stock price performance. In the first three quarters of 2011, Netflix spent $200 million on stock repurchase at an average price of $222. In the same period, Netflix managers and directors sold $90 million of stocks. In November 2011, after the dismal performance of the third quarter was released, Netflix had a secondary offering selling 2.86 million shares at a price of $70 in order to raise $200 million. Needless to say, existing shareholders' value was destroyed by the stock repurchase and the subsequent secondary offering. The insider trades also indicated that the shares repurchase was not a signal that managers believed that Netflix was undervalued. Similarly, firms may have secondary offerings to invest in high growth opportunities instead of signaling to the market that the stock is overvalued. In some cases, managers also invest in the secondary offering themselves. So investors need to spend more time on deciphering the reasons behind shares repurchases and secondary offerings to make more informed decisions.

Institutional Ownership

Transactions by large institutional investors also drive stock prices. Changes in institutional ownership (calculated using quarterly 13F filings) have strong positive correlation with stock returns over the same quarter. Nevertheless, there is no strong positive correlation between changes in institutional ownership in one quarter and stock returns in the next quarter. The reasons that contribute to one quarter's flow may not

---

[39] Agency problem refers to potential conflict of interest between management and shareholders. As the agent of the shareholders, the management is supposed to act in the best interest of the shareholders. But the management may act in their own interest at the cost of shareholders' interest.

persist or may even revert in the following quarter. For example, if investors sell losing funds at year end for tax reasons, or if funds sell losing stocks at year end for window dressing purposes, the selling pressure is unlikely to carry over into the next year. To explore the institutional ownership signal, investors need to build refined versions of institutional ownership changes to predict future returns. Since institutions range from simple index funds to highly sophisticated hedge funds, not all institutional holdings are equal. Some investors only include a selected group of funds with strong historical performance in their universe and aggregate the holdings of this selected group. Others analyze the turnover of the underlying funds. For funds that hold the majority of their positions three months or less, the positions in the 13F filings are already outdated by the time investors receive the information 45 days after the quarter ends. Instead of trying to replicate the buys and sells by institutions in the prior quarter, more sophisticated approaches try to forecast future institutional buys and sells. One strategy is to examine active funds' exposures to typical stock selection signals (e.g., price momentum, earnings yield, and FY1 growth) to identify their factor exposures. Since institutional investors do not change their investment styles overnight, the strategy assumes that the top factors that institutional investors increased exposures to are likely to be favorite factors in the near future. Accordingly, the strategy invests in stocks that have positive exposures to these factors.

Some investors also use institutional holdings and trades to estimate herding risk. For many assets, institutional investors tend to trade in the same direction and overweigh/underweight them in the same period or over several periods. For passive funds, herding in trades often reflect investors' collective asset allocation changes or style/industry rotations. For example, if investors actively move out of European stocks and move into US stocks, many US index funds are likely to buy underlying US stocks in the same period. For active funds, the herding in trades and asset weights often reflects fund mangers' collective betting on specific stock selection factors. One indicator for herding, trade consensus, measures whether institutions are trading in the same direction:

$$NetShr_{t,i} = \sum_{f=1}^{F} \Delta Shr_{t,i}^{f} = \sum_{f=1}^{F} \left(Shr_{t,i}^{f} - Shr_{t-1,i}^{f} \right), \quad GrossShr_{t,i} = \sum_{f=1}^{F} \left| \Delta Shr_{t,i}^{f} \right|$$

$$Trade\ Consensus_{t,i} = \left| NetShr_{t,i} \right| / GrossShr_{t,i}$$

where f is a fund in the universe of F funds included in the analysis;

$Shr_{t,i}^{f}$ and $Shr_{t-1,i}^{f}$ are the numbers of shares held by fund f in stock i at t and $t-1$;

$\Delta Shr_{t,i}^{f}$ is the trade in stock i between $t-1$ and t by fund f.

A trade consensus value close to 1 indicates that all funds are trading in the same direction and more herding risk; a value close to 0 indicates little herding risk. If few funds trade an asset, its trade consensus score is often inflated. An asset with one trade always has a trade consensus score of 1, but it represents no herding risk. So assets with few trades are often removed from the calculation.

Instead of raw shares, we can also calculate active shares relative to a fund's benchmark (if the benchmark is known):

$$ActiveShr_{t,i}^{f} = Shr_{t,i}^{f} - GMV_{t,f} \times \text{Benchmark weight}_{t,i} / Price_{t,i}$$

where $GMV_{t,f}$ is the total gross market value of fund f's positions at t;

  $\text{Benchmark weight}_{t,i}$ is weight of stock i in the benchmark at t;

  $Price_{t,i}$ is the price of stock i at t.

Essentially $GMV_{t,f} \times \text{Benchmark weight}_{t,i} / Price_{t,i}$ is the number of shares that an active manager will hold if he assigns benchmark weight to that asset. So the differences between the true holdings and the benchmark-weight holdings are the active shares.

Institutional ownership data are also used to investigate behavioral biases that explain common anomalies. Using institutional holdings data, Cremers and Pareek (2011) developed a measure to estimate the duration of a stock that has been held in an institutional portfolio and calculate a stock-level average duration (weighted by the number of shares held by each institution). They found that medium-term momentum, short-term reversal, accruals, and share issuance anomalies were all stronger for stocks held primarily by short-term institutional investors.

Short Interest

Investors have long taken an interest in using short interest as a stock selection signal. Many studies rely on public short interest data. The data are released twice a month to show recent short interest in shares for each exchange-listed stock. The short interest is often normalized by shares outstanding (or floating shares if available) or average daily volume to yield short interest ratio and days to cover:

  Short interest ratio = short interest in shares/shares outstanding

  Days to cover = short interest in shares/average daily volume

Shares outstanding reflect the potential supply of shares available for lending. The short interest ratio calculates the percent of supplies currently being used. In comparison, days to cover takes the stock turnover into consideration.

Stock short interest is often viewed as a bearish sentiment measure. Short sellers are more likely to be sophisticated professional investors and some of them may possess negative information about the stocks that they short. So, the stocks they short tend to be overvalued and have lower future returns. One counterargument is that high short interest represents built-in future demand for the security since short sellers will cover their short positions by purchasing the securities in the open market. Furthermore, if everyone has sold or shorted the stock, the stock price is already depressed and is likely to reverse trend. However, empirical evidence supports the argument that stocks with high short interest subsequently experience negative abnormal returns and stocks with low short interest subsequently experience positive abnormal returns. Asquith, Pathak, and Ritter (2005) found that an equally-weighted portfolio with high short interest and low institutional ownership underperformed by 2.15% a month between 1988-2002. When a value-weighted portfolio is used, the underperformance dropped to 0.39% a month and was no longer statistically significant. In recent years, the short interest ratio has proven to be a weak signal for large-cap stocks. However, it is still statistically significant for small-cap stocks. One possible reason is that some S&P 500 stocks are shorted as a general hedge to the market or as an industry hedge. Such hedging does not carry stock specific information and introduces noise to short interest signals. Furthermore, the short interest ratios of S&P 500 stocks tend to be low and often only a handful of names have meaningful short interests. So the difference in short interests reflects more on the noises than the signals themselves.

In practice, the short interest ratio often determines the stock loan borrowing cost, which dampens the profitability of shorting high short interest stocks. High short interest stocks are often hard to borrow stocks that have borrowing costs at a few percent (annualized rate) to dozens of percent. For long/short portfolios, stock loan borrowing costs need to be taken into consideration. For a long-only fund, simply avoiding losing stocks with high short interest may be sufficient. In fact, the raw alpha of the short interest signal is not restricted to the assets with the highest short interests. Assets with low short interest have positive alpha. Boehmer, Huszar and Jordan (2010) found that stocks with low short interest had economically large and statistically significant positive abnormal returns. In their study of stocks listed on NYSE, Amex, and NASDAQ between June 1988 and December 2005, an equal-weighted portfolio of stocks in the lowest decile of short interest ratio had an excess return of 1.3% per month against the Fama-French four-factor model.

One advantage of short interest signals is that they have low turnover, which translates into slow information decay. Short interests tend to stay fairly consistent over a long period of time, which indicates that long-term fundamental portfolios are the main contributors of large short interests in stocks. As a result, some studies found slow decay in short interest's predictive power with lags of up to six months.

Because public short interest data are only available twice a month with delays, investors use vendor data such as Data Explorers for daily data. Vendor data rely on information collected from participants and is not as complete as the public short interest data. Nevertheless, it includes the majority of funds with short positions and has high correlation with public short interest. Although short interest is a slow moving signal, the timeliness of daily data still adds value since it often captures the accumulation of short interests early. Besides short interest demand data, Data Explorers also includes supply information about the number of shares that are available for borrowing and the number of lending agents for each asset. Instead of using shares outstanding as a proxy for supplies, utilization can be directly calculated as the total borrowed quantity divided by total used and unused supplies. The supply data are also used as a more timely proxy for institutional ownership since most securities lending supplies are provided by institutional investors. Some funds also have access to asset-level stock borrowing costs, which allow them to directly include fees as part of the implementation costs when they backtest strategies.

Although on average high short interest indicates lower future returns, the potential built-in demand from short sellers sometimes can push stock returns higher. If many short sellers have to cover their positions at the same time, the stock price will spike—a phenomenon known as a short squeeze. It happens when the supply of borrowable shares disappears and lenders recall their shares from short sellers or when the stock price has risen sharply forcing short sellers to get out of their positions. Short squeezes usually happen to small cap stocks, but occasionally have significant impact on large cap stocks as well. During the 2008 financial crisis, auto industry firms, including German auto maker Volkswagen, were popular choices for shorts. Since most of these firms were large-cap names, short squeeze was not a particular concern. On Sunday October 26, Porsche, the largest shareholder of Volkswagen, disclosed that it raised its direct holding of Volkswagen to 42.6% and had the stock option to increase the holding by another 31.5%. Considering that the second largest holder, Lower Saxony, held 20% of Volkswagen, the perception was that only 6% of the shares were floating shares available for lending. At the moment, the short interest of Volkswagen was more than 12%, resulting in a short squeeze. On October 27, the close price of Volkswagen jumped to €520 from the previous close of €210.85. On October 28, the price of Volkswagen reached as high as €1005, which briefly made it the world's largest company by market cap.

The ongoing stock loan fees and potential recalls by lenders make shorting stocks more costly and riskier than holding long positions. Unlike long positions in stocks, short positions also have unlimited potential losses if the stock price spikes. For example, in early 2012, the price of Sears Holding Corporation (SHLD), one of the most popular shorts among hedge funds, moved up from $31.14 on January 3 to $83.43 on March 15. Besides the heavy losses on the stock price move, hedge funds that shorted the stock also paid an annualized stock lending fee higher than 50% to prime brokers in order to maintain the short positions. Needless to say, investors understand that not all overpriced stocks are good candidates for shorting. For a short position to work out, investors need to have reasonable expectations that the price correction is likely to happen in the near future.

Short interests also influence how stock prices respond when stock-specific news is released. Lasser et al. (2010) examined stock returns in reaction to earnings announcements and found that when significant positive earnings surprises were released, stocks with high short interests had higher positive abnormal returns after the announcements than stocks with low short interests. When significant negative earnings surprises were released, stocks with high short interests had smaller negative abnormal returns than stocks with low short interests. Their evidence indicates that short sellers tend to cover short positions when extreme good news—to cut losses—or bad news—to reap gains—is released, which increases the demand for high short interest stocks and puts upward pressure on stock prices.

Not all short interests are triggered by bearish sentiment. When an acquirer proposes to purchase a target company by (partly) exchanging its own stock for the stock of the target, merger arbitragers often purchase the shares of the target company and short the shares of the acquirer as a hedge. In convertible arbitrage, investors purchase convertible bonds of a company and short sell the same company's stock to hedge price moves. Making adjustments for this "noise" is a difficult task. The impact of merger arbitrage on short interests of the acquirer depends on the relative size of the deal to the acquirer's market cap. Many large companies are involved in multiple acquisitions every year and most targets are relatively small ones that have little impact on the short interests of the acquirer. To estimate the impact of acquisitions, a good database with deal sizes is needed. Similarly for convertible arbitrage, the size of convertible bonds (and their price sensitivity to price moves of the corresponding stocks) is needed. Despite the difficulty, accurately removing short interests due to hedges may improve the performance of short interest signals.

Quality Factors

The quality category is a loose collection of factors ranging from earnings quality to the agency problem between management and shareholders. Exhibit 6-8 shows some of the quality factors that investors use for stock selection:

Exhibit 6-8 Quality Factors

Factor	Description
Working capital to sales	(Inventory + Accounts receivable – Accounts payable) / Sales
Accruals to assets	(Net income – Cash flow from operations) / Average total assets
Percent accruals	(Net income – Cash flow from operations) / |Net income|
Deferred tax	Deferred tax expense / Total assets
Capital expenditure ratio	(Capital expenditure – Depreciation & amortization) / Sales
Investment to assets ratio	(Increase in PP&E + Increase in inventory) / Total assets$_{t-1}$
Asset growth rate	Total assets$_t$ / Total assets$_{t-1}$ – 1
Equity financed M&A	Indicator = 1 if the company has equity financed M&A
R&D to EV	R&D Expense / Enterprise value
Extraordinary item	(Extraordinary loss – Extraordinary gain) / Book value

Earnings Quality

Earnings quality signals gauge whether reported accounting earnings represent a company's true earnings. In general, companies with good earnings quality—conservative accounting—expedite the recognition of costs and delay the recognition of revenues when there are uncertainties about the costs and the revenues. Conservative accounting temporarily depresses current earnings, but leads to higher future earnings. In contrast, companies with poor earnings quality—aggressive accounting—expedite the recognition of revenues and delay the recognition of costs. Aggressive accounting leads to inflated current earnings and lower future earnings when such costs are recognized. As a result, companies with low earnings quality may temporarily have a relatively higher price given higher current earnings. In the future, companies with good earnings quality are more likely to have sustainable earnings growth and have lower negative earnings surprise risk; companies with poor earnings quality are less likely to have sustainable growth and have higher negative earnings surprise risk. Hence, stocks with higher earnings quality are likely to have better future returns.

Most quality signals focus on the difference between a firm's accounting earnings and its cash flows. Traditional quality signals analyze the components in a firm's working capital[40]:

Working capital = Inventory + Accounts receivable – Accounts payable

Working capital gives investors information both on earnings quality and operational efficiency. Excess inventory buildup beyond sales growth impacts future profit in a number of ways. The buildup often reflects weak demand in a company's products relative to supply, which leads to a decline in the company's pricing power. Because of excess inventory, a firm is likely to reduce output in the future. As a result, fixed costs will be spread over fewer goods and will lower the operating profit margin. Inventory buildup also leads to a lack of pricing power as the firm tries to liquidate the inventory. For technology products, existing inventory may become obsolete when new products are released to the market, which leads to large future inventory write-downs. Accounts receivable increases if managers recognize sales prematurely, i.e., before customers pay for their products or if managers reduce allowance for doubtful accounts that covers potential uncollectible bad debt. In many industries, high accounts payable indicates a firm's strong bargaining power over its suppliers and low accounts receivable indicates a firm's strong bargaining power over its customers. Other things equal, higher operating activities—sales or assets—require higher working capital. High level of working capital alone does not necessarily indicate a problem with the underlying business as long as it is part of a solid business development strategy. To incorporate the operating activity difference, working capital to sales ratio normalizes working capital by sales.

Depreciation and amortization expenses impact a firm's accounting earnings but have no impact on operating cash flow. Since firms have flexibility within GAAP guidelines to choose a depreciation schedule, depreciation and amortization expenses contribute to differences in earnings quality. Higher depreciation lowers a firm's current earnings and the values of properties, plants and equipment; such conservative accounting means that the useful lives of assets are longer than the years used by the depreciation schedule. Consequently, these assets continue to generate revenues long after their book values become zero. So, firms using a shorter depreciation schedule temporarily depress their reported earnings and asset values, but have higher earnings and asset values in the long run.

Since Richard Sloan (1996) first documented significant hedged returns by buying stocks with low accruals and selling stocks with high accruals, many academics and practitioners have explored the size and the consistency of the accruals anomaly. Accruals are the difference between net income and cash flow from operations. In Sloan's original paper, he calculated accruals for year t using the following equation:

Accruals $= (\Delta CA - \Delta Cash) - (\Delta CL - \Delta STD - \Delta TP) - Dep$

where ΔCA is the change in current assets (between year $t - 1$ and t);

$\Delta Cash$ is the change in cash and cash-equivalent;

---

[40] A different definition of working capital is current asset minus current liabilities. The earnings-quality version removes cash and cash equivalent from current assets and short-term debt/tax payable from current liabilities since they have no impact on earnings quality.

ΔCL is the change in current liabilities;

ΔSTD is the change in the debt included in current liabilities (short-term debt);

ΔTP is the change in tax payable;

Dep is depreciation and amortization expenses.

Essentially, accruals are the difference between change in working capital and depreciation expenses: increases in working capital increase accruals and increases in depreciation & amortization expenses decrease accruals. This study normalized accruals by the average of total assets at year $t - 1$ and t to account for the difference in assets across companies and asset growth of the same company over time.

Since the cash flow statement has become an important part of financial reporting mandates, we can also directly use net income in the income statement and cash flow from operations to calculate accruals:

Accruals = net income – cash flow from operations

Sloan's study demonstrated that a hedged portfolio that longed stocks with lowest normalized accruals and shorted stocks with highest normalized accruals yielded 10.4% annualized returns between 1962 and 1991. Furthermore, during those 30 years, the hedged portfolio had negative returns in only two years. The existence of such anomaly posed a direct challenge to the Efficient Market Hypothesis. The paper triggered a debate in academia—more than a thousand papers cited Sloan's study in the decade following the paper's publication—about whether accruals anomaly contradicted the Efficient Market Hypothesis or accruals anomaly was caused by systematic risk exposures. In the meantime, active funds jumped on board to exploit the accruals anomaly and made handsome returns. For example, earnings quality signals contributed to the success and the growth of active funds at Barclays Global Investors (BGI) between 2000 and 2005. In 2006, BGI[41] recruited Richard Sloan from the University of Michigan as Director of Accounting Research to expand the firm's research on using accounting information in investment decisions. As the market reached a consensus that accruals anomaly did exist and many funds actively adopted the signal, the profit of the accruals signal mostly disappeared between 2006 and 2010.

In order to revive the signal, researchers investigated alternative ways of constructing the accruals signal. Hafzalla et al. (2010) proposed a change to the definition to normalize accruals by earnings instead of total assets. This new accruals measure, percent accruals, normalizes the accruals by the absolute value of earnings:

Percent accruals = (net income – cash flow from operations)/|net income|

They found that stocks in the first decile (lowest percent accruals) had 5.5% of annualized excess return and stocks in the tenth decile had -6.15% of excess return. Furthermore, the percent accruals have low correlation with traditional accruals measure: only 12% of the stocks in the first decile of the traditional measure are in the first decile

---

[41] Similar to many other quantitative funds, active funds at BGI suffered losses during the 2007 quant meltdown and the 2008 financial crisis. In 2009, Blackrock acquired Barclays Global Investors from Barclays PLC and became the world's largest investment manager by AUM. Many researchers, including Richard Sloan, went back to academia or left the firm to pursue opportunities in other companies.

of percent accruals. Stocks in the highest decile tend to have large positive accruals and net income close to zero.

Another measure of earnings quality is deferred tax expenses. When management uses aggressive accounting to increase current earnings, its reported earnings exceed its taxable earnings as taxable earnings do not recognize some unrealized earnings and require the deduction of some costs. So, a company's tax expense calculated from accounting earnings also exceeds its tax payable. The difference between tax expense and tax payable is deferred tax expense. Since companies with more aggressive accounting are likely to have higher deferred tax expenses, high deferred tax expenses to total assets ratios indicate poor earnings quality.

Agency Problem

The capital expenditure ratio, defined as the difference between capital expenditure and depreciation & amortization costs divided by sales, measures excess capital investments beyond maintaining the necessary asset base:

Capital expenditure ratio = (Capital expenditure – Depreciation & amortization) / Sales

Excessive capital expenditures may sometimes become an agency problem. An example is empire building: Management may have the incentive to invest in projects that have returns lower than the expected cost of capital and to grow the business at the expense of future profitability. Excessive capital expenditure may also reflect management's overly confident and unrealistic view about revenue growth. When revenue growth does not materialize, depressed capacity utilization, higher fixed costs, and lack of pricing power caused by excess capacity all lead to lower profitability. In addition, high capital expenditures may indicate that the company is delaying the recognition of some expenses by recording these as long-term assets, which leads to higher current earnings and lower earnings quality. On the other hand, excessive underinvestment with new capital expenditure significantly below the level of depreciation and amortization may hinder future growth opportunities. Besides, it may reflect that the company cannot generate sufficient cash flows to make necessary capital investments required for growth. Overall, the capital expenditure ratio signal recommends that investors avoid companies that make excessive overinvestment or underinvestment in capital expenditure but invest in companies that make moderate and sustainable levels of capital expenditure to benefit shareholders. Since capital expenditure is reflected by increase in property, plant and equipment (PP&E) and inventory, investment to asset ratio measures the increase in PP&E and inventory as a percentage of the previous year's total assets. Instead of digging into details about capital expenditure and depreciation costs, other investors directly look at asset growth rate. Historically, companies with the highest asset growth rate are often the ones that have low future returns. The agency problem again contributes to the asset growth anomaly.

Historical evidence suggests that companies that pursue organic growth—growth by increasing sales—on average performed better than those that pursue inorganic growth—growth by mergers and acquisitions. Companies with organic growth display greater sustainability of growth in the future. There is a belief that managers focusing on empire building are more likely to acquire or merge with other companies, often at significant premiums, with the hope of creating synergy. When the realized synergy falls short, shareholders suffer losses. Besides paying high premiums for acquisition, companies with inorganic growth are more visible to the market which in turn creates unrealistic high expectations and leads to future disappointment and low returns. That was exactly what happened with the largest merger in history. In 2000, the biggest US internet service provider AOL acquired media behemoth Time Warner for ~$164 billion to form AOL-Time Warner. At the time of the merger, Chairman Steve Case said, *"AOL-Time Warner will lead the convergence of the media, entertainment, communications and Internet industries, and provide wide-ranging, innovative benefits for consumers."* That convergence never materialized and the merger turned out to be a huge failure. After years of internal struggle, Time Warner was separated from AOL-Time Warner in December 2009 at a huge loss to shareholders.

Research and Development (R&D) Expenses and Extraordinary Items

R&D expenses and extraordinary gains/losses are income statement items that may distort investors' view on a company's future earnings. R&D is crucial for future competitiveness in technology and health care companies. US accounting rules require that many R&D costs be expensed instead of being capitalized, which may not effectively reflect the value of R&D as an intangible long-term investment to generate future revenues. Therefore, firms with higher R&D expenses may have more intangible assets that are not included in book value calculations. Expensing R&D costs decreases current earnings with the potential of increasing future earnings. Furthermore, companies that invest heavily in R&D tend to have high cash flows to support R&D, which makes them industry leaders creating a virtuous cycle of higher future sales growth, more cash and more future R&D investment.

The majority of companies do not have a separate line for reported R&D expenses. For example, most financial firms report no R&D expenses. For the firms that do not report separated R&D expenses, we cannot assign zero R&D expenses and compare them with the firms that do report R&D expenses. Chan et al. (2001) documented that companies that reported R&D expenses had similar average returns as firms that did not report R&D expenses. Since R&D expenses are unlikely to be the main driver of future growth for companies that do not report R&D expenses, we need to treat them as a separate group when we incorporate the value of R&D expenses. They also found that the return volatility for companies with high R&D expenses was larger than companies with average R&D expenses. Hence, higher returns on companies with higher R&D expenses may reflect higher risks and those risks are priced by the market to yield a risk premium.

The extraordinary item signal tries to capture possible mispricing because of extraordinary losses and extraordinary gains that affect net income. Extraordinary losses are losses caused by unusual and infrequently occurring events or transactions, e.g., losses incurred in restructuring. Extraordinary losses lower current earnings, but have no impact on future returns. Investors may overreact to current lower earnings without taking into consideration the transitory nature of extraordinary items, which depresses the stock price. But the effects of these events are short-lived. As future earnings improve, the stock price recovers and yields abnormal positive returns. Similarly, investors may overreact to current higher earnings caused by extraordinary gains, which pushes up the stock price. As future earnings revert to the normal level, the stock price drops and yields abnormal negative returns.

Risk Factors

When investor sentiment shifts from risk seeking to risk aversion, we often observe a phenomenon called flight-to-quality. Higher quality assets are less risky and safer investments. Within stocks, flight-to-quality means investors move capital from stocks with high debt to equity ratios, low interest coverage ratios, and high earnings variability to stocks with low debt to equity ratios, high interest coverage ratios and low earnings variability. Empirical evidence also indicates that companies with more stable growth in earnings, cash flows, and sales tend to have higher returns. Exhibit 6-9 lists popular risk factors used for stock selection.

Exhibit 6-9 Risk factors

Factor	Description
EPS variability	Standard deviation of detrended trailing 5-Year EPS / Absolute value of the mean of trailing 5-Year EPS
Sales variability	Standard deviation of detrended trailing 5-Year sales / Mean of trailing 5-Year Sales
Estimate dispersion	Standard deviation of IBES FY1 estimates / Absolute value of the mean of IBES FY1 estimates
Debt to asset ratio	(Long term debt + Short term debt) / Total assets
Debt to equity ratio	(Long term debt + Short term debt) / Book value of equity
Current ratio	Current assets / Current liabilities
Quick ratio	(Cash & cash equivalent + Receivables) / Current liabilities
Cash ratio	Cash & cash equivalent / Current liabilities
Interest coverage ratio	EBIT / Interest expense
Credit rating	Ratings provided by S&P, Moody's, and Fitch
Liquidity risk	Turnover, illiquidity ratio, relative volume, etc.
Beta	Historical beta estimated from trailing 12-month daily returns
Idiosyncratic risk	CAPM or Fama-French residual return volatility
Lottery indicator	Maximum daily return in the past month

Business Risk

Business risk refers to the uncertainty in a firm's ability to generate revenues and profits. EPS variability and sales variability are two common measures of business risk. The EPS[42] variability measure is defined as the standard deviation of the detrended trailing 5-

---

[42] Notice that EPS instead of a company's net income is used. A company may have a quite different capital base over five years if it has secondary offerings. It is for this reason that net income needs to be normalized by the number of shares outstanding.

year EPS divided by the absolute value of the mean of the trailing 5-year EPS. Trend removal is required in EPS variability calculation since the standard deviation of trailing 5-year EPS is high if earnings steadily increase over the years even though steady increase in EPS indicates low risk. The EPS trend is removed by regressing EPS against time as the explanatory variable. Companies with low EPS variability have more consistent earnings and less business risk. Although there is insufficient evidence that stocks with low EPS variability outperform stocks with high EPS variability in the long run, it is well established that stocks with low earnings variability do outperform when overall corporate profit drops and economic growth slows.

Another measure of business risk is analyst forecast dispersion since analyst forecast dispersion likely reflects the uncertainty of a firm's profitability. Diether et al. (2002) presented evidence that stocks with higher dispersion in analysts' earnings forecasts (defined as the ratio of the standard deviation of analysts' current-fiscal-year annual EPS forecasts to the absolute value of the mean forecast) earn lower future returns. They showed that a portfolio of stocks in the highest quintile of dispersion underperformed a portfolio of stocks in the lowest quintile of dispersion by 9.48% per year in 1976-2000.

Financial Risk

Financial risk refers to the uncertainty in a firm's ability to pay creditors and fulfill other financial obligations. Different leverage ratios, liquidity ratios and credit ratings are common factors to assess financial risk.

Firms that have higher leverage tend to have higher financial risk; as a result they are expected to have higher expected long-term returns. Debt to equity ratio, the sum of long term debt and short term debt divided by book value of equity, is one measure of financial leverage. Many financial analysts include only long-term debt in the numerator. Some analysts, on the other hand, include other long-term liabilities such as unfunded pension liabilities and financial leases in the numerator. In recent years, low long-term interest rates have increased the present value of pension liabilities. As a growing number of companies face significant unfunded pension liabilities, broader liability measures have increasingly attracted investor interest. To avoid the problem caused by negative book value of equity—firms with negative book values have high financial leverage even though their calculated debt to equity ratio is negative—we can also use debt to asset ratio, which replaces the denominator with total assets. Stocks with higher debt to asset ratios have higher financial leverage.

Liquidity ratios measure the capacity of a company to service its current liabilities. The current ratio (current assets divided by current liabilities) is often used as a risk factor to measure whether the firm has sufficient resources to cover its liabilities in the next 12 months. A ratio of 1.5 or higher is a sign of safety whereas a ratio of 1 or lower indicates higher bankruptcy risk. Compared to the current ratio, another measure known as the quick ratio removes inventory from the numerator. This is particularly useful for evaluating companies that rely on large inventory (e.g., retail) as they may be unable to quickly liquidate inventory to cover liabilities. To compare these companies, the quick ratio proves to be a better measure. Since the market value of inventory can be different from its accounting value (book value of inventory in the balance sheet), the quick ratio also avoids potential problems in inventory valuation. The cash ratio further excludes accounts receivable from the numerator and includes only cash or liquid marketable securities. This is therefore the most stringent liquidity ratio. Unlike the quick ratio, the cash ratio is not a popular choice for liquidity risk. Many financially solid companies do not maintain a cash ratio above 1. The reason is that cash or cash equivalents do not generate profit for the firm, so high cash or cash equivalents may indicate that the firm's assets are not fully utilized. Interest coverage ratio estimates a company's ability to pay interest on outstanding debt. An interest coverage ratio below 1.5 indicates that the company may not have sufficient earnings to cover its interest expenses; a ratio higher than 2.5 indicates that the company has little risk of not meeting its interest payment obligations.

Credit rating indicators provided by rating agencies to investors signal credit worthiness of a debt issuer or a specific debt issue. S&P, Moody's, and Fitch are the top three rating agencies for corporate bonds as well as for government/municipal bonds. Investors require a risk premium for taking credit risk. This is why the long-term return of riskier non-investment grade (S&P rating BB or under) bonds is higher than the return of investment grade (S&P rating BBB or higher) bonds. Empirical results show that the credit risk is priced in stock returns as well: the long-term return of companies with low credit ratings is higher than the return of companies with high credit ratings. Since stocks with lower credit ratings on average have a smaller market capitalization than stocks with higher credit ratings, size explains part of the credit risk premium. Nevertheless, the credit risk premium still exists after we control for the size factor, which indicates that credit risk is another systematic risk priced in equity returns.

Besides credit ratings, investors also study the relationship between credit rating changes/credit watch and stock returns. Credit rating changes are upgrades and downgrades of a firm's credit ratings. Before credit rating changes, rating agencies sometimes issue a credit watch on possible changes to an issuer's rating. A credit rating change is a lagging factor: stocks tend to have positive abnormal returns in the months before upgrades and tend to have negative abnormal returns in the months before downgrades. One reason is that credit rating agencies are slow to adjust ratings as a company's financial situation strengthens or weakens. As a result, stock price moves often lead downgrades or upgrades. Still, when a credit rating change does happen, the market tends to respond to the change. After the initial market response, upgrades or positive credit watches do not usually lead to longer-term positive abnormal future returns and downgrades or negative credit watches do not usually lead to longer-term negative abnormal returns. Instead, the price tends to revert after the initial response. The downgrade often triggers index funds to sell the company's bonds and stocks either because of investment mandate or managers' unwillingness to take on "extra" credit risk. The negative sentiment and selling pressures do explain the initial price drop and may cause the stock to be oversold. After the selling pressure subsides, the price tends to recover some of the initial losses.

Liquidity Risk

Liquidity is defined as the ability of an asset to be converted into cash quickly and without any price discount. It is a risk factor because illiquidity requires a return premium. Even investors without immediate liquidity needs prefer to hold liquid assets rather than illiquid assets, assuming equal return and risk. As a corollary, in order to entice investors into illiquid assets, it is necessary to offer return enhancement relative to liquid assets.

Since different measures are used to capture different aspects of liquidity, there is no consensus on the best proxy. The following are commonly used liquidity measures.

Effective spread is the difference between the execution price and the mid-price (average of the prevailing bid-ask quotes) divided by the mid-price. Effective spread is the cost that an investor pays for taking liquidity.

Turnover is the average of daily volume divided by shares outstanding in the past T days:

$$TO_{t,y} = \frac{1}{T} \sum_{i=0}^{T-1} \left(V_{t-i,y} / Shrout_{t-i,y} \right)$$

where $V_{t-i,y}$ is the trading volume of stock y on day $t - i$;

$V_{t-i,y} / Shrout_{t-i,y}$ is the number of shares outstanding on day $t - i$;

ILLIQ, introduced by Amihud (2002), is the average ratio of the daily absolute return to the dollar trading volume on the same day:

$$ILLIQ_{t,y} = \frac{1}{T} \sum_{i=0}^{T-1} \left(|R_{t-i,y}| / \$V_{t-i,y} \right)$$

where $|R_{t-i,y}|$ is the absolute return of stock y on day $t - i$;

$\$V_{t-i,y}$ is the dollar trading volume on day $t - i$.

The ratio gives the average percentage price change for each dollar of trading volume, which is a rough measure of price impact. A less liquid stock tends to have higher ILLIQ value. To address the overall market liquidity increase over the years, ILLIQ is further normalized by the average ILLIQ across stocks in the market:

$$ILLIQMA_{t,N,y} = ILLIQ_{t,y} / AILLIQ_t$$

where $AILLIQ_t = \frac{1}{Y} \sum_{y=1}^{Y} ILLIQ_{t,y}$ is the average of $ILLIQ_{t,y}$ across Y stocks in the market.

Illiquidity ratio, a measure similar to ILLIQ, is the ratio of total daily absolute return to the total dollar trading volume: $Illiquidity\ ratio_{t,y} = \sum_{i=0}^{T-1} |R_{t-i,y}| \Big/ \sum_{i=0}^{T-1} \$V_{t-i,y}$

Although it does not have an intuitive interpretation as ILLIQ does, it is a more robust measure of illiquidity for stocks with higher volatility in daily trading volumes.

Return to turnover ratio, an alternative to ILLIQ, is the average ratio of the daily absolute return to daily turnover:

$$TO_{t,y} = \frac{1}{T} \sum_{i=1}^{T-1} \frac{|R_{t-i,y}|}{(V_{t-i,y} / Shrout_{t-i,y})} = \frac{1}{T} \sum_{i=1}^{T-1} \frac{|R_{t-i,y}|}{(\$V_{t-i,y} / Mktcap_{t-i,y})}$$

where $Mktcap_{t-i,y}$ is the market cap of stock on day $t - i$.

Return to turnover ratio normalizes the dollar trading volume by market cap to remove most of the impact of size on trading volume.

Regardless of the proxy used, researchers have mostly demonstrated a negative relationship between stock returns and liquidity. For example, Chordia et al. (2001) showed that stocks with higher stock turnover had lower expected returns. Amihud showed that the expected stock returns were positively correlated with $ILLIQMA_{1,N,y}$ both across stocks and over time. Thus, it is generally accepted that stocks with lower liquidity command a risk premium.

There is significant interaction between size and liquidity factors. In fact, market cap is used as a proxy for liquidity as well. Large-cap stocks have much higher trading volumes than small-cap stocks. As a result, large-cap names naturally have lower ILLIQ and lower illiquidity ratios. Nevertheless, liquidity risk adds value beyond the size effect. After controlling for size, stocks with higher turnover still tend to have lower expected returns. There is also interaction between liquidity and the price-to-book ratio. Growth stocks with high price-to-book ratios tend to have higher turnover than value stocks with low price-to-book ratios.

When the stock universe is restricted to large cap stocks, liquidity premiums disappear. Compared with small cap stocks, large cap stocks are relatively liquid, which is why trading volume differences may have limited impact on the liquidity premium. Instead, large trading volume and high turnover may reflect momentum trading and information trading. As discussed in the technical analysis chapter, high trading volume is often used to confirm price breakouts and moving average crossovers. For relatively liquid stocks, Brown et al. (2009) argued that momentum and information effects might dominate and result in a positive relationship between trading volume and stock returns. When they restricted the universe of stocks to the S&P 500 index or the largest 1000 stocks by market cap, stocks with higher trading volumes and turnover had higher average returns in the following 1-12 months than stocks with lower trading volumes.

Relative volume measure: Besides cross-sectional liquidity measures, investors also use a time series based relative volume measure as a signal:

$$\text{relative vol}_{t,y} = \left(\frac{1}{M} \sum_{i=0}^{M-1} V_{t-i,y} \right) \bigg/ \left(\frac{1}{N} \sum_{i=0}^{N-1} V_{t-i,y} \right)$$

where $V_{t-i,y}$ is the trading volume of stock y on day $t - i$;

Often M is chosen to include one-week to one-month history and N is chosen to include three-month to twelve-month history. Essentially, relative volume is the ratio of a stock's short-term average daily volume to its long-term average daily volume. There are a couple of arguments as to why the relative volume signal may work. First, in technical analysis, the interaction between volume and price indicates that high volume winners are likely to perform better than lower volume winners. Because many informed investors have long-only or long-tilted portfolios, a large increase in volume is more likely to indicate good news instead of bad news. Second, an increase in trading volume compared with its long-term average means that the stock is becoming more liquid than before and the liquidity risk premium is likely to decrease in the future. As liquidity premium decreases, the stock yields higher returns.

Beta and Idiosyncratic Risk

According to the finance theory discussed earlier, investors should be compensated with a risk premium when they take systematic risk. Despite this principle an anomaly is often observed: stocks with low beta and low volatility have *outperformed* stocks with high beta and high volatility. For beta-adjusted returns, this low risk anomaly has existed for the past half a century. As market returns dropped, low risk anomaly has also been true for total returns since 2000. Investments in low-beta and low-volatility stock portfolios have yielded higher average returns at lower standard deviation and a smaller maximum drawdown. Implicit leverage in high beta stocks contributes to the low risk anomaly. CAPM assumes that investors can borrow and lend cash at the risk-free rate. Indeed, hedge funds routinely use leverage to boost their total returns. But the borrowing costs they pay to prime brokers are still higher than the lending yields they receive when they lend to prime brokers. Individual investors are reluctant to use explicit leverage. Even for those who do use leverage, their leverage is limited by margin requirement and Regulation T (it requires 50% initial margin on purchase). When individual investors use margin, brokers charge a substantially higher interest rate than the risk-free rate. As a result, aggressive investors often overweigh assets with higher risk to gain access to higher leverage instead of relying on borrowing on margin. The bias towards riskier assets means that these assets have lower risk-adjusted returns. Ang et al. (2006) showed that stocks with high idiosyncratic volatility—return volatility not explained by Fama and French three-factor model—had low average returns. Using data from July 1963 to December 2000, they found that the quintile portfolio of stocks with the lowest idiosyncratic volatility outperformed the quintile portfolio with the highest idiosyncratic volatility by 1.06% per month. Another interesting observation is the interaction between idiosyncratic risk and momentum: assets in the bottom quintile of 12-month return and top quintile of idiosyncratic risk on average have -2.66% abnormal returns per month. Many funds have jumped on the bandwagon to explore the low risk anomaly in response to the large increase in client demand of low-risk products after the 2008 financial crisis.

Skewness and Lottery Indicator

Since stock returns are non-normally distributed, investors often take higher moments into consideration. Skewness is a measure of the shape of a distribution. It indicates the degree of asymmetry in a distribution (a range of returns). Skewed distributions have more values to one side of the peak or the most likely value—one tail is longer than the other. A skewness of 0 indicates a symmetric distribution. Negative skewness means the distribution is skewed to the left of the mean while positive skewness indicates a skew to the right of the mean. A normal (bell-shaped) distribution of returns has no skewness because it is a symmetric distribution. All other things being equal, assets with positive skewness—assets with a higher likelihood to have large positive returns—are preferred over assets with negative skewness. Barberis and Huang (2008) showed that positively skewed securities tended to be overpriced and had negative excess returns and negatively skewed securities tended to be underpriced and had positive excess returns. Skewness can be directly estimated from historical returns. Nevertheless, skewness depends on tail returns, which happen at low frequency. Skewness measured using lagged returns is often a weak predictor of future skewness and as a result may not be a good predictor of future returns. Instead, Boyer et al. (2010) found that lagged idiosyncratic volatility was a stronger predictor of skewness than the lagged idiosyncratic skewness.

A different indicator of the asymmetry of the distribution, the lottery indicator, directly measures the maximum and minimum of returns. Lottery games have always been popular all around the globe. US state lotteries alone have sales more than $50 billion per year. Even though the expected returns of lotteries are negative, participants are happy to put their money into games in the hope of becoming multi-millionaires overnight. Kumar (2009) showed that, at the aggregated level, investors preferred lottery-type stocks—stocks with a small probability of a huge reward. Bali et al. (2011) used the maximum daily return over the past one month (MAX) as a proxy for the lottery factor and showed that the average monthly raw and risk-adjusted return difference between stocks in the lowest and highest MAX deciles was more than 1%. Investors also prefer stocks with limited downside risk and dislike stocks with a small probability of large losses. Stocks with small minimum daily returns (in absolute values) are preferred and command a lower return premium. Hence, the difference between the daily maximum return and daily minimum return (MAX–MIN) is also used as an indicator: stocks with higher MAX–MIN values have lower expected returns.

Conclusion

In this chapter we discussed a variety of fundamental signals and the rationale behind them:

- Value signals select stocks with good margin of safety.
- Profitability and efficiency signals select companies that are more efficient in managing assets to create shareholder value.
- Growth and fundamental momentum signals select companies with improving efficiency and profitability.
- Sentiment signals select stocks with strong support from corporate insiders, financial analysts, institutional investors and hedge funds.
- Quality signals select companies with conservative accounting, high-quality management teams, and commitment to shareholder value.
- Risk factors select stocks with better risk-adjusted returns.

These fundamental signals have long helped investors make sensible investment decisions. Fundamental signals have contributed to the historic success of and remain the bread and butter of many active equity funds. Given the popularity of these signals, for these are now widely employed by investors, a simple combination no longer consistently generates high risk-adjusted returns. To boost returns and improve return consistency, investors have to dig into the details of financial reports and management notes to look for more information. Instead of analyzing all factors that may impact the price of a stock, fundamental analysts focus on a small number of key drivers at a time. They actively seek information that estimates key drivers better than market consensus and take positions based on their non-consensus view as such positions have the possibility to yield high risk adjusted returns.

Chapter 7

Other Signals

As traditional technical and fundamental signals become widely available to professional investors, these signals have increasingly been incorporated in investment processes. Consequently, their predictive power has gradually deteriorated over time and in some cases has even completely disappeared. In order to maintain an edge, investors actively pursue new data and information to make better investment decisions. In this chapter, we discuss some interesting signals we believe have been less frequently used. Their unique edge perhaps relies on data that is harder to obtain or to clean. When signals are difficult to replicate, decay in signal strength becomes less of an issue. Therefore, research in less attainable or proprietary data often uncovers more valuable investing signals.

Economic Links

A company does not exist in a vacuum. Instead it is economically linked to its customers, suppliers, partners, and competitors. Economic linkages have long been studied and understood by fundamental investors; studying a company's customers, suppliers, partners, and competitors has always been an indispensable part of analyst reports. Fundamental portfolio managers routinely use such information to forecast the company's revenue, profit and stock returns. **Porter's five forces** framework is often used to estimate a company's prospect and profitability. Porter's five forces framework analyzes a company's competitiveness and assesses a company's potential profitability using the following five factors.

1. **Threat of new competitors**: Highly profitable businesses naturally attract new competitors and competition eventually leads to lower profitability. The threat of new competitors is lower if entry barriers are high or if the company has significant cost advantage through economies of scale.

2. **Threat of substitutes**: Even if entry barriers are high, other businesses may produce substitute products to attract customers away. The threat of substitutes is especially high if customers' cost of switching is low.

3. **Bargaining power of customers**: If a company's revenue depends on several large customers, buyer concentration often gives customers more bargaining power. If customers can easily find similar products or substitutes and are sensitive to price, customers have more bargaining power as well.

4. **Bargaining power of suppliers**: If there is high supplier concentration and few substitute inputs, suppliers have more bargaining power.

5. **Rivalry among existing competitors**: If a company is neither a market leader in innovation nor a cost leader, constant competitive pressure will limit a company's revenue growth and profitability.

To capture the relationship between different companies, fundamental analysts often dig into detailed earnings reports, other SEC filings, press releases, and communicate with industry experts to build detailed economic link maps for the companies that they cover. Quantitative researchers were slow to include economic linkage in their stock selection models. The main reason for this seems to be that company performance is often related to its customers, suppliers and competitors in a non-linear fashion. A company may grow its revenue and earnings because of robust industry growth—a rising tide lifting all boats. For instance, when the economy recovers, more companies spend heavily on information technology, which benefits all competitors within the information technology sector. As the pie gets bigger, a company may get bigger without actually increasing its market share. When that happens, similar growth by competitors may not affect a company much. But competitors can also grow by becoming better players within their industry and obtain a larger market share. When this happens, competitor growth augurs bad news. For example, Nokia was the largest cell phone maker when Apple released the iPhone in June 2007. In the following five years, even though consumers spent more on cell phones, Nokia struggled to compete with Apple and other competitors. Nokia's market share dwindled and its stock price dropped 90%.

Economic links also help investors identify the market leader in an industry. William O'Neil's CANSLIM strategy recommends investing in companies that are market leaders in their industries. He found that market leaders outperformed both large-cap stocks and small-cap stocks with considerably less risk. The stock prices of market leaders tend to decline the least in a bear market or in a market correction and rise the most in a bull market. Therefore, understanding linkages between competitors within an industry and identifying the market leader may help investors select a strong company within an industry. Many investors also use the price action of the market leader as the barometer of the price direction of an industry: the market leader tends to rise before other companies in the same industry begin to rise, and the market leader tends to go on to lead other companies in entering the peak and the distribution phase.

Although bargaining power of customers may reduce profitability, the overall observation is that a company tends to perform well when its customers are performing well. In other words, the profit tends to spread across the supply chain. Using a dataset that identified a firm's major customers, Cohen and Frazzini (2008) built a customer momentum strategy that longed the top 20% good customer news stocks—highest average customer stock returns in the previous month—and shorted the bottom 20% bad customer news stocks—lowest customer stock returns in the previous month. The long portfolio outperformed the short portfolio by 1.45% per month between 1981 and 2004. Their results indicate that investors did not fully incorporate customer news into their suppliers' prices. Therefore, lagged customer returns could predict supplier returns.

Order Flow Indicators

Stock prices are determined by supply and demand. When there are more buyers than sellers, the price of a stock is likely to rise; when there are more sellers than buyers, the price of a stock is likely to fall. Order flow indicators provide investors with information on the historical supply and demand of a stock. If imbalance between supply and demand persists, forecasted imbalance helps predict stock price moves.

Order Imbalance

Order imbalance is one measure to capture the imbalance between supply and demand:

$$IMB_t = \frac{\sum_{b=1}^{M} V_{b,t} - \sum_{s=1}^{N} V_{s,t}}{\sum_{b=1}^{M} V_{b,t} + \sum_{s=1}^{N} V_{s,t}}$$

where $V_{b,t}$ is the volume of the b-th buy order on day t;

$V_{s,t}$ is the volume of the s-th sell order on day t;

M and N are the number of buy orders and sell orders on day t.

Essentially, order flow imbalance calculates signed order flows and normalizes it by the total trading volume. If a trade is buyer-initiated, the trade has positive sign and is added to the flow. If a trade is seller-initiated, the trade has negative sign and is subtracted from the flow.

In practice, the direction of a trade is not directly observable. TAQ data are often used to estimate the sign of a trade. The simplest approach is the **tick test**, which relies only on the trade data. A trade is classified as a buy if it happens on an uptick (the price is higher than the price of the previous trade) or a zero-uptick (the price is the same as the previous price and the last price change was an uptick). A trade is classified as a sell if it happens on a downtick or a zero-downtick. The **Lee and Ready algorithm** (1991) combines the tick rule and the quote rule. If the price of a trade is higher than the mid-price (average of the prevailing bid and ask price), the trade is classified as a buy. If the price of a trade is lower than the mid-price, the trade is classified as a sell. When the price of a trade is at the mid-price, the tick test is used to classify the trade.

If the quote price has changed between two consecutive trades, the tick test may result in misclassification of the second trade. Compared with the tick test, the Lee and Ready algorithm generally reduces classification errors by including the quotes in the trade classification. For example, using a NASDAQ proprietary data set that identified trade direction, Ellis et al. (2000) found that the tick rule correctly classified 77.66% of the trades and the Lee and Ready algorithm correctly classified 81.0%. But the Lee and Ready algorithm requires processing quote data, which is many times larger than the trade data. Furthermore, quotes and trades are recorded through different systems and as a result they might not be synchronized correctly. Lee and Ready observed that quotes were more likely to be recorded ahead of the trades and recommended to lag the quotes by five seconds to align them better with the trades. Such a heuristic approach might have worked in the past and was adopted by researchers through the 1990s. With the development of electronic trading, the five second delay became excessive. Bessembinder (2003) recommended the removal of the quote lag, which is consistent with recent years' observations and has become the standard. Ellis et al. (2000) found that quote- and trade-based rules had a very limited success in classifying trades executed inside the quotes. The shrinkage of tick size to one cent made the classification even more difficult.

The development of electronic communication networks (ECNs) as trading venues and the development of high-frequency trading have produced more trades with execution prices between the bid and the ask price. This is likely to increase the classification error. Another known problem is the uptick rule. Before July 2007, the uptick rule prevented short selling a stock unless it was on an uptick or zero-uptick, which caused many short sells to be misclassified as buys. Using a random sample of 200 stocks over a three-month period in 2005, Asquith et al. (2010) showed that the Lee and Ready algorithm only classified 33.4% of their short sales as seller-initiated.

Tick-by-tick data provide the highest sampling frequencies for trade classification, but market microstructure makes trade classification difficult. Traditional money flow indicators used by technical analysts rely on daily price changes to decide whether the money flow is positive or negative, which loses the detailed information embedded in the tick data. Some investors calculate money flow index and order imbalance using 1-minute or 5-minute bars that summarize a stock's trading activities for every 1-minute or 5-minute period within the daily trading session.[43] If the volume weighted average price (VWAP) of a bar is higher than the VWAP of its previous bar, the entire volume within the current bar is considered to be a buy order (positive money flow); if the VWAP of a bar is lower than the VWAP of its previous bar, the entire volume within the current bar is considered to be a sell order (negative money flow). Instead of assigning the entire volume of a bar to buy orders or sell orders, Easley et al. (2012a) proposed a bulk volume classification method to allocate a bar's volume to buy volume $V_{b,t}$ and sell volume $V_{s,t}$:

$$V_{b,t} = V_t \times Z\left(\frac{P_t - P_{t-1}}{\sigma_{\Delta P}}\right) \text{ and } V_{s,t} = V_t \times \left[1 - Z\left(\frac{P_t - P_{t-1}}{\sigma_{\Delta P}}\right)\right]$$

where V_t is the total volume traded during bar t;

$P_t - P_{t-1}$ is the price change between the bars;

$\sigma_{\Delta P}$ is the estimate of volume-weighted standard deviation of price changes between bars;

Z is the cumulative distribution function (cdf) of the standard normal distribution.

Essentially, if the price does not move, the volume is evenly split between the buy volume and the sell volume; if price has a large increase (decrease) relative to the volume-weighted standard deviation, most of the volume is allocated to buy (sell) volume. By testing bulk volume classification method on E-mini S&P 500 futures, WTI oil futures, and gold futures, they found that the method yielded greater accuracy than tick tests even though the bulk volume classification required only a small fraction of the data of the tick test.

Despite its limitations, order imbalance was shown to have good correlation with concurrent stock returns. Bennett and Sias (2001) showed money flow had positive autocorrelation: stocks with high money flows subsequently tend to have high money flows and stocks with low money flows subsequently tend to have low money flows.

---

[43] Similar to daily stock price/volume data, the one-minute bars and five-minute bars include open, close, high, low, volume, and VWAP information. Since the US stock market opens for 6.5 hours on a normal trading day, the trading activities of a stock are summarized by 390 one-minute bars or 78 five-minute bars.

More importantly, they also documented that money flow had predictive power in explaining future stock returns.

Probability of Informed Trading (PIN)

PIN is another indicator derived from TAQ data. It assumes a sequential trade model that involves three players: a market maker, noise traders, and informed traders. Noise traders are uninformed. They, as a group, trade every day with buy orders following a Poisson process at a rate of ε_b and sell orders following a Poisson process at a rate of ε_s. Informed traders only trade when they believe they have special information. If that information is positive, they buy following a Poisson process at a rate of μ; if the information is negative, they sell following a Poisson process at a rate of μ. The market makers have no special information. In order to set the bid and ask prices, they observe the sequence of the trades and assess the probability that the orders come from informed traders. If we further assume that for every day, the probability that an information event occurs is α and the probability that the it is negative information is δ (the probability that it is positive information is $1 - \delta$), we have the PIN model as shown in Exhibit 7-1.

Exhibit 7-1 Probability of information trading (PIN) model

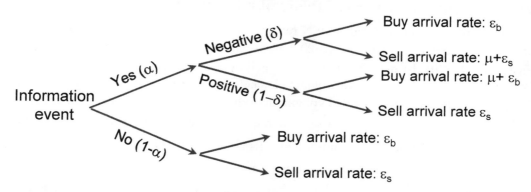

The parameters $\theta = (\alpha, \mu, \varepsilon_b, \varepsilon_s, \delta)$ can be estimated from the trades using the maximum likelihood method. The likelihood function for the PIN model is

$$L\big((B,S)\,|\,\theta\big) = (1 - \alpha)\frac{e^{-\varepsilon_b}\varepsilon_b^B}{B!}\frac{e^{-\varepsilon_s}\varepsilon_s^S}{S!} + \alpha\delta\frac{e^{-\varepsilon_b}\varepsilon_b^B}{B!}\frac{e^{-(\mu+\varepsilon_s)}(\mu + \varepsilon_s)^S}{S!}$$

$$+ \alpha(1 - \delta)\frac{e^{-(\mu+\varepsilon_b)}(\mu + \varepsilon_b)^B}{B!}\frac{e^{-\varepsilon_s}\varepsilon_s^S}{S!}$$

where B and S are the number of buys and sells for a given day.

If every trading day follows the same process and is independent of other days, the likelihood function for T days is the production of daily likelihood functions. Hence, the estimation of parameters can be expanded to multiple days.

Using θ, we can calculate the probability of informed trading as

$$PIN = \frac{\alpha\mu}{\alpha\mu + \varepsilon_b + \varepsilon_s}$$

where $\alpha\mu$ is the arrival rate for informed trades;

$\alpha\mu + \varepsilon_b + \varepsilon_s$ is the arrival rate for both informed and uninformed trades.

Unlike order flow imbalance measures, PIN is an unsigned measure: both informed buys and informed sells yield higher PIN. PIN was originally developed as a model for market makers to estimate potential risks. The market maker sets a bid-ask spread to gain from trading with uninformed traders that compensates the loss from trading with informed traders. For stocks with high PIN values, market makers need to set higher bid-ask spreads. Similarly, investors may demand higher returns for investing in stocks with higher PIN to compensate the risk. Easley et al. (2010) showed that a zero-investment portfolio that longed high PIN stocks and shorted low PIN stocks yielded positive returns that could not be explained by Fama-French three-factor or four-factor models. However, the return premium for high PIN stocks was mainly in the stocks at the bottom three deciles of market cap, which limited its value to institutional investors.

Volume-Synchronized Probability of Informed Trading (VPIN)

The standard approach to calculate PIN requires complex maximum likelihood method to estimate parameters $\theta = (\alpha, \mu, \varepsilon_b, \varepsilon_s, \delta)$ before calculating PIN. To reduce complexity, Easley et al. (2012b) developed volume-synchronized probability of informed trading (VPIN) that relied on equal volume bucketing instead of time bucketing. Let $t = 1, 2, \cdots, T$ be the index of equal volume buckets. For each bucket t, the total volume V is the sum of buy volume $V_{b,t}$ and sell volume $V_{s,t}$. If we further assume that the arrival rates for uninformed buys and uninformed sells are the same ($\varepsilon = \varepsilon_b = \varepsilon_s$), the expected arrival rate of all uninformed and informed trade is $\alpha\mu + 2\varepsilon$ and the expected absolute trade imbalance is $\alpha\mu = E[|V_{b,t} - V_{s,t}|]$. Since each volume bucket has the same volume V, VPIN can be estimated as

$$VPIN = \frac{\alpha\mu}{\alpha\mu + 2\varepsilon} = \frac{\alpha\mu}{V} \approx \frac{\sum_{t=1}^{T}|V_{b,t} - V_{s,t}|}{T \times V}$$

The buy volume $V_{b,t}$ and sell volume $V_{s,t}$ for each volume bucket can be estimated using the bulk volume classification. The amount of volume in each volume bucket V and the total number of buckets T depend on the forecasting horizon. VPIN is often used to estimate intraday flow toxicity. In this case, if we choose V to be the historical average 1-min volume and T to be 50, VPIN measures the probability of informed trading in the volume approximately corresponding to historical average 50-min volume. Since volume bucket is used instead of time bucket, VPIN automatically adjusts to trade intensity changes. As more information arrives, the trade volume often spikes. Using volume bucket allows VPIN to quickly capture the change in the probability of informed trading at shorter time span, which increases its predictive power.

Equity Flow Indicator

The order imbalance relies on trades to estimate net buying (buy – sell) by investors, which naturally makes it a noisy factor. State Street, the world largest custodian, administrates around 15% of the world's tradable assets held by institutional investors. That gives it a sufficient sample of institutional investors and a unique advantage to monitor net buying by institutional investors. Using aggregated position changes of its clients, State Street has built a number of equity flow indicators to track equity flows by country, sector/industry, and styles. State Street's research showed that there was significant period-to-period autocorrelation in flows as well as positive contemporaneous correlation between flows and returns. Furthermore, the correlation between current flows and next period's returns was generally positive as well.

Derivative Market and Bond Market Data

Stock is but one asset class in the integrated financial market. Information from other asset classes such as bonds, credits, derivatives, and commodities is often useful in forecasting stock returns. For instance, informed investors may use options or credit default swaps (CDS) to reflect their views. Therefore, options prices and CDS prices may help forecast future stock price moves.

Option Data

Because of the inherent connection between the stock market and the equity derivatives market, price and volume information of call and put options often carry valuable information in predicting stock returns and risks. One simple approach explores deviations from the put-call parity. Put-call parity indicates that a put and a call on the same stock with the same strike price and maturity should have similar implied volatility.[44] Deviations from the put-call parity often contain information about future stock returns. Cremers and Weinbaum (2010) studied the **volatility spread** (CVOL-PVOL), the difference in implied volatilities between call options and put options with the same strike price and the same expiration date, as a factor to predict stock returns. To take advantage of option pairs at different strike prices, the asset level volatility spread is calculated as the weighted difference in implied volatilities across option pairs with open interest as the weights. Using data between 1995 and 2005, they found that a portfolio that longed stocks with high volatility spreads—calls were more expensive relative to puts—and shorted stocks with low volatility spreads—puts were more expensive relative to calls—earned a value-weighted abnormal return of 50 bps per week. They also observed that the degree of predictability was larger when option liquidity was high and stock liquidity was low. This suggests that for these stocks informed investors were more likely to use options as the trading instrument to reflect their private information. These results suggest possible mispricing of the underlying stocks. The true benefit of such a strategy is less than the return difference though: stocks with the low volatility spreads have high stock-loan borrowing costs, which dampens the returns if we short these stocks.

---

[44] If the options are European options, the theoretical implied volatilities should be the same. In reality, the options are American options and there are market frictions, which is why small deviations are common.

In fact, high stock-loan costs and the limited availability of borrowable stocks are reasons why many informed traders choose the options market.

Bali and Hovakimian (2009) confirmed that a portfolio that longed stocks in the highest CVOL-PVOL quintile and shorted stocks in the lowest CVOL-PVOL quintile earned positive returns. However, their hypothesis was that CVOL-PVOL was a proxy for jump risk (discontinuous jumps in stock prices) since stocks with higher CVOL-PVOL on average had higher jump risk. They also showed that a trading strategy that longed stocks in the highest IVol-RVol (the implied volatility calculated as the average of CVOL and PVOL minus the realized volatility calculated using daily returns in the previous month) quintile and shorted stocks in the lowest IVol-RVol quintile produced a return of 0.6-0.73% per month.

Another approach related to CVOL-PVOL is the **volatility skew**. For equity options, volatility skew refers to the typical downward slope when implied volatilities are plotted against strike prices. For example, Exhibit 7-2 shows that on August 16, 2013, the implied volatility of Tesla Motors (TSLA) options (expiration on September 20, 2013) gradually decreased with increasing strike prices.

Exhibit 7-2 Implied volatility of TSLA options versus strike prices

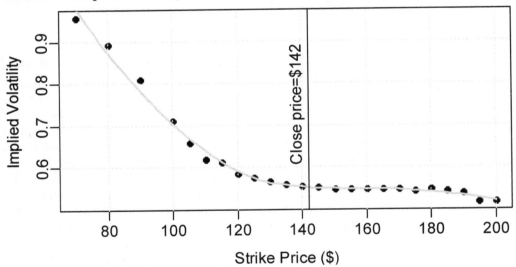

Xing et al. (2010) adopted the following volatility skew measure to investigate its predictive power for future equity returns:

$$SKEW_{i,t} = VOL_{i,t}^{OTMP} - VOL_{i,t}^{ATMC}$$

where $SKEW_{i,t}$ is the calculated skew for stock i at time t;

$VOL_{i,t}^{OTMP}$ is the implied volatility of the out-of-the-money (the ratio of strike price to the stock price between 0.8 and 0.95) put option;

$VOL_{i,t}^{ATMC}$ is the implied volatility of the at-the money (the ratio of strike price to stock price between 0.95 and 1.05) call option.

They found that stocks with the lowest volatility skew—sorted by the one-week moving average of the daily skew—outperformed stocks with the highest volatility skew by 10.9% per year. Furthermore, the predictability of volatility skew persisted for at least 6 months, which indicates reasonably low turnover of the signal. Since they observed that firms with the highest volatility skew experienced the worst earnings surprises, the evidence is consistent with the hypothesis that informed traders with negative news use out-of-the-money options as the trading venue to reflect their private information and the information is then gradually incorporated into the stock market. Lin et al. (2012) confirmed that both the volatility spread and volatility skew had significant predictive power in forecasting earnings surprises and analyst revisions. They found stocks with low volatility spread and high volatility skew tended to have negative earnings surprises, negative analyst earnings revisions, and more downgrades.

Besides the snapshot of implied volatilities, we can also examine the changes in implied volatility. Ang et al. (2010) studied the relationship between changes in volatility and future stock returns. In their analysis, at-the-money call and put options' implied volatilities with a delta of 0.5 and an expiration of 30 days[45] were used to calculate volatility innovation, which was defined as the one-month change of the implied volatility of the call (or put) option:

$$\Delta CVOL_{i,t} = CVOL_{i,t} - CVOL_{i,t-1M}$$

where $\Delta CVOL_{i,t}$ is the change of implied volatility for stock i at time t;

$\quad CVOL_{i,t}$ is the implied volatility of 30-day at-the-money call option;

$\quad CVOL_{i,t-1M}$ is the implied volatility of an at-the-money call one month ago.

They found that an equally weighted portfolio of stocks in the highest quintile of $\Delta CVOL_{i,t}$ (largest increases) outperformed an equally weighted portfolio of stocks in the lowest quintile of $\Delta CVOL_{i,t}$ (largest decreases) by 0.97% per month between 1996 and 2008. A normalized version of implied volatility change, $\%\Delta CVOL_{i,t} = \dfrac{\Delta CVOL_{i,t}}{CVOL_{i,t-1M}}$, also yielded similar results.

CDS Data

Early academic research indicated that stock returns had predictive power in forecasting future bond returns, but bond returns had little power in forecasting future stock returns. In other words, stock returns tended to lead bond returns. One likely explanation is liquidity. Investors tend to reflect their views using liquid stocks because the corporate bond market has low liquidity. Since the credit default swap (CDS) market is more liquid than the corporate bond market, investors often look at the CDS market for credit spread information.

---

[45] In reality, we often do not have options with delta of 0.5 and an expiration of 30 days. But the numbers can be interpolated from existing options. Ivy DB provides an interpolated volatility surface for each security on each day with expiration from 30-730 days at deltas of 0.2-0.8 (negative deltas for puts).

A CDS is a swap where the buyer makes a series of the payments to the seller and receives a predefined payoff from the seller in the event of a corporate bond default or other credit events. Essentially, the buyer of the CDS purchases an insurance against the default risk from the seller. The price of the CDS is quoted as spread, the annualized amount that the buyer pays to the seller. Therefore, an increase in the CDS spread indicates that the credit risk of the underlying bond has increased. Although the CDS market existed in the 1990s, CDS trading did not take off until the 2000s. ISDA (International Swaps and Derivatives Association) Market Survey showed that the total notional value of CDS increased from $0.9 trillion at the end of 2001 to $62.2 trillion at the end of 2007. As the financial crisis unfolded in 2008, the CDS market began to shrink. In 2012, the estimated outstanding notional value was ~$25 trillion. CDS are more actively traded than their underlying bonds. Blanco et al. (2005) showed that the CDS price changes tended to lead the price changes of the underlying bonds. Although the stock price changes still lead the CDS spread changes, the CDS spread changes help predict short-term stock returns. Han and Zhou (2011) showed that the slope of CDS spreads—the spread difference between 5-year CDS and 1-year CDS—negatively predicted future stock returns. Stocks with low slopes outperformed stocks with high slopes by 1% a month in the next six months. They believe that the high slope indicates future credit deterioration that is not fully incorporated in the current stock price. As investors gradually incorporate the information, the 1-year CDS spread tends to increase and the stock price tends to underperform.

Broker and Third-Party Research

In order to maintain an information edge, active investors, especially fundamental portfolio managers, also collect information through brokers and third-party research firms. All large brokers and independent research firms have dedicated web-based research portals to provide clients with research updates. Such updates are detailed analysis of companies based on both quantitative and qualitative information. For instance, since the management team is critical to the success of a company, research reports often analyze the management team's experience, vision, and their ability to execute corporate strategies. Besides routine research on companies on their coverage list, some brokers and independent research firms also conduct custom-tailored research for clients.

Channel Checks and Expert Networks

Many investors rely on published data in financial statements, analyst reports, or management notes to calculate different financial ratios. Some stock pickers, on the other hand, often further scrutinize disclosed numbers. Since all financial statements and management notes are provided by the company itself, fundamental stock pickers may rely on **channel checks**—third-party independent research on a company using supplier, customer, and competitor data—to determine the financial health of the company. Because management compensation is tied to stock price performance, management may be biased to present an overtly optimistic picture to boost the stock price. Sometimes, to avoid damaging relationships with management, analysts may be reluctant to disclose negative information about the companies that they cover. Independent researchers, on the other hand, provide objective views as they have no vested interest. Another advantage of channel checks is their timeliness. Independent researchers collect information from a company's suppliers, manufacturers, distributors, customers, and competitors through interviews or commercial data providers. Therefore, the data are often available before the company releases its earnings statements.

We can see that channel checks are a valuable tool for investors to gather information that is not widely available. If this information is different from and more accurate than the market consensus, trades relying on the more accurate information gleaned from channel checks may yield positive abnormal returns when the company releases its financial reports. For example, many researchers collect information from Apple's suppliers in order to forecast the sales of iPhones and iPads before Apple's earning releases. It is critical, however, to avoid using insider information in channel checks. SEC defines illegal insider trading as buying or selling a security, in breach of a fiduciary duty or other relationship of trust and confidence, while in possession of material, nonpublic information. Channel checks rely on mosaic theory to gather information and evaluate stock prices. Mosaic theory allows investors to collect material public information as well as non-material non-public information about a company and draw conclusions about buying and selling securities based on the combined information mosaic.

Expert networks have attracted a lot of attention in recent years. Expert networks refer to companies that provide client access to experts on specific subjects—any subjects ranging from industry knowledge to government policies—for on-line, telephone, or in-person consultations. Financial service firms, especially hedge funds, are major clients of such expert networks. Expert network consultants help portfolio managers better understand business models, industries and companies, sources of revenues and costs, as well as the competitive landscape. In rare cases, consultants have been known to disclose material non-public information to their clients who subsequently traded on the basis of such information. SEC and federal prosecutors have since convicted dozens of consultants working for such expert networks as well as their clients on insider trading charges. In a well-publicized case, Joseph Skowron, a portfolio manager at the hedge fund FrontPoint Partners (a $7.5B hedge fund), acted on a tip about the result of a clinical trial leaked by Dr. Yves Benhamou, an expert network consultant, and thus avoided $30 million in losses. Insider-trading charges and a subsequent guilty plea in 2011 ultimately brought down the fund. To avoid receiving and using material non-public information, some hedge funds have set up strong guidelines on how portfolio managers communicate with consultants, require official approval from the compliance department for hiring consultants, and have attorneys review the information before incorporating any information from the consultants.

Alpha Capture

Alpha capture is a system for sell-side contributors to submit trade ideas to investors. Through a website[46], salespeople and researchers at investment banks, brokers, and research firms deliver long/short ideas, the rationale behind their recommendations, expected holding periods, target prices, and conviction levels to participating clients. Since the origination, updates and the close of an idea are all time-stamped, investors can easily evaluate a contributor's historical performance as well as monitor performance in

---

[46] E.g., https://tradeideas.youdevise.com/TradeIdeasMonitor/monitor

real time. That provides investors the opportunity to evaluate contributors systematically and to select contributors who have good stock selection skills. Contributors can distribute the same idea to multiple subscribers and often get compensated for the good trade ideas they generate. This gives contributors incentive to research and publish ideas. The system was first introduced by Marshall Wace (a hedge fund in London) in 2001 and has been adopted by a number of providers.[47] In recent years, Trade Ideas Monitor (TIM) Group has become a major provider of alpha capture.

Since alpha capture ideas are submitted by sell-side contributors, one may enquire into the difference between alpha capture ideas and analyst ratings or recommendations? There are indeed a number of differences. Contributors of trade ideas are salespeople and researchers and not analysts. Analysts are bound by Reg FD to disseminate ideas to all clients at the same time. Salespeople and researchers, on the other hand, are allowed to share their knowledge and quick analysis with select clients if they believe that those trade ideas are more suitable for the trading strategies and styles of their clients. Analysts usually make longer term recommendations backed up by detailed analysis and adjust their recommendations infrequently. Trade ideas, by contrast, are short-term in nature. For example, the majority of trade ideas in TIM were closed in a month. The rationale for a trade idea is usually captured in no more than a few sentences and a recommendation may sometimes be simply based on a contributor's gut feeling.

Compared with traditional communication methods, alpha capture platforms reduce the risk of insider trading. It is easier for regulators to monitor alpha capture platforms than to monitor other communication—phone calls or private meetings—since alpha capture trade ideas leave electronic audit trails. Regulators can scan all communications in an alpha capture system to determine whether insider information was passed. In contrast, phone calls and private meetings are difficult to trace. When Wall Street Journal (2009) revealed that Goldman Sachs shared short-term trading ideas with a selected group of favored clients in weekly private meetings that the firm called "trading huddle", some investors and regulators were outraged. Two years later, Goldman Sachs agreed to pay a $10 million fine to the Massachusetts securities regulator and stopped the practice. At the same time, many brokers developed their own web-based systems to distribute trade ideas and market color to subscribing clients without raising eyebrows. Third-party alpha capture platforms, because they incorporate contribution from many providers as well as provide a more objective evaluation of contributors' performance, have grown in popularity among buy-side users.

There are few published studies on the value of alpha capture ideas. Using trade ideas from First Coverage[48], Thomas (2011) built a smart trade signal (STS) that summarized the recommendations of the contributors for each stock:

STS = (Buy − Sell)/(Buy + Sell)

where Buy and Sell are the numbers of buy and sell recommendations on a stock.

The stocks were then sorted by STS and separated into quintiles. For large-cap stocks, the stocks in the top quintile outperformed the Russell 1000 by more than 12% a year before trading costs from June 2007 to December 2009; for small-cap stocks, stocks in the top

---

[47] http://en.wikipedia.org/wiki/Alpha_capture_system
[48] First Coverage merged with TIM Group in 2011.

quintile outperformed the Russell 2000 by more than 15% a year. Although portfolio turnover was high, the strong performance of the STS signal indicated that trade ideas could be a new alpha signal.

Given hefty fees (often through commissions) involved in acquiring trade ideas, most buy-side users of alpha capture are institutional investors. An investment strategy may rely mostly on trade ideas to make investment decisions. In order to achieve better risk-adjusted returns, such a strategy may conduct detailed performance analysis on contributors and select contributors with demonstrated track record of success. More funds now include trade ideas as part of information seeking in their qualitative or quantitative decision making process, rather than relying on trade ideas to make buy or sell decisions.

News, Internet and Social Media

Since investors constantly seek new information on markets and individual companies, they closely follow news releases from news agencies such as Reuters, Bloomberg, and Dow Jones. With the development of the internet, increasingly people have found that just following the traditional news media alone is not sufficient. They therefore also track internet sites, blogs, Twitter and other social media for information.

News Signals

Fundamental portfolio managers and technical analysts use different approaches to trade on news. One approach is "buy the rumor, sell the fact". The stock market moves higher when investors as a group anticipate positive economic news or government actions (e.g., announcement of QE3, the third round of quantitative easing) and declines when the news is actually announced. The argument is that if the announcement is not as positive as the expectation, investors will be disappointed and sell; even if it is consistent with the positive expectation, investors have the incentives to take profits and sell. Some fundamental investors keep a flat position before news announcements unless they have an edge in predicting the news better than the market. Many technical analysts also recommend keeping a flat position before market-level or stock-level news. They argue that it is risky to bet on news. Instead, it is more important to see how the market responds to news and follow market reactions. If the market shrugs off negative news, it indicates that the market has incorporated the information before the news release and is a bullish sign. On the flip side, if the market fails to rally on positive news, it indicates weak demand and is a bearish sign.

High-frequency traders were the first to systematically take advantage of news information. Significant news causes price changes in the same day, often within minutes or seconds. Therefore, it used to be difficult for quantitative portfolio managers with holding period from weeks to months to trade on news signals directly. Instead, they had to focus on post-event price drifts—price moves after the news releases. As more portfolio managers adopted a daily or intraday rebalancing strategy instead of weekly or monthly rebalancing, they began to incorporate news sentiment in trade timing decisions. If a portfolio manager decides to buy a stock because of its long-term potential, instead of taking a position when the stock is beaten down by negative news, he can wait for the news sentiment to stabilize before entering into the position.

Many quantitative investors use news sentiment data from providers such as RavenPack News Analytics and Thomson Reuters News Analytics in their investment process. For each stock, investors calculate stock-level sentiment factors from sentiment scores, relevance scores, and novelty scores (explained in Chapter 2) of historical individual news items. Investors then compare the stock-level sentiment signals across stocks to build portfolios that long stocks with strong sentiment and short stocks with weak sentiment. Using RavenPack's news sentiment data for each stock (relevance score ≥ 90), John Kittrell (2011) calculated the trailing positive news ratio (ρ_1) and the trailing negative news ratio (ρ_{-1}) for the stock:

$$\rho_1 = m_1 /(m_1 + m_{-1}) \text{ and } \rho_{-1} = m_{-1} /(m_1 + m_{-1})$$

where m_1 is the number of positive stories (sentiment score > 50) in the past month;

m_{-1} is the number of negative stories (sentiment score < 50) in the past month.

A 150/50 long/short portfolio that longed stocks with the highest trailing positive news ratios and shorted stocks with the highest trailing negative news ratios yielded an annualized return 19.5% higher than the market return in 2007-2010. When he combined the news sentiment data with securities lending data, the excess return of the long/short portfolio increased to 29.5% a year (before trading costs and securities lending costs).

Using a similar trailing positive news ratio over the past 90 days, Hafez and Xie (2012) found that stocks in the tenth decile of positive news ratio outperformed the stocks in the first decile by 0.63% in the two days after the signal construction (0.53% on the first day and 0.1% on the second day). The two-day spreads were fairly consistent in 2001-2011. The largest spread was 1.29% in 2010 and the smallest spread was 0.41% in 2004. Such a strategy requires high turnover as the return spread between the tenth and the first decile was close to zero after the second day. Nevertheless, if investors could control the one-way trading costs below 10 bps, a portfolio that relied on the signal would have generated good returns in 2001-2011.

The success of the news sentiment signal depends on stock price moves after news releases. Stocks with positive news events are expected to rise further and stocks with negative events are expected to fall. One explanation is that positive (negative) news triggers more positive (negative) news. News agencies often pick up other agencies' breaking news and report similar stories. As more news agencies report the same story, more investors notice the news and act on the information. Another reason is that news sentiment often leads analyst revisions. Research analysts often update their analysis and revise their forecast after news releases. When a news release includes new information about a stock's fundamentals, analysts who incorporate the new information in their analysis subsequently revise their recommendations and forecasts to reflect the new information. However, the value of news sentiment does not mean that the news sentiment signal is a substitute of the analyst revision signal: although news sentiment signal and earnings revision signal are positively correlated, their correlation is usually below 0.5, which indicates both may independently add value.

As the market became more efficient, post-event drifts became smaller and the time span for the drifts became shorter as well. In recent years, the drift has mostly disappeared after a couple of days. Many investors also noticed that post-event drift was weaker or nonexistent after negative news releases. When negative news hit, investors often rushed to sell the stock. As a result, the stock price quickly incorporated bad news. When positive news hit, investors tended to be more cautious and bought the stock at a slower pace. Therefore, stock prices had stronger drifts after positive news releases.

Social Media, Blogs and Other Internet Sites

In recent years, more and more internet users have come to rely on social media, blogs and other internet sites for news instead of using traditional news outlets. In 2013, the SEC released guidance that allowed companies to use social media outlets such as Facebook and Twitter to release information as long as investors were alerted about which social media would be used. These and other changes have profound impact on how investors collect and analyze news information. The market response to a false tweet on April 23, 2013 demonstrated the power of social media. A group of hackers hacked the twitter account of the Associated Press and sent out a false message at 1:07 PM saying *"Breaking: Two Explosions in the White House and Barack Obama is Injured."* In a few minutes, the S&P 500 lost close to 1% in response to the false tweet and then recovered when the rumor was denied. The temporary loss to the US stock market was more than $150 billion. The incident demonstrates that investors closely follow Twitter and other internet news sources.

Overall, news sentiment from internet data and social media has moderate positive correlation with news sentiment from the traditional news media. The moderate positive correlation reflects some difference in the content of traditional news and internet news. Traditional media tends to focus on projected earnings, or revenues and analyst sentiment. In comparison, internet news and social media have more news items on product reviews and customer sentiment. The difference suggests that the internet data adds value beyond the traditional news media. To capture non-traditional news information, Thomson Reuters has introduced News Analytics for Internet News and Social Media. The product aggregates information from more than four million social media channels and fifty thousand news sites. Bloomberg has built functions that allow users to follow tweets of specific companies by selected authors, or to follow social velocity alerts (stocks with unusually high number of social media postings). Specialized data provider Dataminr claims that it "transforms social media streams into actionable signals, providing enterprise clients with one of the earliest warning systems for market-relevant information, noteworthy events, and emerging trends".

Amongst all the internet data, the easiest ones to test are the buy/sell recommendations on blogs and social investing websites. Social investing websites have a large community of stock pickers who share their picks or detailed views on stocks with the public. One may ask why participants would contribute their picks to social investing websites if their picks are good. After all, skilled participants receive no direct financial incentives for making good predictions. An old saying attributed to Napoleon may help explain why skilled contributors may participate in these websites: *"A soldier will fight long and hard for a bit of colored ribbon"*. People get excited about being recognized for doing a good job even if there is no monetary award. On the Motley Fool website, tens of thousands of members make their own buy/sell recommendations. Motley Fool has a CAPS system that assigns positive scores to buy (sell) recommendations that outperform (underperform) the market (S&P 500 index) and negative scores to buy (sell) recommendations that underperform (outperform) the market. The system then rates each contributor on historical accuracy. Members receive different types of CAPS depending on their ratings to recognize members with high ratings. Furthermore, members with the best scores as well as their pitches are highlighted on the website for more investors to follow. Besides recognition, many contributors also find it valuable to exchange ideas with other contributors. Since investors have different information and make different assumptions, explaining the investment thesis and defending investment decisions through discussions with other contributors often help contributors collect more information, adjust their assumptions, and make better investment decisions. Several studies confirm the value of the CAPS rating for stocks. Avery et al. (2011) tested a strategy that longed stocks with the most favorable CAPS ratings and shorted stocks with the least favorable ratings. The portfolio returned 9% a year over their test period between November 2006 and December 2008.

Unlike recommendations on social investing websites, most internet data remain unstructured and require further processing and analysis. The astounding amount of data on the web is both a challenge and an opportunity for investors. Powerful natural language processing software can scan and extract sentiment information from billions of words or sentences on the internet every day. Researchers have found positive contemporaneous correlation between public sentiment extracted from social media data and stock market returns. However, the positive correlation does not mean that the public mood influences future stock market returns. Instead, negative public sentiment may be a response to negative market returns. Evidence that public sentiment influences future market returns is not clear cut and depends on the method used to extract public sentiment. Bollen et al. (2011) analyzed daily Twitter feeds using two mood tracking tools and found that the inclusion of some public mood indicators helped predict daily Dow Jones Industry Average (DJIA) returns while others did not. In their study, a general sentiment factor extracted using OpinionFinder (a software package for sentiment analysis) did not improve the DJIA return prediction while one of the six mood dimensions extracted using GPOM (another software package that measure mood states in six dimensions, i.e., Calm, Alert, Sure, Vital, Kind and Happy), Calm, improved the DJIA return prediction.

It is difficult to extract useful information from social media for cross-sectional stock selection as well. Simple aggregation of information from internet sites and social media rarely works. Although social media sometimes releases information earlier than traditional media, the information released on social media is less reliable than the information from traditional media. There have been instances where anonymous users have used unverified accounts (or hacked verified accounts) to spread rumors on social media sites. Investors therefore need to build proper filters to reduce the number of false inputs without removing timely information. Furthermore, genuine buzzes on social media or all the "like" clicks may not translate to sales for companies. Many companies have found advertising on social media to be ineffective even though the advertisements targeted users who expressed interest. The disconnect between online words or online sentiment and real-life action makes it a difficult task to extract useful information to forecast product sales and stock returns. One reason is that web users who are active on social media may not represent a product's customer base well. Besides, as social media experienced rapid growth, user demographics have not been stationary over time. Investors who can address the differences in demographics and selectively extract high-quality relevant information can effectively use web data to forecast product sales. Since linked companies often show up in online discussions together, the ease of processing news and internet data also helps investors identify economic links that are often neglected by traditional fundamental research. Traditional economic links among different companies are defined by industry classifications or return correlations. The vast amount of data from news and the web now allows investors to identify economic links between companies that may be in unrelated industries.

Industry-Specific Factors

Since key drivers of revenue and profit of companies in different industries vary, investors look beyond standard financial ratios available across all industries and examine industry-specific factors. These industry-specific factors tend to focus on data that shed light on a company's ability to generate current and future revenues and on a company's expenses.

Case Study

A full discussion of industry-specific factors for different industries is beyond the scope of this book. In this section, we illustrate this point by taking the example of the oil and gas exploration and production (E&P) industry. A popular factor in analyzing E&P companies is the recycle ratio:

Recycle ratio = profit per barrel / total cost of discovering and extracting that barrel

Companies with higher recycle ratios have lower costs and higher profit margins. Companies with low recycle ratios are leveraged bets on oil and gas prices and are more sensitive to oil and gas price moves. E&P companies report recycle ratios in their financial statements (often in the Management Discussion and Analysis section). However, these companies have the flexibility to make accounting choices in the calculation of the recycle ratio. Therefore, the numbers from different companies may not be comparable. To address the accounting difference, data providers collect the individual cost components from the financial statements and recalculate the recycle ratio in a way that is more consistent across companies.

Another popular factor for oil & gas companies is reserves-to-production ratio:

Reserves-to-production ratio = known reserves / trailing 12-month production

The known reserves are estimated numbers. The oil and gas industry classifies reserves into three categories:

- Proved reserves (1P) are identified resources that are recoverable with a high degree of certainty based on analysis of geologic and engineering data.

- Probable reserves (2P) are reserves that are less certain to be recoverable but do have at least 50% confidence level of recovery.

- Possible reserves (3P) are reserves with at least 10% certainty of being recoverable.

Generally, only proved reserves are included in the reserves-to-production ratio calculation. Managers have some flexibility in classifying the reserves. When production costs are higher than the oil/gas price, the reserves are removed from the book. Hence, the oil/gas price influences the reserve calculation as well. Other factors such as technology advancement also have large impact on the estimation. Developments in hydraulic fracturing and horizontal drilling technologies have changed the landscape of the U.S. gas and oil production in recent years. These technologies enable E&P companies to recover natural gas and oil that were previously unrecoverable and increased proved and probable reserves. At the same time, the new supplies have had a negative impact on the prices (more on natural gas than on oil), which has put high-cost E&P companies at a disadvantage. Needless to say, detailed information on how these changes influence the recycle ratio and reserves-to-production ratio of individual companies are closely tracked by investors.

At the industry level, investors use specific reports to track the supply and demand of oil, gas, and coal. International Energy agency (IEA) releases a monthly Oil Market Report that includes a variety of information on historical, current, and 12-18 month forecast of oil supply, demand, inventory, and price moves. Energy Information Administration (EIA) releases a weekly Petroleum Status Report at 10:30 AM Eastern time on Wednesday. The report summarizes the supply, imports, exports, inventories, and refinery activity of petroleum products. Therefore, the Oil Market Report and Petroleum Status Report are tracked by investors who invest in E&P companies. EIA also releases a weekly Natural Gas Storage Report at 10:30 AM Eastern time on Thursday. The report provides an estimate of natural gas volume held in underground storage facilities at national and regional levels. Since changes in gas storage reflects the net effect of natural gas supply and usage, unexpected changes impact both natural gas futures prices and the prices of E&P companies. The Association of American Railroads (AAR) publishes a weekly traffic report of carloads of a variety of commodities such as coal, petroleum products, metals & products, iron & steel crap, lumber & wood products, and grain. Since trains are the main vehicles for long-distance shipping of coal in US, increase or decrease in demand of coal can be estimated from AAR traffic of coal over time.

Investors also closely monitor the relative prices and interactions between different energy products. As shale gas produced by hydraulic fracturing and horizontal drilling technologies caused an oversupply of natural gas, the gas price plummeted from $5.83 in January 2010 to $3.34 in December 2012 (EIA data for Henry Hub natural gas spot price). Since most of the crude oil was used to produce gasoline, diesel fuel, and jet fuel that natural gas was not a close substitute in the U.S., the natural gas price drop had limited impact on the oil price. The natural gas price drop, however, made it a competitive alternative to coal for power generation. A number of new environmental policies and regulations to control pollution and greenhouse gas emission also made coal plants more costly.[49] The electricity generated by coal decreased from 44% in 2009 to 37% in 2012 and the electricity generated by natural gas increased from 23% to 30%. Such a shift led to lower coal price and lowered the stock prices of coal companies. In 2010-2012, although SPY was up 36%, KOL (coal ETF) was down 28%.

Many industry-specific metrics are difficult and expensive to collect. By definition, industry-specific factors only apply to a small group of stocks instead of a broad universe of stocks. In other words, they have limited breadth. These limitations prevent them from being broadly adopted by investors. Nevertheless, barriers to entry make them especially

---

[49] Power generation from natural gas produces about half of the carbon dioxide, the main greenhouse gas, for each kilowatts of electricity. Therefore, power generation from natural gas has less environmental impact than power generation from coal.

valuable for informed suave investors who can afford the cost of collecting and processing the data and have the ability to act on less crowded signals.

Economies of scale play a crucial role too. Unlike retail investors, large institutional investors may invest hundreds of millions of dollars in individual stocks in which they have high conviction. Considering the dollar value invested, institutional investors are willing to spend millions of dollars on researching specific industries and the associated companies. A deep understanding of selected industries and companies gives institutional investors the necessary edge to generate alpha, which in turn covers the costs of collecting and analyzing industry-specific data.

Conclusion

In this chapter, in addition to previously described popular signals—calendar effects, economic factors, price and volume patterns, financial ratios, and sentiment indicators—we explored less familiar signals. When investors manage a large number of signals, it is important to avoid analysis paralysis. Analysis paralysis refers to an investor's inability to make a decision because the investor overanalyzes the data and is overwhelmed by different pieces of information. Instead of trying to track and incorporate all the information at the same time, successful investors dedicate their resources to focus on several key drivers at any given time. These drivers are often the key valuation assumptions where consensus is hard to reach or where investors may have a view different from the market consensus. If an investor is better at collecting and analyzing the data and reaches more accurate conclusions on key assumptions, the convergence of market consensus towards the investor's conclusions generates positive alpha.

Although the less frequently explored signals do not get arbitraged away immediately, the market inefficiency reflected in these new signals weakens over time. When one investment team identifies a new signal by exploring new data or by creative ways of extracting information from the existing data, they collect abnormal returns for a period of time. Sooner or later, other investors will begin to explore the same signal, either because they may have independently identified the signal or because members of the original investment team move to other investment firms. As a result, the signal will gradually lose some or even all of its predictive power. Therefore, active investors keep on researching new ideas in order to maintain an edge and to generate sustained alpha.

Chapter 8

Performance Measures

To compare the performance of different strategies, investors use a variety of measures to capture both historical returns and risks. In this chapter, we discuss popular performance metrics to evaluate risk-adjusted returns as well as point out their advantages and disadvantages.

Trade-Level Performance Measures

For simple market timing and technical trading strategies, investors often run trade-level analysis. Let Y be the number of years of trade history, n_w be the number of winning trades, n_l be the number of losing trades, r_w be the average gain/return of the winning trades, r_l be the average loss (absolute value) of the losing trades. A trade-level analysis produces the following performance measures:

- **Gross gain** is the total gain of the winning trades, $n_w \times r_w$.
- **Gross loss** is the total loss of the losing trades, $n_l \times r_l$.
- **Net profit** is the difference between gross profit and gross loss, $n_w \times r_w - n_l \times r_l$.
- **Percent of time in market** is the percent of time that the strategy holds either long or short positions.
- **Number of trades** is the number of round-trip trades executed over the life of the test, $n_w + n_l$.
- **Annual turnover** is the number of round-trip trades per year, $(n_w + n_l)/Y$.
- **Hit rate (% of winning trades)** is the ratio of the number of winning trades to the total number of trades, $n_w/(n_w + n_l)$.
- **Profit factor** is the ratio of the gross profit to gross loss, $(n_w \times r_w)/(n_l \times r_l)$.
- **P/L ratio**, also called **slugging ratio**, is the ratio of the average profit of the winning trades to the average loss of the losing trades, r_w/r_l.

A hit rate higher than 50% means that the majority of the trades are profitable. A slugging ratio higher than 1 means that the winning trades on average generate more profits than the losses of the losing trades. A strategy can be profitable even if its hit rate is lower than 50% as long as its slugging ratio is sufficiently high. For example, many trend following strategies with tight stop loss have lower than 50% hit rate, but the winning trades tend to be far more profitable and fully compensate the small losses of the losing trades.

Exhibit 8-1 shows performance measures of the dual time frame RSI(3) strategy that we discussed in Chapter 5. The cumulative gross gain was 304.7% and the cumulative loss was 99.3% (all the gains and losses are arithmetic sums instead of geometric returns). The profit factor is 3.07, which means the average gain is $3.07 for every dollar of loss. The strategy has a high hit rate of 65%. The slugging ratio of 1.35 indicates that on average the gain of the winning trades is higher than the loss of the losing trades. As a mean-reversion strategy, it was only in the market 13.4% of the time with 18.7 trades every year.

Exhibit 8-1 Performance measures of dual time frame RSI(3) strategy

Performance measure	Value
Gross gain	304.7%
Gross loss	99.3%
Net profit	205.4%
% of time in market	13.4%
Number of trades	355
Annual turnover	18.7
Hit rate	65%
Profit factor	3.07
Average gain of winning trades	1.32%
Average loss of losing trades	0.98%
Slugging ratio	1.35

Portfolio-Level Performance Measures

Active equity investors usually apply one or more strategies to a large number of assets in their investment universe to build a portfolio. Therefore, portfolio-level performance measures based on daily or monthly returns are used to compare different strategies and funds. Let us consider a portfolio that has T days of history with daily returns $r_1, r_2, \cdots, r_T$. A portfolio-level analysis produces the following performance measures.

- Average daily return: $\bar{r} = \dfrac{1}{T}\sum_{t=1}^{T} r_t$

- Annualized average return: $\bar{r}_y = 252 \times \dfrac{1}{T}\sum_{t=1}^{T} r_t$

- Annualized geometric return: $r_g = \left(\prod_{t=1}^{T}(1+r_i) \right)^{(252/T)} - 1$

- Daily volatility (standard deviation): $s = \sqrt{\dfrac{1}{T-1}\sum_{t=1}^{T}(r_t - \bar{r})^2}$

- Annual volatility: Under the assumption that daily returns are uncorrelated, we can add up daily variance across time to yield the annual variance and the reported annualized volatility is calculated as $s_y = \sqrt{252} \times \sqrt{\dfrac{1}{T-1}\sum_{t=1}^{T}(r_t - \bar{r})^2}$

- Maximum daily profit: $r_{max} = \max(r_1, r_2, \cdots, r_T)$
- Minimum daily profit: $r_{min} = \min(r_1, r_2, \cdots, r_T)$
- Hit rate: $\dfrac{1}{T}\sum_{t=1}^{T} I(r_t > 0)$ where $I(r_t > 0) = 1$ if $r_t > 0$ and $I(r_t > 0) = 0$ otherwise
- Gross profit: $\sum_{t=1}^{T} \left(I(r_t > 0) \times r_t \right)$
- Gross loss: $\sum_{t=1}^{T} \left(I(r_t < 0) \times |r_t| \right)$
- Average gain in up days: $\left. \sum_{t=1}^{T} \left(I(r_t > 0) \times r_t \right) \middle/ \sum_{t=1}^{T} \left(I(r_t > 0) \right) \right.$
- Average loss in down days: $\left. \sum_{t=1}^{T} \left(I(r_t < 0) \times |r_t| \right) \middle/ \sum_{t=1}^{T} \left(I(r_t < 0) \right) \right.$
- Slugging ratio: Average gain in up days / Average loss in down days
- Profit factor: Gross profit / Gross loss
- Turnover: If the portfolio weights before rebalancing is $w_t^o = (w_1^o, w_2^o, \cdots, w_N^o)'$ and the portfolio weights after the rebalancing is $w_t^n = (w_1^n, w_2^n, \cdots, w_N^n)'$, the turnover is defined as $turnover_t = \dfrac{1}{2} \times \sum_{i=1}^{N} |w_i^n - w_i^o|$

For fully invested portfolios, the total buy orders and total sell orders have approximately the same value. The total trading required for the rebalancing is twice the turnover: a portfolio with 5% daily turnover trades 10% of the gross market value of the total balance. The inverse of turnover is the holding period: the average holding period of the stocks in a portfolio with 5% daily turnover is 20 days.

When the period between portfolio rebalances is longer than the period for return measurement, we need to calculate the cumulative return of each position between rebalances. For example, some portfolios are rebalanced weekly and monthly while the returns are measured daily. For a long position held over T periods, the cumulative return, r_{long}, is the geometric return calculated from daily returns:

$$r_{long} = \left(1 + r_{long,1}\right) \times \left(1 + r_{long,2}\right) \times \cdots \times \left(1 + r_{long,T}\right) - 1$$

However, for a short position held over T periods, the cumulative return r_{short} is not the geometric return calculated from daily returns:

$$r_{short} \neq \left(1 + r_{short,1}\right) \times \left(1 + r_{short,2}\right) \times \cdots \times \left(1 + r_{short,T}\right) - 1$$

Instead, the cumulative return of the short position is the minus of the cumulative return of a long position:

$$r_{short} = -r_{long} = 1 - \left(1 + r_{long,1}\right) \times \left(1 + r_{long,2}\right) \times \cdots \times \left(1 + r_{long,T}\right)$$

Let us consider a simple example: the stock closes at day 0 at $100, goes up 10% to $110 on day 1, and then goes down 10% to $99 on day 2. The cumulative return over two days if we long the stock is $r_{long} = (1+10\%) \times (1-10\%) - 1 = -1\%$. If we short the position, the daily return is -10% on day 1 and 10% on day 2. The geometric return calculated from daily returns is $(1-10\%) \times (1+10\%) - 1 = -1\%$. The correct cumulative return for the short position is +1% as the price dropped $1 from the initial price of $100.

Sharpe Ratio and Information Ratio

Sharpe ratio and information ratio are by far the most widely used risk-adjusted performance measures. Sharpe ratio is defined as

$$S = \frac{E[\alpha]}{\sigma_\alpha} = \frac{E[r - r_f]}{\sqrt{\text{var}(r - r_f)}},$$

where r is the portfolio return;

r_f is the return of a risk-free asset;

$\alpha = r - r_f$ is the excess return over the risk-free rate;

$E[\alpha] = E[r - r_f]$ is the expected value of the excess return;

$\sigma_\alpha = \sqrt{\text{var}(r - r_f)}$ is the standard deviation of the excess return.

Information ratio replaces the risk-free asset with any selected benchmark:

$$IR = \frac{E[\alpha]}{\sigma_\alpha} = \frac{E[r - r_b]}{\sqrt{\text{var}(r - r_b)}},$$

where $E[\alpha] = E[r - r_b]$ is the expected value of the excess return over the benchmark;

σ_a, **tracking error** or **active risk**, is the standard deviation of the excess return.

Because of its flexibility in benchmark selection, the information ratio is a more versatile measure. For example, many US active long-only mutual funds use the S&P 500 index as their benchmark. For cash-neutral (equal dollar values invested in longs and shorts) hedge funds, the benchmark return is often zero since the portfolio is theoretically self-financed: the proceeds from the shorts can be used to purchase the longs.

The information ratio is not a dimensionless ratio. A good estimation of expected alpha over multiple periods is that the expected alpha grows linearly with the number of periods, T. If we assume that returns are not correlated from period to period, variance σ_α^2 is additive across time: the variance grows linearly with T and the standard deviation grows linearly with the square root of T. Therefore, the IR grows linearly with the square root of T. Although excess returns and its standard deviation are usually measured daily or monthly, the reported information ratios are usually annualized numbers. Monthly and daily information ratios are converted to annualized information ratio using the following equation:

$$IR_{annual} = \sqrt{12} \times IR_{monthly} = \sqrt{252} \times IR_{daily}$$

where $IR_{monthly} = E[\alpha_{monthly}]/\sigma_{monthly}$ and $IR_{daily} = E[\alpha_{daily}]/\sigma_{daily}$.

Since there are 252 trading days in a year, an annualized information ratio of 1 means a daily information ratio of $1/\sqrt{252} \approx 0.063$.

When investors receive a historical track record of a portfolio manager or of a strategy, a natural question to ask is whether the information ratio estimated from the historical excess returns is statistically significantly different from 0. In other words, does a fund manager have skills judging from the track record? Many investors use a simple *t*-statistic to establish the statistical significance of the information ratio using historical daily or monthly excess returns:

$$t = \frac{\overline{\alpha}}{\text{standard error of } \alpha} = \frac{\overline{\alpha}}{\hat{\sigma}_{\alpha}/\sqrt{T-1}} = \frac{\overline{\alpha}}{\hat{\sigma}_{\alpha}} \times \sqrt{T-1} = \overline{IR} \times \sqrt{T-1}$$

where $\overline{\alpha}$ is the mean of historical excess returns, $\overline{\alpha} = \frac{1}{T}\sum_{t=1}^{T}\alpha_t$;

$\hat{\sigma}_{\alpha}$ is standard deviation of excess returns, $\hat{\sigma}_{\alpha}^2 = \frac{1}{T-1}\sum_{t=1}^{T}(\alpha_t - \overline{\alpha})^2$;

$\overline{IR}$ is the estimated information ratio, $\overline{IR} = \overline{\alpha}/\hat{\sigma}_{\alpha}$.

If the daily excess returns α_t $(t = 1, 2, \cdots, T)$ are independent draws from a normal distribution with expected excess return α and standard deviation σ, we can use the following asymptotic distribution (Jobson & Korkie, 1981):

$$\overline{IR} = \frac{\overline{\alpha}}{\hat{\sigma}_{\alpha}} \sim N\left(\frac{\alpha}{\sigma_{\alpha}}, \frac{1}{T}\left\{1 + \frac{\alpha^2}{2\sigma_{\alpha}^2}\right\}\right) = N\left(IR, \frac{1}{T}(1 + 0.5 \times IR^2)\right),$$

where IR is the true daily information ratio.

In other words, information ratio estimated from historical excess returns follows a normal distribution with mean = IR and variance = $\frac{1}{T}(1 + 0.5 \times IR^2)$. The asymptotic z-score of $\overline{IR}$ is $z = \sqrt{T} \times \dfrac{\overline{IR}}{\sqrt{1 + 0.5 \times \overline{IR}^2}}$

Since the z-score for 95% confidence interval is 1.96, we need $\dfrac{1.96^2 \times (1 + 0.5 \times \overline{IR}^2)}{\overline{IR}^2}$ days to reject the null hypothesis that the information ratio is 0 at 95% confidence level. Naturally, the higher the information ratio, the fewer days we need to show such statistical significance. When the annualized IR is 0.5 (daily IR is 0.0315), we need 3875 trading days (15.4 years); when the IR is 1, we need 970 days (3.8 years); when the IR is 3, we only need 110 days (5 months). In other words, if a manager has extremely good skills and achieves an IR of 3, he needs less than half a year's history to demonstrate his skill. In practice, we need to be more cautious and take market conditions into consideration. Many strategies can perform well for a period of time in a certain market regime. For example, SPY had a Sharpe ratio of 4.2 in the half year between September 2010 and February 2011 and a Sharpe ratio of 2.0 in the two years after the market bottomed on March 9, 2009. If we had used a short history of SPY and had taken the Sharpe ratio at its face value, any index manager would have been classified as a skilled active manager.

A criticism about the information ratio lies in its risk measure—standard deviation. Since returns, especially hedge fund returns, do not follow normal distributions, the use of standard deviation may underestimate the risk and overestimate risk-adjusted performance. Skewness and kurtosis capture the tail risks of the returns distribution. Skewness measures the asymmetry of excess returns around the mean. A negatively skewed distribution has a heavier left tail (more large losses) than the right tail (fewer large gains) and a positively skewed distribution has a heavier right tail than the left tail. Kurtosis measures whether the tails are heavier (more large losses or gains) than a normal distribution. To address the problem, Mertens (2002) suggested a variance measure for IR that directly incorporates the skewness or the kurtosis of the return distribution. If the excess returns are not normally distributed, the variance of IR can be estimated as

$$\text{var}(IR) = \frac{1}{T}\left(1 + 0.5 \times IR^2 - \gamma_3 IR + \frac{\gamma_4 - 3}{4} IR^2\right),$$

where $\gamma_3 = E[(\alpha - \bar{\alpha})^3]/\sigma_\alpha^3$ is the skewness estimated from historical returns;

$\gamma_4 = E[(\alpha - \bar{\alpha})^4]/\sigma_\alpha^4$ is the kurtosis estimated from historical returns.

The skewness of a normal distribution is 0 and the kurtosis is 3: a return distribution with negative (positive) skewness has a heavier left (right) tail and a return distribution with kurtosis larger than 3 has fatter tails than a normal distribution. For strategies with negative skewness and high kurtosis, the variance of IR is significantly higher than a normal distribution. So the asymptotic z-score is smaller than a normal distribution and it takes longer time to establish the manager skill.

Other Risk-Adjusted Performance Measures

Besides the information ratio, there are other risk-adjusted performance measures that use risk measures different from the standard deviation. The alternative risk measure that has received the most attention is Value at risk (VaR) since it summarizes the risk to a single number. In the Financial Risk Manager Handbook,[50] VaR is defined as the maximum loss over a target horizon such that there is a low, pre-specified probability that the actual loss will be larger. Given a confidence level $a \in (0, 1)$, the VaR can be implicitly defined as

$$a = \int_{-VaR}^{\infty} f(x)dx,$$

---

[50] *Financial Risk Manager Handbook* by Phillippe Jorion is a comprehensive book covering different aspects of risk management. A classic book for VaR is *Value at Risk*, also by Philippe Jorion.

where x is the dollar profit (loss) or portfolio return;

$f(x)$ is its probability density function of x.

In practice, a is often set to 95% or 99%. Mathematically, it is simply the (negative) fifth or the first percentile of the profit distribution.

VaR is recommended by the Basel Committee on Banking Supervision—a committee that makes recommendations on banking laws and regulations—as a preferred approach for market risk and now widely adopted by banks. Nevertheless, for equity investors, the value that it adds beyond standard deviation is often limited. Many investors use multivariate normal distribution to model portfolio returns, in which case the VaR is equal to dollar-valued standard deviation times a constant. If VaR is simply reported as 2.33 (99% one-tail normal distribution z-score) times of standard deviation, it clearly adds no value beyond standard deviation. To incorporate the non-normality of returns, a different approach uses historical returns to estimate VaR. But we often run into sample size issues when we estimate tail risk. Let us consider VaR at a one-week horizon. Even with 10 years of history, we have only 521 weeks of independent data points and the 99% VaR is determined by five data points on the left tail.

As a percentile-based measure on the profit distribution, VaR does not depend on the shape of the tails before probability $1-\alpha$, so it does not describe the loss on the left tail. When the profit/loss distribution is far from a normal distribution, as in the cases of many strategies, the tail portion has a large impact on the risk, and VaR often does not reflect the real risk.[51] For example, consider a short position in a credit default swap. The underlying asset is bond A with a $1 million notional value. Let us further assume that A has a 3% default probability and the loss given default is 100% (no recovery). Clearly we are facing the credit risk of bond A. Yet if we use 95% confidence level, VaR(A) = 0 since the probability of default is less than 5%.

Furthermore, VaR is not sub-additive and is not a coherent measure of risk: when we combine two positions A and B to form a portfolio C, we do not always have VaR(C) ≤ VaR(A) + VaR(B). For example, let us add a short position in a credit default swap on bond B with a $1 million notional value. Let us assume that B also has a 3% default probability that is independent of A and the loss given default is 100%. Again we have VaR(B) = 0. When A and B form a portfolio C, the probability that at least one bond will default becomes

$$1 - (1 - 3\%) \times (1 - 3\%) \approx 5.9\%$$

So VaR(C) = $1M > VaR(A) + VaR(B). Lack of sub-additivity directly contradicts the intuitive idea that diversification reduces risk. So, we can see from this example that this is a theoretical drawback of VaR.

Conditional value at risk (CVaR) measures the average loss when the loss is at least as large as the value at risk. Unlike VaR, CVaR is sub-additive: when we combine two position A and B to form a portfolio C, we always have CVaR(C) ≤ CVaR(A) + CVaR(B). Therefore, it captures the diversification benefit and directly measures the left-tail risk of a portfolio. We can calculate a **conditional Sharpe ratio** by replacing the standard deviation with CVaR:

$$\text{Conditional Sharpe ratio} = \frac{E[\alpha]}{\text{CVaR of } \alpha}$$

Agarwal and Naik (2004) showed that many hedge fund strategies had significant tail losses as their return distributions were negatively skewed. The traditional mean-variance framework underestimated the tail losses and led to suboptimal returns. When they replaced the mean-variance framework with the mean-conditional-value-at-risk frame, they got higher long-term returns and lower long-term volatility for the hedge fund indices they tested.

Besides CVaR, investors also use other risk measures that focus on the downside risk. **Sortino ratio** replaces the standard deviation, the square root of variance, with the downside deviation:

$$\text{Sortino ratio} = \frac{E[\alpha] - MAR}{\text{Downside deviation}},$$

where MAR is the minimum acceptable return (e.g. zero return or risk-free return);

$N(\alpha < MAR)$ is the number of periods with alpha less than MAR;

$$\text{Downside deviation} = \sqrt{\frac{1}{N(\alpha < MAR)} \times \sum_{t=1}^{T} \left(\min(\alpha - MAR, 0)^2\right)}. \text{[52]}$$

Downside deviation measures the dispersion of all observations that are below the minimum acceptable return. Supporters of the Sortino ratio argue that it is a better risk measure as upside volatility is not risky. It is the downside volatility that investors truly care about. For return distributions with equal mean and variance, a distribution with negative skewness tends to have higher semivariance than a distribution with positive skewness. Therefore, Sortino ratio implicitly includes higher moments in the calculation. Although Sortino ratio is sometimes reported to get a comprehensive view on the portfolio performance, it is seldom used in portfolio construction. There is no computationally efficient method to include semivariance in portfolio optimization as there is no easy approach to aggregate downside deviation across assets.

Calmar ratio replaces the standard deviation with the maximum drawdown as the risk measure:

$$\text{Calmer ratio} = \frac{E[\alpha]}{\text{Maximum drawdown}}$$

Peak-to-trough **drawdown** measures cumulative loss from the peak of the equity value before a date to the equity value at that date. It is a measure investors follow closely since it indicates the maximum loss a strategy may suffer before recovering. **Maximum drawdown** is the maximum loss an investor faces if he had invested at the fund's maximum equity value and sold at the minimum, so it represents the historical maximum loss an investor may suffer. Drawdown and maximum drawdown are often complementary risk measures to standard deviation. Drawdown reflects both negative tail

---

[52] Some investors directly use total number of periods, T, as the denominator in downside deviation calculation.

returns and autocorrelation of negative returns (consecutive losses over multiple periods), so it is a nonparametric measure of downside risk. Another risk measure related to drawdown is **drawdown duration**. Drawdown duration is the duration between the start of a drawdown to the time a new equity peak is reached. In other words, if an investor puts money in at the beginning of the drawdown, how long must he wait to get back his initial investment. If the drawdown duration is long, investors may not have the patience to wait for a fund to recover after poor performance. Since drawdown relies on real or simulated historical return data, it has its limitation. If the history does not include a crisis period that the fund is likely to experience in the future, just looking at historical drawdown may underestimate the risk. For example, when the 2008 financial crisis hit, many hedge funds suffered far higher drawdowns than their historical maximum losses.

Although performance measures using alternative risk measures are complementary to the information ratio, the information ratio is still the gold standard for equity portfolio managers. It is a simple and intuitive measure capturing risk-adjusted returns. Research done by Martin Eling (2008) showed that Sharpe Ratio yielded similar rank ordering of different funds as many other performance measures that used either higher moments or value-at-risk measures. More importantly, using standard deviation (variance) as the risk measure has laid the foundation for mean-variance portfolio optimization, something widely used for portfolio construction.

Leverage

The ultimate goal of investors is to achieve superior risk-adjusted absolute return. That raises the question whether the information ratio is more important than just raw returns when we compare different strategies. After all, a less volatile strategy with a high information ratio may have low expected return. A reason for using the information ratio is to compare strategies when those with low expected absolute return and high information ratio may be leveraged. For equity investments, leverage is defined as the gross exposure—the sum of the absolute value of the long exposures and short exposures—divided by the capital.[53] Many equity funds and individual investors use leverage to boost absolute returns. Besides the typical buying and shorting of securities on margin, investors can also add portfolio leverage by utilizing futures, options, or swaps. If the return on the gross exposure is higher than the borrowing cost, investors achieve higher return through leverage. On the other hand, if the return on the gross exposure is lower than the borrowing cost, the loss is magnified as well.

A proper level of leverage can help investors boost long-term returns. The Kelly criterion provides a theoretical framework to estimate the optimal leverage ratio. The goal of the Kelly criterion is to maximize the long-term geometric return of capital. The original Kelly criterion was developed for binary bets. Let p be the probability of winning a bet, q = $1 - p$ be the probability of losing the bet, and b be the net odds received on the wager (you receive \$b if you wage \$1 and win), the optimal fraction of the current capital to bet is

---

[53] Although the definition of leverage is the gross exposure divided by the capital, some long/short cash-neutral portfolio managers only use one-side exposure to calculate leverage. When \$1 of capital is used to support a portfolio with \$3 long positions and \$3 short positions, they calculate the leverage as 3 instead of 6.

$$f* = \frac{bp - q}{b} = p - \frac{q}{b}$$

The intuition behind the equation is clear: p is the long-term hit rate and b is the slugging ratio. We increase the bet if the hit rate increases or if the slugging ratio increases. If the bet is a sure bet with p close to 1, the optimal fraction is also close to 1.

For a strategy with continuous return distributions, if the returns follow a lognormal distribution with expected return α and standard deviation σ, the Kelly formula for optimal leverage ratio is

$$f* = \alpha / \sigma^2$$

To put the recommended number in perspective, if a long/short portfolio has expected annual return of 5% and standard deviation of 5% (it represents a good portfolio manager with information ratio = 1), the calculated optimal leverage is 20. Clearly such leverage is much higher than the leverage employed in typical funds. The unrealistic assumption behind the Kelly formula explains the lower leverage used in practice. Both the expected alpha and the variance are estimates: the true alpha may be lower and the variance may be higher. Furthermore, the realized standard deviation is actually time-dependent, which means during certain periods the alpha is much lower and the standard deviation is much higher than the long-term average. Besides, strategy returns rarely follow log normal distribution: they usually have fat tails and many are negatively skewed. The Kelly formula also assumes that the portfolio can be adjusted continuously without incurring any trading costs. In practice, even actively managed funds only rebalance their portfolios periodically and face trading costs. To mitigate the problem caused by the assumptions in the Kelly formula, half Kelly—leverage that is half of what Kelly formula recommends— or lower is often adopted. Another ad-hoc approach is to take the volatility of volatility into consideration. For example, instead of using the estimated volatility σ in the denominator, Cooper (2010) recommended replacing it with volatility plus twice the standard deviation of volatility, which he called extreme volatility (EV).

Considering the limit of theory in determining leverage, how do investors determine leverage in practice? The determination often involves two aspects. The maximum leverage is set by brokers. For individual investors, brokers usually use simple rules. For example, Federal Reserve Regulation T allows investors to borrow up to 50% of the purchase price of the underlying security. For hedge funds, prime brokers often use risk-based analysis to determine the maximum leverage. A common approach is to stress test the underlying portfolio using a number of extreme scenarios and to calculate the maximum potential loss before the portfolio can be liquidated. For brokers, the overall goal of these tests is to fully recoup the financing they provide should the underlying portfolio suffer losses. Although many such processes are model driven, the inputs to the model, often selected by using old fashioned human judgment, have a large impact on the margin requirement. Before the 2008 financial crisis, prime brokers often allowed 10-to-1 leverage on long/short market-neutral funds. As the crisis unfolded, model inputs were changed and margin requirements were raised. As the crisis subsided, margin requirements were lowered on account of business pressure: If one prime broker does not provide the leverage that a hedge fund needs and another does, the hedge fund can always move its portfolio to the other broker. Besides, prime brokers also make profits through interest rate spread by providing financing. That said, the prime brokers now maintain tighter capital requirements than they did before the financial crisis. Although the market volatility has dropped to pre-crisis level, the margin requirements have stayed above the pre-crisis level.

Within the boundary set by brokers, fund managers determine the level of leverage using a combination of expected return, risk estimation and investors' risk tolerance. On the return side, typical quantitative hedge funds have less than 5% expected alpha on their holdings and fundamental funds have less than 8% expected alpha. To generate sufficient absolute returns in the 10-20% range after management and incentive fees, a leverage ratio of 2 to 6 is often needed. On the risk side, lower risk strategies can be leveraged higher. Because of non-normality of returns, maximum drawdown instead of standard deviation often plays a larger role in determining the level of leverage. For a hedge fund, a loss of 20% may trigger redemptions and investor capital withdrawal. In practical cases the rule of thumb is to control the leverage below 3 if the maximum drawdown before leverage is 7%.

Conclusion

In this chapter, we discussed a variety of trade-level and portfolio-level performance measures with a focus on the advantages and disadvantages of the information ratio. The information ratio is a popular risk-adjusted return measure that captures the trade-off between risk and returns. Conditional Sharpe ratio, Sortino ratio, and Calmar ratio use alternative risk measures to capture the downside tail risk of strategies and complement the information ratio in evaluating portfolio performance. These performance measures help fund managers determine the amount of portfolio leverage. As we will discuss in the chapter on Portfolio Construction and Risk Management, these risk-adjusted return measures also help fund managers combine different pieces of information to build better portfolios.

Chapter 9

Signal Construction and Testing

Investors explore stock selection signals in a variety of ways. Individual investors tend to take a qualitative approach by using stock selection signals as filters. Brokers and financial websites provide screening tools for investors to identify stocks that fit certain stock selection criteria; price-to-earnings ratios, dividend yield, growth rates, and analyst recommendation are popular choices for stock screeners. A casual examination of the P/E ratio and the PEG ratio can also help individual investors avoid overhyped stocks or becoming victims of the pump and dump scheme—a scheme that market manipulators use to inflate the price of a stock they own by making misleading or even false statements to other investors so that they can sell the stock at a higher price. Professional fundamental stock pickers routinely compare a variety of financial ratios to peers in order to make buy or sell recommendations. Fundamental financial analysts also build Excel spreadsheet models to estimate the value of stocks using detailed forecasts of revenues and costs as inputs. Quantitative portfolio managers apply a more systematic approach to extract value out of signals. To analyze a potential factor, researchers use statistical tests to evaluate a factor's predictive power and investigate the best way to construct the signal. In this chapter, we will focus on systematic approaches to constructing and testing stock selection signals.

Factor Score

A raw factor such as inventory turnover has little meaning unless we compare it to inventory turnovers of other companies, or the company's own historical average. The first step in systematic signal construction is to convert raw factors to factor scores. These measure the factors comparatively, or to their own history and provide further insight.

Factor Z-Scores

Cross-sectional factor z-scores standardize raw factors by removing the mean of all stocks in the investment universe and dividing the result by the cross-sectional standard deviation of raw factors. Since the estimation of the mean and the standard deviation may be heavily influenced by outliers and potential data errors, extreme outliers are often trimmed or Winsorized in the estimation. Trimming simply removes outliers. The outliers are not included in the estimation of the mean (or the standard deviation) and the z-scores of these outliers are set to 0. Winsorization sets all outliers to specified percentiles of the data. For example, a 98% Winsorization sets all data points below the 1st percentile to the value of the 1st percentile and sets all data points above the 99th percentile to the value of the 99th percentile. Then we estimate the mean and the standard deviation using the Winsorized data and calculate the cross-sectional z-scores:

$$z_{i,t} = \frac{x_{i,t} - \bar{x}_t}{\hat{\sigma}_t}$$

where $z_{i,t}$ is the z-score for stock i at t;

$x_{i,t}$ is the Winsorized raw factor value for stock i at t;

$\bar{x}_t$ is the mean of the Winsorized raw factor values of all the stocks in the universe;

$\hat{\sigma}_t$ is the standard deviation of the Winsorized raw factor values.

It is also common practice to further Winsorize the z-scores if the final portfolio position sizes are proportional to the z-scores. The choice to Winsorize, or to trim the outliers depends largely on the source and behavior of outliers. Outliers that are likely caused by data error are usually trimmed. For some factors, stocks with extreme factor exposures behave similarly to others in the top or bottom decile of factor exposures; for others, they behave quite differently. For example, stocks with an extremely high historical earnings yield— i.e., a very higher E/P ratio—often have earnings that may not reflect future earnings power. These high earnings may be on account of one-time events such as the sale of a valuable division. As a result, such stocks tend to underperform the market. In this case, trimming outliers and assigning zero z-scores to these stocks are reasonable choices. However, trimming the z-score causes the final scores to be a discontinuous function of the original z-scores. If ± 3 is used as the threshold, a stock's final z-score will move from 2.99 to 0 when the original z-score moves from 2.99 to 3.01. Such discontinuity around thresholds is questionable and increases the factor turnover. To address the problem, we may introduce a transformation to gradually reduce the transformed z-scores to zero as the absolute values of the original z-scores become large. Exhibit 9-1 shows such a smoothed z-score transformation. As the raw z-score increases from 2 to 4, the transformed z-score is gradually reduced from 2 to 0.

Exhibit 9-1 Smoothed z-score transformation

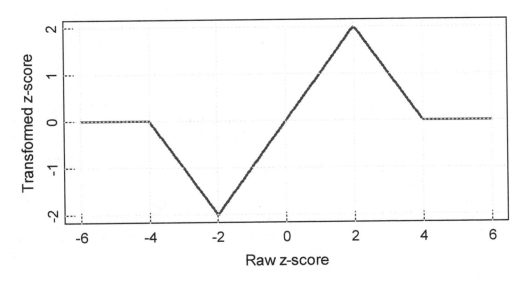

Besides cross-sectional z-scores, **time series z-scores** are used to compare a factor with its own historical average (equilibrium values). For time series z-scores, the mean $\bar{x}_t$ is the average of historic raw factor values of the same stock and $\hat{\sigma}_t$ is the standard deviation of historical values. For example, we use time series z-scores to compare a company's current asset turnover relative to its long term average. If the current value is above the average, it means that the company is more efficient at managing its assets to generate revenues.

When the distribution of raw scores is far from a normal distribution, Winsorization itself may not be sufficient. If we directly calculate z-scores from highly skewed raw scores, the z-scores will be skewed as well. To address the problem, we can transform the raw factors prior to the z-score calculation. For example, the standard measure of company size, market cap, is positively skewed because of a few mega-cap stocks. As demonstrated in Exhibit 9-2, if we directly calculate z-scores using the market caps of the Russell 3000 stocks, even with Winsorization, most of the stocks have negative z-scores that are close to 0 and the mega-cap stocks have z-scores close to 10. Since the factor return is dominated by outliers with huge z-scores, such z-scores carry little information. When we transform raw signals by taking the logarithm of the market caps and then calculate the z-scores using the transformed data, the new z-scores have a much better distribution than the z-scores calculated using market caps directly.

Exhibit 9-2 Transformation of raw scores before z-score calculation

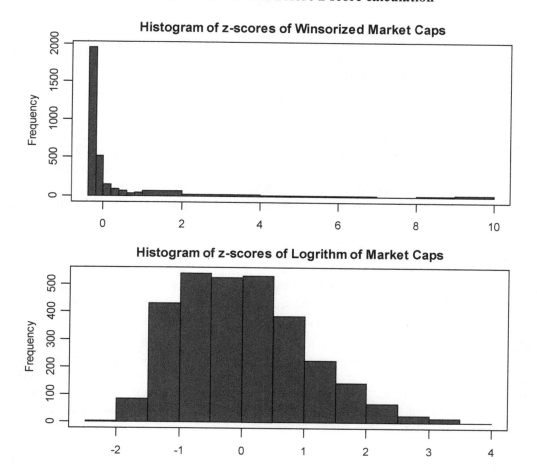

The logarithmic transformation is a special case of the generalized Box-Cox transformation:

$$y_{i,t} = \begin{cases} \left[(x_{i,t} + \delta)^{\lambda} - 1\right]/\lambda, & \text{if } \lambda \neq 0 \\ \ln(x_{i,t} + \delta), & \text{if } \lambda = 0 \end{cases}$$

where λ is a power parameter and δ is a shift parameter to keep all $x_{i,t} + \delta > 0$.

Such transformation preserves the ranks of the raw scores as higher raw scores always lead to higher transformed scores. For financial data, we often choose λ between 0 and 1 to shrink outliers. Theoretically, both λ and δ can be "optimized" using raw scores to make the transformed scores close to data from a normal distribution. Nevertheless, we need to be cautious about such an optimization since the distribution of raw data may not be stationary. For instance, many firms have large negative earnings yields during a recession and far fewer have negative earnings yields during an expansion. The parameters fitted using earnings data from a recession will no longer be a good choice during an expansion. In practice, the transformation involves a careful examination— often visually—of the historical data and to make an intuitive transformation, instead of a transformation based purely on mathematical optimization.

A simpler transformation incorporates only the ranks of the raw scores:

$$y_{i,t} = \text{rank of } x_{i,t} \text{ in } x_{1,t}, x_{2,t}, \ldots, x_{N,t}$$

For tied values, the average rank is used as the transformed value. We can calculate z-scores by subtracting the mean rank from $y_{i,t}$ and then dividing the de-meaned ranks by the standard deviation of the ranks. Since $y_{i,t}/(N+1)$ are uniformly distributed numbers between 0 and 1, if we treat $y_{i,t}/(N+1)$ as the cumulative distribution function (cdf) and take the inverse cdf for the standard normal distribution, we get different z-scores. For example, if a stock's score ranks 2500 among 3000 stocks, the cdf value is 2500/3001. If we take the inverse cdf, we get its z-score 0.966 (for a normal distribution with mean = 0 and standard deviation = 1, there is 2500/3001 probability that a random variable x from the distribution has a value lower than 0.966). As shown in Exhibit 9-3, the z-scores for the top and bottom ranks are amplified in the reverse cdf approach than the z-scores calculated by standardizing the ranks. If a small percentage of stocks with top and bottom raw scores drive the signal performance, the reverse cdf approach is a better choice. The drawback of using ranks is that some information is lost in the conversion from raw scores to ranks. If the scales of the raw scores have information beyond the ranks, z-scores calculated from the ranks are less efficient and may have less forecasting power.

Although z-score is a popular choice for normalizing raw signals, it is not the only choice. The key to factor scoring is to convert raw factor values to scores that reflect expected returns. Many signals work best at the tails, e.g., signals in the top and bottom two deciles. For example, for changes in shares outstanding signals, we only observe significant changes in shares outstanding for stocks in the top and bottom deciles and the rest of the changes may be noise. Indeed, the signal performs better in these two deciles. Instead of z-scores, we can adopt a variety of transformations to better reflect the relationship between raw signals and expected returns. Exhibit 9-4 shows one such approach: the transformed scores remain at 0 when the raw signals are between the 20th and the 80th percentiles; raw factors in the top quintile (large decrease in shares outstanding) have positive scores; raw factors in the bottom quintile (large increase in shares outstanding) have negative scores. Other factors may indicate that stocks with both positive and negative extreme values have lower expected returns. For example, for the capital expenditure ratio, stocks with excessive overinvestment or underinvestment both are likely to have negative expected returns. For such signals, we can assign positive scores to stocks in the middle quantiles and negative scores to stocks in the top and bottom quantiles.

Exhibit 9-3 z-scores from ranks

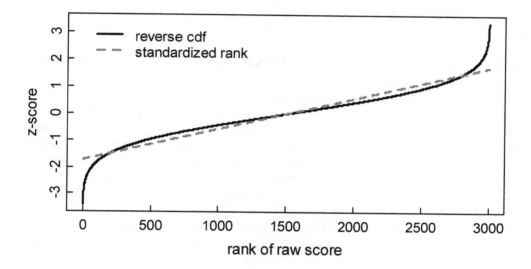

Exhibit 9-4 Transformed scores from signal percentiles

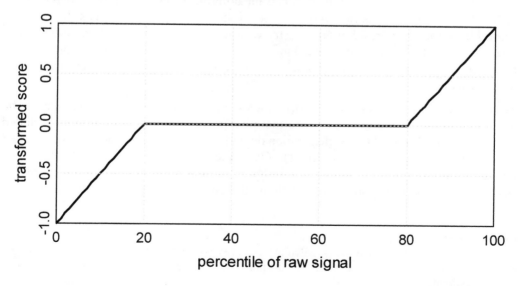

Neutralization

Since business models, profit drivers, and growth potentials vary for different industries, the average z-scores tend to be different among industries as well. Instead of removing the mean of all stocks in the investment universe, we can use industry-neutral z-scores[54] for some factors:

$$\widetilde{z}_{i,t} = z_{i,t} - \overline{z}_{K,t}$$

where $\widetilde{z}_{i,t}$ is industry-neutral z-score of stock i at t; stock i is a member of the K-th industry; $\overline{z}_{K,t}$ is the weighted average z-score of all stocks in the K-th industry:

$$\overline{z}_{K,t} = \left(\sum_{i\in K} z_{i,t} w_{i,t}\right) \bigg/ \left(\sum_{i\in K} w_{i,t}\right)$$

If we assign equal weights to all stocks in the group, $\overline{z}_{K,t}$ becomes the simple average. Equal weights ignore market values of the stocks. In other words, it treats each stock included in the universe equally: a small-cap $300 million stock is treated the same as a mega-cap $300 billion stock. In practice, investors generally believe that large-cap stocks better represent their corresponding industries and should be given higher weights. Besides, many funds put higher weights on large-cap stocks for liquidity reasons. Nevertheless, weighting by market cap may be suboptimal, since a few mega-cap stocks in a group may dominate the weighted average. Active funds are unlikely to invest in a group of selected stocks with weights proportional to their market caps since such a portfolio does not have optimal alpha and has significant exposure to the idiosyncratic risks of mega-cap stocks. We can adopt different weighting schemes that increase the weights of large-cap stocks but reduce the concentrated weights in mega-cap stocks. One popular choice is to use square roots of the market caps as the weights.

For US stocks, grouping by 10 GICS sectors or 24 industry groups yields a sufficient number of stocks in each group to produce meaningful average z-scores. At the GICS industry level, some industries have an insufficient number of stocks to produce meaningful average z-scores. For an industry with few stocks or high asset concentrations, we can incorporate the weighted average z-score of its parent industry group into the industry average. For multi-country stock selection models, factors are often neutralized by country as well.

How do we decide whether to neutralize factor z-scores by industry or country? The general answer is that we should choose the most parsimonious model unless the added complexity of neutralization has clear rationale and yields significant better risk-adjusted returns (higher returns or lower risks). Over the past decade, some of the more quantitative investors have adopted industry neutralization because of the growing popularity of standard industry classifications, the growth of sector ETFs/funds, and the

---

[54] A different approach is to directly calculate z-scores sector by sector using the raw scores instead of removing the industry mean. That approach may add no benefit since the standard deviations estimated from individual industries often become less stable with fewer stocks used in the estimations.

wide usage of factor risk models. For example, an investor may build one model for industry selection and another model to pick stocks within individual industries.

Conditional Factors

In some cases, the z-scores are further adjusted using other stock characteristics (conditioners). The goal of conditional factors is to refine the z-scores to make the final scores better correlated with expected returns. Conditioners should only be added if they are theoretically sound and supported by strong empirical evidence. Let us consider the following theory: when a stock's momentum is exhausted, the stock return volatility should increase as bulls and bears battle to control the direction of the stock price. If the theory is true, we would expect that the momentum signal would work less well on stocks that have had recent volatility higher than their historical volatility. Indeed, the theory is confirmed by the observation that the momentum factor has less predictive power when a stock's recent idiosyncratic risk is significantly higher than its historical risk. To incorporate such an observation into the z-score calculation, we can introduce a time series risk ratio:

$$tratio_{i,t} = \frac{IVOL_{i,t}(1M)}{IVOL_{i,t}(12M)}$$

where $tratio_{i,t}$ is the time series risk ratio for stock i at t;

$IVOL_{i,t}(1M)$ is the idiosyncratic risk estimated using one month of daily returns;

$IVOL_{i,t}(12M)$ is the idiosyncratic risk estimated using 12 month of daily returns.

When recent idiosyncratic risk is higher, the time series risk ratio is higher than 1 and we want to reduce the scale of momentum z-score. To achieve that, we can introduce a weight transfer function to adjust the z-score:

$$\tilde{z}_{i,t} = z_{i,t} \times w_{i,t} = z_{i,t} \times \frac{1}{1 + a \times \exp(b \times (tratio_{i,t} - 1))}$$

where $\tilde{z}_{i,t}$ is the adjusted momentum z-score;

$z_{i,t}$ is the raw momentum z-score;

$w_{i,t} = \dfrac{1}{1 + a \times \exp(b \times (tratio_{i,t} - 1))}$ is the weight transfer function.

The weight transfer function is shown in Exhibit 9-5 if we set $a = 0.1$ and $b = 6$. It clearly demonstrates that the weight is close to 1 when the time series risk ratio is less than 1 and the weight quickly drops towards 0 when the time series risk ratio rises above 1.

Exhibit 9-5 Weight transfer function

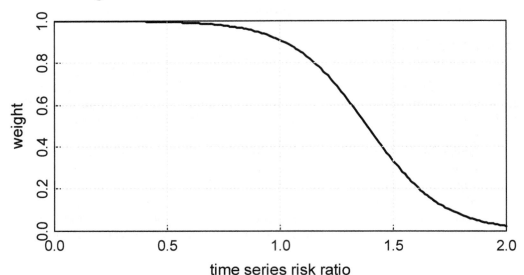

Da et al. (2011) proposed a " frog-in-the-pan" hypothesis to explain the momentum signal: investors underreact to information arriving continuously in small amounts than to discrete information. To test this hypothesis, they introduced an information discreteness (ID) measure:

$$ID = sign(PRET) \times (\%neg - \%pos)$$

where *PRET* is the total return of the signal formation period;

sign(*PRET*) = 1 if PRET > 0, 0 if PRET = 0, and -1 if PRET < 0;

%neg and *%pos* are the percentage of negative return days and positive return days during the formation period.

Large positive ID values indicate more discrete information and negative ID values indicate more continuous information. For example, if a stock has positive total return but has more negative return days than positive return days, it means that a small number of positive returns are likely to contain jumps to make the cumulative return positive. These jumps indicate that the total return is mainly driven by discrete information and the ID value is large. They found that six-month forward return of a typical 12M-1M momentum signal decreased monotonically from 8.86% for stocks with continuous information (low IDs) to 2.91% for stocks with discrete information (high IDs). Therefore, we can also incorporate the ID measure as a conditioner to shrink the original z-scores if ID values are large.

Evaluation of a Single Factor

Having extracted factor scores from raw factors, two approaches may be used to evaluate the performance of the factor scores:

1. Information coefficient: This approach measures the correlation between factor scores and realized future returns.

2. Hedged portfolio return: This approach measures the performance of a long/short cash-neutral portfolio with asset weights determined by factor scores.

In addition, we need to analyze the turnover and the information decay of factor scores, as factors with high turnover and fast information decay require more portfolio rebalancing and incur higher trading costs.

Return Measures

Stock returns are the standard choice in evaluating factor performance. To calculate returns, we need to make two choices.

First we need to decide which time horizon is to use to calculate returns. The horizon depends on the frequency of factor updates and the frequency of portfolio rebalances. In most cases, the decision comes naturally. For a portfolio that is only rebalanced weekly, weekly returns are better choices than daily returns. If we implement a statistical arbitrage strategy that uses a short-term mean version signal, and on average hold a position for 3-5 days, daily returns or intraday returns are better choices.

Second we need to decide whether to use raw returns or risk-adjusted residual returns. This choice has no clear answer. If we use raw returns, the predictive power of a factor may be influenced by exposures to common risk factors. By using residual returns, we evaluate the performance of a signal after removing risk factor returns. Yet, the risk-adjusted residual returns depend on the specific risk model used in the residual return calculation and there is no consensus as to what risk model to use. In most portfolios, the risk penalty only reduces factor exposures instead of completely neutralizing factor exposures, in which cases the portfolio returns are different from residual returns.

Besides residual returns from full risk models, market-beta-adjusted residual returns are often used to evaluate signals. The reason for its popularity is that it is easy to hedge beta exposures using ETFs such as SPY. If a portfolio has beta exposure, we can easily add a SPY hedging position to the portfolio and examine the performance of the final beta-neutral portfolio. If our focus is to select stocks within the same sector, we can also calculate a stock's beta to its sector and estimate residual returns relative to the sector. Sector ETFs are readily available for hedging as well.

Academic researchers also use the Fama-French three-factor model or the Fama-French four-factor model to calculate residual returns. In asset management firms, factor models from providers such as Barra and Axioma are widely used. There are different factor models available from the same provider. For instance, the Barra US Trading model can produce residual returns significantly different from the US Long-Term Model. One drawback of using such commercial factor models is that factor exposure calculation is often opaque and the factor returns are estimated from multivariate robust regressions; so to hedge these risk exposures is not as transparent as to hedge market beta. As a result, factor-model-based residual returns are favorite choices of quantitative portfolio managers since they directly minimize or neutralize factor exposures in the portfolio construction and optimization steps.[55]

---

[55] When using factor risk models, we also need to remove the factor exposures from the raw alpha factors and be careful about the interaction between the alpha factors and risk factors. We will discuss these issues in more detail in Chapter 10.

Information Coefficient (IC)

As discussed in the Fundamental Law of Active Management, IC is a measure of skill or factor performance. When IC is defined as the cross-sectional linear correlation—Pearson correlation—between the z-scores calculated at t and the realized future returns between t and $t + 1$, the expected return of a portfolio with z-scores as the weights, $w = (z_1, \cdots, z_N)'$, is proportional to the IC:

$$r_p = \sum_{i=1}^{N} z_i r_i = \sum_{i=1}^{N} z_i r_i - \sum_{i=1}^{N} z_i \bar{r} = \sum_{i=1}^{N} z_i (r_i - \bar{r}) \Rightarrow$$

$$E[r_p] = \sum_{i=1}^{N} E[z_i (r_i - \bar{r})] = N \times \mathrm{cov}(z_i, r_i) = N \times cor(z_i, r_i) \times \sigma_z \times \sigma_r = N \times IC \times \sigma_r$$

where r_p is the return of the portfolio;

$r_1, r_2, \cdots, r_N$ are the returns of the stocks;

$\bar{r}$ and σ_r are the average and the cross-sectional volatility of the stock returns;

$IC = cor(z_i, r_i)$ is the correlation between factor z-scores and the stock returns.

The derivation of the equation relies on the assumption that z-scores have mean of 0 and standard deviation (or variance) of 1: $\sum_{i=1}^{N} z_i = 0$ and $\sigma_z = 1$. When the mean of the z-scores is different from 0 and variance is different from 1, we can always normalize the z-scores.

IC directly establishes a link between z-scores and forecasted stock returns. Let us consider a linear regression model for stock returns:

$$r_i = \bar{r} + \delta \times z_i + \varepsilon_i$$

where δ is the coefficient that linearly converts the scores to returns;

ε_i is the prediction error, $E[\varepsilon_i] = 0$.

Applying the least square regression, we get $\delta = \dfrac{\mathrm{cov}(z_i, r_i)}{\mathrm{var}(z_i)} = \sigma_r \times IC$ and the forecasted excess return of stock i:

$$E[(r_i - \bar{r}) \mid z_i] = \delta \times z_i = \sigma_r \times IC \times z_i$$

In other words, the expected excess return of a stock increases with cross-sectional stock return volatility, information coefficient, and the z-score of the stock. Using forecasted excess returns, we again confirm that the expected return of a portfolio with z-scores as the weights is proportional to the IC:

$$E[r_p] = \sum_{i=1}^{N} E[z_i (r_i - \bar{r})] = \sum_{i=1}^{N} E[\sigma_r \times IC \times z_i^2] = \sigma_r \times IC \times \sum_{i=1}^{N} E[z_i^2] = \sigma_r \times IC \times N$$

A criticism of using linear correlation as IC is that the result is sensitive to outliers. Rank correlation—Spearman correlation—between factor scores and realized future returns is used as an alternative measure since rank correlation is a robust estimation that removes the impact of outliers. We believe both linear correlation and rank correlation have their own advantages and disadvantages. Spearman correlation achieves robustness at the cost of loss in efficiency, which means that it incorporates less information than the Pearson correlation. Since negative and positive outliers in returns are common, Pearson correlation and Spearman correlation may yield different signs. In some of these cases, the ultimate financial measure, portfolio return, is likely to have the same sign as Pearson correlation instead of Spearman correlation. The following is one of such examples:

Stock	A	B	C	D	E	F	G	H
Factor Score	-2	-1.5	-1	-0.5	0.5	1	1.5	2
Factor Rank	8	7	6	5	4	3	2	1
Forward Return	8.0%	0.5%	1.0%	1.5%	1.5%	2.0%	2.5%	4.0%
Return Rank	1	8	7	5	5	4	3	2

Although the rank correlation is positive (0.33), which indicates that stocks with higher factor values tend to have higher returns, the linear correlation is negative (-0.16) because the return for stock A is an outlier. A portfolio that longs the stocks in the top quartile (G and H) and shorts the stocks in the bottom quartile (A and B) will have a negative return as well. Such difference does not invalidate the value of Spearman IC; it suggests that we should complement Spearman correlation with return analyses.

When a single IC number is reported for a signal, the reported number is the average IC of all periods or the expected IC, $E[IC]$. In practice, the realized ICs are different in different periods. For each period, we can calculate an IC value as the correlation between factor scores at the beginning of the period and the realized stock returns of that period. The return of a portfolio with z-scores as the weights for period t is

$$r_{p,t} = \sigma_{r,t} \times N_t \times IC_t$$

where $r_{p,t}$ is the portfolio return for period t;

   $\sigma_{r,t}$ is the cross-sectional volatility of stock returns;

   N_t is the number of stocks in the portfolio;

   IC_t is the realized IC at period t.

This equation is similar to the equation for the expected return of the portfolio. We add the subscript t to reflect that $\sigma_{r,t}$, N_t, and IC_t can change from period to period. For a given period, the expected portfolio return again becomes

$$E[r_{p,t}] = \sigma_{r,t} \times N_t \times E[IC_t]$$

If we further assume that the cross-sectional volatility and the number of stocks[56] stay stable over time, we can derive both the expected value and the standard deviation of the portfolio return:

$$\left.\begin{array}{l} E[r_p] = \sigma_r \times N \times E[IC] \\ std(r_p) = \sigma_r \times N \times std(IC) \end{array}\right\} \Rightarrow IR(r_p) = \frac{E[r_p]}{std(r_p)} = \frac{E[IC]}{std(IC)}$$

Therefore, the ratio of the expected IC (average historical IC) to the standard deviation of the IC (historical IC volatility) is often used as an estimate of the information ratio of a factor. If the true IC is constant over time, the standard deviation of the realized IC is simply due to sampling error of IC in each period and the estimated standard deviation of realized ICs for a portfolio with N stocks is

$$std(IC) = \sqrt{(1 - IC)^2 / (N - 2)}$$

In other words, if the true correlation between factor scores and next-period returns is constant over time, the volatility of realized ICs is caused only by limited sample size. In each period, the realized IC is calculated as the correlation using a selected sample—N stocks. As N grows larger, the sampling error gradually reduces to 0. For reasonable ICs ($|IC| < 0.1$) and diversified portfolios ($N > 30$), the standard deviation of IC is approximately $\sqrt{1/N}$ and the equation for the information ratio becomes the Fundamental Law of Active Management:

$$IR(r_p) = \frac{E[IC]}{std(IC)} = E[IC] \times \sqrt{N}$$

In practice, the IC itself varies from period to period, which increases the standard deviation of the realized IC. For well diversified portfolios (e.g., $N = 400$), the volatility of the time series of real ICs often has a larger impact on the standard deviation of realized ICs than the sampling error. Furthermore, the expected value of IC may not be stationary and many factors' ICs have decayed towards zero as the factor was discovered and explored by more portfolio managers. To monitor the performance of a factor over time, we plot a time series of ICs. As single-period realized ICs tend to be volatile, researchers also examine a moving average of ICs. The time series plot demonstrates the consistency, or inconsistency, of factor performance. The moving average also reveals the potential decay in the factor's forecasting power over time as well as highlights the cyclicality (*e.g.*, whether the factor performs better in a bull market or in a bear market) of factor returns. Besides the moving average, we can also explore the full distribution of the ICs of all periods to examine the skewness and the kurtosis of factor returns.

---

[56] Although the expected portfolio return increases with the number of stocks in this calculation, the return on each unit of gross investment stays stable. Since the portfolio weights are the z-scores, the total absolute portfolio weight is $\sum_{i=1}^{N}|w_{i,t}| = \sum_{i=1}^{N}|z_{i,t}| = N \times E[|z_t|]$, which increases linearly with N. Once we divide the portfolio return by the total absolute portfolio weight, the normalized return (return on gross market value) does not depend on N. If z-scores are from a standard normal distribution, $E[|z_t|] = \sqrt{2/\pi}$.

Hedged Portfolio Return

The success of a trading strategy is ultimately determined by risk-adjusted returns, which is why portfolio return analysis has always been an intrinsic part of signal construction and testing. A zero-investment portfolio with equal dollar investments in long positions and in short positions is a standard choice for evaluating signal returns. The stocks in the investment universe are sorted using the raw factor scores or z-scores and then divided into quantiles. Terciles, quartiles, quintiles, and deciles are common choices. A typical zero-investment portfolio takes long positions for the stocks in the top quantile and short positions for the stocks in the bottom quantile. Equal weights, market cap weights, and square root of market cap weights are often used to decide the relative weighting of each stock within the quantiles.

Such a zero-investment portfolio ignores the information contained in the stocks that are not in the top or the bottom quantile, and in doing so does not include all available information. To complement the zero-investment portfolio, we also directly plot the cumulative returns of all quantiles overtime. Relative returns are sometimes used instead of absolute returns to remove the market returns; the return of the middle quantile or the average return of all stocks is often used as the benchmark to calculate relative returns. If we plot the rolling 12-month return of a zero-investment portfolio instead of the cumulative return from the inception of the test, we demonstrate the rolling annual performance of the factor along with the periods that the signal adds value and the periods where it incurs losses. This is similar to the plot of the 12-month moving average of ICs with correlation replaced by portfolio returns.

We can also examine the return series of the zero-investment portfolio with weights proportional to their z-scores[57]. This approach includes all stocks in the portfolio and gives stocks at the top and the bottom quantiles higher weights. It may be a more efficient way of using all available information. Since a z-score weighted portfolio has higher breadth (more stocks), it often yields a higher information ratio than a long/short portfolio using only stocks in the top/bottom quantiles. Nevertheless, if most of the alpha is concentrated in the top and bottom quantile, the increase in breath by including more stocks may still yield lower information ratios because of lower returns. If the cross-sectional stock return volatility stays the same over time, the moving average of the return series adds no extra information beyond the moving average of ICs. In reality, cross-sectional volatility varies over time. Furthermore, the IC of a period is often correlated with the cross-sectional volatility of that period. If the correlation between the IC and the cross-sectional volatility σ_r is ρ, the expected portfolio return becomes

$$E[r_p] = N \times E[\sigma_r \times IC] = N \times \left(E[\sigma_r] \times E[IC] + \rho \times std(\sigma_r) \times std(IC)\right)$$

where $std(\sigma_r)$ is the standard deviation of the cross-sectional stock volatility;

$std(IC)$ is the standard deviation of IC.

If the correlation between IC and the cross-sectional volatility is positive, IC tends to be higher when the return dispersion among stocks is higher. Positive correlation increases the long-term portfolio alpha as the signal performs better than average when the stock

---

[57] The total weight on the long (short) side is scaled to 1 (-1).

return dispersion is large and negative correlation decreases alpha as the signal performs worse when the stock return dispersion is large.

Using the historical returns of a hedged portfolio, we can also calculate the hit rate—the percent of periods that the portfolio has positive returns. A signal with a good hit rate delivers returns more consistently through time. If a signal has positive returns with a hit rate well below 50%, the signal relies on a small percentage of positive outliers (high slugging ratio) to add value. Low hit rate indicates higher likelihood of long periods of losses—often this challenges investors' faith in the strategy. Furthermore, missing a couple of profitable periods may be detrimental to the portfolio's long-term performance.

Turnover, Information Decay and Rebalancing

By design, some factors change slowly from one period to the next, whereas others change rapidly. For example, the size factor stays stable over months or even years. Therefore, the single-factor portfolio constructed using size factor has low turnover. In contrast, values of a short-term reversal factor change rapidly from day to day (if the signal works, recent losers become winners and recent winners become losers). Therefore, a single-factor portfolio constructed using a short-term reversal factor has high turnover. Since the turnover depends on how we use a factor to construct a portfolio, there is no standard approach to estimate turnover. One approach is to directly look at a zero-investment portfolio, e.g., the top quintile minus the bottom quintile, to calculate portfolio turnover. A different approach, independent of portfolio construction, measures the serial correlation of factor scores: the correlation between factor scores of the stocks at t and the factor scores of the same stocks at $t + 1$. Higher correlation means that factor scores are more stable over time and indicates lower factor turnover.

Factors with high turnover need to be, and sometimes are, compensated with higher predictive power. If we have a reasonable estimation of trading costs, they can be directly incorporated to estimate after-cost returns and information ratios. Mediocre predictable power and high turnover, however, do not automatically make the factor a poor signal. Investors usually use multiple factors in the portfolio construction and the final turnover depends on the interaction of the selected factors.

The information coefficient that we compute is IC_1 since the scores calculated at t is used to forecast 1-period forward return (returns between t and $t+1$). In general, we can use IC_n ($n \geq 1$) to measure the cross-sectional correlation—Pearson or Spearman—between the scores calculated at t and the $(t + n)$-th period returns (returns between $t+n-1$ and $t+n$). Essentially, we assume that we use information available at t for a later period. The series of IC_n measures the information decay over time. If the information decays slowly, we will see a slow decrease of IC_n as n increases. Slow decay of information implies that we can use lagged information without sacrificing much of the predictive power. Besides, slow information decay indicates lower factor turnover. Some investors also uses lead-lag plot that includes both $n > 0$ and $n \leq 0$. When $n \leq 0$, IC_n shows the signal performance if we had perfect foresight. For example, IC_0 shows how the signal would have performed between $t - 1$ and t if the scores calculated at t were known at $t - 1$.

Once a signal is translated into portfolio weights at t, we can test its performance for different periods of length. To control portfolio turnover, the holding period is often more than one day as signals usually have predictive power beyond one day. If signals can be updated on a daily basis, it means that the signal construction frequency is higher than the portfolio rebalancing frequency. In such cases, we can test portfolio construction from different starting dates to examine the consistency of the signal performance. For example, using five consecutive starting dates, we can build five portfolios that rebalance every five days to examine their cumulative returns. The five time series should show similar patterns for a robust signal. Alternatively, we can use a portfolio with an incremental rebalancing strategy. The portfolio is divided into five independent sub-portfolios each representing one-fifth of the total portfolio value. On each trading day, one sub-portfolio that was rebalanced five days ago is rebalanced. Such an approach strikes a balance between incorporating timely information and controlling for portfolio turnover. The sub-portfolio approach is equivalent to a special case of signal smoothing. Instead of using the latest signal available, signal smoothing uses the simple moving average of the past K-days' portfolio weights:

$$SMA_{t,K} = \frac{1}{K} \sum_{i=0}^{K-1} W_{t-i}$$

where $SMA_{t,K}$ is the smoothed signal;

$\quad W_{t-i}$ can be any portfolio weights constructed using single-day signal on day $t - i$.

For example, if z-scores are directly used for the zero-investment portfolio, then z-scores are W_{t-i} on day $t - i$ if top minus bottom quintile are used in zero-investment portfolio, then W_{t-i} is +1 for any stocks that are in the top quintile and -1 for any stocks that are in the bottom quintile.

Signal smoothing is not restricted to simple moving averages. We can use a variety of weighting schemes to overweigh more recent signals, making for a more versatile approach to incorporating historical signal information. Signal smoothing usually increases the serial correlation of factor scores and lowers the turnover. When the savings from the lower turnover is sufficient to compensate for the loss in raw factor returns, the net returns from the signal will be higher.

The hysteresis approach we discussed earlier in Chapter 5 is a valuable tool for reducing turnover as well. After we enter a long position when the stock moves into the top quintile, we do not necessarily exit the position when it moves out of the top quintile. Instead, we only exit the position if the stock falls below the 60th percentile. Although the expected alpha is lower when the stock falls from the top quintile to the fourth quintile, holding the existing long position does not require extra trading and does not incur trading costs. Similarly, after we enter a short position when the stock moves into the bottom quintile, we only exit the position if the stock moves above the 40th percentile. By using different thresholds for entry and exit, we can reduce the turnover of fast-moving signals and achieve a better trade-off between raw returns and trading costs.

Stratified Models

Many quantitative fund managers adopt a one-size-fit-all approach to test signals on all the stocks in the investment universe. Some choose to remove certain types of stocks on an ad-hoc basis; many remove real estate investment trusts (REITs) from their investment universe as the business models and tax structures of REITs are different from other industries. For example, instead of earnings, adjusted funds from operations (AFFO) are a common profit measure for REITs. Some fund managers remove banks from their investment universe or build a separate model for banks since banks have a unique set of financial ratios that determine their asset values and profits. In recent years, as returns from employing parsimonious one-size-fit-all models drop, increasingly managers have begun to split the stock universe into small groups to investigate the performance of signals for individual groups of stocks. The goal of such stratified models is to look for a subset of stocks which still generate good returns even though the signal is no longer profitable when applied to all stocks.

One natural way of splitting the stocks is to use their sector classifications. As we discussed earlier, business models, profit drivers, and growth potential is different for different sectors. A signal may have better predictive power for a subset of sectors if the factor plays a larger role to differentiate stocks. The GICS sector classification is a popular choice. There are ten GICS sectors, some with a small number of assets. When we further split stocks in each sector to quantiles, the number of quantiles needs to stay small for each quantile to have sufficient number of stocks. For example, telecommunication services have fewer than 40 stocks in the Russell 3000 universe. To increase the number of stocks in each subgroup, some investors further combine similar sectors into subgroups. As shown in Exhibit 9-6, Morgan Stanley's research team (2011) introduced five mega sectors. At a higher aggregated level, we simply classify sectors as defensive (D) or cyclical (C): GICS sectors materials, industrials, consumer discretionary, financials, and information technology are roughly classified as cyclical sectors; GICS sectors energy, consumer staples, health care, telecommunication services, and utilities are roughly classified as defensive sectors. We can investigate a factor's performance separately in cyclical sectors to examine whether a factor is more suitable for a subset of stocks. Overall, the majority of factors tend to be more effective in cyclical than in defensive sectors.

Exhibit 9-6 Classification of GICS sectors

GICS Code	GICS Sector Name	Mega Sectors	Defensive/Cyclical
10	Energy	1	D
50	Telecommunication services		
55	Utilities		
30	Consumer staples	2	
35	Health care		
15	Materials	3	C
20	Industrials		
25	Consumer discretionary	4	
45	Information technology		
40	Financials	5	

It is well established that market cap affects the performance of many factors. Numerous studies confirm that factor performance (IC or factor return) is likely to be stronger in small-cap stocks than in large-cap stocks. One reason for this is that price inefficiency in small-cap stocks is less exploited by large institutional investors, given capacity constraints of small-cap stocks. Many small-cap stocks do not have sufficient depth and liquidity for large institutions to trade in. Instead, they focus on large-cap names such as stocks in the S&P 500 or the Russell 1000 universe. Besides, small-cap stocks also receive less attention from analysts. With less analyst coverage, small-cap stocks are less visible to investors and information is disseminated slower than information about large-cap stocks, which further increases price inefficiency.

To explore the performance difference, we can split stocks into two groups (large cap and small cap) or three groups (large cap, mid cap, and small cap) and analyze the factor performance separately. Russell 3000 provides a natural split between large-cap and small-cap stocks: Russell 1000 includes the top 1000 stocks by market cap[58] and Russell 2000 includes the rest. For three groups, the Russell 2000 index can be further split to two smaller groups by market cap. It is important to take into consideration the trade-off between higher raw returns and higher costs associated with trading small-cap stocks though. A point of practical advice here: Compared with large-cap stocks, small-cap stocks have higher bid-ask spreads, lower liquidity, and higher stock loan borrowing costs. Therefore, higher raw returns in small-cap stocks do not necessarily translate to higher net returns unless the increase in raw returns is sufficient to cover the extra costs.

In addition to the performance difference, the factor scores of small-cap stocks also may behave differently from large-cap stocks. For analyst revision scores and news sentiment scores, if we do not split the stock universe, the extreme deciles tend to be dominated by small-cap companies as they are followed by few analysts and have little news. Whenever there is a single analyst revision or news release, the change may put a small-cap stock in the top or the bottom decile. For large cap stocks, there is steady flow of analyst revision and news releases. Therefore, the sentiment scores fall into the top and the bottom deciles less often. If the market has a strong trend, the market condition may create factor scores in favor of one market cap group over the other. When the market recovered in 2009, most analysts revised their forecasts upward. As a result, small-cap stocks tended to have more (extreme) positive scores resulting in a tilt towards small-cap stocks in the long/short hedged portfolio. To mitigate unintended exposures to the size factor, we can also split the stock universe by market cap to create more homogenous groups for signal testing.

Besides separating stocks by market caps and sectors, some investors also use risk factors to split the stock universe. For example, it is widely believed that high idiosyncratic volatility poses limit to arbitrage. Since arbitragers cannot hedge the idiosyncratic risks of stocks, they are less willing to invest in stocks with high idiosyncratic volatility. Mispricing of high volatility stocks tends to last longer and the returns to arbitrage may be higher for investors who are willing to take on idiosyncratic risk. Hence, many signals

---

[58] In 2007, Russell introduced a percentile banding to reduce index turnover. The change uses a hysteresis approach to keep some existing Russell 1000 stocks in the Russell 1000 index even if their market cap fall slightly below the market cap cutoff; it also keeps some existing Russell 2000 stocks in the Russell 2000 index even if their market caps rise slightly above the cutoff. The overall impact on the stratified models tends to be small.

are stronger among stocks with high idiosyncratic risks. For example, Li and Sullivan (2011) found the accrual and asset growth anomalies occurred mostly in stocks with high idiosyncratic risks. Stocks with the highest volatilities are more likely to fall into the top and the bottom quantiles. For example, the top and the bottom deciles of momentum signals and mean-reversion signals are dominated by high volatility stocks. Splitting stocks by idiosyncratic risks also create groups of stocks with similar risk profiles for signal testing.

Good Modeling Practices

Before we delve deeper into the methods employed to construct portfolios using multiple alpha signals, we dedicate the last section of this chapter to discuss pertinent issues related to signal testing and model development. Extracting signals with predictive power from extremely noisy financial data is inherently difficult and careful examination reveals flaws in many financial studies. Many signals that look deceptively good on paper are far less powerful in practice or even completely useless. It is therefore very important for investors to understand the potential pitfalls in signal testing and model development.

Inaccuracies in Data

In Chapter 2, we have discussed data quality issues in detail. In order to better manage potential data error, we need to have a good understanding of their potential impact and the ability to reduce their impact in backtests. For example, an intraday mean-reversion strategy that relies on tick data is sensitive to data error: for a stock that has been trading at $100, a couple of incorrect ticks at $120 will trigger a sell. If we assume that the trade is executed at $120, when the ticks go back to $100, it appears that the trade has made $20. In reality, that $20 profit is fictitious and it introduces an upward bias to the strategy's profit estimation. An intraday momentum strategy, on the other hand, would have triggered a buy. If we assume that the trade is executed at $120, when the ticks go back to $100, the trade results in $20 fictitious loss. Incorrect tick prices have opposite effects on backtests depending on whether the strategy is based on mean reversion or on momentum: they tend to inflate the backtest returns of mean reversion strategies and decrease the backtest returns of momentum strategies. We can reduce the impact of erroneous prices by avoiding the use of prices that generate signals as the trade prices. If we assume that we can only execute the trade at the volume weighted average price in the minutes after a trading signal is triggered, it will remove most of the fictitious gains/losses in the backtests.

Another important part is to understand the data and their limitation. High/low prices tend to be noisier than open/close prices, since high/low prices are more likely to include erroneous tick data or small order sizes. Given increased popularity of high-frequency trading, mini flash crashes—large price swings in a short period of time— are prone to increase in the market. Besides, execution venues are fragmented. The high/low prices may happen at a venue that a trading system does not route trades to and those high/low prices may often only include a few lots of shares. As a result, if a strategy uses limit prices for entry/exit and assumes that the trades are filled as long as the high/low prices touch the limit prices, we need to treat such a strategy with caution. If the results can be validated by sufficient volume of tick-by-tick trade data, one would have more confidence in the model.

Missing values are common in financial data and fund managers need to understand the sources and the impact of missing values in order to properly handle them. Many financial service companies report no inventory or R&D costs, in which cases we can treat the missing values as zero since they likely hold no inventory and have no significant R&D costs. Another example is that a large percentage of companies do not have reported long-term forecast growth rate in I/B/E/S. This happens when analysts do not make a forecast. In such a case we naturally cannot treat the missing values as zero, for just because a value is missing it does not mean that the expected long-term growth rate is zero. Instead, we suggest that using the average value across a comparable group of stocks is a better choice. Missing prices require more careful handling. Many researchers use last observation carried forward (LOCF) method to handle missing prices. The method essentially assumes that the price on a day with missing value is the same as the previous close price and the return is 0. In reality, if a stock with sufficient liquidity has no trading in a day, it usually means that the stock is halted with news pending. If a strategy generates an entry signal on that day, one cannot initialize the position at the previous close price; if a strategy generates an exit signal on that day, one cannot exit the position until the next day. For bankruptcy filings and fraud cases, it may mean close to 100% loss. For a biotech company that waits for FDA approval or denial of a drug, it may mean the difference between a huge gain and a huge loss. For portfolio with 4% of the balance invested in the stock, using the previous close price can cause the estimated return to be 4% different from realized return. If the portfolio is leveraged 2.5 times, it means 10% difference in return on capital and that single position may be sufficient to make or break a year for a fund.

Data Snooping

Every year, millions of individual and professional investors study the market for patterns in stock returns and potential signals that predict stock price moves. So, the risk of collective data snooping—inappropriate use of data mining[59] to uncover misleading relationships in data—is high. As investors interrogate the same data (e.g., prices and volumes) again and again, some signals always emerge. A few of these observed signals are real; most are spurious. When we use statistical methods to test the significance of a signal, we often use either 95% or 99% confidence interval (p-value 0.05 or 0.01). But even with a 99% confidence interval, about 1 in 100 randomly selected signals appear to work. A professional investor can easily test dozens of signals in a few years. If we include variations in signal parameters, the number of tests can easily reach thousands. It might not cause problems if the world had only one professional investor. In reality, there are tens of thousands of professional investors looking for different signals every day. Even with huge overlaps between signals that investors study, the total number of independent statistical tests is in the millions. We can have thousands of signals that show statistical significance even if none of the signals work. Most spurious signals yield good historical results but have little predictive power in the future.

So, how do we separate the wheat from the chaff?

The first principle is that a signal should be based on solid reasoning. In other words, the signal should make sense. For instance, the Super Bowl Indicator says that a victory in

---

[59] In statistics, data mining is a process to discover new patterns from large data sets.

the Big Game by a team from the old American Football League means a bear market for the coming year and a victory by a team from the old National Football League means a bull market for the coming year. The indicator had an impressive track record with close to 80% success rate for annual Dow Jones returns from 1967 to 2012, which is much better than most market pundits. Nevertheless, serious investors would naturally suspect that the correlation is spurious as there is no sensible causality between the Super Bowl and the stock market. An analysis using more recent data shows that the Super Bowl Indicator had no better odds than always betting that the market was up and the Super Bowl Indicator had the wrong forecast for the 2008 bear market.

The second principle is that the signal should work in different periods, on different assets, and in different markets. All signals may yield good results for a couple of years, but they may not perform in the long run. It is therefore advisable to test a signal over a long period of time. Besides, we can also split the history to different sub-periods and check whether it works for different sub-periods. If we fit the signal using one sub-period (usually an earlier period), we need to test it out of sample on another sub-period (usually a later period) to make sure that the signal still works. If a signal works for one asset or one group of assets, we would expect it to work for similar assets or similar groups of assets as well. For instance, if a market-timing rule works well for SPY (S&P 500), it should work for IWB (Russell 1000) and QQQ (NASDAQ 100) as well. If not, it may be the result of data snooping that over fits SPY data.

The third principle is that a signal should be robust to small parameter changes. When we choose specific parameters for a signal, optimization is often used to choose the parameters that yield the best results in the training data. One sanity check is to make small changes to the "optimized" parameters and analyze their impact on the results. If the signal is robust, we would expect to see good results with the modified parameters; otherwise, the optimized "good" signal may be just the result of data snooping. In our own testing we came across a moving average crossover system with five parameters that generated fabulous backtest results. But when we changed one of signals from an 11-day moving average to a 10- or 12-day moving average, most of the profit disappeared. Needless to say, the "optimized" system was likely to be the result of data snooping. Indeed, the system yielded a loss in the following years.

Look-Ahead Bias

Besides the potential look-ahead bias in historical economic and financial data, we also need to be careful about other sources of look-ahead bias. Inclusion of new data may also introduce a look-ahead bias. For example, hedge fund index databases sometimes backfill historical returns of newly added hedge funds. Since those hedge funds were not available historically in the database and only funds with good performance tend to be added to the index, the overall hedge fund performance calculated using the funds in the database is an overestimation of average fund performance unless proper corrections are made.

Unsynchronized data are another possible source of look-ahead bias. Different markets open and close at different times. For example, trading of broad-based index ETF closes at 4:00 pm and the option trading for these indices closes at 4:15 pm. So we cannot simply take the open/close prices from different markets and treat them as synchronous data. What is often neglected is that even within the same market/exchange, the open/close prices may not be synchronized, especially for stocks with lower liquidity. For example, although the US stock market opens at 9:30 AM, many stocks do not have the first trades until one to five minutes after the open. When the market has significant moves in the first one to five minutes, the open prices of these stocks with delayed first trades capture the market move. So the open prices of different stocks are not synchronized and they reflect different market conditions.

To address the look-ahead bias problem, the time series should reflect the available data at a specific time. Besides better data information, careful backtest design also helps. One strategy is to consider what data are available now if we rely on the data to build a production portfolio to trade. Analyzing the data available today gives us some ideas as to the necessary time lag needed for the underlying data. The ideal solution is point-in-time databases. Such databases allow users to extract all data available up to any time point in the history. Point-in-time databases, however, requires the system to record the timestamp whenever a piece of information is updated. Therefore, point-in-time databases are expensive to build and maintain.

Survivorship Bias

Many studies fail to include the total returns of delisted stocks or funds as these no longer show up in reported databases. Delisting may occur on account of bankruptcy filing, acquisitions, management buy-outs, voluntary delisting or involuntary delisting requested by the exchanges. Different causes have different impact on the returns of delisted stocks. A stock that is removed from an exchange because of a corporate acquisition will have close to zero returns after the delisting; for such a stock usually trade for a period of time after the approval of the acquisition by shareholders and regulatory agencies before the deal is finally closed. For example, TPG capital announced the acquisition of J. Crew (JCG) on November 22, 2010. After the announcement, the price of JCG quickly moved close to the cash acquisition price, $43.50. When the deal was finally closed on March 4, 2011, the close price of JCG was $43.51. So using the last available close price for JCG to calculate total return will not distort the results. In contrast, a stock that is delisted because of failing to meet listing requirement or bankruptcy tends to lose most of its value. For example, on the day before MF Global[60] filed for bankruptcy on October 31, 2011, it closed at $1.25. The subsequent bankruptcy wiped out most shareholder value.

Survivorship bias has a far larger negative impact on traditional value strategies (e.g., price to earnings ratio and price to book ratio) than on growth and momentum strategies since stocks with low prices are often selected by value strategies. Value stocks, many of which are fallen angels with negative business outlook, have a higher probability of getting delisted or filing for bankruptcy. If we do not include delisted stocks in our tests, we introduce a survivorship bias; if we include a delisted stock in historical portfolio construction, we need to calculate returns after it was delisted. If the backtest fails to capture negative returns after stocks are delisted, the calculated return is higher than the return that the strategy can actually achieve. To mitigate the problem in the backtest, a popular filter is to remove stocks with prices lower than five dollars from the stock universe as these stocks have higher delisting risk. Such a choice does not fully address the problem though. Many stocks have prices above five dollars on the day they are delisted, in which cases the filter is insufficient. On the flip side, investors can invest in

---

[60] MF Global bankruptcy was the eighth largest bankruptcy in US history.

stocks with prices below five dollars and many strategies are especially profitable for low price stocks, in which cases the filter causes an underestimation of strategy returns. An alternative approach is to estimate the total return after the delisting. CRSP publishes delisting return—the total return calculated by comparing a value, either the stock price when the stock resumes trading as a pink sheet stock or the total value of distributions to shareholders, against the price on the security's last trading day on the exchange. The availability of return after delisting is one reason why CRSP is a popular choice of researchers.

Return Distribution

Most stock returns are not normally distributed. They have fat tails. Often, willingness to take downside tail risk is rewarded handsomely and profits can exist for extended periods of time. For example, selling credit default swaps has a large likelihood of earning a small profit over a long period, coupled with a small chance of losing a large amount if the underlying asset defaults. Capital Decimation Partners, a hypothetical hedge fund created by Andrew Lo (2001), used a strategy that sold out-of-the-money S&P 500 put options with maturity no more than three months on each month's option expiration dates. Capital Decimation Partners would have made 2721% total returns from 1992 to 1998 with a Sharpe ratio of 1.94. During the same period, the S&P was up 367% and had a Sharpe ratio of 0.98. Furthermore, such a strategy would have had only 6 negative months in those 8 years. The strategy might have looked brilliant at the beginning of 2000, but we all know how such a strategy could well have wiped an investor's entire capital in the subsequent bear market.

The majority of hedge fund strategies have negative skewness and high kurtosis. Part of the negative skewness comes from the negative skewness of the underlying factor returns. In recent years, voluntary and forced hedge fund deleveraging has also contributed to the negative skewness of returns. In the period between September and October 2008, hedge funds experienced unprecedented pressure to deleverage. After the Lehman bankruptcy filing, many prime brokers tightened their margin requirements and even dropped many of their hedge fund clients. At the same time, cash-strapped clients requested massive redemptions. The double whammy of higher margin requirements and redemptions forced hedge funds to close out their existing positions to raise cash. Since many hedge funds held similar long positions as well as short positions, they suffered heavy losses in their rush to close their positions. This is but one example which illustrates the need to take tail risk into consideration when evaluating the potential future performance of a trading strategy.

Stocks with Low Liquidity

It is well established that many signals are stronger in small-cap (market cap between $300 million and $2 billion) or micro-cap stocks (market cap less than $300 million) and are much weaker or even non-existent in large-cap stocks. Yet, the reality is that most funds cannot allocate much capital to small-cap and micro-cap stocks because of the lack of liquidity in those stocks. Individual investors are less constrained, but they cannot invest heavily in micro-cap stocks either. Many academic studies only remove stocks with market cap below $20 million, which keeps about 6000 stocks in CRSP universe. But few funds or investors invest in stocks with market cap as low as $20 million. Instead, if we use $300 million market cap as the filter, the universe is reduced to ~3000 stocks and if we use $1 billion as the filter, the universe is reduced to ~2000 stocks. Besides market cap, the average daily trading volume also constrains stock choice and amount deployable. If a signal mostly relies on investment in small-cap and micro-cap stocks to theoretically make profitable trades, in practice one may not be able to realize much profit by trading on that signal.

Market Friction and Costs

Depending on portfolio turnover, execution costs often have significant negative impact on a strategy's profitability. There is often a trade-off between paper profits from a trading strategy and portfolio turnover: lower-frequency strategies with lower turnover tend to have lower paper profits (without considering costs) and higher-frequency strategies with higher turnover tend to have higher paper profits. For example, traditional value signals such as book to price ratio have very low turnover—often less than 25% annually—and short-term mean reversion strategies have much higher turnover—often as high as 25% daily. For strategies with high turnover, reducing trading costs is crucial. A strategy with a daily turnover of 25% and an assumed trading cost of 10 basis points requires 12.6% annualized before-cost return[61] to break even. High trading costs are the reason why some apparent anomalies are hard to monetize and continue to exist. If the costs to arbitrage an anomaly are higher than theoretical returns, the apparent anomaly can continue to exist in the market as investors cannot exploit it on account of large trading costs. Besides trading costs, investors also incur financing costs, securities borrowing costs and other market frictions. These costs are seldom included in backtests. In practice, these costs may have a meaningful negative impact on realized returns.

High securities lending costs can turn highly profitable trades on paper to unprofitable ones in reality. For example, on February 27, 2009, Citi announced an offer to exchange preferred shares to common shares at $3.25 per share. Since the face value of the preferred shares was $25, it indicated a conversion ratio of ~7.7. Citi share price dropped from its previous close of $2.46 to $1.5. But even at such a low price, 7.7 shares of Citi stocks were valued at $11.55, which was significantly higher than the close price of the preferred stock, ~$8.05. An obvious arbitrage strategy was to long 1 share of preferred stock at $8.05 and short 7.7 shares of common stocks at $1.50. An investor could pocket $3.5 of the price difference initially and convert the preferred stock when the conversion happened to cover the short positions. It would indeed be a "risk free" arbitrage if one did not consider securities lending costs. Unfortunately, the costs were high. At the moment of the announcement, Citi's short interest was only about 3% of the shares outstanding. More than 1 billion shares of the preferred stocks were privately owned. These preferred shares, if converted, would produce more shares than Citi's shares outstanding, 5.5 billion shares. When investors, including many hedge funds, rushed to buy the preferred stock and shorted the common stock, the supply of borrowable common stock was depleted. Lenders recalled the shares from individual investors and charged hedge funds more than 100% annualized lending fees. The potential profit would have covered the lending fees if the conversion happened within 2-3 months as originally anticipated. Instead, Citi

---

[61] Turnover is calculated as dividing either the total amount of buys or total amount of sells over a period by the total net asset value. Each dollar of turnover requires two dollars of trading. So the total annual cost of trading is 25%/day × 2 × 0.001 × 252 days.

delayed the conversion and the deal was not closed until late July. As a result, the "risk free" arbitrage opportunity turned out to be a losing trade for many investors.

Credibility of Simulated Results

Investors, when evaluating portfolio managers, always put more emphasis on real track record instead of simulated backtests. This is because backtests require added scrutiny to ensure that assumptions and costs used are valid. Compared with a real track record, simulated backtests have a number of limitations.

First, simulated results are biased by the selection process or even data snooping. In academia, the review process always has a bias in favor of positive results—identification of new anomalies or improvements of existing anomaly—over negative results. In the financial industry, researchers are inclined to show their best historical results as well. Such self-selection increases the likelihood of data snooping. There are thousands of "optimized" trading systems on the market that show fabulous backtests but very few of them have any real value.

Second, many simulated results fail to properly account for explicit and implicit trading costs. For example, there are numerous reports on the value of simple mean reversion strategies. In testing a mean-reversion signal, we found that the top decile outperformed the bottom decile by more than 25% a year (without considering the trading costs) if the asset filter only removed stocks with market caps below $200 million. However, when we added another filter to removed stocks with prices below $5, the return difference fell to below 15%. The large decrease in returns indicates that part of the return reversal simply reflects bid-ask bounce since the bounce impacts low price stocks disproportionally. Let us consider a stock with a bid-ask spread of 2 cents. For a $20 stock (bid/ask 19.99/20.01), the spread is 10 bps; for a $2 stock (bid/ask 1.99/2.01), the spread becomes 100 bps. On a day when this stock is amongst top losers, investors will be selling the stock and the $2 stock is likely to close at bid price $1.99. When we exit on a day without the selling pressure, this stock is equally likely to close at $1.99 or $2.01 if the market price (mid-price) does not change. Even though the bid/ask prices do not move, the strategy is likely to show a return of 50 bps simply because the close price on the day of the entry is more likely to be the bid price.

Some researchers also inadvertently use incorrect statistics to conclude the statistical significance of some simulated results. Analysis of financial time series is often more difficult than simple statistical analysis. If the analysis is not well designed, we may conclude that a strategy is statistically significant when the statistical power is inadequate to draw such a conclusion. For example, using overlapping intervals is a common practice in backtest. Let us assume that we have five years of monthly data to estimate whether the annual return is larger than zero. If we simply use each year as a data point, we have only five data points. What if we use rolling twelve month returns instead? We now have 49 data points (months 1-12, 2-13, …, and 49-60). If we calculate the mean and the standard error of these 49 data points, we get the t-statistic as the ratio of mean return to the standard error of the return. But is such an approach valid? The answer is a no. The simple t-test requires each data point to be independent. We do have 49 data points, but these 49 data points are clearly not independent. The period of months 1-12 and 2-13 have eleven months in common and only one month difference, so naturally the correlation between their returns is largely positive, which reduces the statistical power.

Without correction, the value of estimated standard error is largely underestimated and the t-statistic is inflated. Since many of the financial time series show autocorrelation as well as heteroskedasticity, we suggest using more sophisticated estimations such as Newey-West standard errors in the statistical tests.

Regime Shift

Nearly all quantitative forecasting methods are based on a study of the historical data. In many cases, history repeats itself. But when the market environment fundamentally changes, the past can no longer be used to predict the future. When we decide on the strength of a signal, we should examine both its performance over the entire history as well as its more recent performance. Overall we would of course prefer to choose a signal that has good overall performance as well as good recent performance.

Many stock selection signals have good aggregated performances over the past thirty years, but their performances have been dismal or nearly non-existent in the past few years. A number of factors contribute to the difference in performance. The first reason seems to be the increased efficiency of the equity market. Back in the 1980s and 1990s, few investors built systematic stock signals to exploit market anomalies and those that did, were rewarded handsomely. As the industry has grown, hedge funds alone have more than $2 trillion under management. Since many of these funds use leverage, the gross market value of their portfolios is even higher. Competition to explore market inefficiency is fierce, and the signal that performed well a decade ago may be irrelevant in today's environment. Another structural change in the stock market was the shift from a fractional trading system to decimal pricing. Before 2000, the tick size of stocks was often 1/8 to 1/16 of a dollar instead of a penny. Since 2001, almost all listed stocks have been traded in decimals, making the smallest bid-ask spread to be a penny. To illustrate the impact of the spread difference, consider a strategy with average holding period of one month invested in stocks with average price $30. If we further assume that we incur the full spread for each round-trip trading, the yearly bid-ask spread cost was 1/8 * 12 = $1.5 when the tick size was 1/8, which was 5% of the average stock price. When the tick size is one penny, the bid-ask spread cost is 0.01 * 12 = $0.12, which is 0.4% of the average stock price. That 4.6% difference alone often explains the difference between a signal's performance before and after 2000. Before 2000, investors could not exploit an alpha of 5% for trading costs would have consumed the alpha. Recently, with lower trading costs, investors can quickly arbitrage away the 5% alpha. Furthermore, before 2000, the stock trading volumes were lower as well. So the market impact of trades was much higher, which put tighter limits on trade sizes.

The regulatory environment also experienced significant changes since 2000. For example, in August 2000, SEC ratified Reg FD (Regulation Fair Disclosure) that requires all publicly traded companies disclose material information to all investors at the same time. Before Reg FD, large institutional investors and financial analysts often received selectively disclosed material information from corporate managers. Reg FD made that practice illegal. After the passage of Reg FD, the predictive power of analyst revisions has deteriorated. Palmon and Yezegel (2011) demonstrated that abnormal return earned by investors following analysts' advice to predict earnings surprises was about 70% lower in the post-Reg FD period than in the pre-Reg FD period. Another significant change was the repeal of the uptick rule in July 2007, prior to which shorting a stock was disallowed unless it was on an uptick or zero-uptick. The purpose of the uptick rule was to prevent short sellers from driving the stock price down using successive short sell orders at lower and lower prices. The repeal of the uptick rule does facilitate momentum trades. As a stock's price falls, momentum traders can easily short sell the stock. The uptick rule also impacts order flow calculation. Because of the uptick rule, more short sells were classified as buys by tick tests or the Lee and Ready algorithm before 2007. The repeal of the uptick rule allows short sells to happen no matter whether the previous trades are on upticks or downticks, which led to better classification of short sells. Therefore, the change introduced a structural difference before and after repeal of the rule.

Since 2000, the rapid development of electronic trading and competition among different trading venues has triggered significant changes to trading. Historically, trading volumes of NASDAQ stocks needed to be adjusted by dividing a factor close to 2 (Anderson & Dyl, 2007) to make them comparable to the trading volumes of NYSE stocks. The reasoning was that NASDAQ was a dealer's market, which meant that market makers stayed between buyers and sellers for each transaction and the volume was double counted as a result. NYSE was mostly an auction market where each transaction was executed between a buyer and seller. The designated market maker, the specialist, only stayed between buyers and sellers in a small percentage of transactions. Since 2000, electronic communication networks (ECNs) have enabled buyers and sellers to directly trade with each other when the prices posted on ECNs are better than quotes from NASDAQ dealers. As a result, ECN has accounted for a growing percentage of volumes of NASDAQ stocks, which reduces double counting. In 2000, NYSE allowed NYSE listed stocks to be traded off the exchange floor. The trading volume of NYSE listed stocks through ECNs and NASDAQ gradually built up in the following years and by 2010, more than half of the trading volumes for NYSE listed stocks were executed off NYSE. So an adjustment factor close to 2 for NASDAQ stocks is clearly no longer a reasonable choice; we no longer use an adjustment factor for NASDAQ stocks.

Given these and other fundamental changes, signal performance prior to 2000 may have limited predictive power in the future. Interestingly, the way that signal performance is presented by academic papers indicates a disconnection between academia and industry. Most academic papers include the (residual) returns by quantiles, the differences between the top and bottom quantiles, as well as t-statistics to show the statistical significance of the quantiles. Few papers have time-series figures for cumulative returns; nor do they have breakdown of returns by years. Practitioners of course are far more interested in examining cumulative returns over time to confirm contemporary signal effectiveness.

Conclusion

We have discussed dozens of signals investigated by technical analysts, fundamental stock pickers, and macro investors. The important question is which signals one should employ for portfolio construction. The overall principle is to choose factors that have good performance and consistency in predicting stock returns balanced against turnover. The information coefficient and the information ratio are two popular choices for performance evaluation. The trading of zero-investment portfolios, serial correlation of factor scores, and alpha decay are used to estimate factor turnover. If trading costs are estimated properly, as they often are for institutional investors, these costs can be directly incorporated into the performance analysis to calculate before- and after-cost information ratio. To evaluate consistency, it is important to investigate a factor's performance in the full period, in the first/second half of the period, as well as in the most recent time period. One can also calculate the information ratio using rolling windows to show its performance over time.

When using statistical models to construct signals and to evaluate the signals' predictive power, we recommend abiding by the following guidelines:

- When constructing a signal, one should ensure that the signal is intuitive and based on solid reasoning. It is important to avoid data snooping that may lead to spurious conclusions.

- When backtesting, one should try to collect high-quality and accurate data free of look-ahead bias and survivorship bias. If some data have quality issues or have potential biases, one should make conservative choices that are more likely to lead to underestimation of returns instead of overestimation of returns.

- When selecting from the investment universe and determining stock weightings, one should take the liquidity of the stocks into consideration.

- When calculating a signal's performance, one should properly account for potential negative impact of market frictions and costs (e.g., trading costs, financing costs, and securities lending costs) on returns. When making assumptions on costs, one ought to make conservative choices that are more likely to lead to overestimation of costs instead of underestimation of costs.

- When evaluating a signal's performance, it is important to consider consistency of results over time. If signal performance decays over time or was concentrated within a few years, one ought to discount the value of that signal.

- When selecting parameters, one should make sure that the selected parameters are sensible and the signal performance is robust to small changes in parameters.

- When evaluating the future predictive power of a signal, one should understand the limitation embedded in models and the potential risks associated with assumptions made to arrive at the model.

As a first step to identify potential useful signals, it is often acceptable to skip a few precautions highlighted here. This helps quickly estimate the value of a new signal. Once a signal with potential value is identified, we recommend building rigorous tests for careful evaluation. The recommendations in this chapter may help in identifying valuable signals as well as averting costly mistakes from including spurious underperforming ones.

Chapter 10

Portfolio Construction and Risk Management

In Chapter 9 we focused on the different approaches to identify and refine individual stock selection signals. In practice, with notable exception of simple style factor-based funds, few investors rely on a single factor to make investment decisions. Instead, investors usually include several to dozens of stock selection factors in portfolio construction for the following reasons:

- Different signals capture different aspects of a company. A combination of different factors provides a comprehensive picture of a company.

- Most factors alone yield low standalone information ratios. A combination of different factors provides significant diversification benefit and generates a higher information ratio.

- Different factors tend to outperform (or underperform) in different economic environments or market conditions. A combination of different factors introduces more consistency to portfolio returns.

- Furthermore, the inclusion of different factors allows investors to explore factor rotation strategies and adjust factor weightings according to market conditions.

In this chapter, we first discuss the mean-variance optimization, a popular approach to construct portfolios using forecasted expected returns and forecasted covariance matrix of stock returns. Then we explore different methods to estimate the covariance matrix of stock returns and forecast the expected returns of stocks by combining stock selection signals. After that, we discuss the Black-Litterman model, a Bayesian model that provides an alternative way to incorporate expected return forecasts in portfolio construction. Last, we draw attention to portfolio constraints used to control for portfolio risk and to increase diversification.

Mean-Variance Optimization

Since Harry Markowitz (1952, 1959) published mean-variance portfolio theory, mean-variance portfolio optimization has gradually become the foundation of modern asset management and is still the most widely used method in portfolio construction. The crux of mean-variance optimization assumes that investors prefer (1) higher expected returns for a given level of risk and (2) lower risk for a given a level of expected return. When standard deviation (variance) is used as the risk measure, portfolios that provide the maximum expected return for a given standard deviation or the minimum standard deviation for a given expected return are efficient portfolios. For a portfolio with N risky assets to invest in, the portfolio return is the weighted average return of the assets:

$$r_p = w_1 r_1 + w_2 r_2 + \cdots + w_N r_N = w' r$$

where $w_i, \forall i = 1, 2, \ldots, N,$ is the weight of asset i in the portfolio;

r_i is the return of the asset i in the portfolio;

$w = [w_1, w_2, ..., w_N]'$ is an $N \times 1$ column vector of asset weights;

$r = [r_1, r_2, ..., r_N]'$ is an $N \times 1$ column vector of asset returns.

The expected return and the variance of the portfolio can be expressed as

$$\mu_p = w_1\mu_1 + w_2\mu_2 + \cdots + w_N\mu_N = w'\mu = \sum_{i=1}^{N} w_i\mu_i$$

$$\sigma_p^2 = \text{var}(w_1 r_1 + w_2 r_2 + \cdots + w_N r_N) = w'\Sigma w = \sum_{i=1}^{N}\sum_{j=1}^{N} w_i w_j \sigma_{i,j}$$

where μ_i is the expected return of asset i in the portfolio, $\mu_i = E[r_i]$;

$\mu = [\mu_1, \mu_2, ..., \mu_N]'$ is an $N \times 1$ column vector of asset expected returns;

$\sigma_{i,j}$ is the variance of the returns of asset i if $i = j$ and the covariance of the returns of asset i and asset j if $i \neq j$;

Σ is an $N \times N$ covariance matrix of the returns of N assets, $\Sigma_{i,j} = \sigma_{i,j}$.

If the vector of the expected returns μ and the covariance matrix Σ are known, for a fully invested portfolio with expected portfolio return μ_p, we can formulate the following mean-variance portfolio optimization problem to assign optimal asset weights to minimize the variance of the portfolio:

$$\min_{w} \tfrac{1}{2} w'\Sigma w$$

$$s.t. \sum_{i=1}^{N} w_i\mu_i = w'\mu = \mu_p, \sum_{i=1}^{N} w_i = w'e = 1$$

where e is an $N \times 1$ column vector with all elements equal to 1.

The problem can be solved in closed form using the method of Lagrange:

$$L = \tfrac{1}{2} w'\Sigma w + \gamma(\mu_p - w'\mu) + \eta(1 - w'e)$$

To minimize L, take the derivative of w, γ and η:

$$\left.\begin{array}{l} \dfrac{\partial L}{\partial w} = 0 \Rightarrow \Sigma w - \gamma\mu - \eta e = 0 \\[2mm] \dfrac{\partial L}{\partial \gamma} = 0 \Rightarrow \mu_p - w'\mu = 0 \\[2mm] \dfrac{\partial L}{\partial \eta} = 0 \Rightarrow 1 - w'e = 0 \end{array}\right\} \Rightarrow \left\{\begin{array}{l} \tilde{w} = \eta\Sigma^{-1}e + \gamma\Sigma^{-1}\mu \quad \text{(minimum variance portfolio)} \\[2mm] \gamma = (\mu_p A - B)/D \\[2mm] \eta = (C - \mu_p B)/D \end{array}\right.$$

where $A = e'\Sigma^{-1}e > 0$, $B = e'\Sigma^{-1}\mu$, $C = \mu'\Sigma^{-1}\mu > 0$, $D = AC - B^2$

So for each specified μ_p, we can easily derive the optimal portfolio weights $\widetilde{w}$ and the corresponding minimum variance $\sigma_p^2 = \widetilde{w}'\Sigma\widetilde{w}$. Combining the results, we get a hyperbolic relationship between the expected return and the standard deviation for the efficient portfolios:

$$\sigma_p^2 = \eta + \gamma\mu_p = \left(A\mu_p^2 - 2B\mu_p + C\right)\big/D$$

The efficient frontier shows that the contribution of a stock to the portfolio risk is not its own volatility, but its covariance with other stocks. Therefore, the efficient frontier shows the importance of diversification: when we allocate stocks among various assets, we can achieve similar returns while reducing the portfolio risk or achieve higher returns while maintaining the portfolio risk. Diversification provides a mathematical explanation on why investors should not put all their eggs in one basket.

To yield a portfolio that has the lowest possible portfolio variance from these risky assets, we set the derivative of portfolio variance to 0:

$$\frac{d(\sigma_p^2)}{d\mu_p} = 2A\mu_p - 2B = 0 \Rightarrow \widetilde{\mu}_p = B/A \Rightarrow \widetilde{\sigma}_p^2 = 1/A, \ \widetilde{w}_p = \Sigma^{-1}e/A$$

The resulted portfolio is called **the global minimum variance portfolio**. Since the global minimum variance, $\widetilde{\sigma}_p^2$, and the asset weights, $\widetilde{w}_p$, depend on A and A only depends on the covariance matrix Σ, the portfolio weights are determined by the covariance matrix alone. In other words, the construction of the global minimum variance portfolio does not require an estimation of the expected returns.

If we introduce a risk-free asset (an asset with zero variance, in nominal term) with return r_f, we can invest part of our wealth in risky assets and the rest in the risk-free asset. The mean-variance optimization problem becomes

$$\min_{w} \tfrac{1}{2}w'\Sigma w$$

$$s.t. \ w'\mu + (1-w'e)r_f = r_f + w'(\mu - r_f e) = \mu_p$$

where w is an $N \times 1$ column vector of weights of investments in risky assets;

$$1 - w'e = 1 - \sum_{i=1}^{N} w_i \text{ is the weight of the investment in the risk-free asset;}$$

r_f is the return of the risk-free asset.

Using the method of Lagrange, we have

$$L = \tfrac{1}{2}w'\Sigma w + \gamma\left(\mu_p - r_f - w'(\mu - r_f e)\right)$$

Taking the derivative of w and γ and setting them to 0, we get the optimal weights:

$$\widetilde{w} = \gamma\Sigma^{-1}(\mu - r_f e)$$

where $\gamma = \dfrac{\mu_p - r_f}{E}$ and the constant $E = (\mu - r_f e)' \Sigma^{-1} (\mu - r_f e) = C - 2r_f B + r_f^2 A$

The relationship between the expected portfolio return and the variance of the efficient portfolio can be expressed as

$$\sigma_p^2 = \tilde{w}' \Sigma \tilde{w} = (\mu_p - r_f)^2 / E$$

The equation is more frequently expressed as

$$\text{Sharpe ratio} = \frac{\mu_p - r_f}{\sigma_p} = \sqrt{E}$$

As shown in Exhibit 10-1, the relationship between the expected portfolio return and the portfolio volatility becomes linear. The addition of a risk-free asset changes the hyperbolic efficient frontier to a straight line, which is tangent to the hyperbolic efficient frontier with only risky assets.

Exhibit 10-1 Efficient Frontier and Capital Market Line (CML)

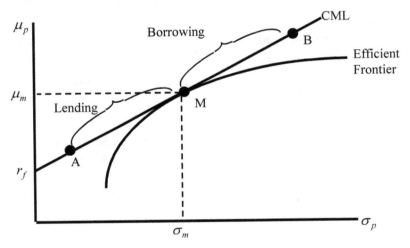

The tangent portfolio, M, is a fully invested portfolio ($\sum\limits_{i=1}^{N} w_i = 1$). When the risk-free asset is available, rational investors should make their investments along the tangent line. When their expected return is lower than the expected return of the tangent portfolio, the investors should invest part of their wealth in the tangent portfolio and the rest in the risk-free asset (e.g., point A). When their expected return is higher than the expected return of the tangent portfolio, they should borrow at the risk-free rate and invest in the tangent portfolio on margin (e.g., point B). Sharpe (1964) and Lintner (1965) showed that the tangent portfolio must be the market portfolio and the tangent line is called the capital market line (CML), which lays the foundation of Capital Asset Pricing Model (CAPM). The expected return of a portfolio can be expressed as a function of the expected market return:

$$\mu_p - r_f = \beta(\mu_m - r_f)$$

where β measures the sensitivity of the portfolio's return to the market return;

μ_m is the expected return on market portfolio.

Utility functions are often used to represent investors' preference on trade-offs between expected return and risk. The mean-variance optimization indicates that the investors have quadratic utility functions:

$$U = \mu_p - \tfrac{1}{2}\lambda\sigma_p^2$$

where U is the utility function;

λ is the risk aversion coefficient.

The constant λ measures the degree of risk aversion: the more risk averse an investor is, the larger the λ is. Therefore, we can also formulate the mean-variance optimization as a problem to maximize the quadratic utility function[62]:

$$\max_w U = \max_w \mu_p - \tfrac{1}{2}\lambda\sigma_p^2$$

Let us apply this alternative approach to the problem of optimizing the portfolio weights when there is a risk-free asset:

$$\max_w U = \max_w \mu_p - \tfrac{1}{2}\lambda\sigma_p^2 = \max_w r_f + w'(\mu - r_f e) - \tfrac{1}{2}\lambda w'\Sigma w$$

Taking the derivative of w and setting the derivative to 0, we have

$$(\mu - r_f e) - \lambda\Sigma w = 0 \Rightarrow \tilde{w} = \frac{1}{\lambda}\Sigma^{-1}(\mu - r_f e)$$

This equation for the weights of investments in risky assets is the same as our previous solution once we set the risk aversion coefficient to be $\lambda = \dfrac{1}{\gamma} = \dfrac{E}{\mu_p - r_f}$.

The simple mean-variance optimization requires only two inputs—the expected return vector and the covariance matrix. The model is based on a formal quantitative objective that will always give the same solution with the same set of parameters. These reasons contribute to the popularity of the mean-variance optimization. The method is not without drawbacks though. The mean-variance frontier is very sensitive to the inputs, and the inputs are subject to random errors in the estimation of the expected returns and the covariance matrix. The naïve mean-variance approach sometimes leads to extreme portfolio weights when the estimates of expected returns or covariance matrix contain small estimation errors. This "error-maximization" phenomenon (Michaud, 1989) often causes the unconstrained mean-variance portfolios to underperform simple weighting schemes such as equal weighting or market-cap weighting. Besides, small and statistically insignificant changes in these estimates also lead to significant changes in the composition of the portfolio weights, which in turn lead to frequent rebalances to stay on this elusive efficient frontier, incurring unnecessary transaction costs. To address these drawbacks, investors build sophisticated and robust methods to estimate the expected

---

[62] As we will show in the following sections, this alternative formulation is valuable in developing the risk-adjusted information coefficient and the Black-Litterman model.

returns and the covariance matrix, include sensible portfolio constraints, and incorporate prior beliefs in the portfolio optimization.

One assumption behind the mean-variance portfolio optimization is that the portfolio return is normally distributed or investors have a quadratic utility function. In reality, the quadratic utility curve is a mere approximation of investors' utility function when returns are close to zero and asset returns are far from normally distributed. Therefore, mean-variance optimization, as other mathematical models, is a simplified representation of the reality. It is well known that stock returns and factor returns are skewed and have high kurtosis. Hedge fund returns in general are negatively skewed as well. Exhibit 10-2 shows the cumulative daily return of a zero investment portfolio that longs Russell 2000 stocks with low short interests and shorts Russell 2000 stocks with high short interests in 2007-2008. Overall, the signal yields a positive annual return of 4.8% (Information ratio = 0.7). The figure clearly demonstrates the cumulative tail risk. During the quant meltdown, the factor returned -6.5% between August 6, 2007 and August 9, 2007. Right after the Lehman bankruptcy, the factor returned -6.0% between September 15, 2008 and September 18, 2008. That is, on two occasions, the signal lost more than one year's average gain in less than a week. Several relative value signals also suffered extreme losses during the same periods. Clearly, the tail risk is significantly higher than what the portfolio variance indicates.

Exhibit 10-2 Tail risk of short interest signal

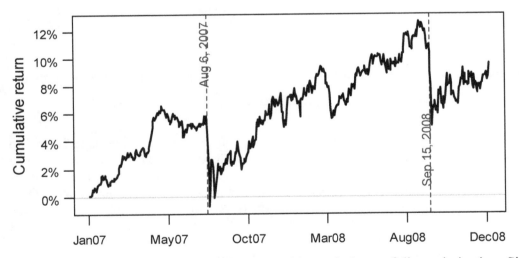

Investors may choose to include skewness and kurtosis in portfolio optimization. Since investors prefer positive skewness—higher likelihood of large positive return than large negative returns—and small kurtosis, theoretically we can include the skewness and the kurtosis in the utility function:

$$U = \mu_p - \tfrac{1}{2}\lambda\sigma_p^2 + \psi \times \text{skewness} - \zeta \times \text{kurtosis}$$

where ψ and ζ are positive numbers that reward positive skewness and penalize large kurtosis.

In practice, models that incorporate skewness and kurtosis are rare. Because of the interactions of factors, co-skewness and co-kurtosis between factors play a large role in determining a portfolio's skewness and kurtosis. Compared with the covariance matrix estimation, which is a difficult task, the co-skewness matrix and co-kurtosis matrix estimations are even more difficult as they rely heavily on tail events. The estimation errors of the estimated matrices are often large, which limits the value of including skewness and kurtosis in portfolio construction.

Risk Forecast

Since the covariance matrix of asset returns or factor returns is a key component in the mean-variance portfolio optimization, researchers have conducted extensive studies on the topic. Methods to estimate the covariance matrix vary in two major choices. The first choice is how much structure we place on the estimation. We can apply little structure to estimate a sample covariance matrix using the historical covariance of each pair of assets. The model is simple and the results are unbiased (the expected value of the calculated covariance is equal to the true covariance matrix). However, the model requires the estimation of a large number of parameters with potentially large estimation errors. Alternatively, we can apply restrictive structure to estimate a one-factor covariance matrix using the market beta of each asset. This model requires the estimation of far fewer parameters and reduces estimation errors. However, the model may fail to capture the complexity of the relationship between different assets and as a result the estimation may be biased. Practical models try to find the right trade-off between sample covariance matrix and a highly-structured estimator. The second choice is how to choose an appropriate historic window size and how to assign weights to different historical data. A short window size with insufficient number of historical returns may be unreliable and the calculated result may not represent the true distribution of the population. A long historical period with large number of historical returns will diminish such a problem. Yet the returns in the distant past may not represent the future population distribution since the underlying (economic, market, regulatory and psychological) fundamentals may well have changed over time. In this section, we summarize popular methods for covariance matrix estimation and explain how the methods handle the trade-offs in the estimation.

Sample Covariance Matrix

The sample covariance matrix is the best unbiased estimator using maximum likelihood method under the assumption of multivariate normality. Let us denote the historical returns for N assets over T periods as R, a $T \times N$ matrix where each row represents the returns of all assets at period t and each column represents the returns of asset i over T periods:

$$R = \begin{bmatrix} r_{1,1} & r_{1,2} & \cdots & r_{1,N} \\ r_{2,1} & r_{2,2} & \cdots & r_{2,N} \\ \vdots & \vdots & \ddots & \vdots \\ r_{T,1} & r_{T,2} & \cdots & r_{T,N} \end{bmatrix}$$

The (i, j)-th element of the sample covariance matrix Σ_T, the covariance of asset i and asset j, is calculated as

$$\Sigma_{T,i,j} = \frac{1}{T}\sum_{t=1}^{T}\left(r_{t,i} - \bar{r}_i\right)\left(r_{t,j} - \bar{r}_j\right)$$

where $r_{t,i}$ and $r_{t,j}$ are the returns of asset i and j at period t;

   $\bar{r}_i$ and $\bar{r}_j$ are the average returns of asset i and j over T periods

In matrix format, the covariance matrix can be calculated as

$$\Sigma_T = \frac{1}{T}(R - e\bar{R}')'(R - e\bar{R}') = \frac{1}{T}R'\left(I - \frac{1}{T}ee'\right)R$$

where $\bar{R}$ is a $N \times 1$ column vector of average returns, $\bar{R} = [\bar{r}_1, \bar{r}_2, \cdots, \bar{r}_N]'$;

   e is a $T \times 1$ column vector with all elements equal to 1;

   I is a $T \times T$ identity matrix.

If daily data are used, we can omit the average returns since the bias introduced by the omission, $\bar{r}_i\bar{r}_j$, is small. The approximation for the sample covariance matrix becomes

$$\Sigma_T = \frac{1}{T}R'R \text{ where } \Sigma_{T,i,j} = \frac{1}{T}\sum_{t=1}^{T}r_{t,i}r_{t,j}$$

To increase the weights for more recent data, the exponentially weighted covariance matrix can be used to overweigh recent data:

$$\Sigma_{T,i,j} = \lambda\Sigma_{T-1,i,j} + (1 - \lambda)r_{i,T}r_{j,T}$$

In the 1990s, J.P. Morgan developed the RiskMetrics variance model that used exponential weighting. For the US market, λ was set to 0.94. Since return time series exhibit volatility clustering (large changes tend to follow large changes and small changes tend to follow small changes) and leverage effects (negative correlation between asset returns and volatility), Generalized Autoregressive Conditional Heteroskedasticity (GARCH) models are often used to address the changes of variance/covariance over time.

Despite the simple computation involved in the sample covariance matrix, this approach has high complexity: the covariance of each pair is estimated as a parameter and the total number of the parameters estimated is $N(N+1)/2$. For a stock universe that contains 2,000 stocks, the number of parameters is 2,001,000! Sample covariance matrix suffers from the problem of high variance, which means that the estimation errors may be significant and lead to erroneous mean-variance efficient frontiers. The problem is further exacerbated if the number of observations is of the same order as the number of assets, which is often the case in applications to select individual securities. When the number of periods, T, is smaller than the number of assets, N, the sample covariance matrix is always singular: the matrix Σ_T has no inverse and we can always find a combination of weights to make the portfolio have an estimated volatility of zero. Naïve mean-variance optimizations using sample covariance matrix often produce extreme portfolio weights instead of diversified portfolios and result in dramatic swings in weights when there are small changes to the expected returns or the covariance matrix. Using longer history to estimate the covariance matrix can help reduce the estimation errors. However, the correlation between stocks may not be stable over time. Besides, many stocks also experience structural changes in their financials and business models over time, which makes historical returns less relevant in determining future risks. Since intraday trading data are readily available through TAQ, some investors use 5-minute returns to calculate the variance and the covariance of stock returns. Compared with daily returns, 5-minute returns increase the number of periods, T, by 78 fold. The number of periods is close to 10,000 in six months, which allows the sample covariance matrix to be estimated using return data from recent history.

To reduce the impact of outliers, to reduce the impact of estimation errors, and to increase diversification, investors often apply robust statistics and Bayesian shrinkage methods to covariance matrix estimation. For example, it is well understood that when two stocks have high estimated correlation (collinearity problem) and different expected returns, the mean-variance portfolio optimization tends to assign large positive weight to the stock with higher return and large negative weight to the stock with lower returns. One simple ad-hoc solution is to shrink the off-diagonal covariance terms. For example, we can simply shrink all the covariance terms by 20% and further cap the correlation between two stocks to be between -0.7 and 0.7. The shrinkage of covariance reduces the absolute value of the correlation between stocks, which in turn increases the estimated benefit of diversification in risk reduction. When the shrinkage methods are applied in the mean-variance optimization, they often yield more diversified portfolios with better risk characteristics.

Fundamental Factor Models

One approach to reduce the number of parameters in the covariance matrix estimation is to create structured multi-factor risk models. In a multi-factor risk model, the returns of a stock are explained as a linear combination of factor returns and residual returns:

$$r_{t,i} = \alpha_i + \beta_{i,1}f_{t,1} + \cdots + \beta_{i,k}f_{t,k} + \cdots + \beta_{i,K}f_{t,K} + \varepsilon_{t,i} = B_i'f_t + \varepsilon_{t,i}$$

where $r_{t,i}$ is the return of asset i for period t;

α_i is the intercept of the factor model for asset i, $i = 1, 2, \ldots, N$;

$\beta_{i,k}$ is asset i's exposure to the k-th factor, $k = 1, 2, \ldots, K$;

$B_i = [\beta_{i,1}, \beta_{i,2}, \ldots, \beta_{i,K}]'$ is a $K \times 1$ column vector of factor exposures;

$f_{t,k}$ is the return of the k-th factor for period t, $k = 1, 2, \ldots, K$;

$f_t = [f_{t,1}, f_{t,2}, \ldots, f_{t,K}]'$ is a column vector of factor returns;

$\varepsilon_{t,i}$ is the residual return of asset i for period t.

In matrix form, the returns of the N stocks can be expressed as

$$r_t = Bf_t + \varepsilon_t$$

where $r_t = [r_{t,1}, r_{t,2}, \ldots, r_{t,N}]'$ is an $N \times 1$ column vector of asset returns;

B is an $N \times K$ matrix, the exposure matrix for all N assets, $B_{i,k} = \beta_{i,k}$;

$\varepsilon_t = [\varepsilon_{t,1}, \varepsilon_{t,2}, \ldots, \varepsilon_{t,N}]'$ is an $N \times 1$ column vector of residual returns.

If we further assume that the correlations of the residual returns of different assets are zero ($cor(\varepsilon_{t,i}, \varepsilon_{t,j}) = 0$, $\forall i \neq j$) and the correlations between residual returns and factor returns ($cor(f_{t,k}, \varepsilon_{t,i}) = 0$) are zero, the covariance matrix of the stocks can be calculated as

$$\Sigma = BFB' + S$$

where F is a $K \times K$ matrix, the covariance matrix of the K factors, $F_{k,l} = cov(f_{t,k}, f_{t,l})$;

S is an $N \times N$ diagonal matrix for the variance of residual returns, $S_{i,i} = var(\varepsilon_{t,i})$.

Unlike the sample covariance matrix, the risk models using K factors only need to estimate at most $NK + K(K+1)/2 + N$ (for B, F, and S, respectively) parameters instead of $N(N+1)/2$ parameters. When K is much smaller than N, the number of parameters that needs to be estimated is much smaller as well. If we use the market return as the factor and market betas as the factor exposures, we have a single-factor model:

$$r_{t,i} = \alpha_i + \beta_i r_{t,mkt} + \varepsilon_{t,i}$$

For this single-factor model, we only need to estimate the variance of the market returns, σ_m^2, and the market beta of the N assets, $\beta = [\beta_1, \beta_2, \cdots, \beta_N]'$. The covariance matrix of the assets can be expressed as

$$\Sigma = \sigma_m^2 \beta\beta' + S.$$

The factors, $f_{t,1}, f_{t,2}, \ldots, f_{t,K}$, are called the common factors in a factor risk model. The asset return risks arising from exposures to common factors is called the systematic risk and the standard deviation (or variance) of residual returns is called specific risk or idiosyncratic risk. Since the model assumes that the residual returns of different assets have zero correlation, we can directly estimate the correlation of any two assets from the factor model:

$$cor(r_{t,i}, r_{t,j}) = \frac{cov(r_{t,i}, r_{t,j})}{\sqrt{var(r_{t,i})} \times \sqrt{var(r_{t,j})}} = \frac{B_i' F B_j}{\sqrt{(B_i' F B_i + S_{i,i})} \times \sqrt{(B_j' F B_j + S_{j,j})}}$$

In practice, the systematic risk arising from exposures to common factors usually explains no more than 75% of an individual stock's total variance and the specific risk explains no less than 25% ($B_i' F B_i < 3 \times S_{i,i}$). Hence, the correlation between two stocks is usually capped at 0.75.

The total portfolio risk, as measured by portfolio variance, can be decomposed to systematic risk and specific risk as well. For a portfolio with weight vector w, the portfolio variance is estimated as

$$w'\Sigma w = w'(BFB')w + w'Sw = \text{systematic risk} + \text{idiosyncratic risk}$$

Among factor models, fundamental factor models are the most popular among institutional investors. Any fundamental factor that can explain the cross-sectional differences in stock returns is a candidate for factor risk models. The factors used are often variables that have proven their explanatory power in equity research. Barra, Axioma and APT offer a wide variety of style factors as well as indicator variables for country and industry exposures. For example, the Barra USE4 model has one country factor, 12 style factors and 60 industry factors. Every US stock has an exposure of 1 to the US country factor. The 12 style factors are growth, size, size nonlinearity, dividend yield, book-to-price, earnings yield, beta, residual volatility, non-linear beta, momentum, leverage, and liquidity. Although Barra has its own definition of different style factors, it is clear from their names that these style factors are used by many portfolio managers for stock selection as well. For most Barra style factors, the factor exposures are robust z-score measures to the underlying factors. Barra assigns industry exposures using the stocks' asset and sales exposures. If a company only has asset and sales exposures to one industry, the stock gets an industry weight of 1 for that industry and 0 for other industries. If a company has asset and sales exposures to multiple industries, the stock may have industry weights for up to five industries and the total weights of the industry exposures add up to 1. Therefore, it is important to note that the factor exposures in the Barra model are often not estimated from regression of stock returns on factor returns. Using robust z-scores as style factor exposures and industry weights as industry factor exposures removes the need to estimate all $N \times K$ parameters in the factor exposure matrix B. The factor returns of the fundamental factor models are estimated using a generalized least square regression:

$$f_t = \left(B'S^{-1}B\right)^{-1}B'S^{-1}r_t$$

Since many of these fundamental factors incorporate up-to-date information of the underlying stocks, they automatically adapt to the structural changes of the companies. Besides explanatory power, stability is another requirement for factors used in factor models. The serial correlation of factor exposures, the cross-sectional correlation between factor exposures of the stocks at t and the factor exposures of the same stocks at $t + 1$, should be close to 1. Otherwise, the instability of factor exposures will introduce high portfolio turnover when investors manage the portfolio risk using the risk model. Therefore, unstable factors such as short-term mean reversion signals are usually not included in the factors even though they have good explanatory power of cross-sectional stock returns.

There is often a trade-off between the responsiveness and the stability of a factor risk model. A model that is more responsive to market changes and underlying stock characteristic changes provides better accuracy in short-term risk forecasting. But to make the model more responsive, we introduce instability to factor exposures and the factor covariance matrix. When we rebalance the portfolio, such instability introduces higher portfolio turnover and higher trading costs. The appropriate trade-off between responsiveness and stability depends on the portfolio diversification and average holding period. For strategies with short holding periods, the instability introduces little extra cost; for strategies with longer holding periods and stable alpha forecasts, frequent changes in risk estimations introduce unnecessary rebalances. Since there is no one-size-fits-all solution, investors use different models to meet their portfolio construction and risk monitoring needs. In response, vendors also provide multiple models. For US stocks, Barra has long-term models, short-term models, trading models, and daily models to satisfy the requirements of different clients. For example, the Barra USE4 model has a short-term version (USE4S) and a long-term version (USE4L). USE4S and USE4L share the same factor exposures and factor returns, but they have different factor covariance matrices and different specific risk forecasts. The short-term model, USE4S, is designed to be more responsive to market changes and provides better predictions. The long-term model, USE4L, sacrifices the responsiveness for more stability in risk estimations.

Economic Factor Models

Although fundamental factor models are more popular, many investors also use economic factor models. For example, Northfield macroeconomic equity risk model measures a stock's exposure to macroeconomic factors and includes the following seven factors: inflation, industrial production, slope of the term structure, investor confidence, foreign exchange rates, housing starts, and oil prices. The difference between fundamental factor models and economic factor models are not simply the differences in the factors: for fundamental factor models, the factor exposures of a stock are usually directly observable and the factor returns need to be estimated. For instance, the size factor is calculated as the z-scores of the log of the market caps. For economic factors, the factor exposures of a stock are not directly observable and the factor returns are observable instead. For instance, the inflation rate is a direct observation. However, a stock's exposure to inflation needs to be estimated. How do we estimate the factor exposure of a stock to an economic factor? One simple approach is to regress historical stock returns against the time series of underlying economic factors. The regression often requires at least three years of data to make the estimated factor exposure stable, which is a limitation of the economic factor models. The factor exposures estimated from the regression may have estimation error. Furthermore, if a stock's fundamentals change in the past years, its factor exposures are likely to change and the regression is an ineffective way of capturing the current exposures. Overall, fundamental factor models tend to have better performance than economic factor models in risk forecasts, which explains the popularity of fundamental models.

Statistical Factor Models

Besides fundamental factors and economic factors, statistical factors such as principal components extracted from historical returns can also be used. Let us start with the sample covariance to calculate the principal components. We can express the covariance matrix using singular value decomposition:

$$\Sigma = VDV' = \begin{bmatrix} V_1 & V_2 & \cdots & V_N \end{bmatrix} \begin{bmatrix} \lambda_1 & 0 & \cdots & 0 \\ 0 & \lambda_2 & \cdots & 0 \\ \vdots & \vdots & \ddots & \vdots \\ 0 & 0 & \cdots & \lambda_N \end{bmatrix} \begin{bmatrix} V_1' \\ V_2' \\ \vdots \\ V_N' \end{bmatrix} \Leftrightarrow V'\Sigma V = D$$

where $V_1, V_2, ..., V_N$ are $N \times 1$ eigenvectors of Σ;

$\lambda_1 \geq \lambda_2 \geq \cdots \geq \lambda_N \geq 0$ are eigenvalues of Σ;

$V = \begin{bmatrix} V_1 & V_2 & \cdots & V_N \end{bmatrix}$ is an $N \times N$ matrix with orthogonal columns, $V'V = I$;

D is an $N \times N$ diagonal matrix of eigenvalues, $D_{i,i} = \lambda_i$.

The sum of the N eigenvalues is equal to the sum of the variance of the N assets:

$$\sum_{i=1}^{N} \lambda_i = \sum_{i=1}^{N} \Sigma_{i,i}$$

Let us transform the original return matrix[63] (mean returns of stocks are removed), R, by V and calculate the covariance matrix:

$$\text{var}(RV) = \frac{1}{T}(RV)'(RV) = \frac{1}{T}V'R'RV = V'\Sigma V = D$$

The columns of the transformed matrix RV are uncorrelated with each other and the covariance matrix of RV is the diagonal matrix D. Each column of the matrix RV is a principal component. Each principal component is a linear combination of the existing assets: $RV_i = R \times V_i$. The principal components can be considered as artificial assets that are uncorrelated with each other and have variances $\lambda_1, \lambda_2, ..., \lambda_N$. These principal components (artificial assets) are factors used in statistical models. If we use all N factors and calculate the factor variance matrix D, we recover the sample covariance matrix of the returns as VDV'. Many factors with smaller variances may be noises that do not explain stock returns. Instead of an exact representation using all N factors, we can approximate Σ using the first K principal components, and the approximation can be expressed as

$$\Sigma \approx V_K D_K V_K' + S$$

where $V_K = \begin{bmatrix} V_1 & V_2 & \cdots & V_K \end{bmatrix}$ is a $N \times K$ matrix that represents the first K columns of V;

D_K is a $K \times K$ diagonal matrix that represents the top-left sub-matrix of D;

S is an $N \times N$ diagonal matrix for the variance of residual returns.

The proportion of the total variance explained by the first K principal components is

$$\sum_{k=1}^{K} \lambda_k \bigg/ \sum_{i=1}^{N} \lambda_N = \sum_{k=1}^{K} \lambda_k \bigg/ \sum_{i=1}^{N} \Sigma_{i,i}$$

The number of principal components is often chosen so that the selected principal components can explain a predefined percent (e.g., 60%) of the total variance. The residual variance of a stock is then calculated as part of the total stock variance that is not explained by the principal components:

---

[63] Principal components can also be extracted from the correlation matrix instead of covariance matrix. When correlation matrix is used, the return matrix represents standardized returns: after removing the mean return of a stock, the returns are further normalized by historical volatility.

$$S_{i,i} = \Sigma_{i,i} - [V_{i,1} \quad V_{i,2} \quad \cdots \quad V_{i,K}] \times D_K \times [V_{i,1} \quad V_{i,2} \quad \cdots \quad V_{i,K}]'$$

A model using K principal components only needs to estimate $NK + K + N$ (for V, D, and S, respectively) parameters. Since principal components are used as factors, statistical models have no dependency on external data. Therefore, the costs of maintaining statistical factor models are significantly lower (many companies pay hundreds of thousands of dollars a year to Barra for fundamental risk models). Although it is widely believed that the first principal component represents a market factor and others may mirror industry specific effects, it is difficult to interpret principal components. That causes problem for risk decomposition and portfolio return attribution. If a portfolio has a factor loading of 0.5 on the long-term momentum factor and the factor returns 40 bps in a day, the portfolio manager can attribute 20 bps of returns to long-term momentum. If we replace the long-term momentum factor with principal component five, it provides little intuitive information. Despite their limitations, statistical factor models sometimes capture risk factors that are not included in the fundamental models. All fundamental factor models have predefined factors. Any common factors that are not included in the model will not be captured. Statistical models, on the other hand, extract factors from recent data and can dynamically capture hidden factors that influence cross-sectional stock returns. Therefore, many risk managers use statistical factor models to complement fundamental factor models.

Limitation of Risk Models

Although factor models are popular choices for equity risk management and are valuable tools in portfolio construction, risk estimation, and risk monitoring, we should have a clear understanding of their limitations. Before 2007, many investors treated the portfolio risk estimated from factor models as a precise measurement of risk. They understood the uncertainty captured by the risk models, but failed to fully understand the uncertainty not reflected in the risk models. Before the second Iraq war, Donald Rumsfeld, the Defense Secretary of the United States said,

"There are known knowns; there are things we know we know. We also know there are known unknowns; that is to say, we know there are some things we do not know. But there are also unknown unknowns—the ones we don't know we don't know."

Ultimately, the unknown unknowns—risks not incorporated in the risk models—often lead to massive losses as they become known. Another potential problem is that the factor risks and residual risks are estimated from history. When the estimations do not reflect the current market conditions, the risk model may underestimate the risks. The rare events may not occur for a long time, but unless the risk models correctly incorporate them, the results can be disastrous. Before the housing crisis started in 2007, many subprime mortgages had AAA credit ratings. One of the main reasons that the risk models assigned little risk to these mortgages was the low mortgage default rate from late 1990s to 2006, which coincided with the period of housing price bubble and huge growth in subprime mortgages. When the housing bubble burst, companies that held such mortgages and companies that provided mortgage insurances suffered catastrophic losses.

In the 2007 quant meltdown and in the 2008 financial crisis, many funds that relied on factor models for risk management suffered losses far more severe than what the models forecasted. In other words, the models failed exactly at the moment when risk management was critical for the survival of those funds. The failure of the factor models during the crises revealed the following model limitations:

- Even with a dozen style factors and dozens of country/industry factors, linear factor models are not sophisticated enough to capture all risks in the financial markets. No model can include all factors that impact stock returns—in this book alone, we discuss dozens of factors that impact stock returns—since it will make the model unmanageable. Besides, the relationship between stock returns and factor returns can be non-linear. Therefore, linear models are approximations instead of accurate descriptions of reality.

- Factor models make the assumption that returns follow multivariate normal distributions. Financial returns, on the other hand, have fat tails and are often skewed. Most factor returns have fat tails as well and are negatively skewed. Therefore, the assumption of normal distribution underestimates the frequencies of tail events.

- One reason why the covariance matrix estimated from factor models is more stable than the covariance matrix estimated from historical returns is the higher stability in factor correlations. The volatilities of factors and their correlations are estimated using a long history to guarantee their stability. But as a market crisis strikes, the volatilities of all factors increase with the market volatility. Therefore, the lag built in the factor models underestimates the factor volatilities.

- During a market crisis correlations between stocks rise dramatically. The models underestimate the correlations between stocks and overestimate diversification benefits during a crisis. Therefore, the underestimation of correlations during market crises also leads to underestimation of portfolio risk.

- When a portfolio is optimized using a risk model, the risk of the portfolio estimated from the same risk model often underestimates the risk. More often than not, the number of factors used in the risk model is much smaller than the number of assets included in the portfolio optimization, so the optimization often forces the final portfolio towards the null space of the risk factors—exposures to risk factors are close to 0. Although the optimized portfolio has low exposures to the common factors in the model, it often has exposures to other systematic risks that are not included in the model. Therefore, the unaccounted systematic risk leads to underestimation of the systematic risk and the total risk in optimized portfolios.

These limitations do not suggest that factor models are not useful in portfolio risk management. Quite the contrary, they are valuable tools that are widely used by investors. We just need to understand the limitations of factor models in order to use the information generated by the models properly. Understanding the limitation of factor models also provides opportunity to further improve portfolio risk forecast and risk management. For example, if we use the same model used in the portfolio optimization to estimate the portfolio risk, we often underestimate the portfolio's true systematic risk and total risk. After optimizing the portfolio using one risk model, using a different risk model with different factors or different time horizon helps investors better evaluate the portfolio's risk exposures.

We can also introduce an adjustment factor to correct the bias in the risk estimation. For an asset or portfolio i with expected return $\bar{r}_i$, if a risk model accurately estimates the risk $\sigma_{t,i}$, we would expect the normalized residual returns, $b_{t,i} = (r_{t,i} - \bar{r}_i)/\sigma_{t,i}$, to follow a normal distribution with mean 0 and variance 1. Therefore, $\sum_{t=1}^{T} b_{i,t}^2$ should follow a chi-square distribution with mean T and variance $2T$. When T is large, $Z_i = \frac{1}{T} \sum_{t=1}^{T} b_{i,t}^2$ is close to a normal distribution with mean 1 and variance $2/T$. If Z_i is significantly larger than 1, it indicates that the realized variance is significantly higher than the model estimated variance. Z_i, the adjustment factor, is then used to scale the model estimated variance. For instance, if we want to control the portfolio risk within 5% and the adjustment factor is 25/16, we control the model estimated risk within 4% instead. Since the adjustment factor depends on stock selection signals and portfolio optimization decisions (e.g., full neutralization of factor exposures versus small reduction in factor exposures), the adjustment factor needs to be tuned to an individual portfolio to make the adjusted variance unbiased.

Once we understand the limitation of the normal distribution assumption, we can incorporate tail risk in our portfolio construction. For instance, merger and acquisition activities introduce tail risk to equity long-short portfolios as acquirers sometimes pay a premium as high as 50 to 100 percent for acquisition targets to facilitate the takeover process. For the majority of long-short portfolios, acquisition targets are more likely to be in the short positions of the portfolio instead of the longs. When acquirers pay large premiums for the acquisition targets, such targets tend to be companies with low profitability and underperforming share prices. The existence of such tail risk prompts many investors to have tighter position size limits on short positions. By limiting the size of individual short positions, the investors can better manage the acquisition risk—the risk that a company is acquired by another company at high premium—in short positions.

Risk-Adjusted Information Coefficient

In Chapter 9 we defined raw IC as the cross-sectional linear correlation between the z-scores calculated at t and the realized future raw returns between t and $t+1$. If the portfolio weights are proportional to their z-scores, the raw IC determines the expected return of the portfolio. Such a portfolio, however, usually has exposures to systematic risk factors. For instance, the raw momentum factors may have significant correlation with market beta. If the portfolio weights are proportional to the z-scores, the constructed portfolio may have significant market beta exposure. In practice, portfolio managers often try to eliminate or limit the exposures to these risk factors. Let us consider the case of a cash-neutral portfolio [64] ($\sum_{i=1}^{N} w_i = e'w = 0$) that is neutral to all common factors

---

[64] Many risk models have a market factor that the factor exposure of every stock is 1. For example, when we build a long/short portfolio and use USE4 model, the cash-neutral constraint is equivalent to zero exposure to the US country factor.

($B'W = 0$). If the forecasted returns are $\alpha = [\alpha_1, \alpha_2, ..., \alpha_N]'$, we apply the mean-variance optimization to maximize the utility function:

$$\max_{w} \alpha'w - \tfrac{1}{2} \times \lambda w' \Sigma w$$

$$s.t. \begin{bmatrix} e' \\ B' \end{bmatrix} w = \tilde{B}'w = 0$$

where α is an $N \times 1$ vector of forecasted asset returns;

$\quad$ B is an $N \times K$ matrix of factor exposures;

$\quad$ $\tilde{B} = \begin{bmatrix} e & B \end{bmatrix}$ is an $N \times (K+1)$ matrix for cash exposures and factor exposures;

$\quad$ Σ is the covariance matrix estimated from the risk model, $\Sigma = BFB' + S$.

Since the portfolio has no factor exposures, the variance of the portfolio $w'\Sigma w$ is equivalent to the variance calculated from the diagonal specific risk matrix:

$$w'\Sigma w = w'Sw$$

If we replace $w'\Sigma w$ with $w'Sw$ and apply the method of Lagrange, we get

$$L = \alpha'w - \tfrac{1}{2}\lambda w'Sw - \gamma'\left(\tilde{B}'w\right)$$

To minimize L, take the derivative of w and γ:

$$\left. \begin{aligned} \frac{\partial L}{\partial w} &= 0 \Rightarrow \alpha - \lambda Sw - \tilde{B}\gamma = 0 \\ \frac{\partial L}{\partial \gamma} &= 0 \Rightarrow \tilde{B}'w = 0 \end{aligned} \right\} \Rightarrow \begin{cases} w = \lambda^{-1}S^{-1}\left(\alpha - \tilde{B}\gamma\right) \\ \tilde{B}'w = 0 \end{cases} \Rightarrow \lambda^{-1}\tilde{B}'S^{-1}\left(\alpha - \tilde{B}\gamma\right) = 0 \Rightarrow$$

$$\begin{cases} \gamma = \left(\tilde{B}'S^{-1}\tilde{B}\right)^{-1}\tilde{B}'S^{-1}\alpha \\ w = \lambda^{-1}S^{-1}\left(\alpha - \tilde{B}\left(\tilde{B}'S^{-1}\tilde{B}\right)^{-1}\tilde{B}'S^{-1}\alpha\right) = \lambda^{-1}S^{-1}\left(I - \tilde{B}\left(\tilde{B}'S^{-1}\tilde{B}\right)^{-1}\tilde{B}'S^{-1}\right)\alpha \end{cases}$$

Let us tackle the mean-variance optimization problem from a different perspective. Since the raw forecasted asset returns have exposures to risk factors, we decompose the forecasted returns into returns from factor exposures and stock-specific returns:

$$\alpha = \tilde{B}f + \alpha_\perp, \text{ where } \alpha_\perp \sim N(0, S)$$

The forecasted factor returns can be estimated using the generalized least squares regression:

$$f = \left(\tilde{B}'S^{-1}\tilde{B}\right)^{-1}\tilde{B}'S^{-1}\alpha$$

The residual stock-specific returns are then estimated as

$$\alpha_\perp = \alpha - \tilde{B}f = \alpha - \tilde{B}\left(\tilde{B}'S^{-1}\tilde{B}\right)^{-1}\tilde{B}'S^{-1}\alpha = \left(I - \tilde{B}\left(\tilde{B}'S^{-1}\tilde{B}\right)^{-1}\tilde{B}'S^{-1}\right)\alpha$$

The residual stock-specific returns have no exposures to risk factors:

$$\alpha_{\perp}'S^{-1}\widetilde{B} = \alpha_{\perp}'\left(I - S^{-1}\widetilde{B}(\widetilde{B}'S^{-1}\widetilde{B})^{-1}\widetilde{B}'\right)S^{-1}\widetilde{B} = \alpha_{\perp}'\left(S^{-1}\widetilde{B} - S^{-1}\widetilde{B}(\widetilde{B}'S^{-1}\widetilde{B})^{-1}(\widetilde{B}'S^{-1}\widetilde{B})\right)$$

$$= \alpha_{\perp}'\left(S^{-1}\widetilde{B} - S^{-1}\widetilde{B}\right) = 0$$

Since the forecasted residual-stock return has no exposures to risk factors, the mean-variance optimization can be simplified as

$$\max_{w} \alpha_{\perp}'w - \tfrac{1}{2}\lambda w'Sw \Rightarrow w = \lambda^{-1}S^{-1}\alpha_{\perp} = \lambda^{-1}S^{-1}\left(I - \widetilde{B}(\widetilde{B}'S^{-1}\widetilde{B})^{-1}\widetilde{B}'S^{-1}\right)\alpha$$

For each stock, the weight is proportional to the forecasted residual stock return divided by the residual variance of the stock.

When we use risk models to control the portfolio exposures to risk factors, risk-adjusted residual returns are used instead of raw returns to estimate the ICs. The residual returns are estimated using a similar generalized least squares regression:

$$r = \widetilde{B}r_f + r_{\perp}$$

where r is an $N \times 1$ vector of realized future raw returns;

r_f is an $(K+1) \times 1$ vector of factor returns;

$r_{\perp} \sim N(0, S)$ is an $N \times 1$ vector of residual returns.

The realized factor returns are estimated as $r_f = (\widetilde{B}'S^{-1}\widetilde{B})^{-1}\widetilde{B}'S^{-1}r$ and the risk-adjusted residual returns are $r_{\perp} = \left(I - \widetilde{B}(\widetilde{B}'S^{-1}\widetilde{B})^{-1}\widetilde{B}'S^{-1}\right)r$.

Let us define $\widetilde{z}_i = \dfrac{\alpha_{\perp,i}}{\sqrt{S_{i,i}}}$, $\widetilde{r}_i = \dfrac{r_{\perp,i}}{\sqrt{S_{i,i}}}$. The risk-adjusted IC, $IC_{adj} = cor(\widetilde{z}_i, \widetilde{r}_i)$, is the correlation between $\widetilde{z}_i$ and $\widetilde{r}_i$. Both $\widetilde{z}_i$ and $\widetilde{r}_i$ approximately follow a standard normal distribution as they are normalized residuals from generalized least squares regressions. The residual return of the optimized portfolio can be estimated as

$$r_p = w'\hat{r} = \sum_{i=1}^{N} w_i \hat{r}_i = \frac{1}{\lambda}\sum_{i=1}^{N}\frac{\hat{\alpha}_i}{S_{i,i}}\hat{r}_i = \frac{1}{\lambda}\sum_{i=1}^{N}\left(\frac{\hat{\alpha}_i}{\sqrt{S_{i,i}}} \times \frac{\hat{r}_i}{\sqrt{S_{i,i}}}\right) = \frac{1}{\lambda}\sum_{i=1}^{N}(\widetilde{z}_i \times \widetilde{r}_i)$$

$$\Rightarrow E[r_p] = \frac{1}{\lambda}\sum_{i=1}^{N}E[\widetilde{z}_i \times \widetilde{r}_i] = \frac{N}{\lambda} \times cor(\widetilde{z}_i, \widetilde{r}_i) \times \sigma_{\widetilde{z}} \times \sigma_{\widetilde{r}} \approx \frac{N}{\lambda} \times IC_{adj}$$

Therefore, the expected residual return of the portfolio is proportional to the adjusted IC. Since the risk-adjusted factors remove the factor exposures, their performance can be substantially different from the raw factors. When the factor exposures of the final portfolio are tightly constrained, the portfolio performance is closer to what the risk-adjusted factors indicate than what the raw factors indicate. If only some of the systematic factors are tightly constrained, we can choose to include the subset of factors that are constrained. When investors decide to hedge exposures to beta, size, and book-to-price factors (Fama-French factors), they may choose to include Barra factors beta, size, and book-to-price in the risk-adjusted information coefficient calculation. Such an approach makes the risk-adjusted information coefficient a versatile tool to handle different portfolio constraints.

Return Forecast

In previous chapters, we discussed a wide variety of seasonality factors, economic factors, technical factors, and fundamental factors that help investors make investment decisions. In this section, we discuss how investors may use quantitative models to combine the information from different factors to forecast stock returns. The process of combining information from different factors is more art than science. There is no standard approach. Instead, investors choose different models that best meet their needs and decisions are often influenced by their experience with the effectiveness of different models.

Factor Group and Composite Factor Scores

Complex quantitative stock selection models may incorporate dozens of factors. By construction, signals that capture similar information are often similar to each other. In the relative value group, we have equity value-based factors and enterprise value-based factors. Within equity value-based factors, we have different profitability measures as numerators. Naturally, these similar factors are correlated. Similar factors are grouped together to form a factor group. For each factor group, the z-scores of these factors are often combined to generate a group z-score. Then group z-scores from different groups are further combined to form a final score for each asset.

There are two methods to identify factors that have high correlation with each other. The first one is to calculate the time series correlation of factor returns: we build long-short zero investment portfolios using individual signals and calculate the correlation of portfolio returns. The second one is to calculate the cross-sectional correlation of factor scores at each period and use the long-term average of cross-sectional correlations. The cross-sectional correlation of factor scores is noisier than the time series correlation of factor returns since factor scores include noise from individual assets. But a time series of cross-sectional correlation of factor scores sometimes yields patterns that are not revealed by the correlation of factor returns. Let us consider the correlation between the 12M-1M momentum signal and the market beta. Both the long-term time series correlation of factor returns and the long-term average cross-sectional rank correlation of factor scores are close to zero. But as Exhibit 10-3 shows, the cross-sectional correlations can be significantly positive or negative at certain time periods and the magnitude of correlation reveals important information.

At the beginning of April 2009, the cross-sectional correlation was -0.75 since low beta stocks had outperformed high beta stocks during the financial crisis. It means that a bet on the momentum signal was largely a bet against market beta, which explained the loss of the momentum signal when the stock market recovered in 2009. One year later, the cross-sectional correlation reached 0.5 as high beta stocks outperformed low beta stocks and a bet on the momentum signal was partly a bet on the market beta. Therefore, the time series of cross-sectional correlations indicate that after extreme market moves, the momentum factor scores have high positive or negative correlation with market betas.

Exhibit 10-3 Correlation between momentum factor and beta

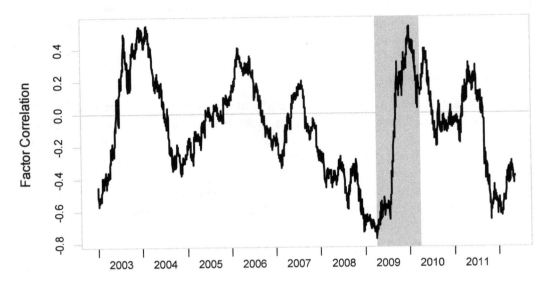

When we have two signals with high correlation, it may be sufficient to include just one of them in the final model. A two-stage regression model is often used to answer whether it is sufficient to select only one of them. Let us consider two signals, A and B. In the first stage, we regress the returns against signal A and calculate the residual returns from the regression. In the second stage, we regress the residual returns from the first-stage regression against signal B. If the coefficient on the signal B is no longer statistically significant (or has the wrong sign), signal A subsumes signal B; otherwise, signal B adds value beyond signal A. Similarly, we can regress the returns against B in the first stage and regress the residual returns from the first-stage against signal A. If the coefficient on signal A is no longer statistically significant, signal B subsumes signal A; otherwise, signal A adds value beyond signal B. When one of the factors subsumes the other, we only need to include one factor; when neither subsumes the other, we often combine both factors. The two-stage model is also used to investigate whether one of the factors dominates the other: if signal A subsumes signal B and signal B does not subsume signal A, A is the dominant factor.

Factors with moderate correlations capture different aspects of a factor group. Hence, similar factors within the same factor group that are not subsumed by other factors are often combined to yield a group score. Group scores from different factor groups are then combined to generate the final forecasts. Using group scores reduces the dimensions of the factors and makes the forecast model more robust. How do we combine factors to yield a group score? In general, we calculate a group z-score for a factor group as the weighted average z-scores of factors within that group:

$$z_{i,t,k} = \sum_{m \in G_k} w_{k,m} z_{i,t,m}$$

where G_k is the factors in factor group k;

$w_{k,m}$ is the weight of factor m in group k, $\sum_{m \in G_k} w_{k,m} = 1$;

$z_{i,t,m}$ is the z-score of factor m for asset i at t;

$z_{i,t,k}$ is the composite z-score of factor group k for asset i at t.

Theoretically, we want to select a set of weights that maximizes the predictive power of the group score in forecasting stock returns using a multivariate linear regression:

$$r_{i,t+1} = \beta_0 + \beta_1 z_{i,t,k} + \varepsilon_{i,t+1} = \beta_0 + \beta_1 \left(\sum_{m \in G_k} w_{k,m} z_{i,t,m} \right) + \varepsilon_{i,t+1}, \quad s.t. \sum_{m \in G_k} w_{k,m} = 1$$

where $r_{i,t+1}$ is the realized future return of asset i between t and $t + 1$;

β_0 and β_1 are the estimated intercept and slope of the regression;

$\varepsilon_{i,t+1}$ is the residual return of asset i between t and $t + 1$.

However, multicollinearity may pose a problem for the linear regression. Although any pair of signals may only have moderate correlation, one factor in the group may be explained by a combination of other factors in the group. Because of multicollinearity, a multivariate regression without constraints is not a good choice in determining the weights of each factor. Although each individual signal has positive expected alpha[65], the weight of the signal may become negative because of multicollinearity. To address the multicollinearity problem, we can add a constraint that the weights of all signals need to be non-negative in the regression:

$w_{k,m} \geq 0, \ \forall m \in G_k$

We can also use Ridge regression to address the multicollinearity problem. Besides minimizing the residual sum of squares as the linear regression does, Ridge regression incorporates a regularization term to penalize large weights: $\min\limits_{w} \sum \varepsilon_i^2 + \lambda \sum_{m \in G_k} w_{k,m}^2$

where the parameter λ controls the amount of regularization. When two factors are similar, the penalty tends to allocate similar weights to both factors instead of allocating most of the weight to one factor. If the group includes only two very similar factors, instead of assigning the factor with higher return a weight close to 1 and the other a weight close to 0, ridge regression moves both factors' weights toward 0.5.

Alternatively, investors calculate the information ratios of individual factors and assign factor weights proportional to their information ratios without estimating their covariance. This alternative approach assumes that each pair of factors within the factor group has similar correlations. This simple approach turns out to be a robust way of generating composite z-scores. The z-scores calculated from simple weightings proportional to the information ratio often yields higher information coefficients than composite z-scores estimated from linear regressions.

---

[65] We can always change the sign of z-scores to make assets with positive z-scores have positive expected alpha.

Factor Interactions, Sequential Screening, and Selection Scores

To combine information from factors in different factor groups, some investors examine factor interactions and conditional factor performances. A popular approach to investigate the interaction between two signals with low correlation is double sort analysis. The assets in the universe are first sorted by one factor, A, to m quantiles; assets within each quantile are then sorted by the second factor, B, to n quantiles. The end result is an $m \times n$ matrix of sub portfolios. The goal is to identify differences in conditional factor performance of the second factor in the smaller universe defined by the values of the first factor. For instance, using double sort analysis, Bali *et al.* (2010) investigated the interaction between value signals and the shares repurchase signal. They found that assets with high book-to-price ratio and net shares repurchase outperformed assets with low book-to-price ratio and net share issuing in 24 years out of the 30 years between 1972 and 2002. The average return difference between the two groups of stocks was ~10% a year. Avramov et al. (2006) used double sort analysis to establish a link between the momentum signal and the credit rating: momentum was large and statistically significant in non-investment grade firms and was small and statistically insignificant in investment grade firms (S&P rating BBB- or better). In their study, returns between month $t - 6$ and $t - 1$ were used for momentum ranking. For firms with investment grade credit ratings, the monthly return difference between assets in the top and the bottom deciles was 0.77% (t-statistic = 1.77); for firms with non-investment grade credit ratings, the difference was 2.12% (t-statistic = 4.29).

We should note that conditioning the scores of B on the quantiles of A restricts the investment universe of B, which reduces the breadth. If we sort the stocks by A to quintiles and then sort stocks within each quintile by B to five sub-groups, the stock universe is split into 25 sub-groups and each sub-group is only 4% of the original universe. Therefore, it is not fair to choose the difference in returns between two sub-groups and compare the conditional return difference with the unconditional return difference of B's top quintile and B's bottom quintile as each unconditional quintile contains 20% of the stock universe. A better benchmark for unconditional performance is the return difference between the top 4% and the bottom 4% of all stocks sorted by B. This way, the long/short portfolios in the conditional and unconditional signal performance tests have the same number of stocks.

Built upon factor interactions, sequential screening is a popular stock selection method, especially among individual investors. It is intuitive as sequential screening allows us to easily incorporate our fundamental views into stock selection. Hence, popular financial websites such as Yahoo Finance and Motley Fool provide sequential screening tools. Let us consider one sequential screening using the Growth at A Reasonable Price strategy. The strategy combines growth and momentum factors with value factors. We use growth and momentum factors such as price and fundamental momentums to select stocks with growth potential; at the same time, we use value factors such as B/P ratio to make sure that we pay for good-quality growth at a reasonable price. The first step is to select stocks with expected growth rates higher than zero and the median of the growth rates of the stocks in the same industry. Within this subset of stocks, we select stocks that have forward earnings-to-price ratios higher than 0.1. Finally, we can further filter the stocks that pass the earnings yield filter by eliminating stocks with price-to-book ratios higher than 1.5.

Sequential screening works well when we have only 2-5 stock selection criteria. Violation of a single criterion eliminates the stock even though it meets all other criteria. As the number of selection criteria increases, sequential screening often yields few assets that meet all the criteria and as a result creates an undiversified portfolio. To mitigate the problem, selection scores are often used to expand the selection. Instead of eliminating a stock when it violates a single criterion, selection score adds up the total number of criteria that each stock meets. If we have 10 stock selection criteria and a stock meets 9 of them, it is assigned a score of 9 and is likely to be included in the long positions. If a stock only gets a score of 1, it is a good short candidate. Some investors use fixed thresholds and allow the number of stocks that pass the threshold to vary; others adjust the cutoff scores to allow similar number of assets that a portfolio selects over time. The FSCORE system to select value stocks and the GSCORE system to select growth stocks both use a combination of sequential screening and selection scores.

Quantitative Linear Models

When quantitative portfolio managers build multi-factor models to forecast stock returns, they often use linear models to combine different factors. The following general principles are used to determine the factor weights:

- Assign higher weights to a factor with higher information ratio since it generates higher risk-adjusted returns.

- Assign higher weights to a factor with lower correlation with other factors since it adds information that is not captured by other factors.

- Assign higher weights to a factor with lower turnover since it reduces trading costs.

The linear model to assign weights to factors is similar to the mean-variance portfolio optimization used to assign weights to assets. The weights depend on the expected ICs (as proxies for factor returns), volatility of ICs, and the correlation of ICs. When we combine different stock signals to produce a composite factor, the information coefficient of the composite factor is the weighted average of the information coefficients of the individual signals:

$$IC_c = w_1 IC_1 + w_2 IC_2 + \cdots + w_K IC_K = w' IC$$

where $w = [w_1, w_2, \ldots, w_K]'$ is a $K \times 1$ column vector of factor weights;

$IC = [IC_1, IC_2, \ldots, IC_K]'$ is a $K \times 1$ column vector of factor ICs.

The expected information coefficient of the composite factor and the variance of the information coefficient can be expressed as

$$E[IC_c] = w_1 E[IC_1] + w_2 E[IC_2] + \cdots + w_K E[IC_K] = w' E[IC]$$

$$\text{var}(IC_c) = w' \Sigma_{IC} w$$

where $E[IC] = [E[IC_1], E[IC_2], \cdots, E[IC_K]]'$ is a $K \times 1$ vector of expected factor ICs;

Σ_{IC} is a $K \times K$ covariance matrix of factor ICs;

$E[IC_c]$ is the expected value of the information coefficient of the composite factor;

$\text{var}(IC_c)$ is the variance of the information coefficient of the composite factor.

If we do not have constraints on the factor weights, the weights can be optimized by applying the mean-variance optimization to the factor portfolio:

$$\max_w U = \max_w E[IC_c] - \tfrac{1}{2}\lambda\, \text{var}(IC_c) = \max_w w'E[IC] - \tfrac{1}{2}\lambda w'\Sigma_{IC}w$$

Taking the derivative of w and setting derivative to 0, we have

$$\widetilde{w} = \frac{1}{\lambda}\Sigma_{IC}^{-1}E[IC] \Rightarrow E[IC_c] = \frac{1}{\lambda}E[IC]'\Sigma_{IC}^{-1}E[IC],\ \text{var}(IC_c) = \frac{1}{\lambda^2}E[IC]'\Sigma_{IC}^{-1}E[IC].$$

In Chapter 9 we derived an approximation for the information ratio as the ratio of the expected IC to the standard deviation of the IC. The same approximation applies to the composite IC as well. Hence, the information ratio of the composite IC is

$$IR_c \approx \frac{E[IC_c]}{std(IC_c)} = \frac{E[IC]'\Sigma_{IC}^{-1}E[IC]\big/\lambda}{\sqrt{E[IC]'\Sigma_{IC}^{-1}E[IC]}\big/\lambda} = \sqrt{E[IC]'\Sigma_{IC}^{-1}E[IC]}$$

The linear model requires the covariance matrix of factor ICs. The covariance matrix is often estimated using a sample covariance matrix of the historical factor ICs (as we discussed in the sample covariance matrix section). To reduce estimation error, factors with high factor return correlations are combined by factor groups before the linear model is applied. Since the number of estimated parameters grows with the square of the number of factors, investors usually prescreen factors to select a small number of factors that have good predictive powers as input signals.

In practice, factor weightings are often not determined by the unconstrained mean-variance optimization of the factor portfolio. The mean-variance optimization involves the estimation of expected ICs, the volatility of ICs, and the correlation of ICs, all of which involve potential estimation errors. After selecting a number of factors with predictable power, if investors have no strong view on the expected ICs and the covariance matrix of the selected factors, they may take a simple agnostic approach and assign all selected factors equal weights. This approach turns out to be a reasonable choice that yields good out-of-sample results in many cases. Therefore, it is often used as the benchmark to evaluate the out-of-sample performance of other factor weighting methods. To evaluate the performance of different weighting methods, the historical information ratios of the portfolios constructed using different weightings are often compared to select a method that yields higher information ratio. Investors also qualitatively compare drawdowns, drawdown periods, and tail risks of different weighting methods to select a weighting method that yields better overall performance.

Some investors implement an ad-hoc approach to factor weighting. They apply the general principle of assigning higher weights to better performing factors and higher weights to less correlated factors. Instead of resorting to an optimization process, they examine the historical performance and correlation of selected factors and manually assign weights following the general principles. If the factors (factor groups) already have reasonably low correlation, investors may choose not to incorporate factor correlation in the weightings. The relative weights of different factors (factor groups) simply become

$$w = [w_1, w_2, \ldots, w_K]' = \left[\frac{E[IC_1]}{Var(IC_1)}, \frac{E[IC_2]}{Var(IC_2)}, \ldots, \frac{E[IC_K]}{Var(IC_K)} \right],$$

Short-Term Signals for Long-Term Investors

By design, some factors change slowly from one period to the next, whereas others change rapidly. For example, size factor stays stable over months or even years. So the single-factor portfolio constructed using size factor has low turnover. In contrast to this, values of a short-term reversal factor change rapidly from day to day. Many technical signals—e.g., one-month return reversal or 5-day RSI—and news/investor sentiment signals are short-term in nature, which means that they have high turnover. When we combine long-term signals with short-term signals in the return forecast without taking turnover and trading costs into consideration, the short-term signals often dominate the model as they have higher before-cost forecasting power. If we include trading costs into the model, the short-term signals are assigned much smaller weights. For funds with significant size, trading costs dominate the model construction and short-term signals are often assigned weights close to zero. The large discrepancy in short-term signal weights between before-cost and after-cost models motivates long-term investors to look for different ways to incorporate the short-term signals. One approach is to use short-term signals for trade timing decisions. Instead of directly including the short-term signals in the expected alpha calculation, we calculate the expected returns without the short-term signals and then adjust the trading decisions using returns calculated from short term signals. For example, if a model using only long-term signals generates a buy signal for Google with 1% expected one-month return, the expected one-day return is about 5bps. If the short-term signals forecast that the expected one-day return is -10 bps, we should not execute the buy trade today since the total expected one-day return is -5 bps. Instead we can wait for one or more days until the short-term signals forecast a positive one-day return. On the flip side, if the short-term model forecasts that the expected one-day return is 10 bps, we should accelerate the buy trade to capture the short-term returns. Since we need to buy Google because of the long-term signals anyway, delaying or accelerating the trade introduces no extra trading costs.

Nonlinear Models and Statistical Learning Approaches

Despite the popularity of linear models, investors generally agree that the assumption of a linear relationship ignores the effect of the nonlinear factor interactions and is too simple to fully utilize the predictive power of the signals. For example, some high-flying firms achieve high accounting earnings growth rates through questionable accounting practices. These companies have top growth scores but bottom earnings quality scores. A linear model that combines the growth scores and the quality scores simply adds the positive growth score and negative quality score to yield a final score close to zero. But these firms may be some of the best short candidates. Clearly, linear models are not designed to capture the nonlinear interaction between two factors unless we explicitly incorporate an interaction term.

Instead of trying to forecast the expected returns or alphas directly, many nonlinear models are classification models that assign stocks to different groups. One favorite classification model among financial practitioners is logistic regression. Investors use logistic regression to forecast the probability that an asset will outperform its selected benchmark (class 0) or will underperform the benchmark (class 1). If the benchmark is zero, we have a classification model for total returns; if the benchmark is the beta-adjusted return, then we have a classification model for residual returns. If the probability that an asset will be in class 0 is $P(G = 0)$, the probability that it will be in class 1 is $P(G = 1) = 1 - P(G = 0)$. The explanatory variables in a classification model, factor z-scores, are theoretically unbounded, whereas the response variable—the probability of outperformance—is bounded between 0 and 1. To project values between negative infinity and positive infinity to values between 0 and 1, the logistic regression uses the logistic function: $f(\zeta) = e^{\zeta}/(1+e^{\zeta})$. The variable ζ, the log of the odds ratio, is estimated by a linear regression:

$$\zeta = \log\left(\frac{P(G=0 \mid Z=z)}{P(G=1 \mid Z=z)}\right) = \beta_0 + \beta_1 z_1 + \cdots + \beta_K z_K = \beta_0 + \beta' z$$

$$P(G=0 \mid Z=z) = \frac{e^{\zeta}}{1+e^{\zeta}} = \frac{\exp(\beta_0 + \beta' z)}{1+\exp(\beta_0 + \beta' z)}$$

$$P(G=1 \mid Z=z) = \frac{1}{1+e^{\zeta}} = \frac{1}{1+\exp(\beta_0 + \beta' z)}$$

where $z_1, z_2, \ldots, z_K$ are the factor scores (e.g., z-scores) of factors 1, 2, ..., K;

$\beta_0, \beta_1, \ldots, \beta_K$ are the estimated model coefficients.

Exhibit 10-4 shows the relationship between log of the odds ratio ζ and the probability of outperformance.

Exhibit 10-4 Logistic function

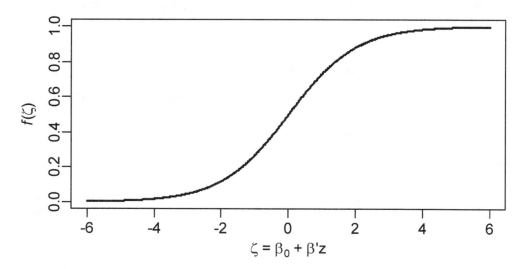

Compared with linear models, logistic regression is less influenced by outliers as it reduces the weights of data points that are far from the decision boundary in the model fitting: If a factor's z-score increases from 0 to 3, it may bring the probability of outperformance from 50% to 95.3% (ζ from 0 to 3 if the model coefficient is 1) and makes a meaningful difference in forecast; If a factor's z-score increases from 3 to 6, it may bring the probability from 95.3% to 99.8% (ζ from 3 to 6 if the model coefficient is 1) and makes a smaller difference.

If investors want to classify the stocks into more than two groups and the groups have a natural order, ordinal logistic regression is often used. For instance, stocks can be classified into five groups: strong sell, sell, hold, buy, and strong buy with the following natural order:

   strong sell < sell < hold < buy < strong buy

When the classification type G belongs to ordered categories $1 < 2 < \cdots < n$, ordered logit model is defined as

$$\text{logit}(G \leq 1) = \log\left(\frac{p_1}{1 - p_1}\right) = \alpha_1 + \beta_1 z_1 + \cdots + \beta_K z_K = \alpha_1 + \beta' z$$

$$\text{logit}(G \leq 2) = \log\left(\frac{p_1 + p_2}{1 - p_1 - p_2}\right) = \alpha_2 + \beta' z$$

$$\vdots$$

$$\text{logit}(G \leq n-1) = \log\left(\frac{p_1 + p_2 + \cdots + p_{n-1}}{1 - p_1 - p_2 - \cdots - p_{n-1}}\right) = \alpha_{n-1} + \beta' z$$

where $p_1, p_2, \ldots, p_{n-1}$ are the probabilities that G is in categories $1, 2, , \ldots, n-1$;

   $z_1, z_2, \ldots, z_K$ are the factor scores (e.g., z-scores) of factors $1, 2, \ldots, K$;

   $\beta_1, \ldots, \beta_K$ are the estimated model coefficients;

   $\alpha_1, \alpha_2, \ldots, \alpha_{n-1}$ are the estimated intercepts, $\alpha_1 < \alpha_2 < \ldots < \alpha_{n-1}$.

Both simple logistic regression and ordinal logistic regression are common classification methods in financial prediction because they are easy to fit and easy to interpret. Another popular choice for classification is tree-based models. CART (classification and regression trees) model builds a hierarchical tree structure to sequentially partition the stocks based on their factor exposures. A tree-based model has the same logic as the decision trees used by business managers, which makes them easy to interpret as well. For example, Exhibit 10-5 shows part of a CART model that classifies stocks as buys or sells using fundamental factors. The first split uses forward earnings yield (E_1/P). If a stock's forward earnings yield is higher than 10%, it is classified as a buy; otherwise, we examine the earnings growth rate. If the growth rate is higher than 15%, the CART model uses the forward earnings yields again: if the stock's earnings yield is higher than 5%, it is classified as a buy; otherwise, it is classified as a sell.

Exhibit 10-5 CART model of buy/sell recommendations

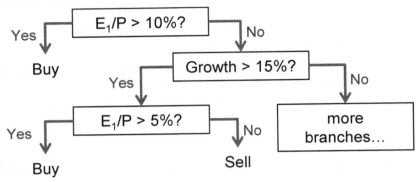

Unlike sequential screening, the CART model may use the same factor in multiple branches, which makes the CART model a much more versatile tool than sequential screening. Since the node split relies on the ordering of factor values, we do not need to transform the factor values or convert them to z-scores. Reliance on the ordering also makes the CART model intrinsically robust—less susceptible to outliers. In deciding the split of the first node, a stock with 50% forward earnings yield has no more influence on the CART model than a stock with 15% forward earnings yield. As a generalized linear model, logistic regression still has difficulty in handling non-linear interactions among factors. Before the logistic function is applied, the signals are combined by a linear model. Unless we manually include factor interactions as part of the inputs, which require prior knowledge of the interactions, the model does not consider non-linear interactions. CART, on the other hand, directly incorporates factor interactions in the tree structure when the model chooses a combination of factors to determine the classification.

The CART model has its own disadvantages though. One obvious disadvantage is its sensitivity to small changes in the factor values as the model produces discontinuous estimates at the split point. The problem is more severe when factors with high correlations are included. The split of a node often switches between factors with high correlation since each split gives similar result. Another potential problem of the CART model is overfitting. If we do not control the size of the tree, it can keep on growing until we assign the correct classification to each stock in the terminal nodes. Such a model may yield good in-sample results, but has little value out of sample. In order to build a tree that works well out of sample, pruning is used to reduce the size of the tree by removing tree branches. Although pruning leads to lower forecasting power for in-sample data, a properly pruned tree yields better out-of-sample forecasts.

To address the overfitting problem of tree-based models, researchers have developed random forest models. Instead of growing one tree using the historical data, a random forest grows a forest of many trees using the following approach to generate each tree:

- The historical data are resampled with replacement to generate a dataset of the same size.

- At each node, a smaller number of k ($k < K$) signals are randomly selected from the K signals and are used to split the node.

Each tree is often fully grown (all samples in a node have the same classification) without pruning. Since each tree gives a classification for a stock, the votes from all trees are tallied and divided by the total number of trees. The forecast chooses the classification with the most votes for the stock. Although each tree clearly has an overfitting problem, using an ensemble of trees addresses the overfitting problem. The disadvantage of random forest is the difficulty in interpreting a forest. Although the factors used to split the nodes close to the tree stems indicate their relative importance, it is difficult to explain which factors determine the classification of a stock to investors without statistical backgrounds.

In most non-linear statistical models, explanatory variables, including the factors that incorporate the interactions of other factors, are fixed. Such approaches require prior knowledge of the interactions between different factors and lengthy process to identify such interactions. For a model with 10 factors, investors need to consider 45 potential pairwise interactions and 120 interactions that involve three factors. Therefore, it is a difficult task to manually examine all of these interactions. To address such difficulty, some non-linear models automatically generate different interaction formulas as explanatory variables, screen the interactions, and incorporate the ones with the best forecasting powers.

One approach is genetic programming. Genetic programming is an optimization method that borrows from Darwin's theory of evolution. Genetic programming starts with a large number of candidate solutions (population) that include different factor interactions, calculates the predictive power (fitness) of each solution, selects the ones with good predictive powers (survival of the fittest), and generates new solutions from the selected solutions (reproduction). To generate new solutions, genetic programming takes a stochastic approach to randomly modify the existing solutions (mutation) and combine components in existing solutions (crossover). The new solutions are then screened to select the fittest to produce the next generation of solutions. The process is repeated for many generations until the best solutions are found. Using a number of valuation, quality, sentiment, and momentum signals, Becker et al. (2006) showed that a genetic programming model significantly increased future stock return ranking capability. When they built a genetic programming model using the returns of the top minus bottom quantiles as the fitness function, the genetic programming model boosted the 1-month forward return spread between the top and bottom quintiles from 0.77% (traditional linear model) to 0.91% and information ratio from 0.76 to 1.24.

Interaction between Return Forecast and Risk Forecast

If a portfolio manager forecasts the absolute returns or relative returns of a number of assets, should the variance and covariance of these stocks be adjusted to reflect the return forecast? In most cases, the answer is no. Many portfolio managers have difficulty accepting such a conclusion for the conclusion is counterintuitive. If a portfolio manager forecasts that Goldman Sachs (GS) will return 5% next month versus 1% expected return for the market, he may believe that GS should have lower risk than the risk model indicates. If he further forecasts that Morgan Stanley (MS) will underperform the market and return -5% next month, he may believe that the correlation between GS and MS should be lower than what the risk model indicates. In practice, the conditional volatility of GS and the conditional correlation between GS and MS after incorporating the portfolio manger's view are close to the unconditional volatility and correlation. The reason is that most views have high uncertainty. Top portfolio managers can achieve monthly ICs in the range of 0.1 to 0.2 (55% to 60% hit rate if slugging ratio is close to 1), which translates to an R^2 of 1% to 4% ($R^2 = IC^2$). Since R^2 is the proportion of the variance explained by the forecasts, 96% to 99% of the variance in stock returns is not explained by the forecasts. Therefore, the conditional volatility after incorporating the forecast is close to the unconditional volatility. In order to reduce the conditional volatility by 20% (variance by 36%), the IC needs to be 0.6 (80% hit rate), which is unrealistic even for top managers' high-conviction bets. Similarly, the forecasts have little impact on the covariance of different stocks. As a result, we do not need to adjust the variance or the covariance of the stocks to reflect the return forecasts.

When we combine factor forecasts with portfolio optimization using factor risk models, however, the interaction between return forecast and risk forecast needs to be taken into consideration. Factors that explain cross-sectional stock returns are potential candidates for risk factors. If such factors have long-expected positive expected returns, they become alpha factors. If investors use factor risk models in portfolio construction, some of the alpha factors that investors use for stock selection may be risk factors in the risk models. When some alpha factors are included in the risk model and others are not, the portfolio optimization may substantially alter the relative weightings of, and the exposures to, different alpha factors. Let us consider a simple return forecast model that includes a momentum factor and an earnings quality factor. If the risk model includes a momentum factor, the portfolio's active exposure to the momentum factor will be penalized more as the exposure increases the style risk. If the risk model does not include an earnings quality factor, the portfolio's active exposure to the earnings quality will be penalized less as the exposure does not increase the model style risk. Therefore, the optimized portfolio has increased exposure to the earnings quality factor and decreased exposure to the momentum factor.

In many cases, a risk factor from commercial risk models is similar to but different from an alpha factor constructed by investors. After the portfolio optimization, the "optimized" portfolio may have exposures to unexpected factors. For example, Lee and Stefek (2008) showed that a portfolio using twelve-month return momentum between month $t - 13$ to month $t - 1$ as the alpha factor and using return between month $t - 12$ to month t as the momentum risk factor has large positive exposure to one-month return momentum between month $t - 13$ and month $t - 12$. The explanation is intuitive: the return momentum between month $t - 13$ and month $t - 12$ is included in the alpha calculation— higher returns yield higher alphas—and is not included in the risk calculation—return variance in that month yields no higher variance in the optimization, so the mean-variance optimization results in positive exposure to one-month momentum between month $t - 13$ and month $t - 12$. Therefore, misalignment between alpha factors and risk factors may lead to unexpected factor exposures. Similarly, many return forecast models include value signals and the construction of these value signals are different from the value signals included in risk models, which may introduce misalignment between alpha factors and risk factors as well.

When portfolio managers use risk models for portfolio optimization, the missing alpha factors in the risk model and the misalignment between alpha factors and risk factors pose a serious problem. The optimization step amplifies the problem by pushing the portfolio towards the factors or the fractions of factors not in the risk model. Quantitative investors often implement two approaches to address the problem. The first approach is to build customized risk models that directly add the alpha factors to the commercial risk model. If an alpha factor is a close substitute of a risk factor, investors may replace the risk factor with the alpha factor. Instead of using the covariance matrix of the factors provided by the vendor, investors need to calibrate the factor covariance matrix and the residual volatility of individual stocks themselves. As we have discussed in the risk forecast section, the calibration of the factor covariance matrix is a difficult task. Investors need to have a good understanding of the models and make choices that best fit their portfolios. The second approach using an alpha alignment factor is to penalize the risk orthogonal to common risk factors in the risk model. When we derived the risk-adjusted information coefficient, we split the raw alpha forecasts to the alpha explained by the risk factors and the residual alpha not explained by the risk factors:

$$\alpha = \alpha_B + \alpha_\perp = \tilde{B}\left(\tilde{B}'S^{-1}\tilde{B}\right)^{-1}\tilde{B}'S^{-1}\alpha + \left(I - \tilde{B}\left(\tilde{B}'S^{-1}\tilde{B}\right)^{-1}\tilde{B}'S^{-1}\right)\alpha$$

where α_B is the portion of alpha explained by the risk factors;

   $\alpha_\perp$ is the residual alpha not explained by the risk factors.

The residual alpha $\alpha_\perp$ captures the misalignment between the alpha forecasts and risk factors. Ceria et al. (2012) recommended augmenting the risk model with an alpha alignment factor, $y = \alpha_\perp / \|\alpha_\perp\|$, to redefine the covariance matrix of the stocks:

$$\Sigma_Y = \Sigma + vyy' = B'FB + S + vyy'$$

where y is the alpha alignment factor that is orthogonal to all common risk factors;

   v represents the systematic variance of y;

   Σ is the covariance matrix estimated from the risk model, $B'FB + S$;

   Σ_Y is the covariance matrix from the augmented risk model.

When we replace Σ with Σ_Y in the mean-variance portfolio construction, the following optimization problem is used to determine the optimal portfolio:

$$\max_w U = \max_w \alpha'w - \tfrac{1}{2} \times \lambda w' \Sigma_Y w$$

The alpha alignment factor y can be estimated from generalized linear regression and the systematic variance v can be estimated from the historical return variance of y. The covariance matrix from the augmented risk model Σ_Y provides a more accurate estimation of the realized portfolio risk. As a result, the augmented risk model mitigates the misalignment problem.

Black-Litterman Model

The Black-Litterman model is a method to address the estimation error and input sensitivity problem of the expected returns. Originally introduced by Black and Litterman in the early 1990s, the Black-Litterman model (1990, 1992) is a Bayesian model that combines the subjective view of investors regarding the expected returns of one or more assets with the market equilibrium expected returns as the prior to generate a posterior estimate of expected returns.

The Black-Litterman model starts with the mean-variance optimization formulation that uses a quadratic utility function for investing in a portfolio with N assets:

$$\max_{w} U = \max_{w} \mu_p - \tfrac{1}{2}\lambda\sigma_p^2 = \max_{w} w'\mu - \tfrac{1}{2}\lambda w'\Sigma w$$

where μ_p is the expected excess return (versus the risk-free return) of the portfolio;

$\qquad$ λ is risk aversion coefficient with larger value of λ indicating higher risk aversion;

$\qquad$ σ_p^2 is the variance of the portfolio return;

$\qquad$ μ is an $N \times 1$ column vector of the expected excess returns, $\mu = E[r]$;

$\qquad$ Σ is an $N \times N$ covariance matrix of the excess returns, $\Sigma = \mathrm{var}(r)$.

To maximize the utility, take the derivative of w:

$$\frac{\partial U}{\partial w} = \mu - \lambda\Sigma w = 0 \Rightarrow \mu = \lambda\Sigma w \ \text{ or } \ w = (\lambda\Sigma)^{-1}\mu$$

If the market weights are used as the equilibrium, through reverse optimization, the market equilibrium returns are derived as

$$\Pi = \lambda\Sigma w_{mkt}$$

where w_{mkt} is an $N \times 1$ column vector of the market weights;

$\qquad$ Π is an $N \times 1$ column vector of the implied excess equilibrium returns.

We can estimate the risk aversion coefficient λ from the historical market risk premium and the variance. Assume that the market weights are optimal, we have

$$\mu_p = w'\mu = \mu'(\lambda\Sigma)^{-1}\mu = \lambda w'\Sigma w = \lambda\sigma_p^2 \Rightarrow \lambda = \mu_p / \sigma_p^2$$

If the expected excess return is 6% and the volatility is 15%, which are approximately the historical average excess return and the volatility of US equities, λ equals 2.7. In practice, λ is often set to a value between 2 and 4 for stock portfolios.

The expected excess return vector μ based on the market equilibrium can be expressed as a joint-normal distribution $\mu \sim N(\Pi, \tau\Sigma)$. A risk multiplier τ is introduced to reduce the scale of covariance matrix since the uncertainty in the expected return is much less volatile than the one-period returns. Studies generally recommended a value close to 0, $0 < \tau \ll 1$. Intuitively, if one considers the expected return as the mean of historical returns of the past T periods, τ can be estimated as $1/T$ since the standard error of the mean is $1/\sqrt{T}$ of the standard deviation of the samples (the central limit theorem). In practice, τ is typically set to between 0.01 and 0.05. For covariance matrix estimated using exponentially weighted moving average with a half life of 36 months, the effective number of T is 52 and τ is 1/52.

Although market capitalization weights are natural equilibrium weights for excess return calculation, we can choose any sensible prior weights. If the portfolio has a benchmark index, the index weights are used. If we start with a list of stocks that analysts recommend buying, we can assign all recommended stocks equal weights as the prior. If we run a long/short cash neutral fund with no benchmark, we can even use all zeros as the prior to yield a vector of zeros for the equilibrium excess returns.

The Black-Litterman model expresses all stock selection signals as views. If a portfolio manager has K views on stock returns, the views can be expressed using the following equation:

$$q = P\mu + \varepsilon_q$$

where q is a $K \times 1$ vector of the returns on the views with expected values Q, $Q = E[q]$;

> P is a $K \times N$ matrix of the stock weights in the views;

> $\varepsilon_q \sim N(0, \Omega)$ represents the uncertainty of the views.

Such a formulation is a versatile approach to incorporate a variety of forecasts. Let us consider a simple portfolio with 5 stocks. Stock 1 and 2 belong to consumer discretionary sector with relative market weights 0.5 and 0.5; stock 3, 4, and 5 belong to consumer staple sector with relative market weights 0.5, 0.3 and 0.2. After analyzing industry trends and individual stocks, we have the following views:

- Stock 3 will have expected return of 10% with 10% estimated volatility.

- Market value-weighted consumer discretionary sector will outperform consumer stable sector by 3% with 4% estimated volatility.

- Using a gross profit signal, a zero-investment portfolio with weights 0.4, -0.6, -0.4, 0.4, 0.2 in stocks 1 to 5 has expected return of 4% with 3% estimated volatility.

We can formulate the views using the following equation:

$$q = P\mu + \varepsilon_q = \begin{bmatrix} 0 & 0 & 1 & 0 & 0 \\ 0.5 & 0.5 & -0.5 & -0.3 & -0.2 \\ 0.4 & -0.6 & -0.4 & 0.4 & 0.2 \end{bmatrix} \begin{bmatrix} \mu_1 \\ \mu_2 \\ \mu_3 \\ \mu_4 \\ \mu_5 \end{bmatrix} + \begin{bmatrix} \varepsilon_{q,1} \\ \varepsilon_{q,2} \\ \varepsilon_{q,3} \end{bmatrix}, Q = E[q] = \begin{bmatrix} 0.10 \\ 0.03 \\ 0.04 \end{bmatrix}$$

For simplicity, Let us assume the views are uncorrelated with each other. Then we have

$$\Omega = \begin{bmatrix} 0.1^2 & 0 & 0 \\ 0 & 0.04^2 & 0 \\ 0 & 0 & 0.03^2 \end{bmatrix}$$

The Black-Litterman model estimates the posterior expected return as a weighted average of the implied equilibrium return vector Π and the expected returns reflected in the views, in which the relative weights depend on the relative confidence in the view versus the confidence in the implied equilibrium returns. Essentially, it is a Bayesian problem with prior distribution $\mu \sim N(\Pi, \tau\Sigma)$ and condition $P\mu \sim N(Q, \Omega)$. To yield the posterior expected returns, the original problem can be formulated as a generalized least squares (GLS) regression problem:

$$\binom{\Pi}{Q} = \binom{I}{P}\mu + \varepsilon, \text{ where } E[\varepsilon] = 0 \text{ and } \text{cov}(\varepsilon) = \begin{bmatrix} \tau\Sigma & 0 \\ 0 & \Omega \end{bmatrix}$$

The linear regression assumes that there is a linear relationship between the response variable Y and the explanatory variables X:

$$Y = X\beta + \varepsilon, \quad E[\varepsilon] = 0 \text{ and } \text{cov}(\varepsilon) = V$$

The GLS estimates the coefficients, β, by minimizing the squared Mahalanobis distance of the residual vector:

$$\min_{\beta} f(\beta) = \min_{\beta} (Y - X\beta)'V^{-1}(Y - X\beta)$$

Taking the first derivative, we have

$$\frac{df}{d\beta} = 2X'V^{-1}(Y - X\beta) = 0 \Rightarrow \hat{\beta} = (X'V^{-1}X)^{-1}X'V^{-1}Y \Rightarrow \text{var}(\hat{\beta}) = (X'V^{-1}X)^{-1}$$

Let $Y = \binom{\Pi}{Q}$, $X = \binom{I}{P}$ and treat μ as β, we can apply equation $\hat{\beta} = (X'V^{-1}X)^{-1}X'V^{-1}Y$ to yield the following expected value for μ:

$$\hat{\mu} = \left[\begin{pmatrix} I & P' \end{pmatrix} \begin{pmatrix} (\tau\Sigma)^{-1} & 0 \\ 0 & \Omega^{-1} \end{pmatrix} \begin{pmatrix} I \\ P \end{pmatrix} \right]^{-1} \left[\begin{pmatrix} I & P' \end{pmatrix} \begin{pmatrix} (\tau\Sigma)^{-1} & 0 \\ 0 & \Omega^{-1} \end{pmatrix} \begin{pmatrix} \Pi \\ Q \end{pmatrix} \right] \Rightarrow$$

$$\begin{cases} \hat{\mu} = \left[(\tau\Sigma)^{-1} + P'\Omega^{-1}P \right]^{-1} \left[(\tau\Sigma)^{-1}\Pi + P'\Omega^{-1}Q \right] \\ \text{var}(\hat{\mu}) = (XV^{-1}X)^{-1} = \left[(\tau\Sigma)^{-1} + P'\Omega^{-1}P \right]^{-1} \end{cases}$$

$\hat{\mu}$ is the weighted average of prior estimation Π and the expected returns implied by the views. We can derive the implied return μ_q in the view equations:

$$P\mu_q = Q \Rightarrow P'P\mu_q = P'Q \Rightarrow \mu_q = (P'P)^{-1}P'Q$$

Expanding the equation for $\hat{\mu}$, we have

$$\hat{\mu} = \left[(\tau\Sigma)^{-1} + P'\Omega^{-1}P \right]^{-1} (\tau\Sigma)^{-1}\Pi + \left[(\tau\Sigma)^{-1} + P'\Omega^{-1}P \right]^{-1} P'\Omega^{-1}Q$$

$$= \left[(\tau\Sigma)^{-1} + P'\Omega^{-1}P \right]^{-1} (\tau\Sigma)^{-1}\Pi + \left[(\tau\Sigma)^{-1} + P'\Omega^{-1}P \right]^{-1} P'\Omega^{-1}P\left((P'P)^{-1}P'Q \right)$$

$$= w_{\Pi}\Pi + w_q\mu_q$$

where $w_{\Pi} = \left[(\tau\Sigma)^{-1} + P'\Omega^{-1}P \right]^{-1} (\tau\Sigma)^{-1}$ and $w_q = \left[(\tau\Sigma)^{-1} + P'\Omega^{-1}P \right]^{-1} P'\Omega^{-1}P$

The sum of w_{Π} and w_q is an identity matrix: $w_{\Pi} + w_q = I$

Alternatively, we can express the equation for $\hat{\mu}$ using the computationally more stable formula from the discrete Kalman filter:

$$\hat{\mu} = \Pi + (\tau\Sigma)P'\left[P(\tau\Sigma)P' + \Omega\right]^{-1}\left[Q - P\Pi\right]$$

$$\text{var}(\hat{\mu}) = \tau\Sigma - (\tau\Sigma)P'\left[P(\tau\Sigma)P' + \Omega\right]^{-1}P(\tau\Sigma)$$

Kalman filter treats $\mu \sim N(\Pi, \tau\Sigma)$ as a system equation and $q = P\mu + \varepsilon_q$ as an observation equation. If $\mu = \Pi$, we'd expect $Q - P\Pi = P\mu - P\Pi = 0$. Hence, if the observed value of $Q - P\Pi$ is different from 0, the difference provides us with new information and we update our estimate as a function of $Q - P\Pi$ and also update the covariance matrix that reflects higher accuracy of the posterior estimation.

$(\tau\Sigma)^{-1}$ and $P'\Omega^{-1}P$ represent the confidence that we have in the equilibrium return Π and the view-implied return μ_q. If we have high confidence in the views, the variances in Ω should be smaller than $\tau\Sigma$ and $\hat{\mu}$ is mostly determined by μ_q. If we have 100% confidence in the views ($\Omega = 0$), we have

$$\hat{\mu} = \Pi + (\tau\Sigma)P'\left[P(\tau\Sigma)P'\right]^{-1}\left[Q - P\Pi\right]$$

On the other hand, if we have little confidence in the views, the variances in Ω should be larger than $\tau\Sigma$ and $\hat{\mu}$ is mostly determined by Π.

Because the posterior expected returns in vector $\hat{\mu}$ are random variables in the Black-Litterman model, the covariance matrix of the returns is no longer Σ. Instead, the distribution incorporates the uncertainty of the expected returns:

$$r \sim N(\hat{\mu}, \hat{\Sigma}), \text{ where } \hat{\Sigma} = \text{var}(r) = \Sigma + \text{var}(\hat{\mu}) = \Sigma + \left[(\tau\Sigma)^{-1} + P'\Omega^{-1}P\right]^{-1}$$

Nevertheless, τ has a value close to 0 and the views further reduce the uncertainty of $\hat{\mu}$ below its prior variance $\tau\Sigma$. Therefore, the elements in $\left[(\tau\Sigma)^{-1} + P'\Omega^{-1}P\right]^{-1}$ are much smaller than the elements in Σ and Σ itself is a good approximation for the covariance matrix of r.

Using the posterior distribution of r, we can again apply the mean-variance optimization to maximize the quadratic utility:

$$\max_{w} U = \max_{w} w'\hat{\mu} - \tfrac{1}{2}\lambda w'\Sigma w$$

For unconstrained problems, we have the new optimization weights $w = (\lambda\hat{\Sigma})^{-1}\hat{\mu}$.

Determining the covariance matrix for the error term of the views, Ω, is the most abstract aspect of the Black-Litterman model since there is no consensus on how to estimate Ω. Although the difficulty in determining Ω hinders its popularity among portfolio managers, it increases the flexibility of the model since investors can express different views through different mathematical formations. For example, two investors may agree on the same view with different confidence levels, which can be easily expressed through the uncertainty of the views. The more confident investor can assign a smaller value (lower variance) to the diagonal elements of the covariance matrix Ω and as a result the view will have a larger impact on the posterior expected returns. To show its flexibility, we now discuss both a qualitative approach and a quantitative approach to estimate Ω.

Thomas Idzorek (2005) developed an intuitive qualitative approach that directly uses the level of confidence in each view. Instead of requiring investors to specify Ω, the method allows investors to express their confidence level in percentage as a vector $[C_1, \cdots, C_K]$ (0 $\leq C_k \leq 1$) for their K views.

For view k with user-specified confidence level C_k, the target weight vector based on the tilt caused by the view can be expressed as:

$$w_{k,\%} = w_{mkt} + tilt_k = w_{mkt} + (w_{k,100\%} - w_{mkt}) \times C_k = C_k \times w_{k,100\%} + (1 - C_k) \times w_{mkt}$$

where $w_{k,100\%}$ is the calculated weights using 100% confidence in view k.

Basically $w_{k,\%}$ is expressed as a weight-average of w_{mkt} and $w_{k,100\%}$ with their relative weights depending on the confidence level C_k. As the confidence level increases, the $w_{k,\%}$ will tilt away from w_{mkt} towards $w_{k,100\%}$.

The steps to incorporate all views and confidence levels can be summarized as the following:

1. Estimate the target weight vector $w_{k,\%}$ based on w_{mkt}, $w_{k,100\%}$, and C_k.

2. Find the value of ω_k (the k-th diagonal element of Ω), representing the uncertainty in the k-th view, that minimizes the sum of square difference between $w_{k,\%}$ and w_k:

$$\min \sum_{i=1}^{N} (w_{k,\%} - w_k)^2$$

$$s.t. \ w_k = [\lambda\Sigma]^{-1} \left[(\tau\Sigma)^{-1} + P'\omega_k^{-1}P\right]^{-1} \left[(\tau\Sigma)^{-1}\Pi + P'\omega_k^{-1}Q\right]$$
$$\omega_k > 0$$

In practice, ω_k can be solved iteratively using numerical methods.

3. Repeat the steps 1 and 2 for all K views, build diagonal matrix Ω with diagonal elements $\omega_1, \ldots, \omega_K$ and solve the new combined return vector:

$$\hat{\mu} = \left[(\tau\Sigma)^{-1} + P'\Omega^{-1}P\right]^{-1} \left[(\tau\Sigma)^{-1}\Pi + P'\Omega^{-1}Q\right] \text{ and } w = (\lambda\hat{\Sigma})^{-1}\hat{\mu}$$

Idzorek's method derives the variance of each view from the user-specified confidence level. Although the computation appears to be complicated, each step only involves the optimization of one variable, ω_k. Therefore, it can be easily solved using a binary search or Newton's method. The key advantage that it enables investors to express their confidence on an intuitive 0 to 100% level justifies the extra effort. The method also removes the need to estimate the scalar τ since the selection of τ does not affect the posterior return vector $\hat{\mu}$.

Since Idzorek's method uses a diagonal matrix Ω, the method assumes investors' views are uncorrelated. Many views are not independent since the views often share common contributing factors. Off-diagonal elements add further flexibility to the model. Two investors can agree on the same two views, as well as on the levels of uncertainty, but have different views on their correlation. The higher correlation of the two views can be expressed as a higher covariance term in Ω. For quantitative signals, we often express expected returns (either relative or absolute) as well as the covariance of different signals based on historical results or simulation. If a model combines different signals to generate forecasted excess returns for all stocks, P becomes an $N \times N$ identity matrix and Q becomes an $N \times 1$ vector of forecasted excess returns:

$$Q = \alpha = [\alpha_1, \alpha_2, ..., \alpha_N]'$$

where $\alpha_1, \alpha_2, ..., \alpha_N$ are the forecasted excess returns for asset 1, 2, ..., N.

If we assume that the covariance matrix of the forecasted excess returns is $\eta\Sigma$, $0 < \eta \ll 1$, the posterior expected excess returns become the weighted average of the implied equilibrium returns and the forecasted returns:

$$\hat{\mu} = \Pi + (\tau\Sigma)P'\left[P(\tau\Sigma)P'+\Omega\right]^{-1}\left[Q - P\Pi\right] = \Pi + (\tau\Sigma)[\tau\Sigma + \eta\Sigma]^{-1}(\alpha - P\Pi)$$

$$= \Pi + \frac{\tau}{\tau + \eta}(\alpha - P\Pi) = \frac{1}{1 + \eta/\tau}\alpha + \frac{\eta/\tau}{1 + \eta/\tau}\Pi$$

The ratio, η/τ, determines the relative weight of α versus Π. If we have high confidence in the model forecast, η/τ is close to 0 and the posterior expected returns are mostly determined by the forecasted excess returns.

Instead of forecasting the excess returns of individual stocks, a quantitative model may simply forecast the returns of the factor portfolios. For the k-th factor, the forecast becomes

$$q_k = w_{k,1}\mu_1 + w_{k,2}\mu_2 + \cdots + w_{k,N}\mu_N + \varepsilon_k = w_k'\mu + \varepsilon_k$$

The factor portfolio weights can be any weight vectors that are used to build the factor portfolio. For instance, it can be a vector of factor z-scores if we assume the portfolio weights are proportional to z-scores. The expected returns, the variance of the factor returns and the covariance between factor returns are estimated from historical factor returns. If we take a quantitative approach to estimate Ω from historical return of signals, we need to recognize that Ω is the covariance matrix of the *expected returns* of the signals; Ω is not the covariance matrix of the *returns* of the signals. Similar to the risk multiplier τ used to adjust the variance of the prior, a multiplier (τ_Ω) close to 0 is needed to adjust the historical covariance matrix of signal returns. The ratio of τ_Ω to τ determines the relative volatility of the returns implied in the views to the volatility of the returns implied in the market weights.

Portfolio Constraints

In practice, investors include a number of constraints in mean-variance portfolio construction. Some constraints are determined by portfolio mandates; some are the results of risk management to control tracking error to a benchmark, to limit exposures to risk factors, and to maintain diversification; some others are used to control portfolio turnover and to reduce market impact. The following are some of common constraints used in portfolio construction.

Risk Constraints

A long-only portfolio requires all asset weights to be non-negative and the portfolio to be fully invested. The total asset weights need to be close to 1:

$$1 - \theta < \sum_{i=1}^{N} w_i < 1 + \theta, \quad w_i \geq 0, \forall i$$

where θ is a small positive number.

A long-short cash neutral portfolio requires the sum of the absolute values of the weights to be close to 1 to guarantee that the total gross exposure is close to the target gross market value and the sum of weights to be close to zero to guarantee that the net cash exposure is close to zero:

$$1 - \theta < \sum_{i=1}^{N} |w_i| < 1 + \theta \text{ and } -\delta < \sum_{i=1}^{N} w_i < \delta$$

where θ and δ are small positive numbers.

For portfolios that are tied to specific benchmarks, risk budgeting is often used. A portfolio is assigned a maximum tracking error (σ_{TE}) constraint to maximize the active return under the risk constraint:

$$(w - w_b)' \Sigma (w - w_b) \leq \sigma_{TE}^2$$

where w_b is the asset weights in the benchmark;

$w - w_b$ is an $N \times 1$ column vector of active (relative to the benchmark) weights;

$(w - w_b)' \Sigma (w - w_b)$ is the estimated variance introduced by the active weights.

Besides limiting tracking error, investors also limit the exposures to common risk factors:

$$L_k \leq \sum_{i=1}^{N} \beta_{i,k} w_i \leq U_k$$

where β_k is the exposure of asset i to risk factor k;

L_k and U_k are the minimum and maximum exposures to risk factor k.

The most common choice for stock portfolio is to limit the portfolio's exposure to market risk, in which case the betas are market betas.

Diversification Constraints

In order to reduce exposure to the idiosyncratic risk of individual stocks, many portfolios also limit exposures to individual assets using holding constraints:

$$L_i < w_i < U_i$$

where L_i and U_i are the upper bound and lower bound of the weights for asset i. The bounds are popular choices to limit the position sizes of the largest long/short positions. Some investors choose tighter limits for short positions to reduce the acquisition risk and the short squeeze risk.

Besides minimum and maximum bounds for individual assets, a portfolio may have a requirement to limit the overall portfolio concentration. Herfindahl index[66], $\sum_{i=1}^{N} w_i^2$, is a proxy for portfolio concentration. It has a value between 0 and 1 with a value closer to 0 indicating a well-diversified portfolio. The inverse of Herfindahl index can be considered as the effective number of assets in the portfolio. As shown in Exhibit 10-6, let us compare two portfolios with 10 stocks in each portfolio. The first portfolio has equal weights for all 10 stocks, so the effective number of assets is 10. The second portfolio is less diversified. Even though the second portfolio still has 10 stocks, 60% of the weight is concentrated in two stocks and the effective number of assets is only 5.

Exhibit 10-6 Herfindahl index of hypothetical portfolios

Portfolio weights	Herfindahl index	Effective number of assets
10% in each of 10 stocks	$10 \times 0.1^2 = 0.1$	$1/0.1 = 10$
30% in 2 stocks and 5% in the other 8 stocks	$2 \times 0.3^2 + 8 \times 0.05^2 = 0.2$	$1/0.2 = 5$

To limit the overall portfolio concentration, we can impose the constraint that the effective number of assets should be no less than a minimum number, $N_{effective}$:

$$1 / \sum_{i=1}^{N} w_i^2 \geq N_{effective}$$

Portfolio managers make different choices on diversification. Many quantitative portfolio managers rely on diversification to achieve breadth. The effective number of assets in their portfolio are often higher than 100. As a result, these portfolios have low volatility and high Sharpe ratios. Top fundamental portfolio managers are willing to accept higher volatility in order to achieve higher expected returns. Many of them achieve higher returns through higher concentration: they invest only in a small number of assets (the effective number of assets is lower than 30) in which they have high conviction. In order to control risk, they continuously monitor the basket to adjust asset weights in response to new market information.

---

[66] Herfindahl index is typically used as an industry concentration measure, in which w_i is the weight of market share of each asset in an industry.

Liquidity and Turnover Constraints

For large portfolios, it is common to have constraints on the maximum percent of the average daily volumes (e.g., 10% of ADV) that the portfolio can invest in. The objective of ADV-based position limits is to reduce the liquidity risk since investors need to be able to liquidate positions within a reasonable time period. Constraints are also used to restrict portfolio turnover. For example, a portfolio usually has stock-level trading limits:

$$\left| w_i - w_{i,o} \right| \leq threshold_i$$

where $w_{i,o}$ is the weight of asset i before rebalancing;

$w_i - w_{i,o}$ is the stock-level turnover;

threshold is the limit that is often a fraction of the average daily trading volume.

We can also have a constraint on the total portfolio turnover:

$$\sum_{i=1}^{N} \left| w_i - w_{i,o} \right| \leq threshold$$

where *threshold* is the maximum total portfolio turnover.

The portfolio-level turnover constraint limits the size of the aggregated trade baskets. When the constraint on the total portfolio turnover is a binding constraint (the size of final trading basket reaches the turnover threshold), it often forces the weight changes of some stocks to zero. In other words, since the total turnover is constrained, the limited turnover is allocated to trades that have larger impact on increasing returns or decreasing risks.

Conclusion

We discussed alpha models to combine different stock selection signals, risk models to capture the variance and covariance of the stocks, portfolio constraints to boost diversification and control risks, and portfolio optimization to generate the final portfolio. Each step of portfolio construction involves numerous choices and many of these involve trade-offs, which makes portfolio construction a complex but potentially rewarding process. Investors who effectively combine different stock selection signals and incorporate portfolio optimization build portfolios with better expected returns, lower volatility, and smaller drawdown risks.

Chapter 11

Dynamic Portfolio Construction

The conventional wisdom, to choose factors that have had good long-term performance and consistency in predicting stock returns, has been challenged in recent years as few factors have generated consistent alpha. Many signals suffered from periods of lengthy large losses as well as significant increase in volatility. In order to improve returns and to reduce volatility, some investors took on the difficult task of identifying genuinely new sources of alpha. Others focused on adapting existing factors and models by incorporating dynamic factor selection and dynamic factor weighting. Dynamic models have long attracted researchers' attentions. Technical analysts were earlier adopters of dynamic models. For many mean-reversion signals, technical analysts gradually shortened the number of days used in the signal calculation based on their observations that markets have moved much faster than in the past. Many investors have also adjusted the number of days used in mean-reversion signals based on market volatility: they shortened the number of days used in the signal when market volatility was high since markets tend to move faster in a higher volatility environment. Dynamic factor models have been used by equity portfolio managers as well. In the first issue of the Journal of Investing, Arnott and his colleagues from the First Quadrant Corporation (1992) proposed the use of economic indicators (producer price index and leading economic indicators), market indicators (market volatility and equity risk premium), and calendar effects to dynamically forecast factor returns and determine factor weights. Nevertheless, dynamic factor models were not widely used by portfolio managers until the August 2007 quant meltdown and the subsequent financial crisis. Several reasons contribute to the slow adoption of dynamic approaches:

- First, many managers are philosophically against using dynamic factor models. They believe that the value of an individual signal is established using long-term (ten years or more) statistics. Therefore, a signal is not expected to work all the time. If a factor works all the time, every investor will jump on board and the signal will be arbitraged away quickly. The inability of a factor to generate positive returns all the time keeps many investors from exploiting it, which is exactly the reason why the factor works in the long term. If we assume that returns follow a normal distribution, a factor with an information ratio of 0.5 is expected to have negative returns in 44% of the months and in 31% of the years. In some periods, it is simply difficult for some signals to succeed. So, it is crucial not to lose faith in a signal because of a period of bad returns for that signal may very well pay off in the long run. In *The Little Book that Beats the Market*, Joel Greenblatt argues that simple strategies continue to work over the long term because few investors stick to a strategy after several bad years, which often happens to be a time when the strategy is likely to rebound.

- Second, since static stock selection models worked well before August 2007, there was little incentive to build dynamic models. Considering the added complexity of dynamic models, investors applied Occam's razor[67] and chose simple static models.

- Third, dynamic factor selections have low breadth. Dynamic factor selections are essentially market timing strategies to select a group of factors, which naturally restricts their breadth compared to securities selection from thousands of stocks.

- Last but not least, dynamic factor selections increase portfolio turnover. The composite factor of a static model adjusts only to changes in asset factor exposures; the composite factor of a dynamic factor model also adjusts to factor weighting changes. The dynamic factor weighting increases portfolio turnover and adds extra trading costs.

A series of market events starting with the massive 2007 quant meltdown changed the views of many portfolio managers. The 2008 financial crisis caused some value signals to underperform the market. The early loss and subsequent recovery of the market in 2009 brought many momentum strategies to their knees. The high correlation and low dispersion between stocks in 2010 made quantitative investing difficult. Wide sentiment swings in 2011 led many active managers to yet another year of losses. Because of fierce competition amongst investors and the increase of market efficiency, many traditional alpha factors with high expected returns and low return volatility have become risk factors with low expected returns and high volatility. A stable tilt—constant exposure to the same set of factors over multiple years—is unlikely to generate consistent outperformance. Instead, factor timing—active exposures to factors under different market environments—may provide better returns and avoid lengthy drawdowns. Needless to say, dynamic factor modeling has always been difficult and is getting even more difficult given increasing competition. Nevertheless, the ability to harness part of its power helps investors enhance alpha returns and reduce risks. In this chapter, we will discuss a variety of strategies that investors explore for purposes of dynamic portfolio construction.

Factor Momentum

Exploring the momentum of factor returns is a popular choice for dynamic factor selection. Similar to stock returns, factor returns also exhibit momentum. Historical factor performances indicate that the best performing factors in the past 12 months tend to outperform in the following month. Unlike stock returns, factor returns also exhibit short-term momentum as indicated by positive autocorrelation: if a factor performs well in one month, it tends to perform well in the next month. Besides momentum, a low volatility strategy works for factor selection as well. Using a database of 45 factors, Mezrich and Feng (2010) showed a strategy that selected factors with low trailing 12-month return volatility and positive returns generated more consistent returns than a simple momentum strategy that selected all factors with positive trailing 12-month returns. The principle of factor momentum is similar to static model factor weighting: select the factors with the best historical risk-adjusted returns. The difference lies in the time horizon. Static models

---

[67] Occam's razor is a principle that says among all the models that have similar performance the simplest one should be selected. It is a principle of parsimony.

estimate the expected factor return and volatility using years of data and assume that they are the current expected return and volatility of the factor. Dynamic models use long-term data to establish the validity of a factor, but estimate the current expected return and the volatility conditioned on its recent performance, instead of using the long-term unconditional return and the unconditional volatility.

Researchers have long established the value of style rotation between large-cap stocks versus small-cap stocks and value stocks versus growth stocks. Barberis and Shleifer (2003) showed that style momentum strategy was as profitable as asset level momentum strategy. Cross autocorrelation—the correlation between one factor's return in a period and another factor's return in the next period—is used for factor selection as well. Wang (2005) used a logit model with one-month lagged Fama-French three factor returns as inputs to predict the probability that small cap stocks outperform large cap stocks and the probability that value stocks outperform growth stocks in the following month:

$$prob(SMB_t > 0) = \frac{\exp(a_{10} + a_{11}MKT_{t-1} + a_{12}SMB_{t-1} + a_{13}HML_{t-1})}{1 + \exp(a_{10} + a_{11}MKT_{t-1} + a_{12}SMB_{t-1} + a_{13}HML_{t-1})}$$

$$prob(HML_t > 0) = \frac{\exp(a_{20} + a_{21}MKT_{t-1} + a_{22}SMB_{t-1} + a_{23}HML_{t-1})}{1 + \exp(a_{20} + a_{21}MKT_{t-1} + a_{22}SMB_{t-1} + a_{23}HML_{t-1})}$$

The parameters $a_1 = (a_{10}, a_{11}, a_{12}, a_{13})$ and $a_2 = (a_{20}, a_{21}, a_{22}, a_{23})$ were fitted using 10-year (120-month) rolling window. A strategy that longed predicted winning styles and shorted predicted losing styles generated a monthly return of 1.13% (t-stat = 3.9) between 1970 and 2000.

Style rotation and investor flows may explain factor momentum. Investors often gradually reallocate their capital towards certain styles over a period of months. The reallocation introduces positive order flows into the stocks with positive exposures to such styles. The tendency of investors to chase recent returns also contributes to the positive autocorrelation of factor returns. As funds with exposures to certain factors outperform others, investors pour more money into those funds. To deploy the new capital, those funds increase existing positions within the same assets or enter into new positions with similar factor exposures, which further drives up the performance of chosen factors.

Factor timing based on factor momentum and the autocorrelation of factor returns has its limitation. The positive autocorrelation estimated using many years of history may break down for months or even years. Part of the persistency of factor returns is due to market sentiment, which can last for months; in periods where market sentiment is unstable, the persistency of factor returns breaks down. In 2008-2010, the negative monthly and quarterly correlation of factors returns—one quarter's top performing factors yielded negative returns in the following quarter—caused many quant funds to underperform. Furthermore, if crowdedness is a reason why many factors stopped working, factor momentum strategies only exacerbate the problem. When investors race into a factor that has had good historical performance, factor crowdedness naturally increases. Sooner or later, the factor will have periods of negative returns. The underperformance triggers some funds to reduce factor exposure, which further negatively impacts factor returns and in turn triggers more funds to reduce factor exposure. When factor return reversal happens, it often causes sharp drawdown in a short period of time. Therefore, chasing factor returns facilitates the formation of bubble-and-bust cycles for factors.

In general, crowdedness means that many arbitragers are actively trading on a factor, which ultimately leads to lower alpha or even the disappearance of alpha and increased volatility. Market catalysts, sometimes unrelated to the factor itself, may trigger a sharp drawdown of the factor return. Occasionally, some funds are forced to unwind their equity positions to raise cash because of losses in other asset classes. For crowded trades, the unwinding causes losses for other participants who use similar factors. As many participants reduce their factor exposures to control risk, they suffer even more losses. In the end, the feedback accelerates the disorderly unwinding of crowded trades and causes steep losses to affected market participants. In September 2006, Amaranth Advisors—a multi strategy hedge fund with more than $9 billion assets under management—was forced to liquidate their multi-billion dollar equity portfolio to meet margin calls after the fund lost more than $5 billion on natural gas futures. The liquidation had limited impact on the overall equity market, but many equity long/short hedge funds that held similar positions as Amaranth suffered heavy losses around September 15, 2006. After a disorderly unwinding, investors often observe a rebound of factor returns as the liquidity impact dissipates and fundamentals take over. Hence, funds that weather the storm without cutting their positions actually may recover part of their losses whereas the funds that dramatically cut their positions may not.

The risk of factor crowdedness raises the question of whether we can detect crowdedness. Investors have developed a number of methods that use portfolio positions, portfolio returns, short interest ratios, and valuation spreads to estimate factor crowdedness. If a portfolio's positions are available, we can use portfolio holdings to calculate the portfolio's exposure to any factor. In this approach, we simply get the factor exposures of each stock in the portfolio, multiply the factor exposures by the portfolio weights, and then aggregate the exposures to the portfolio level. Holdings-based style analysis is widely used for internal risk analysis and return attribution. Investors also use portfolio positions from 13F data to estimate factor exposures of institutional investors. When portfolio holdings are not available, investors resort to returns-based style analysis. In returns-based style analysis, we run a regression of the returns of a portfolio on the contemporaneous factor returns to estimate the portfolio's factor exposures. If the portfolio manager consistently bets on a factor such as expected growth rate, the coefficient (exposure) on that factor is positive and statistically significant. When we combine the exposures to a factor across a collection of funds and calculate a weighted exposure using portfolio sizes as the weights, we get an estimation of the aggregated factor exposure across the funds.

Both holdings-based style analysis and returns-based style analysis have proven to be useful tools in analyzing active mutual funds. The approach has limited success for equity hedge funds though. Hedge funds are not required to submit short positions, so aggregating factor exposures from the long positions of a fund ignores the potential hedges of those factors by the short positions. Unlike mutual funds, neither the returns nor the portfolio sizes of hedge funds are readily available. Furthermore, the factor exposures of an individual hedge fund often evolve over time as portfolio managers refine their stock selection criteria, make factor timing decisions, or adjust their strategies in response to capital flows. As a result, it is difficult to run returns-based style analysis for hedge funds. Since hedge funds have become a major force in active equity management, we need alternative measures for crowdedness. Because short positions are mostly used by sophisticated investors such as hedge fund managers to bet against stocks, short interest is a logical choice for estimating factor crowdedness. If many portfolio managers include the same factor in their stock selections, stocks with unfavorable factor scores are likely to have high short interests and stocks with favorable factor scores are likely to have low short interests. One approach is to rank the stocks by the factor scores to quantiles, calculate the average (or median) short interest ratio of stocks within each quantile, and monitor the difference in average short interest ratio (or utilization of securities lending supplies) between the bottom quantile and top quantile. As the signal becomes crowded, the difference in average short interests of the stocks in the bottom and the top quantile is likely to be much higher than its historical average. Hence, we can build Bollinger Bands of the short interest difference to detect "overbought" condition and reduce the factor exposure if we believe that a factor's return is likely to reverse because of factor crowdedness.

Simple difference in short interests between quantiles does not account for the differences caused by common risk factors such as market cap and sector. Stocks with the highest market caps and lowest market caps on average have lower short interests. Although market-cap weighting is popular for funds that are benchmarked against market-cap weighted indices, few funds would have short positions proportional to market caps. Therefore, mega-cap stocks tend to have low short interests. At the other end of the spectrum, micro-cap stocks often have low institutional holdings and low supplies for securities lending. Hedge funds also avoid shorting micro-cap stocks due to liquidity risk. Therefore, micro-cap stocks tend to have low short interests as well. We can use regression to remove the differences in short interests caused by differences in market caps and sectors[68]:

$$ SR_{i,t} = f_{\text{market},t} + \sum_{l=1}^{10} f_{\text{size},l,t} I_{i,l,t} + \sum_{m=1}^{10} f_{\text{sector},m,t} I_{i,m,t} + \sum_{n=1}^{10} f_{\text{factor},n,t} I_{i,n,t} + \varepsilon_{i,t} $$

where $SR_{i,t}$ is the short interest ratio of asset i at t;

$f_{\text{market},t}$ is the average short interest of all assets at t;

$I_{i,l,t}, I_{i,m,t}$, and $I_{i,n,t}$ are indicator variables for size deciles, sectors, and factor deciles: if asset i belongs to size decile l, sector m, and factor decile n, then $I_{i,l,t}$, $I_{i,m,t}$, and $I_{i,n,t}$ are ones and other indicators are zeros;

$f_{\text{size},l,t}, f_{\text{sector},m,t}$, and $f_{\text{factor},n,t}$ are the short interest differences caused by size deciles, sectors, and factor deciles;

$\varepsilon_{i,t}$ is the residual short interest ratio for asset i at t.

---

[68] Indictors for other common factors such as decile indicators for B/P ratios and turnovers are sometimes included in the analysis as well.

The decile differences, $f_{\text{size},l,t}$, $f_{\text{sector},m,t}$, and $f_{\text{factor},n,t}$, are estimated from cross-sectional regression using short interest ratios of individual stocks. The difference between the short interest ratios of the bottom decile and the top decile, $f_{\text{factor},1,t} - f_{\text{factor},10,t}$, is used to estimate signal crowdedness. When the difference is significantly higher than its historical average, the signal may have become crowded.

Another approach to estimate crowdedness is to examine the spreads in valuation multiples (e.g., price-to-book ratio) between stocks in different quantiles. If active investors take positions for the stocks in the top quantile, one would expect the prices of the stocks in the top quantile to go up and the stocks command a premium to their book values; if active investors take short positions for the stocks in the bottom quantile, one would expect that the prices of the stocks in the bottom quantile to go down and the stocks sell at a (relative) discount to their book values. The spread is defined as the difference between the median price-to-book value of the stocks in the top quantile and the median price-to-book value of the stocks in the bottom quantile. When the spreads of the valuation multiples between stocks in the top quantile and the stocks in the bottom quantile become extreme (e.g., two standard deviations higher than historical average), the signal is likely to be crowded and the risk of signal return reversal is high.

In the long run, crowdedness translates to lower alpha. In the short term, the relationship between crowdedness and alpha is more complicated. Although crowdedness ultimately will lead to a reversal of the signal performance accompanied by heavy losses, the timing of the reversal is highly uncertain. Crowdedness may last for a long time or even accelerate before it crashes. Therefore, many investors choose to stay away from crowded signals instead of betting against the crowd. Others may watch for signs of reversal and try to bet on the reversal only when the signal performance clearly indicates a reversal.

Macroeconomic and Market Factors

Another dynamic factor timing strategy explores the relationship between exogenous variables such as economic factors and alpha factors. The macroeconomic environment directly contributes to the existence of positive autocorrelation of factor returns. There is empirical evidence of factor return differences in different macroeconomic environments. The following are some general historical observations:

- Earnings yield signal outperformed in slow earnings growth environments and underperformed in high growth environments.

- Quality signals outperformed when market volatility was high and underperformed when market volatility was low.

- Price and fundamental momentum factors outperformed during periods of robust economic growth.

- Stocks with high book-to-price ratios and high financial leverage had strong performance following bear market bottoms.

- Dividend-paying stocks outperformed non-dividend-paying stocks in bear markets and non-dividend-paying stocks outperformed dividend-paying stocks in bull markets.

Therefore, investors try to identify current economic conditions, market regimes, and investor sentiment in order to dynamically select the factors that are more likely to perform well in the current environment.

Economic Conditions

Fiscal/monetary policies and the state of the economy (e.g., inflation, interest rate, and GDP growth rates) have a significant impact on factor returns. Arnott et al. (1992) found that rising inflation led stocks with high dividend yields to underperform the market. The rising inflation tended to push up interests rates, which had a negative impact on stocks that paid stable cash flows and had lower nominal growth rate. The inclusion of macroeconomic information in factor selection helps investors avoid costly mistakes in chasing past factor returns. The implementation of major monetary or fiscal policies can trigger the start of a new market trend and reverse factor performance. Since companies with high book-to-price ratios tend to be less profitable and generate less cash, the book-to-price ratio signal performed poorly in 2008 because investors were deeply concerned about the bankruptcy risk of deep-value stocks with high book-to-price ratios. Price momentum, on the other hand, had decent performance as investors continued to dump high risk stocks in favor of low risk ones. In order to stabilize the economy, Congress implemented a number of fiscal policies such as Troubled Asset Relief Program (TARP) in late 2008 and American Recovery and Reinvestment Act (the Stimulus Bill) in early 2009. More importantly, the Federal Reserve started the Quantitative Easing (QE) program to inject money into the economy. Although the programs' impact on long-term government debt as well as the moral hazard of too-big-to-fail remains to be seen, these programs achieved the goal of stabilizing the economy in 2009 and reversed the direction of many factors' returns. As the recession ended in the second quarter of 2009 and the economy gradually recovered, the financial bankruptcy risk of distressed companies decreased. The 12-Month price momentum signal suffered unprecedented losses in 2009 and the book-to-price signal had a strong year as stocks with high bankruptcy risk quickly recovered. Investors who recognized the impact of those government interventions adapted their strategies and changed their factor weightings accordingly to avoid the losses caused by factor reversal.

Significant economic changes can bring extra challenge to the usage of fundamental data. The reason is that companies do not release their annual or quarterly reports simultaneously. When the economic situation rapidly deteriorated, as in the fourth quarter of 2008, the book value, earnings, and cash flow of many companies deteriorated as well. Before a company's fourth quarter's (Q4) report was released, the data up to the third quarter of 2008 (Q3) were usually used in financial ratio calculations. Since investors preferred the latest available data, they naturally incorporated the Q4 results in their cross-sectional analysis as companies began to release their quarterly earnings. As a result, those companies which reported earnings earlier had lower scores than those that reported later—the former had updated Q4 fundamental data and the later still had the Q3 data. Therefore, the asynchronous nature of fundamental data makes cross-sectional analysis less meaningful when there are abrupt changes in the economy.

Some investors build classification models using macroeconomic indicators to determine whether the current economic environment is a good environment for a particular factor to be effective. Arshanapalli et al. (2007) built logistic regression models to forecast the relative performance of Russell 1000 value, Russell 1000 growth, Russell 2000 value and Russell 200 growth indices. They used macroeconomic and market factors such as changes in consumer price index and bond yields as inputs. A market timing strategy that longed the best predicted index outperformed all four Russell indices. The monthly return of the market timing strategy was 1.78% in 1984-2000, which was 46 bps higher than the monthly return of the Russell 1000 value index, the best performing buy-and-hold strategy among the four Russell indices. Instead of using binary classification models to decide whether the current environment is good for a factor or not, other investors use distance models to measure how similar the current environment is relative to historical economic environments. Essentially the models try to identify historical periods that had similar economic readings as the current readings. Investors then forecast the performance of various signals based on the efficacy of these signals in similar historical macro-periods. Specifically, investors generate a forecast for each factor as a weighted average of its historical performance by assigning similar macro-periods higher weights.

Despite the value of building dynamic models conditioned on macroeconomic factors, the statistical power of such models may be limited as there were few economic cycles in a backtest period of ten to twenty years. Dynamic factor timing strategies for momentum signals would have yielded better backtest results than a static model if they had avoided or even bet against the momentum signals during the 2003 and 2009 market recoveries. Nevertheless, it is difficult to draw a statistical conclusion from just two correct timing decisions. Instead, users of such dynamic models need to understand the economic reasoning behind timing decisions and have confidence that the dynamic weighting is likely to reduce the weighting of the momentum signals in a future market recovery.

Market Regimes

Market returns influence the returns of many factors as well. Some factors have exposures to market beta. For instance, growth stocks on average tend to have higher beta exposures than value stocks. High momentum stocks tend to have higher beta exposures after a bull market and have lower beta exposures after a bear market. Even after removing the linear exposure to market beta, some factors still have different responses to large positive or negative market moves. For example, stocks with low earnings variability tend to outperform stocks with high earnings variability when the market crashes after controlling for the beta difference. Therefore, whether the market regime is bull or bear serves as useful information for dynamic factor selection. Although it is difficult to forecast the market regime accurately, several simple market timing strategies (e.g. 10-month moving average crossover) have had some predictive power. Using such market timing strategies to forecast the market regime and to adjust the factor weightings has the potential to yield better predicted alphas than static factor weightings.

Classification of market regimes is not restricted to market returns. We can also use market volatility (cross-sectional dispersion of stock returns or simply the volatility of market index returns) and classify the market as either a high volatility regime or a low volatility regime. If the realized daily market volatility in the past 3 months is higher than the 36-month average, it is a high volatility regime; otherwise, it is a low volatility regime. Unlike market returns, market volatility exhibits much higher consistency because of volatility clustering. As a result, it is easier to forecast the volatility regime. Some signals have different risk-adjusted returns in a low volatility regime versus in a high volatility regime. Technical analysts have long recognized that trend following signals are more effective when the market is quiet (low volatility regime) and trending. The 12-Month momentum signal, as a trend following signal, tends to lose its predictive power when the near-term market volatility is significantly higher than the long-term average. Book-to-price premium, on the other hand, tended to be higher after high-volatility periods. Stivers and Sun (2010) showed that the market's recent return dispersion (σ_t), defined as the cross-sectional standard deviation of the monthly returns of underlying assets, was negatively correlated with subsequent momentum factor payoffs and positively correlated with subsequent book-to-price factor payoffs.

The market volatility also influences factors that rely on analyst forecasts. Since forecasted earnings yields use analysts' consensus earnings forecasts in the factor construction, the effectiveness of these factors depends on the reliability of earnings forecasts. When there was significant uncertainty in the economy, as in the 2008 financial crisis and the 2009 recovery, earnings forecasts tended to be unreliable, which reduced the effectiveness of forecasted earnings yields. The economic uncertainty was often reflected in high market volatility. As a result, when the 3-month market volatility was significantly higher than the 36-month moving average, forecasted earnings became less reliable and the forecasted earnings yield signal became less effective. Economic uncertainty also led to significant dispersion of earnings forecasts amongst analysts and significant increases in earnings revisions. Both the dispersion and the number of revisions can be aggregated across assets to estimate the reliability of earnings forecasts. When the dispersions and revisions were higher than historical averages, forecasted earnings yields were less effective factors. Historical earnings yield (E_0/P) was less effective when the market volatility was high as well. When there was significant uncertainty in the economy, the market volatility tended to be higher and the historical earnings did not represent future earnings well. Therefore, historical earnings yield became less effective in high-volatility environments.

Investors also monitor the average correlation between stocks. One approach to calculate the average correlation is to calculate the correlation of each pair of stocks in an index and then average the correlations of all pairs. However, such an approach requires the calculation of a large number of pairwise correlations when an index includes hundreds of stocks. For the S&P 500 index, it requires the calculation of 124,750 ($500 \times 499/2$) pairs. Since the index volatility and stock volatility are readily available, we can extract the average pairwise correlation from the volatility of the index and the volatility of the underlying stocks:

$$\sigma_p^2 = w'\Sigma w = \sum_{i=1}^{N} w_i^2 \sigma_i^2 + \sum_{i=1}^{N} \sum_{j=1,j\neq i}^{N} w_i w_j \sigma_i \sigma_j \rho_{i,j} \Rightarrow \overline{\rho} = \frac{\sigma_p^2 - \sum_{i=1}^{N} w_i^2 \sigma_i^2}{\left(\sum_{i=1}^{N} w_i \sigma_i\right)^2 - \sum_{i=1}^{N} w_i^2 \sigma_i^2}$$

where σ_p is the volatility of the index;

   $w_i, \forall i = 1, 2, ..., N,$ is the weight of stock i in the index;

   $\sigma_i, \forall i = 1, 2, ..., N,$ is the volatility of stock i.

When stock returns are mainly driven by macro-economic factors, stock price moves are largely driven by macroeconomic news and investor sentiment instead of the fundamentals of individual stocks. High average correlation between stocks indicates that stock returns are driven by common factors and thus is a difficult environment for stock picking.

Investor Sentiment

A drawback of macroeconomic factors is that they are slow signals. While economic cycle lengths vary greatly, they take years rather than months to complete. Unlike economic cycles, investors' risk appetite can change far more frequently. Without meaningful changes to the state of the economy, greed and fear drives stock markets. For a few weeks, investors may focus on just the positives; in the next few weeks, those same investors may subsequently focus on just the negatives. When investors are risk seeking, high-risk stocks are in demand and have higher returns than low-risk stocks; when investors become risk averse, high-risk stocks fall out of favor and have lower returns than low-risk stocks.

Market sentiment indicators such as the VIX are used to measure investors' risk appetite. As the direction of the VIX changes, investors may observe a reversal of factor performance, especially for risk and growth related factors. The TED spread, the difference between the three-month LIBOR rate and the three-month T-bill rate, is another indicator for risk appetite. As investors become more risk averse, the TED spread increases. Hence, changes in the TED spread capture changes in market sentiment. Other investors directly examine the return difference between high beta stocks and low beta stocks. If investors' risk appetite increases, high beta stocks are expected to outperform low beta stocks.

We can rank S&P 500 stocks by their beta and separate the stocks into quintiles at the beginning of a measurement period. The period ranges from a week to three months depending on estimation horizon. The return of a zero-investment portfolio that longs the stocks in the top quintile (equally-weighted high beta stocks) and shorts the stocks in the bottom quintile (equally-weighted low beta stocks) is used to determine the risk appetite. If the return of the zero-investment portfolio is positive, investors are risk-seeking; otherwise, investors are risk-averse. Alternatively, we can calculate the rank correlation between the stock betas and stock returns. If the correlation is positive, investors are risk-seeking; otherwise, investors are risk-averse. Essentially, we treat beta as the systematic risk factor and measure the return of the hedged portfolio or the information coefficient for the factor. The information coefficient often has the same sign as the S&P index return, but sometimes it does not. The divergence happens when the market return is driven by a few mega-cap stocks without broad participation of other stocks. When the market is up (down) while the majority of the high beta stocks are down (up), the information coefficient is negative (positive). Therefore, the divergence of the index return and the risk appetite is a potential leading indicator of market reversal.

Trading by corporate insiders can be used to predict factor returns as well. Using the insider trades of individual companies, Knewtson et al. (2010) computed the net aggregate insider demand as the ratio of the net number of insider purchases over 1-6 months to the number of all insider transactions over the same period:

$$\text{Aggregate insider demand} = \frac{\text{number of purchases} - \text{number of sales}}{\text{number of purchases} + \text{number of sales}}$$

With the exception of the 2009 market recovery, the net aggregate insider demand was strongly negatively correlated with the subsequent month's value premium (return difference between value stocks above the 70th book-to-market percentile and growth stocks below the 30th book-to-market percentile). When the aggregate insider demand was at the bottom one-third of last 60 months' aggregate insider demand, the monthly value premium was ~1% in 1983-2008. When the aggregate insider demand was at the top one-third of last 60 months' aggregate insider demand, the monthly value premium was -0.5%. The difference in value premium was mainly explained by the return difference in growth stocks. Insiders sold (bought) when growth stocks were overvalued (undervalued) and growth stocks subsequently underperformed (outperformed) value stocks.

Valuation Spreads

The spreads in valuation multiples (e.g., price-to-book ratio and price-to-earnings ratio) between stocks in different factor quantiles provide valuable information on signal crowdedness. If active investors take long positions in the stocks in the top quantile, we would expect the prices of the stocks in the top quantile to go up and command a premium to their book values; if active investors take short positions within the stocks in the bottom quantile, we would expect that the prices of the stocks in the bottom quantile to go down and sell at a discount to their book values. The spread is defined as the difference between the median price-to-book value of the stocks in the top quantile and the median price-to-book value of the stocks in the bottom quantile. When the spreads of the valuation multiples between the stocks in the top quantile and the stocks in the bottom quantile become extreme (e.g., two standard deviation higher than the historical average), the signal is likely to be crowded and the risk of signal return reversal is high. On the other hand, when the valuation multiples between the stocks in the top quantile and the stocks in the bottom quantile are below the historical average, the signal is less crowded and the signal tends to outperform.

The spreads in valuation multiples that are used to detect signal crowdedness can also be used to identify less crowded and more effective factors. Asness et al. (2000) expanded the relative price approach by incorporating forecasted future earnings growth rate. The expected return of a stock depends not only on its current earnings yield but also on the future earnings growth. They followed a version of the Gordon growth model:

$$E[R] = E/P + g$$

where E[R] is the expected return of a stock;

E/P is the stock's earnings yield;

g is the expected earnings growth rate (I/B/E/S long-term EPS growth).

A growth stock with low earnings yield can have good returns if the growth rate is high. The expected spreads between the value stocks and growth stocks can be expressed as

$$E[R_{value} - R_{growth}] = (E/P_{value} - E/P_{growth}) - (g_{growth} - g_{value})$$

where $E[R_{value} - R_{growth}]$ is the expected return spread between value and growth stocks;

$(E/P_{value} - E/P_{growth})$ is the value spread;

$(g_{growth} - g_{value})$ is the growth spread.

The value premium is determined by both the value spread the growth spread. Their study demonstrated that for different value measures (E/P, B/P, and S/P), a combination of value spreads and growth spreads was better at predicting next year's value premium than value spreads alone.

When the paper was written at the end of October 1999, value signals had been suffering because of the large positive returns of growth stocks during the internet bubble. As shown in Exhibit 11-1, the Russell 1000 value index underperformed the Russell 1000 growth index[69] by 23.1% (15.6% versus 38.7%) in 1998 and 25.8% (7.3% versus 33.2%) in 1999. Needless to say, the late 1990s were difficult years for value investors. Value investors needed to decide whether the value signals were just temporarily out of favor and were positioned for a turnaround, or the signals might be permanently impaired and would never recover in the future because of changes in the market. Instead of being dazzled by the new internet economy, Asness et al. forecasted that the return spread between value and growth stocks was near historical highs and value stocks would outperform. Soon after the paper's publication, the wheel of fortune reversed. When the internet bubble burst, the Russell 1000 value index outperformed the Russell 1000 growth index by 29.4% (7.0% versus -22.4%) in 2000 and 14.8% (-5.5% versus -20.4%) in 2001. In fact, for seven consecutive years from 2000 to 2006, the value index outperformed the growth index every year. The success of the value signals laid the foundation for the rapid growth of quantitative equity strategies in 2000-2006.

Exhibit 11-1 Return difference between Russell 1000 value and growth indices

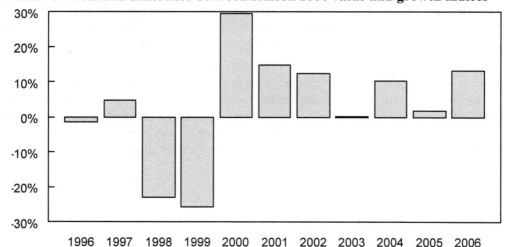

---

[69] Although Russell uses book-to-price ratios to select value stocks, I/B/E/S forecasted growth rates and historical sales per share growth rates are used to select growth stocks.

Seasonality

Similar to stock market returns, factor returns also exhibit seasonal effects. For example, the 12-month momentum signal tended to perform better in the last month of each quarter—March, June, September, and December. One possible explanation is that some fund managers engage in window dressing before the quarter ends. To achieve better appearance, they buy stocks with better performance and sell stocks with worse performance, which further increases the returns of winners and depresses the returns of losers before quarter ends. Besides windowing dressing, tax planning reasons may also contribute to the signal's performance in December. Investors often sell losing stocks in December to realize losses to claim capital losses or use capital losses to reduce capital gains. The selling pressure further pushes down the prices of losing stocks and boosts the gain of the momentum signal.

The optimism cycle is often used to explain the "Sell in May and Go Away" seasonal effect on stock market returns. Consistent with the hypothesis that investors are more optimistic between November and April, there are also observations that risk factors tend to have better performance during these six months than in the other six months. Although stocks with high EPS variability, high debt to equity ratios, low interest coverage ratios, and high liquidity risk underperform the stocks with lower risks between May and October, these stocks tend to outperform between November and April.

Many factors exhibit January effects as well. The 12-month momentum signal often had negative returns in January; 1-month return reversal signals, on the other hand, had good performance in January. Since stock-level return reversals may coincide with possible factor reversals, last year's best performing factors may show reversal (underperform) in January. Value signals also tended to outperform in January. Arnott (1992) found that the January effect of the book to price signal was three times in magnitude as the small-stock effect in January. A possible explanation of the outperformance of 1-month return reversal signal and the book to price ratio signal is that investors sell losing stocks in December for tax reasons (stocks with high book to price ratios are more likely to be losing stocks), which further pushes down the prices of these losing stocks in December and leads to subsequent recoveries in the following January.

Conclusion

Alpha factors, portfolio optimization, and dynamic factor timing are three pillars of quantitative portfolio management. After discussing alpha factors and portfolio optimization in previous chapters, we discussed a number of systematic approaches for dynamic factor timing in this chapter. Besides incorporating systematic signals, investors may incorporate their own view of economic conditions and market regimes in dynamically selecting or increasing the weights of factors that have higher expected returns and lower risks. This works if investors have skills in forecasting the economy or the market. Many investors rely on their market knowledge and experience to make judgment calls on factors that will likely outperform in the near future. The combination of systematic forecast with market experience further boosts investors' ability to dynamically manage their portfolios to achieve better risk-adjusted returns.

Chapter 12

Statistical Arbitrage

The returns of similar assets are expected to be similar. When their returns diverge, the expectation is that they may again converge at an indeterminate time in the future. Statistical arbitrage is a trading strategy that exploits future expected convergence when prices of similar stocks diverge. Although statistical arbitrage is often considered to be an invention of the quants, swing traders have long exploited trading rules to bet on the convergence of similar assets. Both swing traders and quants often hold statistical arbitrage positions ranging from a day to a few weeks, during which capital is put to work while avoiding exposure to long-term price risks. Quants take a systematic approach to statistical arbitrage by making a large number of bets with positive expected returns. The benefit of diversification lowers portfolio volatility and increases the information ratio.

Pairs trading is a traditional statistical arbitrage strategy that exploits the temporary divergence in prices of two similar securities. It models the relationship between the two securities' prices or cumulative returns. When the price difference between the two securities deviates from the model, the difference is expected to revert to its model mean over time. If the current difference is above the mean, it is expected to decrease to its mean; if the current difference is below the mean, it is expected to increase to its mean.

Dual-Class-Shares Based Pairs Trading

One natural choice for pairs trading is dual-class shares. Dual-class shares are shares issued by the same company. They usually have the same cash flows (dividend payment) but different voting rights. For example, Discovery Communications has share class DISCA with voting rights and share class DISCK without voting rights. The prices of dual-class shares of the same company usually are close. Two factors influence the relative price of a voting share to a non-voting share:

- Voting premium: The share class with voting rights commands a premium. The premium is small if the control of the company is not in question and the value goes up when the control is contested.

- Liquidity premium: The share class with more liquidity—higher floating shares and higher trading volumes—commands a premium.

Except for the dates close to contentious shareholder meetings that impact the control of a company, one would expect that the relative price of a voting share to a non-voting share to stay fairly constant, and the ratio of their prices to be a mean-reverting process. Major voting contests, e.g., proxy fights to replace board of directors, may distort the price ratio around the events. As contests settle, the price ratio reverts to a normal level. If the price difference becomes too large compared to its historical average, it is likely to decrease and if the price difference becomes too small, it is likely to increase.

We now examine the DISCA/DISCK pair to show how one may potentially exploit the price difference. As shown in Exhibit 12-1, the prices of DSICA and DISCK in general move together, but there is still significant volatility in the DISCA to DISCK price ratio. When we overlay the price ratio with its 6-month Bollinger Bands, it is clear that the ratio is mean-reverting. As the ratio reaches beyond the upper or lower band, we can take a position and wait until the ratio reverts to the middle of the band. On February 26, 2010, DISCA was added to the S&P 500 index and DISCK was not. The addition to S&P 500 pushed DISCA up relative to DISCK and the price ratio crossed the upper Bollinger Band (DISCA closed at \$31.15 and DISCK closed at \$26.55; Price ratio was 1.17). The price ratio soon reverted to the middle band on March 8 (DISCA closed at \$31.68 and DISCK closed at \$27.95; Price ratio was 1.13). If we had bought DISCK and shorted DISCA at the close of February 26 and then closed the positions on March 8, we would have made 1.8% on the gross investment (total value of long and short) in less than two weeks.

Exhibit 12-1 Prices of DISCA/DISCK and Bollinger Bands of the price ratio

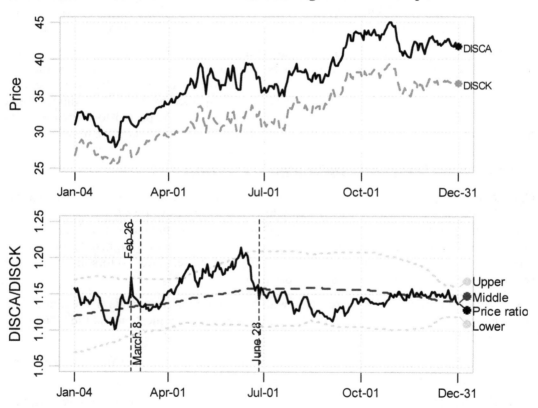

For risk management purposes, it is better to have equal dollar values invested in the longs and shorts instead of equal number of shares, especially if one is expecting large share price moves or if the share prices converge slowly. Let us use an example—a somewhat theoretical one since the positions could have been closed earlier—to show why that is the case. If we had bought 1000 shares of DISCK at the close of February 26, 2010 at \$26.54 and shorted 1000 shares DISCA at \$31.15 and closed the trade on June 28,

2010 when DISCK closed at \$32.74 and DISCK closed at \$37.44. The DISCA premium decreased from 17.4% to 14.4%; How about the profit? It is ((-26.54 + 31.15) + (32.74 − 37.44)) × 1000 = -\$90. Even without considering trading costs, this is, as apparent, an unprofitable trade. If we had used equal dollar approach: bought 1174 shares of DISCK and shorted 1000 shares of DISCA, the gross profit becomes (-26.54 × 1174 + 31.15 × 1000) + (32.74 × 1174 − 37.44 × 1000) = \$988.8 and the annualized raw return is 4.3%.

Although dual-class shares are the natural pairs to trade, a strategy limited to dual-class shares has limited scope and limited trading opportunities. The main reason is that few companies have dual-class shares and for the ones that do have them, one of the share classes tends to be too illiquid to be traded in meaningful sizes by institutional investors.

Correlation-Based Pairs Trading

Since dual-class shares have limited scope, investors have expanded the candidates to all stock pairs that move together. How does one determine whether two stocks move together? One popular choice is to examine the correlation between the returns of two assets. Let us consider an ETF, IYF, and its leveraged pair, FAS. IYF is an ETF that tracks the Dow Jones US Financial index and FAS is a leveraged ETF whose daily returns track three times the daily returns of the Dow Jones US Financial index. As shown in Exhibit 12-2, the daily returns of FAS and IYF were highly correlated with a correlation of 0.996 in 2009. The daily returns of FAS were very close to three times the daily returns of IYF. Pairs with such high correlations are potential candidates for short-term mean reversion pairs trading.

To trade the IYF/FAS pairs, the general principle is to long FAS and short IYF when FAS return is significantly lower than three times the IYF return or to short FAS and long IYF when FAS return is significant higher than three times the IYF return. Let us consider a portfolio that longs \$1 of FAS and shorts \$3 of IYF and track its daily returns:

Portfolio return on day t = FAS return on day t − 3 × IYF return on day t

Using the portfolio return as a signal, we can develop the following trading rules:

Position	Entry at close	Exit
Long \$1000 FAS and short \$3000 IYF	Portfolio return on day t is less than -50 bps; no ex-dividend date for FAS or IYF between t-3 and t+3; sum of portfolio return between t-4 and t-1 is less than -60% of portfolio return on day t	Next day
Long \$3000 IYF and short \$1000 FAS	Portfolio return on day t is more than 50 bps; no ex-dividend date for FAS or IYF between t-3 and t+3; sum of portfolio return between t-4 and t-1 is more than -60% of portfolio return on day t	Next day

50 bps is chosen as the threshold so that the strategy can easily cover trading costs. A higher threshold suggests fewer opportunities, but it also yields a higher success rate and higher returns per trade. The purpose of an ex-dividend date filter is to avoid investing in FAS and IYF around ex-dividend dates. Since the tax rate for dividends is different from capital gains and dividends accrued at ex-dividend dates are not paid until the dividend

payment dates, we avoid days close to ex-dividend dates to avoid the noise introduced by dividend traders. The filter that checks the past four day cumulative portfolio return difference versus today's portfolio return avoids entering a position when today's return is simply a reversal of the previous days' cumulative difference. For example, if today's portfolio return is -60 bps and the cumulative portfolio return difference for the past four days is 50 bps, today's return is likely just a reversal of the previous abnormal returns instead of a valid entry signal.

Exhibit 12-2 Daily returns and cumulative returns of IYF and FAS in 2009

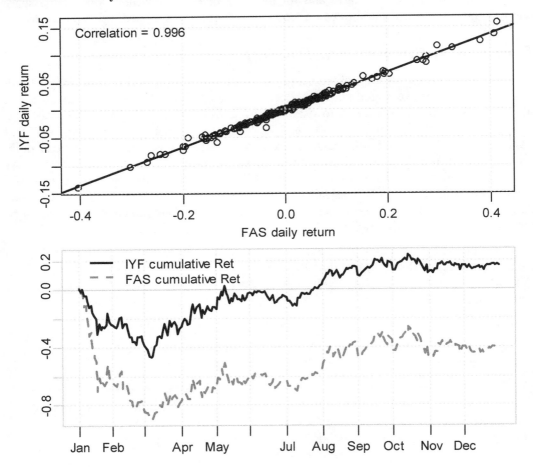

We now further clarify the trade using an example. On October 3, 2011, IYF was down 4.60% and FAS was down 11.96%. The portfolio return was -11.96% − 3 × -4.60% = 1.84%. In other words, FAS did not fall as much as three times as IYF. Since there was no ex-dividend date close to October 3 and the cumulative portfolio return in the previous four days was 0.3%, we longed $3000 IYF and shorted $1000 FAS. On the next day, IYF was up 3.94% and FAS was up 9.09%. We closed the pairs positions to yield a profit of $3000 × 3.94% − $1000 × 9.09% = $27.3.

The strategy held no position in most of the days between 2009 and 2011. During the three year period, 64 trades were executed. As shown in Exhibit 12-3, before trading costs, the total cumulative return was 47.8% for a four-time leveraged ($1 capital for $1 investment in FAS and $3 investment in IYF) portfolio. The strategy had a hit rate of 75% and had little downside risk. The gross gain was 50.8% and the gross loss was only 3.0%. Nevertheless, most of the trades and returns were concentrated in 2009 when the volatility was high (and likely the strategy was less explored and exploited).

Exhibit 12-3 Cumulative return of IYF/FAS pairs trading strategy

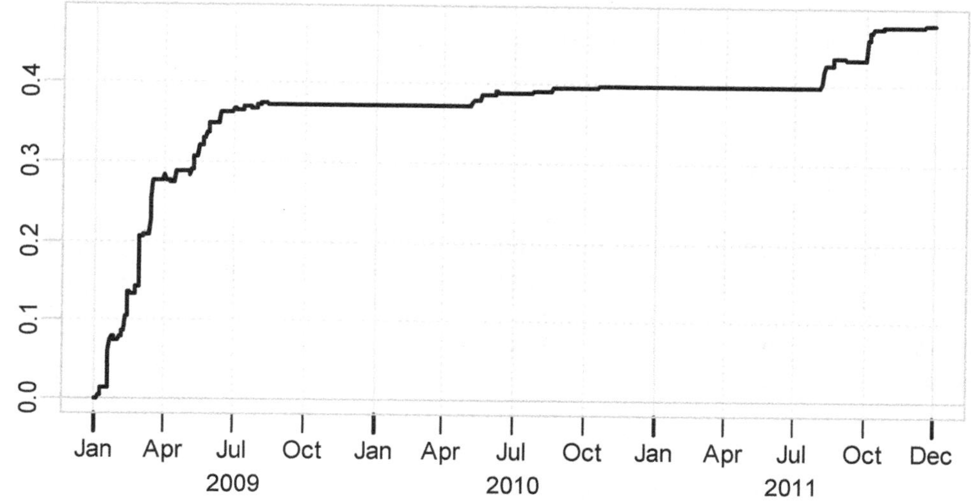

Cointegration-Based Pairs Trading

Pairs trading strategy using daily correlated pairs should be short-term trades as daily correlation measures the short-term relationship between two assets. Assets that have high correlation in daily returns may have drastically different long-term returns. Let us again consider the IYF and FAS pair. Their daily return correlation was 0.996 in 2009. But did their cumulative returns move together in the long run? As shown in Exhibit 12-2, even though the daily returns of FAS were very close to three times of the returns of IYF and they had near perfect daily correlation, their long term cumulative returns diverged. In 2009, IYF was up 16.8%; FAS was down 41.5% instead of yielding three times of IYF returns, +50.4%.

Why did FAS have miserable returns if it accurately replicated the three times of the daily IYF return? Let us consider the following example:

Day	Daily Return		Position Value		Net Return	
	IYF	FAS	IYF	FAS	IYF	FAS
Day 1	5%	15%	1.05	1.15	5%	15%
Day 2	-5%	-15%	0.9975	0.9775	-0.25%	-2.25%

IYF is up 5% on day 1 and then down 5% on day 2. Its cumulative return after two days is -0.25%. If the daily return of FAS is exactly three times of the daily return of IYF, FAS is up 15% on day 1 and then down 15% on day 2. The cumulative return of FAS after two days is -2.25%, which is worse than three times of IYF's cumulative return. The rebalancing of FAS explains the total return difference. Let us consider $1 investment in FAS at the end of day 0, the FAS position has $3 exposure to IYF (futures are often used to provide the leverage). At the end of day 1, since IYF is up 5%, the exposure to IYF becomes $3.15 ($3 × 1.05). Because of leverage, the (equity) value of FAS increases to $1.15. To maintain the three-time exposure to IYF, the fund increases the exposure to $3.45 ($1.15 × 3). The leveraged ETF buys after the underlying index has gone up and sells after the index has gone down. For an index with average daily return μ and volatility σ, the compound daily return of a β-time leveraged ETF can be approximately expressed as

$$r \approx \beta\mu - 0.5 \times (\beta\sigma)^2$$

The first term on the right hand side is simply the average daily return of the leveraged ETF (β can be any number; if $\beta=1$, it is just a normal ETF; inverse ETFs have negative betas); the second term is an adjustment to the compounding return caused by volatility. Both the daily average return and the volatility are proportional to the leverage ratio, β. The variance, however, grows with β^2, which means that high β may lower the compound daily return. To maximize the compound return, the optimal leverage is given by the Kelly formula:

$$\tilde{\beta} = \mu / \sigma^2$$

When the leverage is higher than the optimal leverage, the compound daily return decreases quickly as the decay caused by volatility increases quadratically with the leverage ratio, β. Because of such decay, the prices of over leveraged ETFs move toward zero over a long period of time. That was the case for FAS. In 2009, IYF had an average daily return of 12.5 bps and volatility of 3.6%. The daily compound return of IYF was ~6.1 bps and the cumulative return was $(1+0.00061)^{252} - 1 \approx 16.6\%$. The compound daily return of FAS was

$$r \approx 3 \times 0.00125 - 0.5 \times (3 \times 0.0036)^2 = -0.00208$$

Based on the model, the annual cumulative return of FAS in 2009 was $(1 - 0.00208)^{252} - 1 \approx -40.8\%$. The optimal leverage ratio that maximized the compound return was ~1. Therefore, the three-time leverage in FAS was far from optimal and resulted in heavy losses.

Pairs that move together in the long-term are cointegrated: their price series are both non-stationary, but we can find a linear combination of their price series that is stationary. In less technical terms, the two price series have the same trend and we can find a linear combination of their prices that is mean-reverting over time. Statistical methods use 9 months to 18 months of cumulative returns to identify stock pairs that move together. Longer history increases the statistical power of the tests, but carries the risk of including stale data. Since the fundamental drivers of a company's return vary over time, historically cointegrated pairs may no longer move together if their fundamentals change. To identify cointegrated pairs, Gatev et al. (2006) chose a simple sum-of-squares test. The test first calculates the cumulative returns of each stock using daily total return (dividend return included) data:

$$R_{t,i} = \prod_{k=1}^{t}(1+r_{k,i})-1, \ \forall t = 1, 2, \ldots, T$$

where $r_{k,i}$ is the return of stock i on day k;

$\qquad$ $R_{t,i}$ is the cumulative return of stock i up to day t.

For each pair, the test subtracts two cumulative return series from each other and calculates the distance as the sum of the squares of the differences:

$$D(i, j) = \sum_{t=1}^{T}(R_{t,i} - R_{t,j})^2 = \sum_{t=1}^{T}u_t^2$$

where $u_t = R_{t,i} - R_{t,j}$ is the difference of cumulative return of i and j on day t;

$\qquad$ $D(i, j)$ is the distance of i to j.

The test then calculates pair-wise distances $D(i, j)$ for all pairs in the investment universe and chooses the pairs with the smallest distances as potential candidates for pairs trading.

The sum-of-squares test is a good choice if $R_{t,i} - R_{t,j}$ is stationary[70]. A more general test for cointegration is the Dickey-Fuller test. It tests whether $R_{t,i} - \beta \times R_{t,j}$ is stationary. β captures the return (and volatility) difference between two otherwise similar stocks. The general test first runs a regression of $R_{t,i}$ on $R_{t,j}$ to estimate β. Then it calculates all the residuals $u_t = R_{t,i} - \beta \times R_{t,j}$ and test whether u_t is non-stationary using the Dickey-Fuller test:

$$u_t = c + \phi u_{t-1} + \varepsilon_t$$

The null hypothesis is $\phi = 1$, which means that u_t is non-stationary. If the test rejects the null hypothesis, the pair is a potential candidate for pairs trading.

Pairs selected by statistical methods may require further filtering as some selected pairs are not good candidates for pairs trading. For example, the Dickey-Fuller test may identify two stocks as co-integrated if they happen to have huge price moves on the same day even though they do not move together. One filter is to select only pairs within the same industry. Another filter directly estimates the similarity between two assets' risk profiles. For two stocks to move together, they should have similar risk factor exposures. In other words, their fundamental characteristics and risk exposures are similar so that they are likely to move together. Choosing pairs with similar fundamental characteristics, and within the same industry, lowers the risk of the pairs trading and results in a higher information ratio.

---

[70] Some investors use the log of cumulative total return, $\log(1 + R_{t,i}) - \log(1 + R_{t,j})$, instead of cumulative returns since the distribution of cumulative total return is closer to log normal than to normal distribution. In practice, the results are similar.

Having identified pairs of stocks that move together, one may track the prices/returns of those pairs to make trading decisions. Similar to other pairs trading strategies, investors take a long position in one stock and a short position in the other expecting that the long position will have better returns relative to the short position. Bollinger z-scores (Bollinger Bands) of the residuals are often used to determine the entry point:

$$z_B = \frac{u_t - \overline{u}}{\text{standard deviation of } u_t} \quad \text{where } u_t = R_{t,i} - \beta \times R_{t,j}$$

For example, we calculate the 12-month moving average of the residuals ($\overline{u}$ may simply be set to 0) and the standard deviation of the residuals. If the current residual is two standard deviations away from the moving average ($z_B > 2$), stock i is overvalued relative to stock j and we enter a trade to long stock j and short stock i. The selection of the entry threshold—the number of standard deviations away from the moving average—involves a trade-off between the potential profit and the number of opportunities. With a low threshold, we can participate in more trades since the threshold is reached at higher frequency. But the potential profit is smaller when the pair converges and the pair is more likely to further diverge before converging. A high threshold, on the other hand, triggers fewer trades but the potential profit of each trade is larger. A backtest using different thresholds can help determine the proper threshold. Sometimes investors wait until the residual has peaked and head towards the moving average for a day or two before they enter a pair.

If the residual u_t returns to equilibrium, we take the profit and exit the trade. For example, if we entered a trade when the Bollinger z-score is higher than 2, we can unwind the trade when the z-score falls below 0 or 0.5. What if the pairs move further apart instead of converging? For such cases, we need to decide whether and when to use a stop loss trigger. If we entered a pair when the residual reached two standard deviations and the pairs kept on drifting against us to four standard deviations, what should we do? If we still believe in the original premise, the opportunity looks even more attractive and we should hold or even add more shares. If we believe the cointegration breaks down, we should cover the pairs. To determine whether the cointegration breaks down, we may look at the history for guidance. If the historical divergence has never exceeded four standard deviations, we can put a stop loss at four standard deviations. When the difference goes beyond it, it likely means that our original premise has broken down.

Some investors actively examine the fundamentals of the two stocks to determine whether the pair still moves together. If the further divergence is caused by changes in fundamentals such as earnings surprises in one stock because of its increasing competitive advantage, the pair is unlikely to converge and we should close the trade. Many pairs trading strategies also have a maximum holding period (time stop). If the pairs do not converge within a predefined number of days, the trade is closed.

Another decision pertains to managing corporate events. Since the dates for earning announcements and other corporate events such as spin-offs are usually known before the events, some investors use an event calendar to avoid entering into positions before corporate events. Others pursue trading opportunities precisely around these events. For example, earnings announcements cause significant moves in stock prices. If we have no capability of forecasting earnings surprises and market responses, we may want to avoid holding securities close to earnings announcement dates to reduce portfolio volatility. On the other hand, traders with better views actively identify opportunities around corporate events.

One trading strategy exploits the earnings announcement date difference of the underlying pair. Let us consider Bank of America (BAC) and Citigroup (C) as a pair for a hypothetical trade. Assuming BAC releases its earnings before C and assuming it is a negative surprise, the BAC price falls that day while C has a smaller drop. By analyzing detailed economic linkage between BAC and C, a trader draws the conclusion that C is likely to have negative earnings surprise as well and the market has not fully incorporated that information. The trader will short C and long BAC in expectation of the return convergence when C releases its earnings.

Although earlier pioneers of pairs trading such as Morgan Stanley and D.E. Shaw made huge profits, as the strategy became widely known, the market for pairs trading became more efficient and profits dropped. Gatev et al. (2006) observed a significant decrease in pairs trading return in their study: the excess return of the top 20 pairs dropped from 118 bps per month in 1962-1988 to 38 bps per month in 1989-2002. In recent years, the profit of simple pairs trading has mostly disappeared. In order to revive the pairs trading strategy, investors have dug deeper to improve returns. One approach is to select stocks in the industries that are more amenable to pairs trading. Stock pairs with lower idiosyncratic risks relative to systematic risks are more likely to converge after their prices diverge. Since utility stocks and financial stocks are mainly driven by the economy and regulations, they have historically been good candidates for pairs trading. Biotech companies, on the other hand, have high idiosyncratic risks. Therefore, biotech companies are not good candidates for pairs trading.

Other investors examine the characteristics of historical residuals. Not all pairs with strong cointegration are good candidates for pairs trading. Unless the residuals, $u_t = R_{t,i} - \beta \times R_{t,j}$, have sufficient volatility over time, we may not find price deviations large enough to cover trading costs. In other words, if the residuals (u_t) always stay close to 0, there may not be a tradable opportunity once trading costs are taken into consideration. Besides sufficient volatility, the pair needs to have a good probability of converging at a reasonable time period after the divergence of their prices. Otherwise, the return on capital will be low as the pair is likely to remain open for a long time after we enter a trade. Do and Faff (2010) recommended using the number of zero crossings of the residuals over the nine to eighteen month formation period as a gauge of the convergence speed and found selecting the pairs with higher number of zero crossings substantially increased pairs trading returns. Alternatively, we can directly model the residuals using an autoregressive process:

$$\Delta u_{t+1} = u_{t+1} - u_t = \theta(\bar{u} - u_t)dt + \varepsilon,$$

where Δu_{t+1} is the change of the residual on day t + 1;

$\quad$ $\bar{u}$ is the long-term mean of the residuals;

$\quad$ θ is the speed of the mean-reversion, $\theta > 0$;

$\quad$ ε is the random noise, $\varepsilon \sim N(0, \sigma^2)$.

The expected value of the residuals, $E[u_t]$, is $\bar{u}$ and the variance, $\text{var}(u_t)$, is σ^2/θ. $\theta(\bar{u} - u_t)$ captures the mean reversion of the residuals. When $u_t > \bar{u}$, $\theta(\bar{u} - u_t)$ is negative and Δu_t has negative drift; when $u_t < \bar{u}$, $\theta(\bar{u} - u_t)$ is positive and Δu_t has positive drift. The parameter θ measures the speed of the mean reversion. Larger θ means that the residuals converge towards the mean faster. The inverse of θ, $1/\theta$, estimates the time scale for the mean reversion. Using historical data for the residuals, we can estimate θ and select pairs that have sufficiently large θ to increase the likelihood of convergence within a reasonable period of time.

Benchmark-Based Statistical Arbitrage

The traditional pairs trading approach still faces the difficulty of finding pairs of stocks that are similar to each other. Instead of identifying another stock that is similar, investors create a benchmark portfolio using a basket of stocks that have similar risk characteristics as the stock. When the stock return diverges from the portfolio return, their future relative returns tend to reverse the divergence: if the stock significantly underperforms the benchmark portfolio, it is likely to outperform in the next period; if the stock significantly outperforms the benchmark portfolio, it is likely to underperform in the next period.

Chen et al. (2012) tested an approach to build a benchmark using stocks that have the highest correlations with selected stocks. At the end of each year, their strategy uses the monthly return data for all stocks in the past five years to calculate the pairwise correlation of the stocks. For each stock, 50 other stocks that have the highest correlations with the stock are selected and the benchmark portfolio return is the equal-weighted average return of these 50 selected stocks. To account for the volatility difference between the stock and its benchmark, the monthly excess returns (versus the risk-free return) of the stock in the past sixty months is regressed against the excess returns of the benchmark portfolio to yield the stock's beta, β^C. For a month t in the next year, if the stock return is $r_{i,t}$ and the benchmark return is $r_{b,t}$, a variable $diff_{i,t}$ is used to capture the divergence between the stock return and the benchmark return:

$$diff_{i,t} = \beta^C (r_{b,t} - r_{f,t}) - (r_{i,t} - r_{f,t})$$

where $r_{f,t}$ is the risk-free return for month t.

All the stocks are sorted by $diff_{i,t}$ at the end of month t to form ten deciles. A long-short portfolio is constructed to long the stocks in the highest decile—stocks that underperform their benchmarks the most—and short the stocks in the lowest decile—stocks that outperform their benchmarks the most. For a market value-weighted portfolio, such a portfolio returned 1.4% a month on average in 1931-2007. For an equal-weighted portfolio, the average return was 3.59%. Similar to the pairs trading strategies, they also observed a significant decrease in the return over time, which perhaps reflects an increase in market efficiency. Their results also indicated that the short-term mean reversion signal significantly contributed, but did not fully explain, the performance of the statistical arbitrage strategy.

The benchmark portfolio is not limited to a basket of stocks. Instead, investors also create a synthetic benchmark using factors. Avellaneda and Lee (2010) used a synthetic benchmark extracted from principal component analysis (PCA). Using one-year history of daily returns of US stocks, they extracted the top 15 principal components that explained 40%-60% of the variance of returns. The stock returns were then modeled as factor returns from the exposures to these principal components plus residual returns. Their statistical arbitrage strategy that longed the stocks with significant negative residual returns and shorted the stocks with significant positive residual returns had an average Sharpe ratio of 1.44 between 1997 and 2007 after accounting for 5-bp one-way trading costs. Similarly, they observed lower returns in later years: the average Sharpe ratio was 0.9 between 2003 and 2007.

Compared with pairs trading, benchmark-based statistical arbitrage makes position size management easier. Traditional pairs trading tracks a predefined number of pairs. The numbers of pairs that have active positions, however, have a large variation over time. If investors allocate the same capital to each pair, most of the capital may stay idle and generate no returns; if investors allocate more capital to the pairs that generate signals earlier, the new positions that are triggered later may not get capital allocation. If the new positions have a higher alpha than stale positions, as they often do, investors need to dynamically close existing positions in order to free up capital for new positions. Using the benchmark-based statistical arbitrage strategies, investors can decide the number of assets to invest in each period as well as the amount of capital to put into each asset.

Statistical arbitrage strategies suffered heavy losses during the 2007 quant meltdown, which indicates that they were widely used by quantitative funds. Even with improvement, the annual return of successful statistical arbitrage strategies has fallen to low- to mid-single percentages before leverage. Both risk management and trading cost management is crucial for the success of statistical arbitrage strategies. The return distribution of statistical arbitrage tends to be negatively skewed: the majority of the pairs yield small gains and a small percent of pairs yield large losses. Since the loss may be large when an asset does not converge towards its benchmark, successful arbitragers need to be skilled in controlling such losses. Once the tail risk is well controlled, the portfolio risk is low and the strategies can be leveraged to generate higher returns. Since the strategies tend to have low holding periods (days to weeks), trades are usually executed through algorithm trading and the trading costs may determine the viability of a strategy. Similar to the mean-reversion strategies, statistical arbitrage strategies tended to work better in a high volatility market environment and yielded good profit during the 2000-2002 recession and the 2008-2009 financial crisis.

Conclusion

In this chapter, we discussed a number of statistical arbitrage strategies that exploit the expected convergence of similar securities after divergence in their prices. Although the expected returns of such strategies have been small as the market has become more efficient, well-designed statistical arbitrage strategies have the potential to generate a positive return with low risk. Furthermore, the returns of the statistical arbitrage strategies have low correlation with the returns of many other stock selection signals. It is for these reasons that statistical arbitrage still provides valuable opportunities for active investors.

Chapter 13

Other Investment Strategies

In previous chapters we discussed methods to apply seasonal effects, economic indicators, technical signals, and fundamental factors to select stocks. We also delved into the application of portfolio construction and risk management ideas to build equity portfolios with high risk-adjusted returns. Even though this book is primarily about active equity management, especially equity long/short investment, it is important to remember that within the financial market, actively managed equity strategies are inextricably linked to a broader universe of asset classes and hybrid instruments. Many trading strategies initially developed for equity investing also tend to work for other asset classes as well. In this chapter, we will discuss a variety of investment strategies that use similar signals for security selection and portfolio construction.

Other Strategies

Besides fundamental or quantitative active long-only and long/short equity funds that focus on stock selection, many other funds also explore possible inefficiency in the equity market and the mispricing of equities relative to other securities. In this section, we explain how alpha signals and risk factors can be used to build low risk strategies, risk arbitrage portfolios, and convertible arbitrage portfolios.

Low Risk Strategies

During the financial crisis, the S&P 500 index lost 55% of its value from its peak in October 2007 to its bottom in March 2009. The massive loss fostered investors' interests in equity strategies with less volatility and significantly less drawdown risk than those in broad equity indices. In response, fund managers built a variety of low risk portfolios catering to more risk-averse investors. These portfolios mostly rely on the low risk anomaly: stocks with low beta and low volatility outperformed stocks with high beta and high volatility. Therefore, low risk strategies tend to long stocks with low risks and some may even short stocks with high risks. There are a number of ways to select low risk stocks and to determine portfolio weights:

- **Low beta strategy** uses market beta as a measure of stocks' market risks and invests in stocks with the lowest betas (lowest market risks). Historically, low-beta stocks have had positive alphas and high-beta stocks have had negative alphas after removing the beta returns. Baker et al. (2013) showed that $1 invested in the lowest risk portfolio of US equities—stocks in the lowest quintile of 5-year historical beta—grew to $70.50 in 1968-2011. In the same period, $1 invested in the highest risk portfolio—stocks in the highest quintile of 5-year historical beta—grew to only $7.61 at the end of 2011. They observed similar patterns in the global equity market as well. A dollar invested in the lowest-risk portfolio of global equities grew to $6.40 in 1989-2011 and a dollar invested in the highest-risk portfolio of global equities broke the buck and ended with $0.99.

- **Low volatility strategy** simply selects stocks with the lowest historical volatility. Equal weights can be assigned to the selected stocks. A different approach, equal-risk budget strategy, assigns the same risk budget to each stock in the selected low-volatility stocks without considering the correlation between stocks. In other words, an asset's weight is determined by the inverse of its volatility, so stocks with lower volatility have higher weights. SPLV, the PowerShares S&P 500 low volatility portfolio, uses such an approach. Every quarter, the fund sorts the stocks in the S&P 500 index by their realized volatility over the past year and selects 100 stocks with the lowest volatility. Among these 100 stocks, an individual asset's weight is inversely proportional to its historical volatility.

- **Minimum variance strategy** tries to achieve the lowest estimated portfolio volatility with a number of constraints. Earlier on, in the section on mean-variance portfolio optimization, we discussed the global minimum variance portfolio that depends only on the covariance matrix of the stocks and not on the expected returns. Since the covariance matrix used in the optimization contains estimation error, the global minimum variance portfolio usually contains many short positions and sometimes has extreme weights for individual stocks. To mitigate the estimation error problem and control portfolio turnover, minimum volatility products include a number of constraints. For example, ACWV, iShares MSCI Global Minimum Volatility ETF, does not allow short positions and restricts the maximum weight of any stock to the lower of 1.5% or 20 times the weight of the stock in MSCI World index.

Despite the differences in portfolio composition, low risk portfolios share common characteristics. They tilt the portfolio heavily toward defensive stocks in the utilities and consumer staple sectors. The outperformance of these defensive sectors is a main contributor to the success of the low risk strategy. Baker (2013) attributed the low risk anomaly to two effects: the macro effect that selects low risk countries or industries contributes to higher returns with modest impact on risks; the micro effect that selects low risk stocks within industries and countries contributes to lower risks with modest impact on returns. Low risk portfolios also tilt heavily towards low beta stocks. Although some low risk strategies do not directly use beta as the risk measure, the interaction between beta and total volatility increases the weights of low beta stocks. Since the cross-sectional correlation between realized volatility and beta is usually higher than 60%, stocks with the lowest volatility have the lowest betas as well. Because low-beta stocks deliver higher risk-adjusted returns than high-beta stocks, minimum variance portfolios prefer to long the low-beta stocks (and hedge the risk by shorting some high-beta stocks if the portfolio allows for short positions). Since the market cap is not part of the portfolio weighting in many low risk strategies, low risk portfolios have negative exposures to the size factor when the portfolio assigns equal weights to stocks or uses an equal-risk budget strategy. In other words, low risk strategies invest more heavily in small-cap stocks and less liquid stocks than market-cap weighted indices. As a result, the size effect contributes to better portfolio returns too.

Although low risk strategies have lower volatility and lower drawdown risk, they are not without risk. These portfolios are still exposed to equity market risk and usually have negative returns when the market drops. The style factor exposures of low risk strategies introduce factor risks. Because SPLV tilts towards utility and consumer staple stocks and these stocks tend to have higher dividend yields, SPLV has positive exposure to the dividend yield factor. In May 2013, investors' concerns about Fed's tapering (gradual withdrawal from quantitative easing) led to a 42-bp increase in the yield of 30-year Treasuries. The negative impact of higher interest rates on high-dividend yield stocks contributed to SPLV's 3.6% loss in May even though SPY was up 2.4%. In addition, low risk stocks tend to underperform both the market and high risk stocks when the market rallies. During the risk-on rally from January 2012 to March 2012, SPLV underperformed SPY by 6% when SPY rallied 12.7%. Compared with the corresponding market indices, low risk strategies are better at preserving capital when the market crashes. Better capital preservation during tough times is the key to the long-term success of low risk strategies.

Risk Arbitrage

Risk arbitrage, also called merger arbitrage, takes long/short positions in the stocks of the companies that are involved in mergers and acquisitions. When an acquisition is announced, the acquirer agrees to purchase the shares of the target in cash, in shares of the acquirer's stock, or a combination of cash and stock. The acquirer usually pays a premium (relative to the close price of the target right before the announcement) for the target. After the announcement, the price of the target immediately moves towards the acquirer's bid price. Since the acquisition may not complete and it takes time for the acquisition to close, there is usually a spread between the bid price and the price of the target after the announcement.[71] For cash acquisition, risk arbitragers long the stock of the target company and wait for the stock price to converge to the deal price. For stock acquisition, risk arbitragers long the stock of the target company and short the stock of the acquirer and wait for their stock prices to converge.

Risk arbitragers carefully collect information about the acquisition and estimate the likelihood that the acquisition will be completed:

- They calculate the acquisition premium offered by the acquirer and compare the premium with similar deals. Higher premiums are more likely to win approval from the shareholders of the target company.

- They assess the response of the target company. A friendly takeover with the blessing of the directors of the target company is more likely to succeed; a hostile takeover, on the other hand, has lower likelihood of success and may involve proxy battles.

- They study the characteristics of the target company and the acquirer. The success rate is high for a large company with solid financing to acquire a small company; a reverse takeover, the acquisition of a larger company by a smaller company (the new company often retains the name of the larger company) may have more difficulty in securing financing from banks or investors. Leveraged buyouts tend to have higher failure rates too.

- They evaluate the overall market environment. Strong market sentiment and industry sentiment not only increase the likelihood of deal closure but also

---

[71] Occasionally, the stock price is higher than the bid price if investors believe that the target company may negotiate a better price or other potential acquirers may provide competing bids.

increases the possibility of revised higher bids from the same acquirer or competing bids from other acquirers.

The participation of risk arbitragers increases the probability of deal approval: risk arbitragers who purchase the shares of the target company will subsequently vote in favor of the deal. When they take positions in a deal in concert with others, unintentionally in pursuit of profits or intentionally in anticipation of others' participation, they collectively facilitate the acquisition process and increase the odds of deal closure.

Part of the returns from risk arbitrage is attributed to the risk premium for taking on the tail risk that the deal may fall through. Let us consider a case where the acquirer offers a 30% acquisition premium for the target company in a cash deal. The market responds to the news and the price of the target is up 26%. The 4% residual premium is mostly caused by the 5% probability that the regulators may block the deal on antitrust grounds, in which case the price of the target will be down 20%.[72] The expected return of investing in the target is

$$4\% \times 95\% - 20\% \times 5\% = 2.8\%.$$

Although the expected return is 2.8%, there is 5% probability that the loss will be 20%. Since investors in general prefer stocks with positive skewness instead of negative skewness, many investors are unwilling to accept such a high downside risk. As a result, investors who are willing to accept such tail risk are expected to be compensated for taking on the tail risk. Merger arbitragers rely on diversification across a number of deals to manage the tail risk. Essentially, merger arbitragers are selling put options on targets to collect the residual premium. In most cases, individual deals have little correlation with each other and the risk of holding a portfolio of diversified deals is small.

Nevertheless, merger arbitrage still faces systematic risk. Mitchell and Pulvino (2001) analyzed the historical returns of a tradable merger arbitrage strategy and found that returns were uncorrelated with market returns when the market was flat or up. The returns, however, were positively correlated with market returns when the market dropped. The correlation reflected the nonlinear systematic risk of the merger arbitrage strategy. When the economy deteriorated and the stock market plunged, fewer deals were announced. The competition among merger arbitrage funds to participate in a smaller number of deals led to smaller expected returns for the successful deals. At the same time, a higher percentage of the announced deals failed, which led to higher losses in failed deals. Exhibit 13-1 shows the HFRI monthly index (published by Hedge Fund Research, Inc.) for merger arbitrage strategy. The strategy has been one of the most consistent hedge fund strategies that generated 8.2% of annual returns from 1989 to 2013 with an information ratio of 2.0. The loss in 2008 and the 8.3% drawdown confirmed the systematic risk of the merger arbitrage strategy.

---

[72] The price of the target usually does not fall to the level before the deal announcement even if the deal fails to close. Investors generally believe that the indication of the interest from an acquirer reflects the potential value of the target.

Exhibit 13-1 HFRI Merger Arbitrage Index and Convertible Arbitrage Index

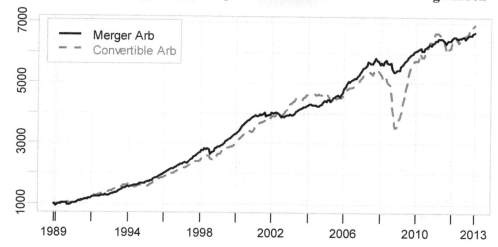

Convertible Arbitrage

Convertible arbitrage is a long/short strategy that longs convertible securities and shorts common stocks of the same issuer. Convertible securities (convertible bonds or convertible preferred stocks) are securities that may be converted into a predetermined amount of common stock within a particular period of time. A convertible bond may pay a fixed coupon rate on its par value and have a fixed maturity. What makes a convertible bond different from a normal bond is the conversion term; the bond holder can exchange the convertible bond for common stocks at a predefined conversion price or conversion ratio. The price of a convertible bond includes the investment value of a normal bond and the value of a call option on the stock. Similar to the value of a normal bond, the investment value is determined by its coupon rate and the prevailing yield of corporate bonds with comparable credit rating and maturity. The investment value increases if the market interest rate declines, the credit quality of the company improves, or the credit spread shrinks. The credit standing of the issuer and other factors may also have an effect on the convertible security's investment value. The conversion value of a convertible security is determined by the market price of the stock and the volatility of the stock. As convertible bonds usually sell as a hybrid of corporate bonds and stock options, they have interest rate risk, credit risk and equity risk. Since many have low trading volumes, they also have liquidity risk. Some convertible bonds are callable that allow the issuer to redeem the bonds at predefined prices. In such cases, investors are usually given rights to convert the bonds to common stocks if the conversion values (stock price × conversion ratio) are higher than the redemption prices. Such a feature further complicates the pricing of convertible bonds. It is for these reasons, convertible bonds are complex financial instruments and their market is less efficient than the stock market.

When a convertible bond is undervalued, convertible arbitrage strategies buy the bond and short the underlying common stock to hedge the equity risk. The coupon payment from the convertible bond and the rebate payment from the cash received from the short stock position generate positive cash flows. Since the convertible bond is undervalued relative to the stock, the convergence towards the fair value also generates positive returns. Since the sensitivity of the call option from the conversion term is hedged by the short stock position, the long/short portfolio has little exposure to stock price moves when price moves are small. The success of the hedge depends on accurate estimation of the sensitivity of the call option to the stock price moves. If the hedge ratio is wrong, the long/short portfolio is subject to equity risk. Since the hedge ratio changes with large stock price moves, the portfolio needs to be rebalanced to maintain the low exposure to equity risk.

Before 2008, investors considered convertible arbitrage a low risk strategy as the short position in the common stock was expected to hedge the equity risk of the convertible bonds. Indeed, as shown in Exhibit 13-1, the strategy returned 8% a year and the standard deviation was only 3.5% before 2008. The perception of low risk was shattered in 2008 when the index lost 40% in a year and wiped out the gains of the previous six years. The huge drawdown demonstrated that most convertible arbitrage funds were exposed to credit risk in a distressed market. As the market crashed in 2008, the credit spread spiked and many convertible bonds became junk bonds: conversion rights had little value since the stock prices were much lower than the conversion prices; the distressed convertible bonds behaved more like equities as the bankruptcy risk of the companies skyrocketed. Therefore, the performance of the convertible arbitrage strategies was highly correlated with the performance of junk bonds, which in turn was highly correlated with the stock market. Not surprisingly, as the prices of junk bonds rallied in 2009, the convertible arbitrage strategy had 60% returns in 2009. In the end, the 2008-2009 period had limited impact on the long-term expected return of the convertible arbitrage strategy. However, it increased the volatility of the strategy to 6.6% and made investors painfully aware of the credit risk embedded in the strategy.

Commodities

After two decades of sluggish performance in the 1980s and 1990s, commodity prices quickly took off in the first decade of 2000s. The commodity boom attracted great interest from investors. Two commodities that attracted most investors' attention were oil and gold. At the beginning of the 2000, the spot price of WTI (West Texas Intermediate) sweet crude oil was at ~$25. The price gradually rose and peaked in the summer of 2008 at above $140 before the subsequent crash to lower $30's around the beginning of 2009. The price has since recovered and traded at $90-$110 in 2014. Because of a surge in investor interest in commodities, commodities are sometimes considered an asset class equivalent to stocks and bonds. As an asset class, commodities may offer the following benefits:

- Commodities provide protection against inflation: Unlike paper currencies, which depreciate fast in a high inflation environment, commodities such as oil and copper have intrinsic value and may serve as a hedge against inflation.

- Commodities provide protection against event risks: When events such as wars or natural disasters occur, they often depress the stock market and boost the value of hard assets. Such events also cause disruptions in the supply or transportation of some commodities, which increase prices as well.

- Commodities provide diversification benefits to stocks and bonds. Since commodity returns have historically had low correlation with stock market and bond market returns, including them within portfolios leads to higher risk-adjusted returns.

There are two ways to invest in commodities: physical assets and paper assets. Investors who hold physical assets are subject to the risk of spot price moves. As the spot price increases, the value of the physical asset increases as well. It is of course difficult for investors to hold physical assets though, as most commodities (precious metals such as gold are exceptions) have significant storage costs. Hence, more investors use paper assets such as futures to invest in commodities. The risk premium for futures is fundamentally different from the risk premium for equities. Erb and Harvey (2006) showed that the average and median geometric excess return of 36 commodity futures had been close to zero. In other words, a simple buy-and-hold strategy that longs all commodity futures generates no better returns than risk-free assets. Instead, the risk premium for futures depends on how futures prices deviate from expected future spot prices. The hedging pressure hypothesis of Keynes (1930) provides an explanation for the existence of (positive or negative) futures risk premiums. Many participants in the futures markets are businesses that use futures to hedge their commodity price exposure. Since these hedgers are willing to pay premiums to reduce their risk exposures, speculators who are willing to take the opposite sides of the trade are compensated accordingly. If risk-averse hedgers (e.g. oil companies) sell futures to hedge their future long exposures, they put downward pressure on the futures price. The futures price is likely to be lower than the expected future spot price and the expected return of the futures is likely to be positive, in which case an investor (speculator) should long the futures. If risk-averse hedgers (e.g., airlines) buy futures to hedge their future short exposures, the expected futures return is likely to be negative, in which case an investor should short the futures.

The total return of a fully collateralized futures portfolio is split into two or three components:

Total return = collateral return + price movement of futures

= collateral return + spot return + roll return

The collateral return is the return of the collateral. In reality, the futures market has fairly low margin requirements that provide investors with high leverage. To estimate the unleveraged futures return, we assume that the futures positions are fully collateralized with the remaining cash invested in risk-free assets. Therefore, the collateral return is close to the risk-free return. The sum of the spot return and roll return is the risk premium for futures. The spot return is the change in the spot price of the underlying commodity. The roll return is the change of the futures price relative to the change of the spot price. The roll returns often depend on the term structure of the futures prices.

Different term structures are classified as either **Contango** or **Backwardation**: Contango is the condition when the spot price is lower than the futures prices and the futures prices increase with maturity; backwardation is the condition when the spot price is higher than the futures prices and the futures prices decrease with maturity. In other words, when futures prices are in Contango (backwardation), the term structure of the futures prices is upward (downward) sloping. The two cases in Exhibit 13-2 explain why the roll return and the term structure are important for futures returns. In both cases, spot prices do not change and the term structures stay the same in a month. In the first case, the futures prices are in Contango. The spot price is $100 at t; the futures price of the near month futures that expires in one month ($t + 1$) is \$101; the futures price of the next month futures that expires in two months is \$102. Since the spot price does not change in a month, the spot return is 0. The near month futures price converges to the spot price at $t + 1$ and the roll yield is -1/101. In the second case, the futures prices are in backwardation. The spot return is still zero, but the roll yield becomes 1/99.

Exhibit 13-2 Roll returns and futures returns

Time	Contango				Backwardation			
	t	t+1	t+2	t+3	t	t+1	t+2	t+3
t	100	101	102	103	100	99	98	97
t+1		100	101	102		100	99	98

For investors who invest in futures or ETFs that hold futures, it is important to understand that the returns of futures are substantially different from the spot price changes. The spot price moves explain most of the futures return volatility. The roll returns, however, play a larger role in explaining the long-term futures returns. Exhibit 13-3 shows the price history of spot price of WTI sweet crude oil and an oil ETF, USO, from the inception of USO in April 2006 to the end of 2009. USO uses oil futures, forwards, and swaps to track the movement of WTI sweet crude oil prices. The daily correlation between WTI oil price changes and USO price change was 0.9, which means that the volatility of the spot prices explained most of the volatility of USO. Nevertheless, USO clearly did not track WTI oil price well in the long run. WTI oil price was up 15.4% and USO was down 42.2%. The largest return difference was in 2009: WTI oil price was up 77.9% and USO was up only 18.7%. In 2009, the oil futures prices were mostly in Contango. Therefore, USO suffered heavy losses on roll returns and significantly underperformed the spot price.

Exhibit 13-3 WTI spot oil prices and USO prices

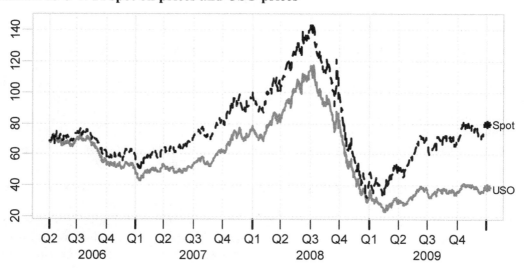

Momentum Strategies

Momentum strategies, backwardation strategies, and hedging pressure strategies are common systematic strategies for futures investments. Since momentum has been shown to be a valuable tool across many financial instruments, investors use absolute momentum strategies and relative momentum strategies for commodity futures as well.

- Absolute momentum: Long the futures with positive returns in the past N (N = 1-12) months and short the futures with negative returns in the past N months.[73]

- Relative momentum: Rank different commodity futures by their past N-month performance. Long the futures with the best performances and short the futures with the worst performances.

Investors have the flexibility to use different lengths of history (seasonality is a concern though). Some strategies test whether futures exhibit short-term mean reversion and remove recent returns from momentum signals if they do. Since futures have huge differences in volatility, some investors use information ratios to rank futures and select the futures with the highest information ratios. To address the volatility difference, futures with lower volatility may be leveraged up to make different positions have similar dollar volatility.

Miffre and Rallis (2007) tested a variety of relative momentum strategies using historical 1, 3, 6, 12-month returns to rank 31 US commodity futures and built a long/short portfolio that longed the futures in the top momentum quintile and shorted the futures in the bottom momentum quintile. Each portfolio was held 1, 3, 6 or 12 months. Among the 16 combinations, only the 12-month momentum signal with 12-month holding period yielded negative returns and 13 of the profitable momentum strategies were statistically significant with 9.38% average return a year between January 1979 and September 2004. The results clearly indicated the value and the robustness of the relative momentum signal.

Backwardation Strategies

Backwardation strategies explore the term structure of the futures prices—the relation between the futures prices and the maturity of the futures contracts. When the current inventory of a commodity is low (high), the futures prices often show backwardation (Contango). Investors use absolute backwardation, time series backwardation, and cross-sectional backwardation to select long/short futures positions.

- Absolute backwardation: Long the futures if the spot price is at least x percent (e.g., 1%) higher than the near month futures price and short the futures if the spot price is at least x percent lower than the near month futures price.

- Time-series backwardation: Long the futures if the ratio of the near month futures price to the next month futures price is above its 52-week average and short the futures if the ratio of the near month futures price to the next month futures price is below its 52-week average.

---

[73] Absolute momentum is also called time series momentum as it uses an asset's own price or return time series. Relative momentum is also called cross-sectional momentum as it measures relative strength of one asset among multiple assets.

- Cross-sectional backwardation: Long the futures with the highest ratios of the near month futures prices to the next month futures prices and short the futures with the lowest ratio of near month futures prices to next month futures prices.

Historical futures returns showed that the average total returns and the average roll returns were positive when the futures were in backwardation and the average returns were negative when the futures were in Contango. The absolute backwardation tries to capture the roll yield. For example, if the spot price is 1% higher than the near month futures price, the difference indicates a potential roll yield of 1% in a month if the spot price stays the same. In the time-series backwardation, the 52-week average of the term spread is used as the threshold. Investors have the flexibility to choose different thresholds. The cross-sectional backwardation takes a cross-sectional approach instead of a time-series one to long the futures with strong backwardation and short the futures with strong Contango.

USCI, an ETF managed by United States Commodity Funds, tracks the total return of the SummerHaven Dynamic Commodity Index (SDCI). The equally-weighted SDCI index relies on both backwardation and momentum to select 14 commodities out of the 27 energy, metal, grain, livestock, and soft (coffee, cocoa, cotton, and sugar) commodities. The index first chooses 7 commodities with the greatest backwardation and then chooses 7 commodities with the greatest 12-month momentum from the remaining 20 commodities. For each of the 14 commodities, SDCI selects the futures contract with the greatest backwardation from a list of futures contracts that expire in the following months.

Hedging Pressure (Normal Backwardation) Strategies

For futures and options with significant market interest, the Commodity and Futures Trading Commission (CFTC) publishes the Commitment of Traders (COT) report every Friday at 15:30 ET with Tuesday's aggregated open interests for commercial traders, non-commercial traders and non-reportable traders.

Non-commercial traders are large speculators who trade futures for profit; commercial traders are hedgers who trade futures as hedges to their cash business; non-reportable traders are small speculators. Exhibit 13-4 shows COT report for light sweet crude oil as of February 19, 2013.

Exhibit 13-4 COT report for crude oil as of February 19, 2013

Trader Type	Long	Short	Spreads
Non-commercial	380,355	122,437	607,471
Commercial	577,086	847,034	
Non-reportable	85,299	73,269	
Total	1,042,740	1,042,740	607,471

The aggregated long positions and short positions of non-commercial traders, commercial traders, and non-reportable traders are reported separately. The total long positions are always equal to the total short positions. For non-commercial traders, the COT report also includes the spreads—the long positions that are offset by short positions. The total open interest can be calculated as either the sum of total long positions and spreads or the sum of total short positions and spreads. For the crude oil futures in the exhibit, the open interest was $1,042,740 + 607,471 = 1,650,211$ contracts (each contract is 1000 barrels).

Using the COT data, we can calculate commercial hedging pressure or speculator hedging pressure:

$$\text{commercial hedging pressure} = \frac{\text{commercial long}}{\text{commercial long} + \text{commercial short}}$$

$$\text{speculator hedging pressure} = \frac{\text{non commercial long}}{\text{non commercial long} + \text{non commercial short}}$$

Low commercial hedging pressure indicates that there are relatively more hedgers (commodity producers) who sell futures than hedgers (commodity consumers) who long futures. When risk-averse hedgers sell futures to hedge their exposures, they are willing to accept prices lower than the expected future prices to reduce their exposures. The hedgers put downward pressure on futures prices and the futures prices tend to show backwardation. In these cases, it pays to long commodity futures. On the other hand, if there are more hedgers who buy the futures than hedgers who sell the futures, the commercial hedging pressure is high and it pays to short the commodity futures. Investors use absolute commercial hedging pressure, absolute non-commercial hedging pressure and relative commercial hedging pressure to select long/short futures positions.

- Absolute commercial hedging pressure: Long when the commercial hedging pressure is below 0.5 (or 52-week average) and short when the commercial hedging pressure is above 0.5 (or 52-week average).

- Absolute non-commercial hedging pressure: Long when the non-commercial hedging pressure is above 0.5 (or 52-week average) and short when the non-commercial hedging pressure is below 0.5 (or 52-week average).

- Relative commercial hedging pressure: Long the futures with the lowest commercial hedging pressures and short the futures with the highest commercial hedging pressures.

- Relative non-commercial hedging pressure: Long the futures with the highest non-commercial hedging pressures and short the futures with the lowest non-commercial hedging pressures.

Many research papers and reports have confirmed the value of hedging pressure in forecasting futures risk premium. For example, Basu and Miffre (2013) tested the relative hedging pressure signals using 27 commodity futures. The hedger-based portfolio longed 15% of the futures with the lowest average commercial hedging pressure over the past 4, 13, 26, or 52 weeks and shorted 15% of the futures with the highest average commercial hedging pressure. The long/short portfolios were held for 4, 13, 16, or 52 weeks. For all 16 combinations of signal formation periods and holding periods, the portfolios yielded positive returns with an average annual excess return of 5.63% and Sharpe ratio of 0.52. The speculator-based portfolio longed 15% of the futures with highest average non-commercial hedging pressure over the past 4, 13, 26, or 52 weeks and shorted the futures with the lowest average non-commercial hedging pressure. All combinations yielded positive returns too with an average annual excess return of 5.78% and Sharpe ratio of 0.53.

Although momentum strategies, backwardation strategies, and hedging pressure strategies use different signals for entry and exit, they have significant positive correlations. Generally momentum strategies buy futures with downward-sloping term structures and sell futures with upward-sloping term structures. Futures with high commercial hedging pressures tend to have upward-sloping term structures and futures with strong non-commercial hedging pressures tend to have downward-sloping term structures. As a result, the roll returns drive the long-term positive risk premiums of all three strategies.

Currency

The foreign exchange market is one of the largest financial markets in the world. It is also one of the most liquid markets with trillions of dollars of average daily trading volume across spot trades, forwards, swaps, and options. The foreign exchange market is less efficient than the stock market as three of the major participants in the foreign exchange market do not trade foreign currencies for profit:

- Central banks trade foreign currencies to stabilize financial imbalances or to push the exchange rates toward a specific direction (often to weaken local currencies).

- Corporations trade foreign currencies to hedge the currency exposures of future revenues or costs.

- Individuals trade foreign currencies to meet their travelling needs.

Although the liquidity and the lack of efficiency attract many active investors, it is difficult to trade foreign currencies. Unlike equities, foreign currencies have no positive risk premium. For a currency pair, the appreciation of one currency means the depreciation of the other currency. Therefore, there is no simple buy-and-hold currency basket with positive expected risk premiums as in the stock market. In order to generate positive returns, currency investors need to forecast the exchange rate changes. The following are some fundamental drivers of exchange rates.

- Economic growth: the currency of a country with strong economic growth tends to appreciate.

- Inflation: the currency of a country with high inflation rates tends to depreciate.

- Interest rate: the currency of a country with high real interest rates (nominal interest rate minus inflation) tends to appreciate as high real interest rates indicate robust economic growth.

- Balance of trade: the currency of a country with trade surplus/deficit tends to appreciate/depreciate.

- Commodity prices: the currency of a commodity exporting country tends to appreciate with increasing commodity prices.

- Government intervention: easy monetary policies, which often involve printing more local currencies, tend to depreciate the local currency.

Fundamental traders carefully analyze the impact of different economic and fundamental drivers to make selected bets based on their analysis. George Soros, the person who helped break the Bank of England, is a high profile currency trader who relied on economic fundamental drivers to make investment decisions and realized more than $1 billion gains in a bet against the British Pound in 1992. In October 1990, Britain had signed up to the European Exchange Rate Mechanism (ERM), following which the British government needed to prevent significant depreciation of the British Pound against the German Mark. The problem was that Britain's inflation rate was three times that of Germany's. Furthermore, Britain ran a large trade deficit with its major trade partner, the United States, as the US Dollar depreciated. As fundamental drivers pushed the Pound down, the Bank of England increased its interest rate and sold billions of Pounds of foreign currency reserves to prevent the Pound from falling below the minimum level required by the ERM. Speculators, including Soros, piled up their short positions to bet that the British government ultimately had to give in to market forces. On September 16, 1992, the British government withdrew from ERM.[74] In the following weeks, the British Pound depreciated 15% against the German Mark and 20% against the US Dollar. Twenty years later, Soros made another $1 billion in a bet against the Japanese Yen. Unlike his bet against Bank of England, he followed the lead of Bank of Japan in 2012. In October to November 2012, it gradually became clear that the new Japanese government would pursue monetary-easing policies in order to lift its economy out of deflation. As the Bank of Japan started aggressively printing money, Soros betted that the Yen would tumble. Indeed, the Japanese Yen fell 15% from November 2012 to January 2013 and Soros again reaped hefty returns on his investment.

Other traders take a more systematic approach to currency trading. The interest rate (similar to dividend yield), momentum, and value strategies also work for currency selection. The carry trade is one of the best-known currency trading strategies. In a carry trade, investors invest in a currency with high interest rate (e.g., Brazilian Real) financed by borrowing a currency with low interest rate (e.g., US Dollar). If the currency with low interest rate does not appreciate more than the interest rate difference, the trade will be profitable. The Brazilian Real and the US Dollar were one of the most successful pairs for carry trade in 2009 and 2010. The short-term interest rate of the Brazilian Real was close to 10% in 2009-2010 and the short-term interest rate of the US Dollar was below 1%. Had the exchange rate stayed the same, a carry trade that longed the Brazilian Real and financed by shorting the US Dollar would have collected the 9% a year interest rate difference. During the same period, the Brazilian Real appreciated from $0.429/Brazilian Real to $0.602/Brazilian Real, adding another 20% a year return to the carry trade. Even without leverage, the trade had 29% annualized returns. The risk of a carry trade is that when the currency with low interest rate appreciates more than the interest rate difference, the trade will result in a loss. Such losses often happen when the country with the higher interest rate cuts its interest rate. As the interest rate falls, many traders choose to unwind the carry trade. The selling pressure from the unwinding often pushes down the currency that the traders long. In 2012, Brazil implemented multiple interest rate cuts to stimulate the economy. The interest rate cut triggered many traders to unwind the Brazilian Real/US Dollar carry trade by selling the Brazilian Real and buying the US Dollar. The

---

[74] ERM was a major step in creating the single currency across multiple European countries. The 1992 crisis was a reason why Britain did not adopt the Euro.

unwinding contributed to the 16% drop of Brazilian Real from March to May and the traders who held the pair suffered losses.

The carry trade captures the phenomenon of forward rate bias. According to interest rate parity, the interest rate differential between two countries is equal to the differential between the forward exchange rate and the spot exchange rate. If the forward exchange rate is an unbiased estimation of the future spot exchange rate, carry trades will have zero expected returns. In reality, the forward exchange rate tends to underestimate the future spot exchange rate of the currency with higher interest rate, which leads to profitable carry trades. Some investors believe that the forward rate bias represents market inefficiency, while others believe it is a risk premium for taking on the currency risk.

Momentum signals work for currencies too. A momentum strategy longs the best performing currencies—the ones that appreciated the most—and shorts the worst performing currencies—the ones that depreciated the most. Menkhoff et al. (2011) studied 1-month to 12-month cross-sectional currency momentum strategies that longed winning currencies and shorted losing currencies. They found that such strategies had an average excess return of up to 10% a year before costs. The momentum signals had little correlation with the carry trades. Similar to stocks, the momentum signals were much stronger in less liquid minor currencies. Furthermore, the returns of the momentum signals were highly time-varying and had larger than 20% drawdowns.

The value signal is based on the purchasing power parity (PPP) argument. According to the PPP, the same basket of goods, commodities, and assets should have the same price when exchange rates are taken into consideration. For instance, if a comparable basket of goods is worth 1.6 million US Dollars and 1 million British Pounds, 1 Pound should be worth $1.6. Theoretically, when the Pound is worth $1.5 (undervalued if PPP holds), an arbitrager can borrow 1 million British Pounds, buy the basket of goods, sell the goods for $1.6 million, and exchange $1.5 million for 1 million British Pounds to repay the lender. After all the transactions, the arbitrager pockets the $0.1 million difference. In reality, PPP does not hold because of the difficulty in defining a comparable basket of goods. People in different countries put different values on the same type of goods (and services) and the quality of the goods may be different in different countries too. Many goods are not transportable between countries. For goods that are transportable, the transportation from one country to another may be expensive. Therefore, theoretical arbitrage may not happen for the PPP to hold. Although PPP did not hold, major floating currencies did converge towards PPP in the long run. MacDonald and Marsh (1999) showed that the currencies that were undervalued based on PPP tended to appreciate in the long run and the currencies that were overvalued tended to depreciate.

Deutsche Bank has currency return indices for carry, momentum and value signals. All indices use 10 liquid currencies (USD, EUR, JPY, GBP, CHF, AUD, NZD, CAD, NOK, and SEK). The carry index allocates 1/3 long position to each of the 3 currencies with the highest 3-month Libor rates and 1/3 short position to each of the 3 currencies with the lowest 3-month Libor rates. The index is rebalanced every three months to capture the changes in interest rates. The momentum index allocates 1/3 long position in each of the 3 currencies with the highest spot exchange rate changes (appreciation) against the US Dollar in the last 12 months and 1/3 short position in each of the 3 currencies with the lowest spot exchange rate changes against the US Dollar. The index is rebalanced every month to capture the momentum changes. The valuation index allocates 1/3 long position in each of the 3 currencies that are most undervalued based on OECD (Organization for Economic Co-operation and Development) PPP and allocates 1/3 short position in each of the 3 currencies that are most overvalued based on OECD PPP. The index is rebalanced every 3 months to capture the change in PPP. Exhibit 13-5 shows the cumulative excess returns (versus T-bill rates) and annualized excess returns of the individual indices and the composite index constructed from these indices in 1994-2013. Although the carry index and the valuation index yielded better average returns than the composite index, they had significantly higher volatility and higher drawdown risk. As a result, the composite index had the highest Sharpe ratio because of the diversification benefit of three different signals. The composite index had 3.25% annual excess return with 5.21% volatility. The Sharpe ratio of 0.65 was 70% higher than the S&P 500 index's Sharpe ratio of 0.37 in the same period. The correlation between the composite currency index excess returns and S&P excess returns was only 0.13. This suggests that the composite currency index provides significant diversification benefit to equities.

Exhibit 13-5 Excess return of Deutsche Bank Currency Indices

Index	Carry	Momentum	Valuation	Composite
Excess Return	4.97%	1.56%	3.94%	3.49%
Annualized StDev	10.09%	10.05%	8.54%	5.35%
Sharpe Ratio	0.49	0.16	0.46	0.65
Worst Drawdown	36.1%	28.7%	16.7%	8.8%

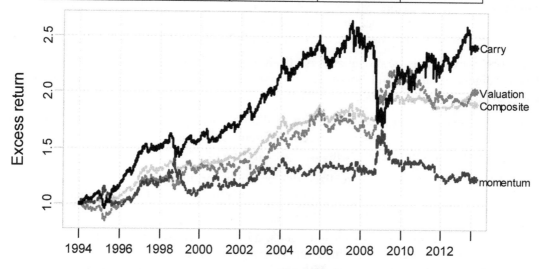

Investors mostly participate in the commodities and currency markets through managed futures accounts. Commodity Trading Advisors (CTAs), advisors registered with Commodity Futures Trading Commission (CFTC), are the managers for managed futures accounts. Although momentum, backwardation, and hedging pressure lay the foundation for systematic commodity futures trading strategies, CTAs apply rigorous statistical tests to filter the raw signals and use stop loss to manage the drawdown risk. Successful CTAs often combine a number of strategies and invest in a large variety of commodities, currencies and equity/bond indices in order to achieve a better information ratio. Individual futures strategies on a single asset tend to have low information ratios (0.2-0.5)

and a large drawdown risk. For instance, the Deutsche Bank carry index had 35% drawdown in 2008. The composite index, on the other hand, had only 8.7% drawdown. The diversification across assets and across strategies allows CTAs to make a large number of independent bets. The increase in breadth boosts the top-tier CTAs to have an information ratio greater than one.

Asset Allocation

Investors generally believe that long term strategic asset allocation is the single most important factor determining 70-90% of the variability in portfolio performance. The objective of asset allocation is to find the right asset mix that provides the appropriate combination of expected return and risk that will allow investors to achieve their financial goals. Traditional strategic asset allocation recommends predefined weights for different asset classes. For allocation between stocks and bonds, conventional asset allocation models often recommend a 60/40 allocation (60% of the capital invested in stocks and 40% in bonds). When the weights differ from the predefined allocation, the portfolio is rebalanced to get the asset classes back to the target weights. The optimal allocation may vary depending on an investor's age and risk tolerance. Life-cycle investing recommends allocating higher percentage of capital in stocks when investors are young. Since young investors are decades away from retirement, they are better at managing potential stock losses and have more time to wait for the stock market to recover. Investors who are financially secure and are more risk tolerant should also allocate a higher percentage of capital to stocks. Investors who are close to retirement, on the other hand, should shift more money to bonds. Since bonds on average have lower risk, investors face less drawdown risk when they need the cash from the investments after they retire.

Investors' views on asset allocation have been evolving over the years. Instead of having fixed weights in stocks and bonds, many investors tackle the asset allocation question using the following approaches:

- Risk versus return: Investors estimate the risk premium of different asset classes, risks, and the correlation between different asset classes to better allocate asset weights in order to achieve higher risk-adjusted returns.

- Market timing: Since the realized risk premium for different asset classes vary over time, investors with skills to forecast asset returns or risks apply their skills to dynamically allocate asset weights.

- Risk factors: Besides stocks and bonds, other asset classes or risk factors may also provide risk premiums. Since the risk premiums of these asset classes or risk factors have low correlation with stocks and bonds, investors incorporate them in the asset allocation to increase portfolio diversification and achieve a higher information ratio.

Risk Parity Strategies

Risk parity is an asset allocation approach that focuses on allocation of risk instead of allocation of capital. It is the principle driving the All Weather Portfolio, the flagship portfolio of Bridgewater Associates (one of the largest hedge funds with more than $100 billion under management in 2013). Compared with conventional asset allocation models, risk parity tries to increase the risk diversification and improve risk-adjusted returns. Despite the popularity of 60/40 stock/bond allocation, such a portfolio has high correlation with the stock market and has significant volatility. The reason is that the stock returns have had much higher volatility than bond returns. Let us use the S&P 500 index returns as stock returns and Bloomberg US 7-10 year government bond index returns as bond returns to explain the risk/return profile of the portfolios. The following are the average annual excess returns (versus T-Bills) and the covariance matrix of the S&P 500 index (s) and the bond index (b) in 1992-2012:

$$\begin{bmatrix} \mu_s \\ \mu_b \end{bmatrix} = \begin{bmatrix} 6.62\% \\ 4.11\% \end{bmatrix}, \begin{bmatrix} \sigma_s^2 & \rho\sigma_s\sigma_b \\ \rho\sigma_s\sigma_b & \sigma_b^2 \end{bmatrix} = \begin{bmatrix} 0.184^2 & -0.29 \times 0.184 \times 0.078 \\ -0.29 \times 0.184 \times 0.078 & 0.078^2 \end{bmatrix}$$

where μ_s and μ_b are the expected returns of the S&P index and the bond index;

σ_s and σ_b are the volatility of the S&P index and the bond index;

ρ is the correlation between the S&P index returns and the bond index returns.

Historically, the excess return of the S&P index, 6.62%, was 1.6 times the excess return of the bond index, 4.11%. The average T-bill return was 3.3%. The volatility of the S&P index, 18.4%, was 2.4 times the volatility of the bond index, 7.8%. The correlation between bond returns and stocks returns was negative. The excess return of the 60/40 portfolio was 5.61% and the volatility was 10.6%. The Sharpe ratio was 0.53. The correlation between the 60/40 portfolio returns and the S&P 500 index returns was 0.96. In other words, the 60/40 portfolio was highly correlated with the stock market and the bond component provided little diversification benefit. The risk-parity portfolio tries to maximize the Sharpe ratio. For mean-variance portfolio optimization with a risk-free asset, the tangent portfolio has the highest Sharpe ratio. As shown in Exhibit 13-6, the estimated stock/bond allocation of the risk-parity portfolio was 25.5/74.5. The portfolio put three quarters of the weight in bonds. The excess return for the risk parity portfolio was 4.75% and the volatility was 6.33%. The Sharpe ratio was 0.75, which was 40% higher than the Sharpe ratio of the 60/40 portfolio. Furthermore, the correlation with S&P 500 was only 0.48. Clearly, the risk-parity portfolio was more diversified and had higher risk-adjusted returns.

What if an investor prefers higher expected returns than the expected return of the risk-parity portfolio? If we choose to assign higher weights to stocks to boost returns, the Sharpe ratio is lower than the risk-parity portfolio. Instead, supporters of the risk-parity portfolio argue that investors should leverage the risk-parity portfolio to achieve the same expected return with lower risk or to achieve higher expected return with the same risk. Instead of investing in a 60/40 portfolio, if an investor leveraged the risk-parity portfolio so that the portfolio has the same volatility as a 60/40 portfolio, the leveraged portfolio had 7.9% excess return. The risk-parity framework can be easily expanded to asset allocation with more than two asset classes. For example, AQR's risk parity fund includes investments in equities, government bonds, corporate bonds, commodities, and currencies. The use of leverage and the inclusion of multiple asset classes make risk party a versatile tool to achieve better risk-adjusted returns through diversification across multiple asset classes.

Exhibit 13-6 Mean-variance efficient frontier of stock/bond allocation

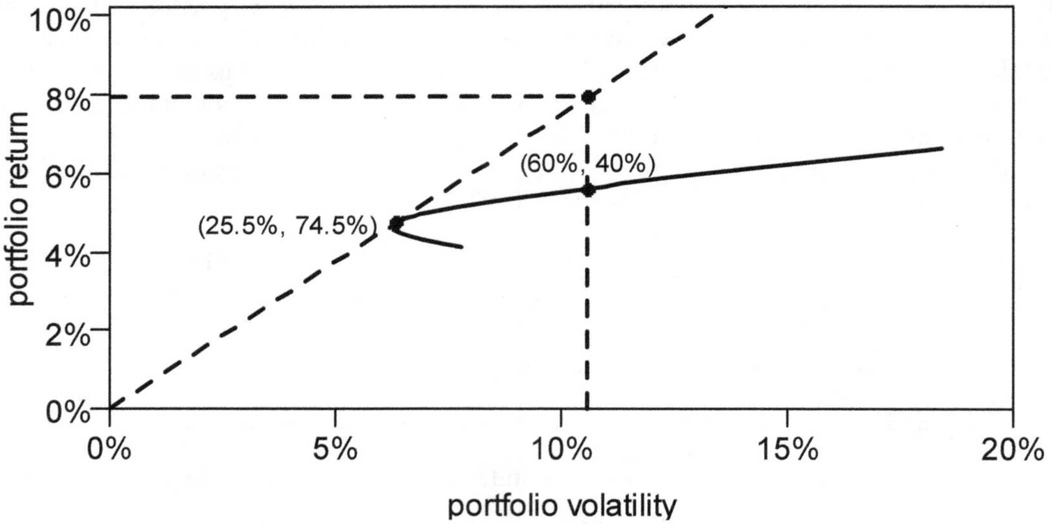

Given historical success, there has been a surge in the popularity of risk parity products in recent years. The success of risk-parity strategies can be largely explained by the strong risk-adjusted returns of bonds since the 1980s and the negative correlation between bond returns and stock returns. The risk parity portfolio construction depends on the forecasted expected returns of different asset classes and their covariance matrix. We need to be cautious as historical success does not guarantee its future success.

It is improper to extrapolate past returns and volatility to the future. Can we expect the next decade to produce similar returns and volatility for bonds as was in the past two decades? From 1983 to 2012, the 10-year Treasury yield dropped from 10.5% to 2%, which drove bond's high risk-adjusted returns. With the 10-year Treasury bond yield at ~2.5% in the summer of 2014, rational investors would not expect 4.11% risk premium (versus T-bills) for long-maturity Treasury bonds in the future. At the beginning of the 1940s, the 10-year Treasury yield was also close to 2%. In the following 40 years (1941-1980), the 10-year Treasury bond had a meager return of 2.65%, 79 bps below the T-bill return of 3.44%. During the same period, the stock market returned 12.73%.[75] Therefore, risk parity portfolio managers ought not to simply take average historical returns, volatility, and correlation as inputs for asset allocation. Instead, portfolio managers need to make their own forecasts of future risk premiums of different asset classes.

For some asset classes, volatility does not give a full picture of the risk. For strategies that invest in less liquid assets (e.g., convertible arbitrage, distressed securities, fixed income relative value), monthly returns show strong positive autocorrelation. In other words, monthly losses tend to be followed by more monthly losses. Positive autocorrelation of returns leads to significant tail risk where volatility only represents one aspect of risk. Rare tail events such as the losses in convertible bonds in 2008 may not happen for years or even decades. In retrospect, the risk estimation for convertible bonds at the beginning of 2008 was clearly an underestimation. Therefore, investors might benefit from

---

[75] Historical return data for stocks, Treasury bills, and Treasury bonds are from professor Aswath Damodaran's data collection: http://people.stern.nyu.edu/adamodar/

considering the use of stress tests to evaluate the performance of different asset classes under extreme market scenarios in order to estimate the combined portfolio's risk. The following are some historical periods commonly used in stress tests:

- 2011 summer: The market (S&P) lost 19% from late July to early October and the US debt was downgraded from AAA to AA+ by S&P on August 5th.

- 2008-2009 financial crisis: The market lost more than 55% from its peak on October 9, 2007 to its bottom on March 9, 2009 before recovering more than 50% from the bottom in 2009.

- 2007 quant meltdown: Many hedge funds and quantitative strategies suffered unprecedented losses between August 6, 2007 and August 9, 2007 even though the market itself was stable.

- 2000-2002 internet bubble burst and recession: The S&P lost more than 40% during the recession and the NASDAQ composite index lost more than 70%.

- 1998 Russian default: The Russian government devalued the Ruble and defaulted on its debt on August 17, 1998. The default triggered a flight-to-quality and led to the demise of hedge fund Long Term Capital Management (LTCM) in September.

- 1997 Asian financial crisis: Thailand abandoned the pegging to US Dollar after currency traders' speculative attacks and let its currency depreciate. The crisis spread to other Asian countries including South Korea and Indonesia escalating currency depreciation and economic recession in multiple countries.

- 1994 US bond crash: From February to early May, the yield of the US 10-year Treasury bond increased by 1.5%, which led to the bond market crash.

- 1990 Gulf War: Iraq's invasion of Kuwait on August 2, 1990 triggered the First Gulf War. Oil price spiked from $17 a barrel in July to $36 a barrel in October, which triggered a stock market drop of 19%.

- 1987 Black Monday: On October 19, 1987, the stock markets crashed and the S&P 500 lost 20.5% in a single day.

Tactical Asset Allocation

With the exception of Treasuries, most asset classes (e.g., stocks, REITs, corporate bonds, and commodities) suffered heavy losses during the 2008-2009 crisis. As all markets got hammered and assets moved in tandem, traditional diversification benefits from investing in different asset classes, different countries and different industries disappeared. Investors who followed the 60/40 rule or other fixed asset allocation strategies lost substantial amounts of their wealth during the crisis. In response, some investors shifted their focus to tactical asset allocation (TAA). Unlike static asset allocation strategies that allocate fixed weights to different asset classes, TAA dynamically adjusts the weights of different asset classes to improve risk-adjusted returns. Instead of using long-term (often decades of) history to estimate the expected risk premium, volatility and correlation of different asset classes, TAA make short-term forecasts using the current economic conditions or market information. The objective of TAA is to create more accurate short-term forecasts on returns and risks so that the investors can build more efficient portfolios.

Typical TAA strategies use a variety of seasonal effects, economic indicators, market indicators, technical indicators, and fundamental signals to make timing and industry (country, commodity, or currency) rotation strategies. Because of the simplicity of the momentum signals, they are popular choices for timing and rotation strategies. In Chapter 5 we demonstrated the value of simple trend following signals such as 10-month moving average crossover or 12-month momentum in timing the US Equity market. Doeswijk and Vliet (2011) showed that 1-month momentum, 12-month momentum, and Sell-in-May signal were all valuable inputs for industry selection. Investors found that trend following strategies worked for most of the risky asset classes. Faber (2007, 2013) tested the 10-month moving average crossover on five asset classes (S&P 500 index for US stocks, MSCI EAFE index for foreign stocks, US 10-Year Government Bond index, National Association of Real Estate Trusts for real estate, and Goldman Sachs Commodity Index for commodities) and compared the following two allocation strategies:

- Static asset allocation: each asset class is assigned 20% of the portfolio weight at the monthly rebalancing.

- Dynamic asset allocation: each asset class is assigned 20% of the portfolio weight if the month-end price is above its 10-month moving average; otherwise that 20% of portfolio weight is invested in 90-day Treasury Bills.

In 1973-2012, the dynamic asset allocation strategy returned 10.48% a year with 6.99% volatility while the static asset allocation strategy returned 9.92% a year with 10.28% volatility. Furthermore, the dynamic strategy reduced the maximum drawdown from 46% to 9.54%. To avoid overfitting the data, Faber did not try to use moving averages of different lengths for different asset classes (e.g., 12-month moving average works better for S&P index) and did not screen whether the timing strategy adds value for individual asset classes. Since different asset classes had different expected returns and risk characteristics, other investors investigated the value of market timing for different asset classes and chose different parameters for different assets. Overall, momentum signals were robust to parameter selection. Moskowitz et al. (2011) systematically studied the one to twelve month momentum signals on 58 liquid instruments across equity, bond, commodity, and currency futures and found that the momentum signals worked for most assets. They also found that a diversified portfolio using 12-month momentum signals across all asset classes yielded substantially better risk-adjusted returns than a passive portfolio that invested in all asset classes.

The momentum signal Faber explored is an absolute momentum signal that relies on an asset's own historical returns. We have discussed relative momentum strategies that long recent winners (and short recent losers) as useful signals to trade commodities and currencies. If we split equities by countries or by industries and split bonds by countries or by credit risks (e.g., Treasuries, investment-grade, and high yield), we can apply the relative momentum strategies to equities and bonds. For long-only strategies, we can also combine relative momentum with absolute momentum. Within a broad asset class, we first apply the relative momentum strategy to select the sub-classes that are the best performers. Then we apply the absolute momentum strategy to invest in a selected sub-class if its return is above Treasury bill return and invest in Treasury bills otherwise.

Furthermore, we can combine momentum strategies with risk parity. Using sub-classes[76] in equities, bonds, commodities, and real estates, Clare et al. (2012) built a relative momentum strategy with absolute momentum as the filter and volatility-adjusted weights. The dynamic portfolio yielded 15.65% a year in 1994-2011 with 12.44% volatility. The minimum rolling three-year return was always higher than 4.5%.

Instead of building market timing strategies to forecast the risk premium of different asset classes, which is inherently difficult, some investors set a relatively modest goal to forecast volatility. Whilst the volatility of asset returns may change substantially over a long period of time, it is more consistent in the short term (volatility clustering). For instance, the volatility of S&P 500 was 41% in 2008 and 13% in 2012. However, the correlation between volatility in one quarter and in the next was more than 60%. Therefore, investors were much better at forecasting volatility as recent realized volatility itself was a good estimator of the near-term volatility. Market history also showed that investors were not compensated with higher market returns when the market volatility was high. The contemporary correlation between quarterly volatility and quarterly returns were negative while the quarterly volatility had close to zero correlation with next quarter's returns. As a result, the risk premium per unit of risk was significantly lower when the market volatility was higher.

Volatility-based asset allocation reduces exposure to a risky asset class when its volatility is high and increases the exposure when its volatility is low. Instead of a fixed 60/40 allocation between stocks and bonds, an investor allocates more than 60% capital to stocks when the stock market volatility is low and allocates less than 60% to stocks when the volatility is high. When the investor maintains a long-term average allocation of 60/40, volatility-based asset allocation achieves better time diversification of risk. The time diversification distributes risk evenly over a long time horizon. It significantly reduces the risk, especially drawdown risk, during market crashes. Consequently, the dynamic asset allocation yields better risk-adjusted returns than fixed allocation.

Alternative Beta Strategies

In this chapter, we have discussed the basic building blocks (e.g., momentum strategies, carry trades, and low risk strategies) investors use in their investment processes. These factors have contributed to a large percentage of historical performance of hedge funds. In fact, the majority of hedge fund returns can be explained by systematic exposures to factors. Since institutional funds can implement these strategies with low costs, investors may argue that the returns from exposures to systematic factors are simply risk premium for factor exposures. In other words, a hedge fund's return is a combination of the manager's alpha, alternative beta return, and random noise.

$$r_t = \alpha_t + \beta_1 f_1 + \cdots + \beta_k f_k + \cdots + \beta_K f_K + \varepsilon_t = \alpha_t + \sum_{k=1}^{K} \beta_k f_k + \varepsilon_t$$

$$= \text{manager's alpha} + \text{alternative beta return} + \text{random noise}$$

where r_t is the return of a hedge fund for period t;

---

[76] The study included equity indices of 24 developed markets and 16 emerging markets, 19 government bond markets, 23 commodities markets and 13 country level real estate markets.

α_t is the alpha attributed to the manager's skill;

β_k is the manager's selected beta exposure to the k-th factor, $k = 1, 2, ..., K$;

f_k is the return of the k-th factor;

ε_t is the random noise, $E[\varepsilon_t] = 0$;

$\sum_{k=1}^{K} \beta_k f_k$ is the total return from alternative beta exposures.

Although they are called alternative betas, they can be exposures to any risk factor that generates positive risk premium, including the US stock market. Some studies have shown that the majority of the hedge fund returns are from alternative beta exposures instead of "pure" alpha. For instance, Pojarliev and Levich (2008) investigated the returns of Barclay Currency Traders Index (BCTI), an equally weighted composite of professionally managed currency funds, over the 1990-2006 period. They found that the average annual return was in double digits until mid-1990s and gradually diminished over time. The average monthly return over the whole period was 62 bps and the excess return versus the one-month USD LIBID (London Interbank Bid Rate) was 25 bps. 34 bps of excess returns can be explained by exposures to four systematic factors—carry, momentum, value, and volatility. Once the beta exposures to these factors were included, the residual alpha became -9 bps per month. The mediocre average alpha after removing returns from beta exposures to alternative risk factors is not surprising. Similar to the stock market, the bond, commodity, and currency markets have become increasingly dominated by professional investors. Therefore, it is difficult for an average active investor to generate alpha. That said, alternative beta strategies do not replace skilled managers. In every asset class, there are skilled managers who generate significant positive alpha in the long run. Although Pojarliev and Levich (2008) showed that an average professionally managed currency fund had no alpha, they also found that 24 percent of the best performing managers generated an average alpha of 104 bps per month.

For most investors, it is a challenging task to invest with skilled managers. First, the investors need to have skills themselves (or pay extra fees to consultants or a fund of funds) to identify skilled managers. Since luck plays an important role in managers' performance, evaluating historical returns and risks alone may not be sufficient to separate the skilled managers from the lucky ones. Because of capacity constraints, some successful managers with long track records close their funds to new investors or charge high fees that investors are not willing to accept. Furthermore, even a long successful track record does not guarantee future returns. As the market adapts, the existing strategies of successful managers may no longer work in the future. The successful track record may not fully capture the potential risk of a fund. Both Long-Term Capital Management and Amaranth Advisors had excellent track records before their quick demise. The fee structure[77] also pushes some hedge funds to pursue highly-leveraged risky bets or strategies with significant tail risk.

---

[77] Hedge funds often do not have clawback provisions. If a hedge fund returns 15% in a year, the manager gets paid incentive fee on the 15%; when the fund loses 30% in the second year, the

For investors who have no skills in analyzing hedge fund managers or have no access to top-notch managers at reasonable costs, alternative beta strategies become an attractive choice. Alternative beta strategies identify a variety of risk factors across different asset classes and build a diversified portfolio to capture the risk premium of these factors. An investment in an alternative beta has significant return volatility and often has substantial drawdown. Most of the factors yield low standalone information ratios and different factors tend to outperform (underperform) in different economic environments or market conditions. Therefore, alternative beta strategies explore the diversification benefit of different factors to improve risk-adjusted returns. Compared with investing in hedge funds, investing in alternative beta strategies has the following advantages:

- Lower fees: Alternative beta funds often charge a fixed management fee of ~1% of assets under management (AUM) a year with no incentive fees. These fees of course often depend on product complexity. Managers who research and maintain sophisticated models to explore more risk factors across multiple asset classes and actively manage the downside risk are compensated by higher management fees. Hedge funds often charge 2% management fee on the AUM and 20% incentive fees on any positive after-management-fee returns.

- Lower netting risk: Alterative beta strategies provide diversification across different asset classes and different strategies. Most hedge funds, however, focus on a single asset class or a single type of strategy. Therefore, investors need multiple hedge funds to achieve diversification. When investors invest in a hedge fund, the 20% incentive fees means that investors collect 80% of the after-management-fee gains while facing 100% of the after-management-fee losses. If two thirds of the hedge funds are positive with average before-management-fee return of 10% and one third of the funds are negative with average before-management-fee return of -8%, the average return before incentive fees across all funds is 4%. If incentive fee is applied after netting across the hedge funds, the return to the investor is 3.2%. In practice, investors receive 8% return from the positive funds and -8% from the negative funds and the final return was 2.67%. Because the factors driving the different hedge fund strategies are different, it is common that some strategies have positive returns while others have negative returns. As a result, investors face netting risk when they invest in multiple strategies.

- Lower trading and financing costs: Each hedge fund builds portfolios optimized for its own strategy. This means that one fund's long positions may be another fund's short positions. For instance, a momentum fund that focuses on cross-sectional momentum signals tends to long high-flying growth stocks. A value fund that focuses on relative value signals tends to short high-flying growth stocks because they have high P/E ratios. Since the positions are held in two different funds, the value fund needs to pay securities lending fees on the short positions and marginal costs if it uses leverage even though the momentum fund longs the same positions. If the momentum fund and the value fund were combined, the consolidated fund would have lower securities lending costs and lower financing costs (because of

---

manager gets no incentive. He does not need to pay back part of the previous year's incentive fee. They do have high watermark provisions though.

lower gross market value) than the sum of two individual funds. Similarly, many of the trades in the two funds may be of opposite direction and a consolidated fund would have smaller trading costs. Alternative beta strategies systematically combine a variety of factors. The consolidation step leads to lower gross market value and lower trading, which in turn lead to lower costs.

Conclusion

In this chapter, we extended some common signals used by active equity funds to other investment strategies. Value, momentum and low volatility are three common themes that provide better risk-adjusted return across a variety of asset classes.

- Value: An asset class with high yield tends to have positive future returns. Within an asset class, assets with high yields perform better than assets with low yields. Stocks with higher earnings yields and cash flow yields tend to have better returns. Currencies with higher interest rates tend to have better returns. Commodities with high convenience yields (backwardation) tend to have better returns.

- Momentum: An asset class that has positive 3-month to 12-month historical returns tends to have positive future returns. Within an asset class, assets with high 3-month to 12-month historical returns tend to perform better than assets with low historical returns.

- Volatility: In periods when an asset class has lower volatility than its historical average volatility, it tends to have better risk-adjusted returns. Within asset classes, low-volatility assets tend to have better risk-adjusted returns than high-volatility assets.

Chapter 14

Implementation

Perold (1988) introduced a concept called the implementation shortfall, which measures the difference between the returns of a paper portfolio where all trades are executed at prices at the time of the investment decision and the actual returns of the real portfolio. Implementation shortfall reflects a variety of costs and financial market frictions associated with managing a real portfolio. Trading costs are often the largest component of the implementation shortfall. For long/short portfolios, securities lending costs and margin costs contribute to the implementation shortfall as well.

Trading Costs and Trading Risk

Since trading costs substantially reduce or even eliminate theoretical paper returns, investors spend significant effort on estimating, monitoring, and controlling trading costs. Although reducing trading costs is not a topic as fascinating as generating alpha is, it is nevertheless a rewarding process. After all, returns and alphas are uncertain, whereas costs are relatively predictable and certain. Trading cost management tends to have a large information ratio since it increases net returns with little or no extra risk.

Trading Cost Components

In order to monitor and control trading costs, we first need to understand the constituents of trading costs. Trading costs[78] are categorized as either explicit costs or implicit costs. Explicit costs are the costs that are easily observable and can be estimated accurately. Implicit costs are the ones that are not directly observable and have to be estimated with less accuracy. Exhibit 14-1 lists typical explicit trading costs and implicit trading costs. Explicit costs—as a percentage of a fund's balance—tend not to increase with a fund's trading volume; in fact, large funds often receive commission reductions from brokers. Implicit costs, on the other hand, are sensitive to the trade size and usually increase as the trade size increases.

Exhibit 14-1 Trading cost components

Explicit costs	Implicit costs
Commissions	Delay cost
Fees	Alpha decay
Bid-ask spread	Market impact
	Opportunity cost

---

[78] Taxes on capital gains and dividends may be part of the costs as well. Mutual funds and hedge fund managers often do not directly take tax costs into consideration though since they pass through income and associated taxes to beneficial owners.

Commissions and Fees

Commissions are payments to brokers for their service in facilitating trades. There are significant differences in commission rates. While some trading desks in large banks do not pay commissions for their trades, retail investors may pay $10.99 to trade a couple of hundred of shares through a full-service broker. Large funds tend to use multiple brokers instead of the one with the lowest commissions since brokers that charge higher commissions often provide research and investment advisory services. Some funds also have soft dollar arrangements with brokers that allow fund managers to direct part of the commissions to pay for research, trade ideas and services by the brokers or other research providers. Besides, some brokers are better at executing difficult trades—trades in low liquidity stocks or large trades relative to market volume—and have better execution quality—at more favorable execution price.

Fees include exchange fees, clearing and settlement costs, and SEC fees (sellers pay the SEC fees). Although these fees change over time as the exchanges and SEC adjusts rates, they are fixed at any given time and are treated as explicit trading costs - fees are usually a small fraction of trading costs. In August 2014, the rate of SEC fee was $22.1 per million dollars of sales proceeds.

Bid-Ask Spread

Bid-ask spread is the difference between the lowest ask price and the highest bid price. To execute an order immediately, investors demand liquidity. So they pay the ask price to liquidity providers (e.g., market makers) to purchase a stock and receive the bid price from liquidity providers to sell a stock. Mid-price, the average of the bid price and the ask price, is often considered to be the prevailing market price at the time of the trade. In practice, small orders often pay a spread less than half of the bid-ask spread since trades sometimes happen within the quotes if orders get price improvement from liquidity providers. A liquidity provider may provide prices within the quotes to capture the order flow. Effective spread is twice the distance between the transaction price and the mid-price:

Effective spread $= 2 \times I \times$ [transaction price − mid-price]

where I is an indicator variable that equals 1 for buy trades and -1 for sell trades.

Bid-ask spread is explicit as the bid/ask prices and the derived mid-price at the time of the trades are observable. Bid-ask spreads vary across assets and across time. SPY, arguably the most liquid name, often has a bid-ask spread of 1 cent, which is less than 1 bp as its price hovers above $170 in 2014. Many microcap stocks, on the other hands, often have bid-ask spreads of more than 20 bps. The main factors that impact the bid-ask spread are order processing costs, inventory risk, option effect, and adverse selection.

Order processing costs: Liquidity providers need to build and maintain infrastructure that collects and distributes quote information, routes and executes orders, and finally clears and settles orders. With the development of automated technology, order processing costs have become a small component in bid-ask spreads.

Inventory risk: Liquidity providers need to hold inventory since buyers and sellers of an asset seldom execute opposite trades of the same size at the same time. If adverse public information surfaces after the trade, the liquidity provider will suffer a loss. The expected value of holding inventory is zero as new information can be either positive or negative. Being risk-averse, market makers need to be compensated for bearing the inventory risk. Since the inventory risk directly correlates with price volatility, stocks with higher volatility have higher bid-ask spreads.

Option effect: Bid prices and ask prices are essentially limit prices posted by liquidity providers. If new public market information or stock-specific information arrives and the liquidity provider cannot adjust the quotes before trades get executed at the bid/ask prices, liquidity providers essentially provide options to traders at no costs: A bid gives the seller a put option to sell a stock at the bid price; an offer gives the buyer a call option to buy a stock at the ask price. So, liquidity providers need to be compensated for giving out the options. Option effect is also a small component in bid-ask spreads. With the development of automatic market making, the numbers of shares at best bid/ask prices are small and the market makers can adjust quotes almost instantaneously. When there is market or stock-specific news pending, market makers also increase the bid-ask spreads and lower the quote sizes to reduce the option effect.

Adverse selection: Studies suggest that liquidity providers as a group do not possess information superior to average traders. When informed traders who possess private information trade with liquidity providers before the information becomes public, liquidity providers usually lose in those trades. Uninformed traders possess no private information. Their trades introduce noise to stock prices, but liquidity providers do not lose on average when they trade with uninformed traders. Bid-ask spreads compensate the liquidity providers for their losses to traders with private information. When the percentage of informed traders is higher, the bid-ask spread is higher.

There is fundamental difference between inventory risk and adverse selection. The inventory risk is caused by possible adverse public information after the trade or random price movements; public information after trades can be either positive or negative, so the expected value of the inventory risk is zero. The adverse selection is caused by the existence of private information before the trade that is revealed after the trade is done. Traders with private information only trade in the direction that is in their favor, so the expected value of the adverse selection for market markers is negative.

Delay Cost

Delay cost is the loss caused by the price move between the time an investment decision is made and the time the order is released to the market. Different funds and strategies have various delay costs. Quantitative funds that take a snapshot of the market information to make investment decisions and then submit the trade basket electronically have little delay cost. If a fund relies on close price to make a decision and then trades on the morning of the next day, the stock price move from close to next open is the delay cost. Many funds have designated traders to handle trades submitted by portfolio managers. In this case the communication between portfolio managers and traders and the traders' decision on when to start working on the trades may cause delays. In these cases, it is difficult to determine the exact release time of the trades. Investors often use the difference between decision-time price and the mid-price just before the first trade is filled to calculate delay cost.

Alpha Decay

Since investors buy stocks with positive expected alphas and sell/short stocks with negative expected alphas, the stocks that investors buy are likely to trend up (relative to the benchmark) during the trading period and the stocks that investors sell are likely to trend down during the trading period. Therefore, the alpha decay—the disappearance of alpha as time goes by—is an implicit cost that active investors need to take into consideration. Fundamental portfolio managers make subjective estimates of the expected short-term alpha before they place trades and adjust the trade speed accordingly. Quantitative portfolio managers rely more on the analysis of historical data to determine the expected short-term alpha and incorporate the expected alpha into trading algorithms.

Market Impact

Market impact is the price move caused by the trade. Market impact includes two components: (i) temporary impact and (ii) permanent impact. The temporary impact is an inventory effect caused by the temporary market imbalance between supply and demand. When we trade, we demand liquidity and have to provide price incentives to motivate a counterparty to supply the liquidity. In other words, when we buy shares, we pay a higher price to motivate the liquidity providers to sell; when we sell shares, we accept a lower price to motivate the liquidity providers to buy. To reduce inventory risk and adverse selection, liquidity providers adjust the bid/ask prices in response to order flow: they increase both the bid price and the ask price as buy orders accumulate and decrease both the bid price and the ask price as sell orders accumulate. Since a trade only causes a temporary imbalance between supply and demand, its effect is temporary and disappears over time after the trade finishes. Other investors' actions also reduce the imbalance over time. If buy orders temporarily drive up the price, the higher price makes the stock less attractive to other investors, which leads to decreased demand from other investors.

Besides triggering temporary market imbalance, trades often convey information to the market as they express investors' views and some trades may reflect private information. Since trades may carry information about the value of the underlying stocks, they cause revisions to consensus price of the stocks. Therefore, the market adjusts the stock price by incorporating the new information. In contrast to temporary impact, the permanent impact does not disappear after the trade finishes.

The market impact of a trade is not directly measurable as it is the difference of price move with or without the trade. If the trade is not executed, one will not observe the price path with the trade; if the trade is executed, one will not observe the price path without the trade. To estimate the market impact, the price difference between the trade's average execution price and the market price of the stock at the start of the trade is often used as a proxy for market impact:

$$\text{market impact} = \frac{\overline{P} - P_0}{P_0}$$

where P_0 is the market price (mid-price of bid and ask) just before the start of the trade;

$\overline{P}$ is the average trading price of the trade.

Such a measure is different from the true market impact measure in four aspects:

1. Observed price difference, $\overline{P} - P_0$, reflects half of the effective bid-ask spread.

2. Observed price difference reflects market volatility and stock price volatility.

3. Observed price difference reflects the impact of other investors' trades.

4. Observed price difference reflects the time decay of alpha.

Despite its limitations, the proxy is widely used. If we want to separate the bid-ask spread component from the rest of components in the estimated market impact, we can compare the trade prices with the quote prices at the time of the trades to recover the effective bid-ask spreads and aggregate the results to yield the bid-ask spread cost. Market volatility and stock price volatility introduce uncertainty to the execution price, but the expected value is zero. If an investor's trades have little correlation with other investors' trades, the expected impact of other investors' trades is close to zero as well. If an investor's trades tend to have positive correlation (herding) or negative correlation (contrarian) with other investors' trades, the cumulative market impact of all investors is what the investor faces constantly and is part of the implicit costs. Similarly, if an investor's trades have little alpha, the expected impact of alpha decay is close to zero. If an investor's trades have positive expected alpha, the investor usually actively manages the trading span to strike the right balance between the market impact and the alpha decay. In that case, the alpha decay during the trading span becomes part of the implicit costs as well.

The theory that market impact includes both temporary impact and permanent impact is consistent with empirical observations. When large trades are being executed, stock prices tend to move in the direction of the trades—buy trades push the prices up and sell trades push the price down. After the completion of these trades, the post-trade prices do on average revert in the opposite direction of the trades. During the execution period of a large trade, as market makers and high-frequency traders observe continuous order flow and trade imbalance in the direction of the trade, they often expect the order flow to continue. In response, they actively adjust the bid/ask price in the direction of the order flow in anticipation of future flows in the same direction. Some traders may accumulate shares themselves in hopes of reversing the position at more favorable price later. When a large trade gets done, the expected future order flow no longer materializes and the price tends to revert. Nevertheless, the reversion is on average smaller than the total market impact, which suggests that trades have permanent impact on the equilibrium prices.

Since the temporary impact dissipates after execution, the difference between the post-trade price and the market price at the start of the trade is an estimation of the permanent impact:

$$\text{Permanent impact} = \frac{P_{post} - P_0}{P_0}$$

where P_{post} is the market price m minutes (m is sufficient large for temporary impact to disappear) after the trade ends. The market mid-price 30 minutes to one hour after the trade ends is often used as the post-trade price.

The permanent impact is the cumulative effect of the information carried in the trades and is usually modeled as a linear function of the total trade size. The first share is traded when the permanent impact is 0. As more shares are traded, the prices of the shares executed later reflect the impact of the shares traded earlier and the last share is traded at the full permanent impact of the total trade size. Therefore, the cost to the traded basket is half of the permanent impact and the temporary impact component is estimated using the following equation:

$$\text{temporary impact} = \text{market impact} - 1/2 \times \text{permanent impact}$$

$$= \frac{\overline{P} - P_0}{P_0} - \frac{1}{2} \times \frac{P_{post} - P_0}{P_0} = \frac{\overline{P} - 1/2 \times (P_{post} + P_0)}{P_0}$$

Opportunity Cost

Opportunity cost is the cost associated with failing to execute planned trades. For those investors who trade liquid US stocks and do not rely heavily on limit orders, opportunity cost is a small component of the total trading cost since trade completion is close to 100%. For investors who short stocks in markets with uptick rules such as in Hong Kong, uptick rules may result in unfinished trades if the stock has no uptick at the end of the trading period. Occasionally the opportunity cost is significant. If market liquidity is insufficient for a planned trade, a trader may not find enough shares to complete the trade. Such a scenario happens if the desired order size is large relative to the total trading volume during the trading period. For example, it is extremely difficult to trade 20% of the daily volume unless the trader is willing to pay a hefty market impact cost.

Now let us put all the trading cost components together by considering a trade executed between time 0 and T. The total trading cost is the sum of commissions and fees, delay cost, market impact[79], and opportunity cost:

Total cost = commissions and fees + delay cost + market impact + opportunity cost

where commissions and fees are explicit costs charged by brokers, exchanges, and the SEC;

delay cost is calculated as $(P_0 - P_d) \times N$;

market impact is calculated as $(\overline{P} - P_0) \times N_X$;

opportunity cost is calculated as $(P_{post} - P_0) \times N_L$;

N is the number of shares to trade;

N_X is the number of shares executed between 0 and T;

N_L is the number of shares not executed, $N_L = N - N_X$;

B_0 is the bid price at the beginning of the trades;

A_0 is the ask price at the beginning of the trades;

P_0, arrival price, is the mid-price at the beginning of the trades, $(A_0 + B_0)/2$;

---

[79] As discussed, both the bid-ask spread and the alpha decay are included in the estimated market impact.

P_d, decision price, is the market price when the trade decision is made;

$\overline{P}$ is the average trading price of the executed shares;

P_{post} is the post-trading price after the temporary impact dissipates.

We now further clarify the above definitions with an example. A portfolio manager constructs a new portfolio and decides to buy 1000 shares of A. At the time of decision, the stock price is $50. The order is sent to the trading desk for execution. At the beginning of the trading, the mid-price is $50.1. Because of limited liquidity, 900 shares are traded at an average price of $50.25 and the remaining 100 shares are canceled at the end of the trading period. The commission is $1 per 100 shares. The market price at the end of trading period is $50.4. Thirty minutes later, the stock price moves to $50.5. The trading cost components and the total trading costs are calculated as the following:

$N = 100$, $P_d = \$50$, $P_0 = \$50.1$, $N_X = 900$, $N_T = 100$, $\overline{P} = \$50.25$, $P_T = \$50.4$, $P_{post} = \$50.5$

Commission and fees = $9

Delay cost = $(P_0 - P_d) \times N = (50.1 - 50) \times 1000 = \$100$

Market impact = $(\overline{P} - P_0) \times N_X = (50.25 - 50.1) \times 900 = \$135$

Opportunity cost = $(P_{post} - P_0) \times N_L = (50.5 - 50.1) \times 100 = \$40$

Total cost = commission and fees + delay cost + market impact + opportunity cost

$\qquad = 9 + 100 + 135 + 40 = \$284$

Trading Risk

Both stock prices and volumes have substantial uncertainty during the period of the trade execution. Furthermore, market participants such as market makers and high-frequency traders may respond to trade flows, which may introduce adverse price moves as well. Therefore, the realized trading costs reflect the impact of price risk, liquidity risk, and signaling risk.

Price risk is caused by stock price volatility. During the execution, stock prices may move in response to market information, stock-specific information, and order flows from other traders. As a result, such price moves introduce uncertainty to the final execution price. The price risk is significant if the trade basket has a significant market exposure (e.g., net long) or exposures to other factors. Similar to portfolio risk, the risk of a trade basket can be estimated using factor risk models. Since the stock price volatility increases with time, the price risk of the trading basket increase as the trading period increases.

Liquidity risk is caused by uncertainty of market volumes. Although we can estimate the market trading volume using information such as average daily volume, historical intraday volume profiles, and intraday trading volume before the start of the trading, the volume during our trading time period may be different from our forecasts. The historical volatility of a stock's trading volume can be used to forecast the volatility of trading volume during the trading period. The coefficient of variance, defined as the ratio of the standard deviation of the trading volume to the expected trading volume, is used to estimate liquidity risk.

Signaling risk is the risk of conveying information about trading intentions to market participants. There are several ways trade information may be leaked to other market participants:

- When one searches for counterparties through brokers, both the brokers and the counterparties contacted get some information about potential trades.

- When trades are executed through brokers, many of whom are market makers, such brokers may use the information to adjust their views on inventory risk.

- When orders are split into smaller trades and executed over time, other market participants can infer the trade direction and the order size from order flows.

- When orders are posted to an alternative trading system, a high-frequency trading desk may ping the alternative trading system to test the presence of large orders.

When large buy orders are executed, dealers may increase ask prices to control their inventory risk. If dealers believe that such orders are being submitted by informed traders—funds with a good track record—they may increase the ask prices to protect themselves against adverse price moves. If a high-frequency trading desk infers that a fund has a large number of shares to trade, they may front run trades to take the existing market liquidity and resell the shares to the fund at higher prices later. For hedge funds, especially the ones with good alphas, effectively hiding their trades is even more important since market markers tend to aggressively move the prices if they believe the trades have high alphas.

Pre-Trade Analysis

Investors actively manage trading costs to alleviate its impact on net returns. The trading cost management starts long before the trade basket is submitted. When portfolio managers make investment decisions, they usually take stock liquidity and trading costs into consideration. For fundamental portfolio managers, it is often a quick estimation of the expected trading costs of the planned trade size versus the expected returns; for quantitative portfolio managers, portfolio optimization often directly incorporates liquidity constraints and estimated trading costs. Accurate estimation of the trading costs help investors make better portfolio rebalancing decisions and achieve better net returns. Therefore, investors spend significant effort on building trading cost models and analyzing a variety of factors that influence trading costs.

Trading Cost Models

When we trade the baskets using a strategy that is close to a volume-weighted average price (VWAP) strategy between 0 and T, we can use a generalized version of the Almgren's equity cost model (2005) to estimate trading costs:

$$\text{cost} = \sigma^k \left(A + B|X/VT|^\beta + C|X/V| + \varepsilon \right)$$

where cost is the market impact cost as a fraction of the dollar value of the trade;

σ measures a stock's volatility;

X is the trade size in shares;

V is the average daily volume;

VT is the estimated market trading volume between 0 and T;

ε is the noise introduced by random price moves and volatility in impact cost;

k measures the relationship between volatility and trading cost, $0 < k \leq 1$;

β measures the relationship between X/VT and the temporary impact, $0 < \beta \leq 1$;

A, B, C are positive estimated coefficients.

Since the dollar value of the trade is approximately $|X| \times P_0$, where P_0 is the arrival price of the stock, the expected dollar cost of the trade is

$$\$cost = (|X| \times P_0) \times cost = P_0 \times \sigma^k \left(A|X| + B|X|^{1+\beta}/|VT|^{\beta} + CX^2/V \right)$$

The first component, A, captures the bid-ask spread and alpha decay during the trading period. X/VT, the ratio of executed shares to the total market trading volume during the trading period, is called the participation rate. Higher participation rate leads to higher temporary impact. For the same trade size X, the participation rate is higher when the trading period T is shorter and the trade speed is faster. Therefore, the temporary impact increases as the trade speed increases. $B|X/VT|^{\beta}$ captures the temporary impact of the trade. The exponential component β determines the shape of the temporary impact curve. Although there is no consensus on the exact value of β, it is usually chosen as a value between 0.5 and 1. Using an inventory risk model, Grinold and Kahn (1999) recommended setting β to 0.5. If a liquidity provider absorbs the total size of the trade, the inventory of the liquidity provider will increase by X shares. The expected time to clear out the X shares from the inventory, τ_{clear}, is proportional to the ratio of X to daily volume V. Since the volatility of a stock increases with the square root of the time, the inventory risk, $\sigma_{inventory}$, increases with the square root of X/V:

$$\tau_{clear} \propto |X/V| \Rightarrow \sigma_{inventory} \propto |X/V|^{0.5}$$

Under the assumption that the liquidity provider demands a return proportional to the inventory risk, the temporary impact—price incentive paid to the liquidity provider—is proportional to the inventory risk and the square root of X/V. Using the market impact data of more than 700,000 US stock trades executed by Citigroup Equity Trading desks, Almgren (2005) estimated that β was 0.600 ± 0.038. Overall, our own experience indicates that the temporary impact is indeed sublinear—when the trade quantity doubles, the impact cost does not. The concave function is also consistent with another common observation: when VWAP algorithms are used, the price tends to respond faster to the earlier trades than to the later trades. If the price impact of a trade basket is 10 bps, the market impact often reaches 7 basis points when less than half of the trade basket is finished. $C|X/V|$ captures the permanent impact of the trade. The theoretical permanent impact is linearly related to the total shares traded. The linear relationship means that the permanent impact depends only on the trade size and is independent of the trading strategy.

If a portfolio has a sufficiently long trading history, the best approach to estimate the parameters k, β, A, B, and C is to use the portfolio's own historical stock trading data. Even if we have months of trading history of a portfolio that trades hundreds of assets a day, the fitted parameters have substantial estimation errors. First of all, the R^2 is likely to be low because of the noise component ε. The noise includes market volatility of stocks. Let us assume that T is 1.5 hours and the average market impact is 8 bps with a standard deviation of 10 bps (variance of 100 bps^2). For an asset with an annual volatility of 30%, the 1.5-hour standard deviation of the stock price is 85 bps (variance of 7225 bps^2). Even if the model captures 70% of the variance in the market impact, the R^2 is only ~1%. To reduce the variance of the estimated parameters, investors have adopted a number of methods to reduce the noise and increase the estimation accuracy. Since market volatility is a main contributor to stock volatility, removing beta-adjusted returns helps reduce the price volatility. For example, consider the hypothetical case of IBM trading at $200 at the start of the trade and a trade is executed at $201 an hour later. In that hour the market is up 45 bps and IBM's beta is 0.8. If we do not adjust for the market move, the estimated market impact for that trade is 50 bps (1/200). Since the market is up 45 bps, the expected beta return of IBM is 36 bps. Removing the beta return of 36 bps means the estimated market impact becomes 14 bps, which is a more accurate measure of the trade impact. After adjusting for beta returns, the individual trades are often grouped by their participation rates to yield grouped data before the regression. For example, all trades with a participation rate between 1.8% and 2% may be grouped, their (value-weighted) average participation rate is used as the explanatory variable and the (value-weighted) average market impact cost is calculated as the response variable of the whole group. Besides grouping by participation rates, trades can also be grouped by stock volatility to better estimate the relationship between volatility and market impact costs. Since large price moves are likely caused by price volatility instead of pure market impact, some models also use robust regression to reduce the weights of trades with large price moves.

A simple trading cost model may use the same coefficients across all stocks. Others estimate different coefficients for buy orders and sell orders. More complex models treat the coefficients as a function of stock characteristics such as growth versus value, sector, market cap, and index membership. Although more complex models may provide more accurate forecasts, simple models work reasonably well in estimating portfolio trading costs. The underlying data used to fit the model coefficients play a more important role in determining the accuracy of the model forecast. The coefficients estimated from a portfolio's own trading history usually yield better forecasts than coefficients provided by brokers. The accuracy of the coefficients depends on a range of factors: the trading time, the range of trade sizes, the range of participation rates, alpha decay, basket style (e.g., intraday momentum versus intraday contrarian), information leakage, and trading algorithms. The brokers fit the model using a large number of client trades that include baskets with vastly different trading strategies and liquidity profiles. Therefore, the estimated coefficients may not accurately reflect the trading costs of a specific portfolio. Since the characteristics of the trade baskets of a portfolio tend to stay relatively stable over time, coefficients estimated from the historical trades accurately forecast the future trading costs of the same portfolio.

Portfolio Optimization with Trading Costs

In Chapter 10 we discussed the mean-variance portfolio optimization without considering trading costs. In this section, we discuss portfolio optimization with explicit cost modeling. Let $w_0 = [w_{0,1}, w_{0,2}, ..., w_{0,N}]'$ be the vector of asset weights before rebalancing, $w = [w_1, w_2, ..., w_N]'$ be the vector of the target weights after rebalancing, and gmv be the target gross market value of the portfolio. To change the weight of asset i from $w_{0,i}$ to w_i, the dollar value of the trade is $\$X_i = gmv \times (w_i - w_{0,i})$. In the portfolio optimization, the following simplified dollar cost is often used:

$$\$\text{cost}_i = \theta_i \times |\$X_i| + \phi_i |\$X_i|^2 = \theta_i \times gmv \times |w_i - w_{0,i}| + \phi_i \left(gmv \times (w_i - w_{0,i})\right)^2$$

where θ_i is the coefficient for commissions/fees and bid-ask spreads;

ϕ_i is the coefficient for market impact costs.

The commissions/fees and bid-ask spreads of a stock depend on the characteristics of the stock. Therefore, the dollar cost of commissions/fees and bid-ask spreads is a linear function of the dollar value traded. Instead of separating the market impact cost (as a fraction of the dollar value traded) to temporary impact and permanent impact, the simplified model assumes that the impact is a linear function of the trade size. The dollar cost of the market impact is a quadratic function of the dollar value traded. The reason for removing the sublinear term in portfolio optimization is to keep the mean-variance optimization problem a quadratic programming problem that can be easily solved. Such a choice does introduce a bias in the trading cost modeling: it may underestimate the price impact of small to medium-size trades and overestimate the costs of large trades.

The dollar cost as a fraction of the portfolio's gross market value becomes

$$\$\text{cost}_i / gmv = \theta_i \times |w_i - w_{0,i}| + gmv \times \phi_i (w_i - w_{0,i})^2$$

This equation estimates the reduction of raw return on gross market value caused by the trading of asset i. The total cost of trading all stocks reduces the return on gross market value by

$$\theta' |w - w_0| + (w - w_0)'(gmv \times \Phi)(w - w_0)$$

The linear cost component $\theta' |w - w_0|$, where $\theta = [\theta_1, \theta_2, ..., \theta_N]$, captures the reduction of raw returns caused by commissions/fees and bid-ask spreads. It does not depend on the size of the portfolio. The quadratic cost component $(w - w_0)'(gmv \times \Phi)(w - w_0)$ captures the reduction of raw returns caused by market impact costs. It grows linearly with the size of the portfolio. Φ is usually a diagonal matrix with $\Phi_{i,i} = \phi_i$ under the assumption that the trading costs of different stocks are uncorrelated. More sophisticated models may include off diagonal terms to reflect the cross impact of the correlated stocks (e.g., buying Citigroup shares may increase the price of Bank of America).

Since trading costs reduce the return on gross market value of the portfolio, a mean-variance optimization that incorporates the trading costs becomes

$$\max_{w} U = \max_{w} w'\alpha - \tfrac{1}{2}\lambda w'\Sigma w - \theta'\mid w - w_0 \mid -(w - w_0)'(gmv \times \Phi)(w - w_0)$$

Although the logic of adding trading costs appears to be straightforward, the optimization is actually far more complicated. Let us consider a portfolio with daily rebalancing. The expected alpha and the portfolio variance used in the portfolio optimization are one-day forecasts. One of the stocks has 63 bps of expected returns in the following month and 3 bps for the next day. Without considering the trading cost, the optimization will initiate a new long position to replace an existing long position that has no expected alpha. If the linear trading cost component (commissions and half of the spread) is more than 3 bps, the inclusion of trading costs may push the trade to zero as the trading cost is higher than the one-day expected alpha. The cost of putting on the new position is a one-time cost. The expected alpha, however, is a recurring one in the following month. That means the long-term benefit will outweigh the short-term cost. Therefore, using one day expected alpha with trading costs may yield a suboptimal target portfolio. In theory, multi-period portfolio optimization is needed to address the horizon difference between expected returns and trading costs. In practice, investors usually modify the one-period optimization problem since multi-period portfolio optimization is difficult to tackle. One approach is to reduce the impact of trading costs on the utility function:

$$\max_{w} U = \max_{w} w'\alpha - \tfrac{1}{2}\lambda w'\Sigma w - \lambda_2 \theta'\mid w - w_0 \mid -\lambda_3 (w - w_0)'(gmv \times \Phi)(w - w_0)$$

where λ_2 and λ_3 are numbers between 0 and 1.

The parameters λ_2 and λ_3 were selected using simulation of the portfolio history. Smaller λ_2 and λ_3 produce portfolios that are closer to the mean-variance optimal portfolio without considering the trading costs; the portfolio has higher expected raw returns and higher expected trading costs. Larger λ_2 and λ_3 produce portfolios that are different from the mean-variance optimal portfolio without considering the trading costs; the portfolio has lower expected raw returns and lower expected trading costs. λ_2 and λ_3 are selected to better manage the trade-off between raw returns and trading costs to achieve higher net returns.

When we use simulated portfolio history to select parameters λ_2 and λ_3, a full trading cost model that accurately captures the trading costs of the strategy's trades should be used to calculate historical trading costs and net returns of the simulated portfolios. Underestimation of trading costs leads to excess portfolio turnover and significant underperformance of the portfolio in production versus the simulated return. Overestimation of trading costs, on the other hand, may lead to pleasant surprise as the production portfolio yields better return than the simulated portfolio. However, overestimation of trading costs often slows down trading and leads to degradation of raw returns. Therefore, the overestimation of trading costs causes the net return to be suboptimal as well. Accurate trading cost estimation yields the best trade-off between loss of raw returns and trading costs. Portfolio optimization with accurate trading cost components often significantly reduces turnover and trading costs with little impact on portfolio risk and a small decrease in raw returns.

Volume and Volatility Patterns

To estimate the market trading volume of a stock during the trading period, VT, we need to understand the volume pattern. Trading volumes clearly exhibit a variety of seasonal patterns. Market volumes tend to be low on the day before a market holiday. The Friday after Thanksgiving, the day before Christmas, and the day before Independence Day tend to have the lowest volumes among all trading days as many traders leave for holidays. These days are sometimes half trading days (market closes at 13:00 EST) and the volumes are 40-60% lower than average trading days. The day for the Russell index reconstitution is a day with abnormally high volume. In 2012, June 22 was the date for Russell to determine the final list of additions and deletions to Russell 1000 index and Russell 2000 index. On that day, the trading volumes were 70% higher than average and the highest of all trading days in 2012. Trading volumes exhibit monthly and weekly patterns as well. August is usually the month with the lowest trading volumes among all twelve months as many traders are on summer vacation. Monday has the lowest trading volumes on average among all week days.

Trading volumes exhibit a U-shaped intraday volume pattern. Exhibit 14-1 shows the half-hour intraday stock volume profiles for Russell 1000 stocks and Russell 200 stocks in 2012. The U-shaped pattern demonstrates that there is more trading volume at the open and close: the first half an hour 9:30-10:00 (labeled as 9:30) accounts for 11-14% of the daily volume and the last half an hour 15:30-16:00 (labeled as 15:30) accounts for 17-18% of the daily volume.

If we do not need to trade early in a trading day, the intraday volumes of the earlier periods provide valuable information for the estimation of later periods. At stock level, the trading volume in the morning (9:30-13:00) is a stronger predictor of the afternoon (13:00-16:00) volume than the 21-day ADV. In 2012, when the ADVs of the past 21 days were used as the explanatory variable to forecast the afternoon volumes, the R^2 was 0.65; when the morning volumes were added as the second explanatory variable, the R^2 increased to 0.84.

Exhibit 14-2 Intraday volume pattern

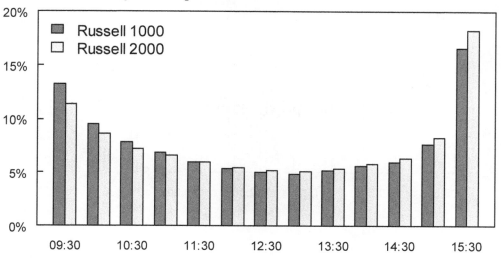

Return volatility has clear intraday pattern as well. Exhibit 14-3 shows the average half-hour stock intraday volatility in 2012. The intraday volatility is the highest early in the morning as the overnight economic news and stock-specific information gets incorporated into stock prices. The volatility then gradually decreases during the morning hours. The volatility is mostly stable in the afternoon with small increase in the last half an hour. The intraday bid-ask spread pattern is similar to the intraday volatility pattern. Bid-ask spreads are the highest at the first half an hour after the market open because of high volatility, potential information asymmetry, and adverse selection. In response, liquidity providers demand higher compensation for higher risk. Bid-ask spreads are sometimes higher at the end of day because of inventory control—many market makers, especially high-frequency trading groups, avoid holding inventory overnight. Since market open and market close are also the periods in a day with the highest trading volumes, many investors actively trade in these periods to take advantage of the liquidity. To estimate the trading costs of a portfolio, we need to take the intraday volatility pattern into consideration. Since the intraday volatility and bid-ask spreads are higher early in the morning, the cost may be higher to trade the same baskets shortly after open.

There is a U-shaped relationship between recent returns and trading volumes—that is, when the stocks have large positive or negative returns, their trading volumes are higher. Market shocks contribute to the U-shaped relationship. During market shocks, volumes increase, the volatility rises, and spreads widen. Stock-specific news such as earnings announcements contributes to the U-shaped relationship as well. The trading volume of a stock increases sharply around the earnings announcement and often remains elevated in the week following the announcement. At the same time, earnings surprises often lead to large price moves, increased volatility, and wider bid-ask spreads. Although a market volume spike results in lower participation rate for the same trade, the market impact may not decrease because of higher volatility and higher spreads.

Exhibit 14-3 Intraday volatility pattern

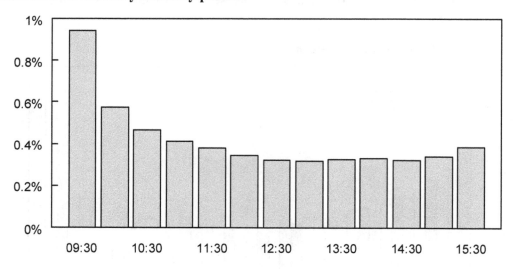

Pre-Trade Report

It is common for portfolio managers or traders to review a pre-trade report before the trading basket is released to the market. The report collects information on current positions, target positions, average daily volumes, intraday volumes, and risk exposures of individual stocks in the portfolio. A pre-trade report may include the following information:

- Total number of shares and dollar values of the trades as well as breakdowns by side (buy, sell, and short sell), sector, and market cap.

- Distribution of asset-level trade sizes by dollar values and as percentages of ADVs or percentages of forecasted market volumes.

- Top-level summaries that estimate the expected trading costs and the trading risks of the basket using trading cost models and price risk models.

- Detailed breakdowns of expected costs and risks to identify the most expensive trades and the most risky trades.

Investors rely on the pre-trade report for an early estimate of the trading cost and the risk of a trading basket. The characteristics of the trading basket allow investors to identify previous trading baskets with similar characteristics and select a broker or a trading algorithm with the best performance in trading similar baskets. The pre-trade reports also alert investors to potential problems in the portfolio construction. For example, an unusually large trading basket and violations of the ADV boundaries set by the optimizer indicate errors in portfolio construction. In such a case, catching the problem before the basket starts trading often prevents potential losses caused by the wrong trades.

Trading strategies

To select an appropriate trading strategy, it is important to understand available choices that are consistent with the characteristics of investment portfolios. Trading strategies try to reach a proper balance between two competing goals:

- Reduce market impact by trading slowly and providing liquidity.

- Reduce alpha decay and trading risk by trading fast and consuming liquidity.

Many trading strategies combine the expected trading cost with the variance of trading cost to form a mean-variance optimization problem:

$$\min_{x(t)} \big(E(x) + \lambda V(x) \big)$$

where $x(t)$ is the trade schedule determining how orders are sliced over time;

$E(x)$ is the expected value of trading cost;

$V(x)$ is the variance of trading cost;

λ is risk aversion coefficient with large λ indicating higher risk aversion.

If an investor is less risk-averse (small λ) or the trading basket has little risk exposure, reducing the expected trading cost is the primary goal. If an investor is more risk-averse or the trading basket has significant risk exposure, reducing the trading risk becomes more important. Since institutional investors often trade baskets of stocks, the trading risk needs to be examined at a portfolio level. Overall, the trading directions of individual stocks and the correlations between stocks have much larger impact on the trading risk than on the expected cost. For example, an index fund deploying new cash inflows is subject to significant price risk and need to trade faster. A long/short value fund rebalancing a cash neutral and beta neutral long/short basket faces much smaller price risk and can trade slower.

Execution Methods

There are several ways through which investors can access the trading market with different levels of broker involvement.

High-touch trades: In general, all trades that are manually handled by traders are high-touch trades. For example, larger block trades are typically handled by brokers manually. When a client asks for a broker to sell a large block trade, the broker advertises the block trade to seek an indication of interest (IOI) from a selected group of clients and serves as the intermediate for possible price negotiations so that clients on both sides of the trades can remain anonymous.

Low-touch trades: In the current stock market, the majority of trades are executed by algorithmic trading. Algorithmic trading refers to the use of computerized electronic trading systems to enter orders with a trading algorithm deciding the timing, order type, quantity, and price of the orders. Many investors rely on broker algorithms for execution. A broker often provides several types of algorithms to meet different client needs and clients can select a variety of parameters for each type of algorithm. For investors who decide to use algorithmic trading, it is important to have an understanding of the underlying algorithms. Most trading algorithm decisions involve the trade-off between the market impact and the trading risk.

Zero-touch trades: Direct market access (DMA) requires essentially no intervention—zero touch—from brokers. DMA refers to the electronic trading facilities provided by brokers that allow investors to interact with the order book of the exchanges directly. In other words, DMA allows investors to use the brokers' trading infrastructure[80] to place orders on exchanges. Brokers provide monitoring tools and risk analysis tools to help manage trading. For example, an order management system can have trade limits to prevent the submission of possible wrong trades. Some sophisticated funds develop their own trading algorithms that are tailored to their trading baskets and implement the algorithms through DMA. DMA does not require algorithm trading though: buy-side traders can work a trade over time by manually posting market or limit orders. For investors, DMA provides full control of order execution, offers low commissions, and still allows investors to hide their identity as the trades show up in the exchange as the trades of the broker that provides the DMA.

---

[80] Another type of access, sponsored access (SA), does not use the broker's trading infrastructure. High-frequency trading firms often rely on SA to build ultra-low latency systems. Because of the hefty cost involved in building the in-house infrastructure, SA is not a popular choice among traditional long/short funds.

To decide whether to use high-touch, low-touch, or zero-touch trades, investors take costs, performance, and efficiency into consideration.

Costs: High-touch trades have the highest commissions and zero-touch DMA algorithm trading has the lowest commissions. However, investors need to make heavy investments in both infrastructure and human capital in order to develop and implement efficient trading algorithms.

Performance: Individual investors and small funds tend to use broker algorithms instead of DMA as broker algorithms may provide better execution performance. The execution desks of large brokers have dedicated teams to research and develop trading algorithms that few investors have the resources to match. If investors select proper broker algorithms, these algorithms usually effectively limit the market impact and control the trading risk. On the other hand, brokers are unlikely to have deep understanding of the trading baskets (e.g., expected alpha of the individual trades) as investors themselves do. Therefore, ad-hoc broker algorithms designed to fit the needs of most clients, may not be optimal for sophisticated funds that have different alpha forecasts for different trades.

Efficiency: Economies of scale also help large brokers execute trades more efficiently. Since brokers maintain a liquidity pool that connects natural buyers and sellers, crossing client orders is common. For instance, some brokers use trajectory cross to cross algorithmic orders over optimally selected time intervals. Let us consider an example. Before market open, consider that client A places an order to buy 5000 shares of IBM using a VWAP algorithm between 9:30 and 12:30 and client B places an order to sell 8000 shares of IBM using a full-day VWAP algorithm. Based on intraday volume profile, trajectory cross estimates that 50% of client B's shares will be done between 9:30 and 12:30. Instead of sending client orders to the market, where clients need to pay half of the effective bid-ask spread for trading, the trajectory cross will cross 4000 shares between client A and client B. The price of the crossing will be determined by the VWAP between 9:30 and 12:30. The remaining 1000 shares of client A's buy order will be traded in the market between 9:30 and 12:30 and the remaining 4000 shares of client B's sell order will be traded in the market between 12:30 and 16:00.

No matter which execution method one chooses and how complex the trading system is, it is important to have an independent monitoring system to analyze filled trades during the trading period. Without close monitoring, human errors or erroneous trading algorithms may lead to heavy losses. Exhibit 14-4 shows an interesting intraday price action of Coca-Cola (KO) on July 19, 2012. In every hour between 10:00 AM and 3:00 PM, the price moved up in the first half an hour and then moved down in the second half. IBM, McDonalds, and even Apple showed similar intraday price actions on that day. Although the source of the trades that drove the price pattern remains a mystery, investors generally agree that the price pattern reflects a trading algorithm error: instead of allocating the buy orders evenly over the whole hour, the algorithm allocated the volume in the first half an hour. Two weeks later, a software glitch cost Knight Capital—a leading market maker and electronic execution provider—$440M on the morning of August 1, 2012. These events demonstrate that technology advancement alone does not replace a solid trading monitoring system.

Exhibit 14-4 Intraday price of the Coca-Cola Company (KO) on July 19, 2012

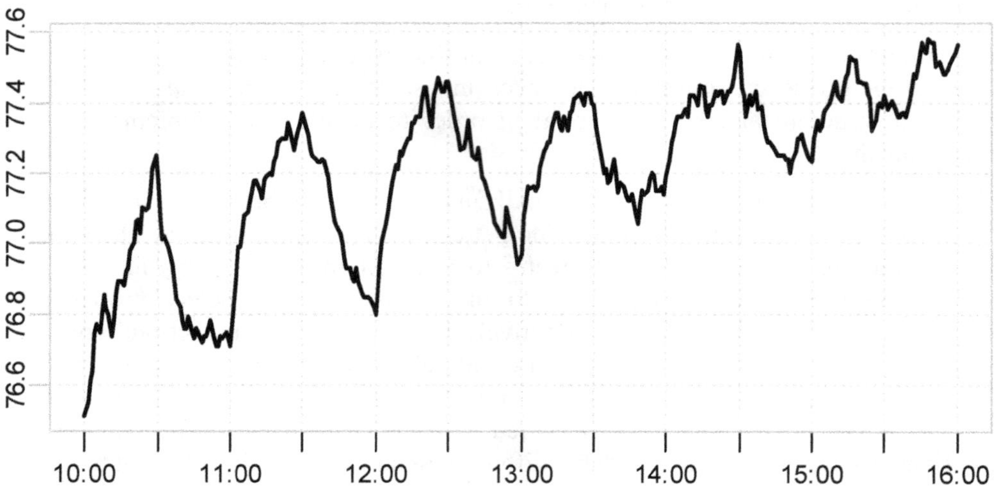

Orders

Investors also use different order types to execute their trades. Orders are specific instructions on how trades should be executed. The two order types that are most commonly used are market orders and limit orders. A market order executes the trade immediately at the current best market prices available. A limit order buys a stock at prices no higher than the preset limit price and sells a stock at prices no lower than the preset limit price. The execution price of a market order is not guaranteed. The bid/ask prices may move before the market order is executed. Besides, the best bid/ask prices have quantities associated with them, usually no more than several hundred shares. If a market buy order has a size larger than the quantity of the best ask, it moves up the order book to trade at increasingly higher prices. In rare cases, the final fill prices are worse than the price that the trader expects. Limit order fixes the worst execution price. But part of, or even all of, the order may not get executed if the market price moves away from the limit price. If the **"immediate-or-cancel (IOC)"** instruction is given with a limit order, the unfilled shares are canceled. Otherwise, the order is considered to be **"good for the day"** and the unfilled shares are left in the order book. Another special type of time-in-force instruction, **"fill or kill"**, specifies that the order must execute immediately in full or not at all. To avoid the risk of adverse price, a trading algorithm can also use marketable limit order—a limit order to buy/sell at or slightly above/below the best ask/bid price. Marketable limit orders allow at least part of the order to be filled unless the price suddenly moves away from the national best bid and offer (NBBO) at the time of trade submission; the limit price prevents the execution of a trade at a very bad price in case that liquidity disappears at the time of the trade submission.

Whether to use market orders or limit orders and how aggressive to pursue liquidity depend on a variety of factors. In general, if a strategy has slow alpha decay, passive trading often reduces trading costs; but if the alpha decays fast, market orders are preferred to take liquidity. The higher the confidence in estimating the alpha decay, the more likely a trader will use market orders. Intraday trend following momentum strategies often need to be more aggressive so that the trades are executed before the price move consumes too much alpha. Intraday mean reversion strategies, on the other hand, can be more passive. Since the trades are against the current price trend, traders can provide liquidity by buying at the bid prices and selling at the offer prices. Another observation is that limit orders can outperform market orders in high volatility environments, especially in a volatile range-bound market. High volatility increases the probability that the limit order will be filled. Another factor is the bid-ask spread. Limit orders are preferred when the bid-ask spread is high as reducing the effective spread using passive orders adds more benefit.

The pricing structure for taking and adding liquidity influences the decision on which order types to use as well. Exchanges and alternative trading venues often charge fees for orders that remove liquidity and offer rebates for orders that add liquidity. In general, marketable orders remove liquidity and non-marketable orders add liquidity. Let us consider a stock with ask price $20.00. If a trader sends a market buy order or a marketable limit buy order with limit price no less than $20.00, the order will be executed (maybe partly if the limit order size is large). The trade removes liquidity from the order book and will be charged a fee. If a trader sends a limit buy order with limit price $19.99 instead, the order will not be executed. The limit order will be added to the order book. If a market sell order comes and causes the limit order to be filled, the limit order provides liquidity and receives rebates. If marketable orders pay 22 cents/100 shares for removing liquidity and non-marketable orders receive 18 cents/100 shares for providing liquidity, the difference is 2 bps on a $20.00 stock. Therefore non-marketable limit orders are preferred when fees and the rebate rates are high as it is more profitable to provide liquidity.

Most venues allow **hidden orders** that are not displayed in the order book. Hidden orders are useful if the orders have a large quantity associated with them as the orders are not visible to other traders. However, hidden orders have only price priority and no time priority. Therefore, hidden orders have lower priority than displayed orders with the same price. An **iceberg order** divides the shares in a large order to two components: a small volume is displayed and the rest of the order is hidden. Whenever the displayed volume is traded in the market, another slice is cut from the remaining shares and displayed. When a slice is displayed, it is put in the queue after the existing displayed orders that have the same price. Since most trading venues apply time priority to execute orders that are posted earlier when multiple orders have the same price, the new slice has lower priority than the existing displayed orders.

Some investors use stop orders to protect profits and reduce sudden losses. **Stop orders** are conditional orders used to reduce losses or to protect profits. A buy stop order is triggered when the stock price touches or moves above the stop price; a sell stop order is triggered when the stock price touches or moves below the stop price. Once a stop order is triggered, it becomes either a limit order or a market order depending on its specification. A stop market order becomes a market order when the stop price is triggered. A stop-limit order, on the other hand, becomes a limit order at a pre-specified limit price.

Trade Schedule

Traders or trading algorithms break large orders into smaller ones and trade the smaller orders successively over a period of time. Trade schedule determines how large orders are sliced into smaller ones over the trading period. The market impact cost, trading risk, and alpha decay are the main forces that determine trade schedules. If we push the trades too hard, the high participation rate causes large imbalance between buy orders and sell orders and the price may move faster against our trades. If we trade too slowly, the price may move away from the arrival price and the price risk increases. The price moves may be simply random moves, in which case slow trading adds to trading risk but the expected value of the price moves is close to zero. In the cases where the trades have high alphas, the price moves may reflect alpha decay—the prices of the assets with positive alphas move higher when we buy them and the prices of the assets with negative alphas move lower when we sell them—and the expected value is always negative. Good trade schedules effectively balance the trade-offs between the market impact and the price risk/alpha decay. Some common trade schedules are volume-weighted average price (VWAP), time-weighted average price (TWAP), percentage-of-volume (POV), passive in-the-money (PIM), aggressive in-the-money (AIM), and implementation shortfall (IS) strategy.

VWAP and TWAP algorithms are popular choices for reducing market impact costs. VWAP is the ratio of total value traded to the total volume over a defined trading period:

$$VWAP = \left(\sum_i P_i Q_i \right) \bigg/ \left(\sum_i Q_i \right)$$

where i represents each trade over the defined trading period;

Q_i is the quantity of trade i;

P_i is the price of trade i.

Since VWAP is considered to be the average price to pay for a passive trader, it is a valuable benchmark to evaluate the execution quality. For a VWAP strategy, an average execution price close to or better than the VWAP is considered good performance. Since it is impossible to participate in each trade, a VWAP strategy tries to match the percent of trading for each sub-interval in proportion to the percentage of the market volume. The strategy trades more when market liquidity is high and trades less when liquidity is low, which minimizes the market impact cost. To determine the trade schedules, VWAP algorithms often use average historical intraday volume profiles. For morning trades, the orders are tilted towards the beginning as the market volume is higher after the open; for afternoon trades, the orders are tilted towards the end as the market volume is higher before the close. The market trading volume profile is usually similar to the historical profile, but occasionally the realized volume pattern is significantly different from the historical profile, which leads to suboptimal execution. While some simple VWAP algorithms have the same volume profile estimated from all stocks in a trade basket, more complex ones build different volume profiles for stocks with different characteristics and dynamically incorporate live trading volumes in the volume profile estimation.

The TWAP algorithms try to trade similar number of shares within each uniform time slice. For example, if the trade duration is two hours, a TWAP algorithm may slice the duration to 20 six-minute time slices and try to trade 5% of the total trades within each time slice. Its benchmark, TWAP, is the average price over all time slices (the typical price for each small time slice is often the VWAP for that period).

VWAP and TWAP algorithms that follow a rigid volume schedule or time schedule have high signaling risk since it is easy for other market participants to decipher the pattern. Once other participants identify the trade pattern, they can use the consistent order flow to their advantage. To mitigate the signaling risk, more sophisticated strategies allow more flexibility for the total trades to deviate from the schedule. Some algorithms introduce randomness to the trade schedule to avoid a consistent trade pattern. Avoiding predictable trading patterns lessens the signaling risk, but the realized trading prices often deviate more from the VWAP or the TWAP benchmark. Brokers also provide guaranteed VWAP execution: for an extra predetermined fee, the brokers guarantee that the execution price is the VWAP. Essentially, the brokers assume part of the execution risk for a fee.

Despite its popularity, for trades that present a significant percentage of total market volume, VWAP is not a good benchmark since these trades themselves drive the VWAP. As the trade reaches close to 100% of the trading volume, the average trade price becomes VWAP. Compared with algorithms that front load the trades, the VWAP algorithm may have high price risk as its primary objective is to reduce market impact instead of minimizing the price risk. For trading baskets that have high price risks, the VWAP algorithm may expose the trading baskets to unnecessarily high risks. For trades with high alpha information, the VWAP already reflects the alpha decay. Hence, the VWAP is not as good a benchmark as the arrival price to evaluate a trade and VWAP strategies may not be suitable choices. For example, if the VWAP moves up 30 bps versus the arrival price, the total implementation cost is at least 30 bps if the trade is executed at the VWAP. Investors use VWAP tilt strategy to reduce price risks and alpha decay. Instead of following the volume profile, investors add predefined formula to tilt the order allocations towards the start of the trading period.

Percentage-of-volume (POV) algorithms try to participate in a fixed percentage of the market volume. For example, a 5% participation rate means that the algorithm tries to match 5% of observed market volume. Since the future market volume is unknown, POV adjusts the volume profile estimation dynamically using live trading volumes. POV is more opportunistic as it increases trading when there is more liquidity and decreases trading when there is less liquidity. Unlike VWAP and TWAP algorithms, the end time of the trades are determined by market volumes and different trades in a trade basket finish at different times. If we trade a balanced long/short basket, POV algorithms may introduce imbalance and market exposure: When all trades are set to have similar participation rate, the trades that represent smaller percentages of daily volumes are filled earlier. If the buy or the sell side has more trades that are smaller percentages of market volumes, those trades will finish first and expose the rest of the basket to market moves.

POV algorithms that follow a rigid participation rate schedule carry signaling risk as well since the algorithms release constant order flows as a percentage of the market volume. To mitigate the problem, some algorithms allow sufficient flexibility so that the realized participation rate can deviate from the initial target participation rate. Allowing the participation rate to be behind or before schedule may also reduce market impact. A short spike in trading volume because of large block trades causes the algorithm to be behind the schedule. But the liquidity may be low after the volume spike and trying to catch up the participation rate will result in large market impact. The added flexibility prevents the algorithms from chasing the volume spike. Alternatively, the POV algorithms may apply more sophisticated approaches to smooth volume spikes and dynamically forecast the market liquidity.

Passive in-the-money (PIM) algorithms trade more passively when the price moves in the trader's favor and more aggressively when the price moves against the trader. For a buy order, PIM algorithms slow down the trades when the price drops and speeds up the trades when the price goes up. **Aggressive in-the-money (AIM)** algorithms, on the contrary, trade more aggressively when the price moves in the trader's favor and more passively when the price moves against the trader. PIM algorithms assume that the price trend is likely to continue: when the price moves in favor, it is likely to continue to move further in favor. By trading passively, one can get a better price later. When the price moves against the trader, it is likely to continue to move further against. By trading more aggressively, the trader may lock in the current price and reduce potential future losses. AIM algorithms assume that the price trend is likely to reverse. Lorenz and Almgren (2011) showed that AIM algorithms could improve the mean-variance optimization if investors preferred to reduce the variance of implementation shortfall. Essentially, by trading more aggressively when the price moves in favor, AIM algorithms spend trading gains on reducing trading risk and achieve better trade-off between market impact cost and trading risk.

Instead of purely focusing on reducing market impact as VWAP/TWAP algorithms do, Chapter 1algorithms directly take the interactions between market impact, the alpha decay, and timing risk into consideration. The benchmark of implementation shortfall algorithms is the arrival price instead of the VWAP/TWAP. In order to make execution prices closer to the arrival price and to reduce timing risk, implementation shortfall algorithms often adopt the following changes:

- Shorten trade horizons for trades that are small relative to market trading volumes. Since the market impact cost is likely to be small, shortening the trade horizons makes the trade prices closer to the arrival price. The algorithm tries to identify an optimal participation rate that strikes a balance between market impact and timing risk.

- Shorten trade horizons for stocks with high volatility. The goal is again to reduce timing risk by sacrificing some market impact costs.

- Tilt the trades towards the beginning if the trades have higher expected alpha and larger expected alpha decay. Needless to say, the tilts depend on the type of the strategies as well as the type of the trades. A simple rebalance trade basket to control risk is unlikely to have high alpha and a small tilt or no tilt works. When we initialize new long positions, we often have higher alpha expectations and require a significant tilt for earlier entries; when we reduce stale existing positions to make room for new positions, we may still have positive alpha expectations (just not as good as the new positions) and are in no rush to trade. For these trades a tilt towards the end of the trade period may help.

Trading Venues and Order Routing

In 2014, U.S. stocks and ETFs are traded on more than 10 exchanges and 30 alternative trading systems (e.g., dark pools). The exchanges accounted for about two thirds of the total trading volumes and the alternative trading systems (ATS) accounted for the remaining one third. Among the exchanges, NASDAQ is the largest by volume that accounts for ~18% of the total trading volume. There has been an on-going debate on whether market fragmentation harms market quality and reduces liquidity. Critics of ATS argue that consolidated market brings all buyers and sellers together to increase liquidity and speed up price discovery. Since most small investors have no access to ATS, the existence of ATS also raises the fairness question. In April 2013, the CEOs of three major US exchanges (NYSE, NASDAQ, and BATS) asked the SEC to increase the regulation on dark pools. Supporters of ATS, on the other hand, argue that the additional trading venues add liquidity and competition among different trading venues and reduce trading costs. For example, O'Hara and Ye (2011) found that more fragmented stocks had lower transaction costs and faster execution speeds.

For traders, market fragmentation is both a challenge and an opportunity. On the negative side, market fragmentation means that trading algorithms have to search for liquidity at multiple trading venues in order to access all available liquidity. After using a trade schedule to decide the slice size, trading algorithms need to split each slice to smaller child orders and to submit them to different venues. For each ATS, traders need to estimate the hidden liquidity, the probability of successful execution, and the fee structure. On the plus side, if traders can effectively route the trades to high-quality ATS and avoid the toxic ones with high information leakage risk, using ATS lowers trading costs. Therefore, algorithm traders have been spending significant effort on smart routing to search for liquidity in different venues and avoid toxic venues.

In response to the market fragmentation, the SEC passed Regulation NMS (National Market System) to improve fairness in price execution and access to market data:

- The Order Protection Rule provides intermarket price priority by requiring execution venues to route an order to another venue that offers the best price.

- The Access Rule requires execution venues to provide fair and no-discriminatory access to their quotation data.

- The Sub-Penny Rule prohibits market venues from accepting or displaying quotations in a pricing increment less than a penny unless the stock price is less than $1.00.

- The Market Data Rule facilitates the consolidation and distribution of market data from different execution venues.

Because of the Order Protection Rule, a trading venue cannot execute the (whole) order if other venues have the best bid/offer prices. Instead, the trading venue needs to route (part of) the order to another venue that has the best bid/offer prices. Such a behavior is not always what the traders want. It is common for a trading algorithm to simultaneously send multiple orders to different trading venues at the same time. To prevent orders from being routed to other trading venues, trades can send **intermarket sweep orders (ISO)** to execute trades at a specific venue. Intermarket sweep orders are limit orders that require they be executed in one specific venue even if another venue is publishing a better quote, disobeying the order-protection rule.

Let us consider a simple case for IBM with two trading venues showing the following ask quotes:

Venue	Price	Size
1	$200.00	500
2	$200.00	800
2	$200.01	1500
1	$200.03	1200

If a trader sends a market buy order for 1500 shares to venue 1, venue 1 executes 500 shares at $200.00 and needs to route part of the trades to venue 2 since the 800 shares on venue 2 have the best offer price. If the trader labels the order as an intermarket sweep order instead, all 1500 shares will be executed at venue 1 (500 shares at $200.00 and 1000 shares at $200.03). In practice, traders, especially informed traders, use intermarket sweep orders to take liquidity from multiple exchange simultaneously. When the trader believes that the price is likely to move to $200.10 soon, he is likely to send intermarket sweep orders to both venue 1 and venue 2 to sweep the existing ask quotes.

Brokers and independent vendors set up dark pools for investors to trade away from the exchanges. Dark pools are crossing networks that do not post bids/offers or publish order books. The trade price is often derived from the midpoint of the bid price and the ask price on the primary exchange at the time of trade. When a trade occurs, it reports the trade to a trade reporting facility which prints the trade to the consolidated tape without going through the exchanges. Sophisticated investors use dark pools to decrease the effective spread as well as to reduce market impact. Stocks that have wider bid-ask spreads (in basis points of the mid-price) and higher market impact costs increase the advantage of using dark pools. Hence, investors are more likely to trade small-cap stocks, high-volatility stocks, and low-priced stocks in dark pools. Although dark pools are beneficial to some sophisticated investors who have the resources to use them to reduce trading costs, the existence of the dark pools reduces the volume available on public exchanges. For those investors who lack the resources to access or effectively explore dark pools, such pools effectively decrease both available liquidity and price transparency.

Post-Trade Analysis

Post-trade analysis evaluates the overall trading quality, the relative performance of different trading algorithms or brokers, and the validity of trading cost models used in the investment decisions. The report from post-trade analysis may include the following components:

- A breakdown of trading costs to commissions, fees, spread costs (effective spreads estimated using prevailing bid/ask prices at the time of the trades), permanent impact (estimated using post-trade prices), and temporary impact.

- Performance of trade prices against different benchmarks such as arrival prices, first-fill prices, and VWAP.

- A breakdown of trading costs by buckets of trade participation rates or percent of average daily volumes.

The trading cost measures from the post-trade analysis are used as inputs to pre-trade analysis to help portfolio managers better estimate different components of trading costs, build accurate trading cost models, and incorporate more accurate trading costs in investment decisions. The post-trade analysis also helps investors make better trading decisions. Let us consider a simple hypothetical case: at 10:00 AM each day, a trader needs to choose the trading horizon for his trading basket to achieve the best trade-off between reducing the market impact costs and reducing the alpha decay. After trading the baskets with 1-hour, 2-hour, and 3-hour horizons, the post-trade analysis, Exhibit 14-5, shows the average price trajectory of the trade basket. The price change is measured against the arrival price at 10:00 AM. Positive price change indicates higher prices for buys and lower prices for sells/shorts. For the trading baskets with 1-hour horizon (A), the aggressive trading pushed the market prices up by 18 bps on average and the market prices quickly reverted after the trades stopped. In general, large and quick price reversals after the trades stopped trading indicated that the baskets caused too much temporary impact. For the trading baskets with 3-hour horizon (C), the passive trading significantly reduced the market impacts. Therefore, the price reversal was small after the trades stopped. The slow trading, however, significantly increased alpha decay costs. The trading basket with 2-hour horizon (B), achieved overall better balance between the market impact costs and the alpha decay costs. The overall advantage of the 2-hour horizon should be confirmed by the trading costs against the arrival prices: we would expect that strategy B has better slippage against the arrival prices than A and C and is a better choice for the trading horizon.

Exhibit 14-5 Average price trajectory of the trade basket

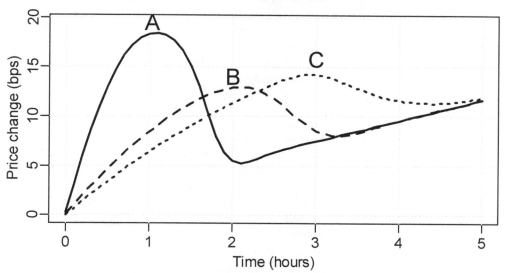

Furthermore, the post-trade analysis is a valuable tool to evaluate the relative performance of two brokers or two trading algorithms. Using trading baskets with similar characteristics, we can compare their performance against different benchmarks. If the objective is to reduce the market impact and the trade baskets are not dominated by trades with high market participation rates, VWAP is often a good benchmark to compare two brokers or algorithms. If the objective is to reduce the implementation shortfall, arrival price is usually the best benchmark. To evaluate the performance of two trading algorithms, the daily trade baskets are split to two smaller ones with similar characteristics (large trades should be evenly allocated and market beta exposures should be similar). Investors then monitor the performance of the two algorithms on a daily basis to evaluate whether one outperforms the other.

Impact of High-Frequency Trading

High-frequency trading groups have become major players in equity trading and accounted for about half of the daily trading volumes in 2013. It is estimated that high-frequency firms generate $7-10 billion dollars of revenues a year. Let us consider high frequency trading in the framework of the previously mentioned Fundamental Law of Active management:

$$IR = IC \times \sqrt{N}$$

Unlike long-term investment strategies that make a few trade decisions on an asset in a year, HFT strategies can make multiple trade decisions on an asset in a day. As a result, the number of independent bets (N) that HFT strategies make in a year is hundreds of times of the independent bets that long-term investment strategies make. Even with lower edge (information coefficient), HFT strategies may yield significantly higher information ratios when compared to long-term investment strategies. It's not uncommon for top HFT firms to have information ratios higher than 10. Building and maintaining an edge in HFT are difficult tasks though. The fierce competition among HFT firms is often described as an arms race. The success of a HFT firm depends on its ability to collect a large amount of trade and quote information in real time, process the information, generate trades, and place the orders on different trading venues. Speed is the key as a difference in milliseconds or even microseconds determines whether one trade is able to get ahead of others. In response, HFT firms have been on the frontier of trading technology. They co-locate their servers with the exchanges' servers, purchase special hardware to increase computing speed, and build efficient computing codes to process the data. Some even set up their own microwave networks to speed up data communications. The competition however has significantly increased the costs and lowered the profits of HFT.

The role of HFT is a topic of conversation in the financial press. Proponents of HFT argue that HFT firms increase market liquidity. They often point to the overall increase in market volume and lower quoted bid-ask spreads as evidence. High-frequency trading firms compete with traditional market makers to provide bids/offers. The competition increases the size of the order book and narrows bid-ask spreads. For individual investors who trade a small number of shares and small institutional funds, high-frequency firms facilitate order execution by increasing the sizes of the order books and provide lower bid-ask spreads. However, for institutional investors that demand market liquidity for their large trades, high-frequency trading may increase their trading costs.

Although the number of shares for the quotes and the depth of the open order books have increased, such increases may not translate to meaningful increase in liquidity for institutional investors. The quotes from HFT desks may change in less than a second. Some HFT strategies may use quote stuffing, placing a large number of quotes and cancelling them almost immediately, to overwhelm the exchange message system and to gain an advantage over competing algorithms. Quote stuffing forces other market participants to process a large number of uninformative messages, slowing down their trading decisions. During the flash crash on May 6, 2010, many stocks had hundreds or even thousands of quotes per second that bogged down the market, which caused a delay in dissemination of quote data and forced many investors to trade without valid market information. Another reason for quote stuffing is to create false mid-prices in order to influence the trade prices in the dark pools. Let us consider a case that an HFT wants to sell a stock when the NBBO is $40.00/$40.04. There are also buy orders pegged to the mid-price in a dark pool. If the HFT directly sells the stock in the dark pool, the sell price is the mid-price, $40.02. Instead, HFT can post a bid price of $40.02, sell in the dark pool, and immediately cancel the bid quote. At the time of the execution, the NBBO is $40.02/$40.04, so the sell price is the new mid-price $40.03. By stuffing the bid quote, the HFT increases the selling price by 1 cent. In such a case, the new quote adds no real liquidity and increases the buyer's trading cost. To reduce the problems caused by quote stuffing, some exchanges begin to charge additional fees for excessive numbers of quote changes.

The increase in the sizes of the order books may not benefit institutional traders. Without HFT, institutional trades are more likely to cross when one buys and the other sells the same stock. The crossing happens at the mid-price and save both the buyers and the sellers half the bid-ask spread. HFT firms, through their high speed market making capability by posting large numbers of bids and offers, intercept the directional trades and position themselves as intermediaries between buyers and sellers before the natural buyers and sellers can trade directly with each other. The buyers are forced to buy at the offer price; the sellers are forced to sell at the bid price; HFTs pocket the bid-ask spread as revenues and the exchange rebates for "providing" liquidity. Interestingly, HFTs are more active in stocks that already have sufficient natural liquidity and have low prices since they can easily flip the trades and the relative spread (as a percent of the stock price) is higher.

Hirschey (2012) found that HFT firms tended to aggressively buy shares before aggressive buying by non HFT firms and aggressively sell shares before aggressive selling by non HFT firms. The study shows HFT firms' ability to forecast order flows in the next 1-5 minutes and suggests that they actively trade on such forecast. Such activities may increase institutional investors' trading costs. Let us consider a case that an institutional investor needs to buy 5% of the ADV over the next three hours. For the trades to balance, the investor either needs a sufficient number of market makers to absorb the temporary imbalance by putting the imbalance into the market markers' inventory or pay higher price to attract more investors to sell their shares. Since high-frequency traders operate at timescales far shorter than three hours, they are unlikely to absorb much of the imbalance caused by the institution's trades. HFT firms use algorithms to sniff out the intention of the institution and jump in ahead of trades in a practice called gaming. When an institution uses iceberg orders, the gamers unleash small sell orders to uncover the hidden buy orders. Alternatively, HFT firms infer the existence of the large order from order flows. Once they sniff out the existence of the large trade, they can easily front run the large order multiple times during the three hour period. Each time, they bid ahead of a child order of the large trade (and pay the fees for taking the liquidity if necessary) to build a long position. Then they turn around and post a limit sell order slightly above the current offer price. As more child orders from the large trade push the prices up, the sell limit order is filled. The high-frequency traders collect the price differences (and the rebates). Since the trading algorithm splits the large trades and gradually releases the child orders, high-frequency traders can repeatedly enter small positions and flip them multiple times over the three-hour period. In appearance, these

HFT firms provide liquidity by selling shares to the investor and increase the market trading volume. In reality, they do not absorb any order imbalance and may force the investor to purchase shares at worse prices.

Similar to their response to market fragmentation, institutional traders have adapted their trading systems and trading algorithms to manage the impact of the prevalent HFT. To avoid trading predictably, investors introduce some randomization to the time of portfolio construction, trade release time, trading horizon, and the parameters in the trading algorithm. Traders also build systems to measure the HFT participation rates in different trading venues. For trades that require significant liquidity, they actively look for natural counterparties in the trading venues that had less HFT participation. Since most high-frequency trading desks do not hold overnight positions, they are less likely to trade close to the end of the day. Thus, the risk of front running from HFT is lower in the last hour. Some investors shift their trading towards the close and use market-on-close orders to capture the close prices.

Other Implementation Costs

For many long-only investors, total cost of trading constitutes most of the implementation shortfall. For long-short funds and funds that use leverage, financing costs and securities lending costs contribute to the implementation shortfall as well. The interest rate on debit cash balance—cash or margin investors borrow from brokers—is always higher than interest rate on credit cash balance—the cash balance investors have with the brokers. For individual investors, the lowest spreads that the brokers provide is close to 50 bps. A broker may charge benchmark rate plus 25 bps when clients borrow money and pay benchmark rate minus 25 bps when clients lend money. For some mutual funds and hedge funds, the spreads may be lower than 25 bps.

Theoretically, a cash-neutral long/short strategy is self-financed: the cash proceeds from the shorts can fully fund the longs. In practice, investors need to borrow stocks to make delivery when they short stocks. In the United States, securities lending agreements usually require a borrower to post cash collateral that is equivalent to at least 102% of the value of the shorted stocks, which means that the cash proceeds from the shorts cannot be used to buy the longs. Securities lenders pay interest on the cash collateral. Most stocks are easy to borrow and these stocks are called general collateral. The interest rate—often called the rebate rate—on general collateral is again determined by a benchmark rate. For example, a hedge fund may receive Fed Open rate minus 25 basis points from its prime broker. The 25 basis points are securities lending fees paid to lenders for their service. When many investors short the same stock, the borrowing demand for the stock increases relative to supply, the stock becomes special. Special stocks command securities lending fees much higher than general collateral. In some cases, investors need to pay an annualized fee of tens of percent in order to borrow a stock. Overall, large-cap stocks, especially S&P 500 stocks, have low average borrowing costs since they usually have sufficient supplies from index funds. Small-cap stocks and micro-cap stocks have much higher average borrowing costs because of limited supplies. In some cases, when supplies are depleted, investors cannot short some stocks when they fail to locate shares that they can borrow to make delivery. In some cases, the prime brokers may even recall the shares that the funds have already borrowed. The unavailability of shares for borrowing is another opportunity cost that adds to the implementation shortfall.

Conclusion

In this chapter, we discussed a variety of costs that contribute to the implementation shortfall with a focus on trading costs. Trading cost management is an integral component of the investment process. For investors, understanding the impact of trading costs and effectively managing them reduce portfolio turnover and boost net returns. Although portfolio managers do not necessarily need to understand the details of trade execution, it is beneficial to have a good grasp of the benefits and drawbacks of the high-level choices that traders make. Pre-trade analysis, post-trade analysis and constant communication between the portfolio managers and traders usually improve execution quality and reduce trading costs. As the market has become more efficient, the implementation edge derived from effective cost management has become an important contributor to overall investing success.

Index

References

Abrams, D., & Walker, S. 2010. MR Swing: a quantitative system for mean-reversion and swing trading in market regimes. Working Paper.

Agarwal, V., & Naik, N. Y. 2004. Risks and Portfolio Decisions Involving Hedge Funds. The Review of Financial Studies, 17(1): 63-98.

Almgren, R., Thum, C., Hauptmann, E., & Li, H. 2005. Direct Estimation of Equity Market Impact. http://www.math.nyu.edu/~almgren/papers/costestim.pdf.

Amihud, Y. 2002. Illiquidity and stock returns: cross-section and time-series effects. Journal of Financial Markets, 5(1): 31-56.

Anderson, A. M., & Dyl, E. A. 2007. Trading volume: NASDAQ and the NYSE. Financial Analysts Journal, 63(3): 79-86.

Ang, A., Bali, T. G., & Cakici, N. 2010. The Joint Cross Section of Stocks and Options. http://ssrn.com/abstract=1533089.

Ang, A., Hodrick, R. J., Xing, Y. H., & Zhang, X. Y. 2006. The cross-section of volatility and expected returns. Journal of Finance, 61(1): 259-299.

Ariel, R. A. 1990. High Stock Returns before Holidays: Existence and Evidence on Possible Causes. The Journal of Finance, 45(5): 1611-1626.

Arnott, R. D., Dorian, J. L., & Macedo, R. 1992. Style Management: The Missing Element in Equity Portfolios. The Journal of Investing, 1(1): 13-21.

Arshanapalli, B. G., Switzer, L. N., & Panjiu, k. 2007. Equity-style timing: A multi-style rotation model for the Russell large-cap and small-cap growth and value style indexes. Journal of Asset Management, 8(1): 9-23.

Asness, C. S., Friedman, J. A., Krail, R. J., & Liew, J. M. 2000. Style Timing: Value versus Growth. The Journal of Portfolio Management, 26(3): 50-60.

Asquith, P., Oman, R., & Safaya, C. 2010. Short sales and trade classification algorithms. Journal of Financial Markets, 13(1): 157-173.

Asquith, P., Pathak, P. A., & Ritter, J. R. 2005. Short interest, institutional ownership, and stock returns. Journal of Financial Economics, 78(2): 243-276.

Avellaneda, M., & Lee, J.-H. 2010. Statistical Arbitrage in the US Equities Market. Quantitative Finance, 10(7): 761-782.

Avery, C., Chevalier, J. A., & Zeckhauser, R. J. 2011. The "CAPS" Prediction System and Stock Market Returns. NBER Working Paper.

Avramov, D., Chordia, T., Jostova, G., & Philipov, A. 2006. Momentum and Credit Rating. http://ssrn.com/abstract=739324.

Baker, M. P., Bradley, B., & Taliaferro, R. 2013. The Low Risk Anomaly: A Decomposition into Micro and Macro Effects. http://ssrn.com/abstract=2210003.

Bali, T. G., Cakici, N., & Whitelaw, R. F. 2011. Maxing out: Stocks as lotteries and the cross-section of expected returns. Journal of Financial Economics, 99(2): 427-446.

Bali, T. G., Demirtas, K. O., & Hovakimian, A. 2010. Corporate Financing Activities and Contrarian Investment. Review of Finance, 14(3): 543-584.

Bali, T. G., & Hovakimian, A. 2009. Volatility Spreads and Expected Stock Returns. Management Science, 55(11): 1797-1812.

Barberis, N., & Huang, M. 2008. Stocks as Lotteries: The Implications of Probability Weighting for Security Prices. American Economic Review, 98(5): 2066-2100.

Barberis, N., & Shleifer, A. 2003. Style investing. Journal of Financial Economics, 68(2): 161-199.

Basu, D., & Miffre, J. 2013. Capturing the Risk Premium of Commodity Futures. Journal of Banking & Finance, 37(7): 2652-2664.

Becker, Y. L., Fei, P., & Lester, A. 2006. Stock Selection - an Innovative Application of Genetic Programming Methodology. http://ssrn.com/abstract=914198.

Bennett, J. A., & Sias, R. W. 2001. Can money flows predict stock returns? Financial Analysts Journal, 57(6): 64-+.

Bessembinder, H. 2003. Issues in assessing trade execution costs. Journal of Financial Markets, 6(3): 233-257.

Black, F., & Litterman, R. 1990. Asset Allocation: Combining Investor Views with Market Equilibrium. Goldman, Sachs & Co, Fixed Income Research.

Black, F., & Litterman, R. 1992. Global Portfolio Optimization. Financial Analysts Journal, 48(5): 28-43.

Blanco, R., Brennan, S., & Marsh, I. W. 2005. An Empirical Analysis of the Dynamic Relation between Investment-Grade Bonds and Credit Default Swaps. The Journal of Finance, 60(5): 2255–2281.

Boehmer, E., Huszar, Z. R., & Jordan, B. D. 2010. The good news in short interest. Journal of Financial Economics, 96(1): 80-97.

Bollen, J., Maoa, H., & Zeng, X. 2011. Twitter mood predicts the stock market. Journal of Computational Science, 2: 1–8.

Bollerslev, T., Tauchen, G., & Zhou, H. 2009. Expected Stock Returns and Variance Risk Premia. Review of Financial Studies, 22(11): 4463-4492.

Bouman, S., & Jacobsen, B. 2002. The Halloween indicator, "sell in may and go away": Another puzzle. American Economic Review, 92(5): 1618-1635.

Boyer, B., Mitton, T., & Vorkink, K. 2010. Expected Idiosyncratic Skewness. Review of Financial Studies, 23(1): 169-202.

Brown, J. H., Crocker, D. K., & Foerster, S. R. 2009. Trading Volume and Stock Investments. Financial Analysts Journal, 65(2): 67-84.

Carhart, M. M. 1997. On persistence in mutual fund performance. Journal of Finance, 52(1): 57-82.

Ceria, S., Saxena, A., & Stubbs, R. A. 2012. Factor Alignment Problems and Quantitative Portfolio Management. The Journal of Portfolio Management, 38(2): 29-43.

Chan, L. K. C., Lakonishok, J., & Sougiannis, T. 2001. The stock market valuation of research and development expenditures. Journal of Finance, 56(6): 2431-2456.

Chen, H.-L., & Bondt, W. D. 2004. Style momentum within the S&P-500 index. Journal of Empirical Finance(11): 483 - 507.

Chen, H. J., Chen, S. J., & Li, F. 2012. Empirical Investigation of an Equity Pairs Trading Strategy. http://ssrn.com/abstract=1361293.

Chen, L., Novy-Marx, R., & Zhang, L. 2011. An Alternative Three-Factor Model. http://ssrn.com/abstract=1418117.

Chordia, T., Subrahmanyam, A., & Anshuman, V. R. 2001. Trading activity and expected stock returns. Journal of Financial Economics, 59(1): 3-32.

Clare, A., Seaton, J., Smith, P. N., & Thomas, S. 2012. The Trend is Our Friend: Risk Parity, Momentum and Trend Following in Global Asset Allocation. http://ssrn.com/abstract=2126478.

Clarke, R., de Silva, H., & Thorley, S. 2002. Portfolio constraints and the fundamental law of active management. Financial Analysts Journal, 58(5): 48-66.

Cohen, L., & Frazzini, A. 2008. Economic links and predictable returns. Journal of Finance, 63(4): 1977-2011.

Cohen, L., Malloy, C. J., & Pomorski, L. 2010. Decoding Inside Information. http://ssrn.com/abstract=1692517(NBER Working Paper Series, Vol. w16454, pp. -, 2010).

Cooper, M. J., Gutierrez, R. C., & Hameed, A. 2004. Market States and Momentum. The Journal of Finance, 59(3): 1345-1365.

Cooper, T. 2010. Alpha Generation and Risk Smoothing Using Managed Volatility. http://ssrn.com/abstract=1664823.

Craig, S. 2009. Goldman's Trading Tips Reward Its Biggest Clients, Wall Street Journal.

Cremers, M., & Pareek, A. 2011. Can Overconfidence and Biased Self-Attribution Explain the Momentum, Reversal and Share Issuance Anomalies? Evidence from Short-Term Institutional Investors. http://ssrn.com/abstract=1571191.

Cremers, M., & Weinbaum, D. 2010. Deviations from Put-Call Parity and Stock Return Predictability. Journal of Financial and Quantitative Analysis, 45(2): 335-367.

Da, Z., Gurun, U. G., & Warachka, M. 2011. Frog in the Pan: Continuous Information and Momentum. Working Paper.

Da, Z., & Schaumburg, E. 2011. Relative valuation and analyst target price forecasts. Journal of Financial Markets, 14(1): 161-192.

Diether, K. B., Malloy, C. J., & Scherbina, A. 2002. Differences of opinion and the cross section of stock returns. Journal of Finance, 57(5): 2113-2141.

Do, B. H., & Faff, R. W. 2010. Does Simple Pairs Trading Still Work? Financial Analysts Journal,, 66(4): 83-95.

Doeswijk, R., & Vliet, P. V. 2011. Global Tactical Sector Allocation: A quantitative Approach. The Journal of Portfolio Management, 38(29-47).

Doeswijk, R. Q. 2008. The optimism cycle: Sell in May. Economist-Netherlands, 156(2): 175-200.

Easley, D., Hvidkjaer, S., & O'Hara, M. 2010. Factoring Information into Returns. Journal of Financial and Quantitative Analysis, 45(2): 293-309.

Easley, D., Prado, M. M. L. d., & O'Hara, M. 2012a. Bulk Classification of Trading Activity. http://ssrn.com/abstract=1989555.

Easley, D., Prado, M. M. L. d., & O'Hara, M. 2012b. Flow Toxicity and Liquidity in a High Frequency World. Review of Financial Studies, 25(5): 1457-1493.

Eling, M. 2008. Does the Measure Matter in the Mutual Fund Industry? Financial Analysts Journal, 64(3).

Ellis, K., Michaely, R., & O'Hara, M. 2000. The accuracy of trade classification rules: Evidence from Nasdaq. Journal of Financial and Quantitative Analysis, 35(4): 529-551.

Erb, C. B., & Harvey, C. R. 2006. The Strategic and Tactical Value of Commodity Futures. Financial Analysts Journal, 62(2): 69-97.

Estrella, A., & Mishkin, F. S. 1996. The Yield Curve as a Predictor of U.S. Recessions. Federal Reserve Bank of New York Current Issues In Economics and Finance, 2(7).

Faber, M. T. 2007. A Quantitative Approach to Tactical Asset Allocation. The Journal of Wealth Management, 4: 69-79.

Faber, M. T. 2013. A Quantitative Approach to Tactical Asset Allocation. http://ssrn.com/abstract=962461.

Fama, E. F., & French, K. R. 1992. THE CROSS-SECTION OF EXPECTED STOCK RETURNS. Journal of Finance, 47(2): 427-465.

Fama, E. F., & French, K. R. 1993. COMMON RISK-FACTORS IN THE RETURNS ON STOCKS AND BONDS. Journal of Financial Economics, 33(1): 3-56.

Gatev, E., Goetzmann, W. N., & Rouwenhorst, K. G. 2006. Pairs Trading: Performance of a Relative-Value Arbitrage Rule. The Review of Financial Studies, 19: 797-827.

Gray, W. R., & Vogel, J. 2011. Analyzing Valuation Measures: A Performance Horse-Race Over the Past 40 Years. http://ssrn.com/abstract=1970693.

Greenblatt, J. 2005. The Little Book That Beats the Market (1 ed.): Wiley.

Grinold, R. C., & Kahn, R. N. 1999. Active Portfolio Management: A Quantitative Approach for Producing Superior Returns and Controlling Risk (2 ed.): McGraw-Hill.

Hafez, P. A., & Xie, J. 2012. Short-Term Stock Selection Using News Based Indicators. http://ssrn.com/abstract=2155679.

Hafzalla, N., Lundholm, R. J., & Winkle, M. V. 2010. Percent Accruals. http://ssrn.com/abstract=1558464.

Han, B., & Zhou, Y. 2011. Term Structure of Credit Default Swap Spreads and Cross-Section of Stock Returns. http://ssrn.com/abstract=1735162.

Hartzmark, S. M., & Solomon, D. H. 2011. The Dividend Month Premium. http://ssrn.com/abstract=1930620.

Heston, S. L., Korajczyk, R. A., Sadka, R., & Thorson, L. D. 2011. Are You Trading Predictably? Financial Analysts Journal, 67(2): 36-44.

Heston, S. L., & Sadka, R. 2008. Seasonality in the cross-section of stock returns. Journal of Financial Economics, 87(2): 418-445.

Hirschey, N. H. 2012. Do High-Frequency Traders Anticipate Buying and Selling Pressure? Working Paper.

Idzorek, T. 2005. A step by step guide to the Black Litterman Model.

Jain, S., Yongvanich, A., & Zhou, X. 2011. Alpha Characteristics of Hedge Funds.

Jansen, I. P., & Sanning, L. W. 2010. Cashing in on Managerial Malfeasance: A Trading Strategy Around Forecasted Executive Stock Option Grants. Financial Analysts Journal, 66(5).

Jegadeesh, N., & Titman, S. 1993. Returns to Buying Winners and Selling Losers - Implications for Stock-Market Efficiency. Journal of Finance, 48(1): 65-91.

Jobson, J. D., & Korkie, B. M. 1981. Performance Hypothesis-Testing with the Sharpe and Treynor Measures. Journal of Finance, 36(4): 889-908.

Kaufman, P. 1995. Smarter Trading: Improving Performance in Changing Markets (1st ed.): McGraw-Hill.

Kestner, L. 2003. Quantitative Trading Strategies: Harnessing the Power of Quantitative Techniques to Create a Winning Trading Program (1st ed.): McGraw-Hill.

Keynes, J. 1930. A Treatise on Money. London: Macmillan.

Kittrell, J. 2011. Behavioral Trends and Market Neutrality Working paper.

Knewtson, H. S., Sias, R. W., & Whidbee, D. A. 2010. Style Timing with Insiders. Financial Analysts Journal 66(4): 46-66.

Kroll, B., Trichilo, D., & Braun, J. 2005. Extending the Fundamental Law of Investment Management. JP Morgan Asset Management.

Kumar, A. 2009. Who Gambles in the Stock Market ? Journal of Finance, 64(4): 1889-1933.

Lakonishok, J., & Smidt, S. 1988. Are Seasonal Anomalies Real? A Ninety-Year Perspective. Review of Financial Studies, 1(4): 403–425.

Lasser, D. J., Wang, X., & Zhang, Y. 2010. The Effect of Short Selling on Market Reactions to Earnings Announcements. Contemporary Accounting Research, 27(2): 609-+.

Lee, C. M. C., & Ready, M. J. 1991. INFERRING TRADE DIRECTION FROM INTRADAY DATA. Journal of Finance, 46(2): 733-746.

Lee, J. H., & Stefek, D. 2008. Do risk factors eat alphas? Journal of Portfolio Management, 34(4): 12-+.

Li, X., & Sullivan, R. N. 2011. The Limits to Arbitrage Revisited: The Accrual and Asset Growth Anomalies. Financial Analysts Journal, 67(4): 50-66.

Lin, T.-C., Lu, X., & Driessen, J. 2012. Why Do Options Prices Predict Stock Returns? http://ssrn.com/abstract=2168566.

Lintner, J. 1965. The Valuation of Risk Assets and the Selection of Risky Investments in Stock Portfolios and Capital Budgets. The Review of Economics and Statistics, 47(1): 13-37.

Lo, A. W. 2001. Risk Management for Hedge Funds: Introduction and Overview. Financial Analysts Journal, 57(6): 16-33.

Lorenz, J., & Almgren, R. 2011. Mean-Variance Optimal Adaptive Execution. Applied Mathematical Finance, 18: 395-422.

Loughran, T., & Vijh, A. M. 1997. Do long-term shareholders benefit from corporate acquisitions? Journal of Finance, 52(5): 1765-1790.

Lucca, D. O., & Moench, E. 2013. The Pre-FOMC Announcement Drift. http://ssrn.com/abstract=1923197.

Maberly, E. D., & Pierce, R. M. 2004. Stock market efficiency withstands another challenge: Solving the "Sell in May/Buy after Halloween" puzzle. Econ Journal Watch, 1(1): 29-46.

MacDonald, R., & Marsh, I. 1999. Exchange Rate Modelling: Springer.

Markowitz, H. 1952. Portfolio Selection. Journal of Finance, 7(7): 77-97.

Markowitz, H. 1959. Portfolio Selection (1 ed.): Blackwell.

McConnell, J. J., & Xu, W. 2008. Equity returns at the turn of the month. Financial Analysts Journal, 64(2): 49-64.

Menkhoff, L., Sarno, L., Schmeling, M., & Schrimpf, A. 2011. Currency Momentum Strategies. http://ssrn.com/abstract=1809776.

Mertens, E. 2002. Comments on Variance of the IID estimator. Working Paper.

Mezrich, J. J., & Feng, J. 2010. Low Volatility: A Simple Tool for Factor Selection. Nomura Securities International Inc, Global Quantitative Research.

Michaud, R. 1989. The Markowitz optimization enigma: Is optimized optimal? Financial Analysts Journal, 45: 31-42.

Miffre, J., & Rallis, G. 2007. Momentum Strategies in Commodity Futures Markets. Journal of Banking & Finance, 31(6): 1863–1886.

Mitchell, M., & Pulvino, T. 2001. Characteristics of Risk and Return in Risk Arbitrage. The Journal of Finance, 56(6): 2135-2175.

Mohanram, P. S. 2005. Separating Winners from Losers among Low Book-to-Market Stocks using Financial Statement Analysis. Review of Accounting Studies, 10: 133-170.

Moskowitz, T. J., Ooi, Y. H., & Pedersen, L. H. 2011. Time series momentum. Journal of Financial Economics, 104: 228-250.

Ni, S. X. Y., Pearson, N. D., & Poteshman, A. M. 2005. Stock price clustering on option expiration dates. Journal of Financial Economics, 78(1): 49-87.

Novy-Marx, R. 2010. The Other Side of Value: Good Growth and the Gross Profitability Premium. NBER Working Paper.

O'Hara, M., & Ye, M. 2011. Is market fragmentation harming market quality? Journal of Financial Economics, 100(3): 459-474.

O'Neil, W. 2002. How To Make Money In Stocks: A Winning System in Good Times or Bad (3 ed.): McGraw-Hill.

Ogden, J. P. 1990. TURN-OF-MONTH EVALUATIONS OF LIQUID PROFITS AND STOCK RETURNS - A COMMON EXPLANATION FOR THE MONTHLY AND JANUARY EFFECTS. Journal of Finance, 45(4): 1259-1272.

Palmon, D., & Yezegel, A. 2011. Analysts' Recommendation Revisions and Subsequent Earnings Surprises: Pre- and Post- Regulation FD. Journal of Accounting, Auditing and Finance 26(3).

Parker, A. S., Ortega, A., Neuhart, P., & Kausar, N. 2011. Introducing MOST: MOrgan STanley's Quantitative Stock-Selection Model. Morgan Stanley Research.

Perold, A. F. 1988. THE IMPLEMENTATION SHORTFALL - PAPER VERSUS REALITY. Journal of Portfolio Management, 14(3): 4-9.

Piotroski, J. D. 2000. Value Investing: The Use of Historical Financial Statement Information to Separate Winners from Losers. Journal of Accounting Research, 38: 1-41.

Pojarliev, M., & Levich, R. 2008. Do Professional Currency Managers Beat the Benchmark? Financial Analysts Journal, 64(5): 18-32.

Pontiff, J., & Woodgate, A. 2008. Share issuance and cross-sectional returns. Journal of Finance, 63(2): 921-945.

Rachev, S., Jasic, T., Stoyanov, S., & Fabozzi, F. J. 2007. Momentum strategies based on reward-risk stock selection criteria. Journal of Banking & Finance, 31(8): 2325-2346.

Reinganum, M. R. 1983. The anomalous stock market behavior of small firms in January : Empirical tests for tax-loss selling effects. Journal of Financial Economics, 12(1): 89-104.

Schutte, M., & Unlu, E. 2009. Do Security Analysts Reduce Noise? Financial Analysts Journal, 65(3): 40-54.

Sharpe, W. 1964. Capital Asset Prices: A Theory of Market Equilibriums under Conditions of Risk. The Journal of Finance, 19(3): 425-442.

Sharpe, W. P., & Alexander, G. 1990. Investments. (4 ed.). Prentice Hall.

Sloan, R. G. 1996. Do Stock Prices Fully Reflect Information in Accruals and Cash Flows. The Accounting Review, 71(3): 289-315.

Stivers, C., & Sun, L. C. 2010. Cross-Sectional Return Dispersion and Time Variation in Value and Momentum Premiums. Journal of Financial and Quantitative Analysis, 45(4): 987-1014.

Swinkels, L. A. P., & Vliet, P. V. 2010. An Anatomy of Calendar Effects. http://ssrn.com/abstract=1593770.

Thomas, J. W. 2011. Capturing Alpha in the Alpha Capture System: Do Trade Ideas Generate Alpha? The Journal of Investing, 20(1): 11-18.

Wang, K. Q. 2005. Multifactor evaluation of style rotation. Journal of Financial and Quantitative Analysis, 40(2): 349-372.

Witte, H. D. 2010. Outliers and the Halloween Effect: Comment on Maberly and Pierce. Econ Journal Watch, 7(1): 91-98.

Wu, Y., & Zhu, Q. 2011. When is Insider Trading Informative. http://ssrn.com/abstract=1917132.

Xing, Y. H., Zhang, X. Y., & Zhao, R. 2010. What Does the Individual Option Volatility Smirk Tell Us About Future Equity Returns? Journal of Financial and Quantitative Analysis, 45(3): 641-662.

CPSIA information can be obtained
at www.ICGtesting.com
Printed in the USA
BVHW062005010821
613278BV00005B/504